I WOULDN'T TAKE

NOTHIN'
FOR MY
JOURNEY

Emancipation Oak stands by rivers of water. It sheltered a school when rebellion was all around. It still lives and shadows a Seat of Learning, though rebellions come and rebellions go.

author's photo, 1969

"And He shall be like a tree planted by the rivers of waters, that bringeth forth His fruit in His season."

Psalms 1:3

I WOULDN'T TAKE

NOTHIN'
FOR MY
JOURNEY

Two Centuries of an
Afro-American Minister's Family

By Leonidas H. Berry M.D.

 Johnson Publishing Co., Inc., Chicago, Illinois

Library of Congress Cataloging in Publication Data

Berry, Leonidas H., M.D.
I Wouldn't take nothin' for my journey!

Bibliography: p.
Includes index.
Summary: Chronicles the impact of the African Methodist Episcopal Church
on the lives of several generations of one Afro-American family.
1. Berry family. 2. African Methodist Episcopal
Church—History. [1. Afro-Americans—Religion.
2. African Methodist Episcopal Church—History. 3. Berry
family] I. Title.
CT274.B46B47   973'.0496073 [B]   80-84628
ISBN 0-87475-079-7   AACR2

Norman L. Hunter, Layout and Design

Text, Jansen Linotype, 12/14
Chapter Headings, Garamond Bold, 30 point

Published in the United States of America
by Johnson Publishing Company, Inc.
Manufactured in the United States of America
By Rand McNally and Company

To the Memory
of
Mom and Pop

Author's Preface

I WOULDN'T TAKE NOTHIN' FOR MY JOURNEY is part of an expressive stanza in a Negro spiritual. It says that life on this earth is only a journey. It can be an experience of success and joy in spite of overwhelming hardships. There is reward in the struggle itself and in the spirit of survival. The spirit eminates from Heaven; the journey leads back to Heaven or to "Mt. Zion," from which the spirit came.

The narrative which follows is a true story of an Afro-American minister and his family. It is a genealogical inquiry and documentation into the lives of the Rev. and Mrs. Llewellyn L. (Beulah Harris) Berry, their forbears and offsprings. They are here identified as the Jenifer-Berry-Harris-Jordan family clan. The story unfolds the identification and achievements of individuals who make up a continuous multi-nuclear family unit, across the generations, for two centuries on American soil. It emphasizes cultural progress against formidable odds. It points out the discovery and recognition of the ingredients of continuous family adhesiveness and love that held together blood related but separate nuclear families across the decades. These ingredients were developed before the Civil War despite the divisiveness of slavery, when family adhesiveness and love were essential to physical and spiritual survival.

When marriage acquired legal sanction these blood relatives continued to feel the necessity and compelling desire for family love and unity. Since the Civil War the families of the Jenifer-Berry-Harris-Jordan family clan have been of the nuclear variety. That's to say they have had the presence and support of father as well as mother during formative and other years in each family unit. The African Methodist Episcopal Church has had a most important influence in maintaining family stability, through its unique spirituality and its preachments for education since the pre-organized founding of the church under Richard Allen in 1787. In its establishment of Wilberforce University of Ohio in 1856, the first Negro College, the church has promoted the cultural progress and achievements observed in this family clan.

The author has been prompted to tell this story because of a strong personal feeling of family love and closeness across the generations. More importantly he has felt for many years that it is time to tell more stories of single related Black families who have developed and achieved on their own individual economic resources. There has been far too much of a continuous, "mass"-analysis and "statistical" treatment, more often depreciatory, of the "total family" and special "racial" categories of Black American families. In telling this story the author has relived his own rendezvous with destiny. The first dramatic episode begins with the escape of "Doc" Henry Jenifer from St. Mary's County, Maryland to Canada by way of the Underground Railroad in 1848. His brother, Nace Jenifer, father of Nancy Jenifer Berry and grandfather of Rev. L. L. Berry was born in 1816. Their parents were slaves in Maryland during the preceding generation.

The second dramatic episode involves the escape of Nace Jenifer's son Sam Jenifer and John Berry who joined the Union Army in 1864 and fought in strategic battles of the Civil War. The story continues in a chronological sequence of episodes of the up-and-down struggles and progress of family members to the present generation with optimistic hopes for the future.

There is no claim of family exclusiveness. Tens of thousands of Black families have climbed the same mountains to achieve middle-class status and bi-parental relationships. To get there, they have fought the same battles against racial prejudice, unequal opportunities and poverty. The present youngest generation of the Jenifer-Berry-Harris-Jordan family shows striking evidence of accelerated cultural growth and exciting prospects for the future of individuals and Black American families. The research and writing of this story over a period of the last twenty-five years have been a very rewarding personal experience. The extent to which this story identifies and relives the destinies of individuals, of their families and their contributions to the quality of life for themselves and their fellow man must be left to the readers judgment.

Leonidas H. Berry, M.D.

About the Author

LEONIDAS Harris Berry, B.S., M.S., M.D., (Hon.) Sc.D., was born on his maternal grandfather's tobacco farm in Woodsdale, Person County, N.C., July 20, 1902, where his mother Beulah Harris Berry was a county school teacher. His father, Rev. L. L. Berry, the principal personality in this book, was a commuting African Methodist Episcopal Minister of small churches in his native state of Virginia. He spent the remaining two decades as Secretary of Missions for the AME church. Dr. Berry lived in many parsonages during his pre-school years in Winston-Salem and Chapel Hill, N.C. He spent most of his childhood in Norfolk and the surrounding Tidewater area of Virginia and is a product of the "separate but equal" Abraham Lincoln grammar school and Booker T. Washington High School of Norfolk. After college at Wilberforce University in Ohio, in 1924 he moved to Chicago where he has remained since. There he received a second Bachelor of Science Degree and M.D. at the College and the Rush Medical School of the University of Chicago. Later he received the M.S. degree in Pathology at the University of Illinois Medical School and the honorary Doctor of Science from Wilberforce University. He reared his family and practiced the speciality of Internal medicine and digestive diseases with a major interest in Endoscopy in Chicago and in some of its best known hospitals.

The author likes to think of himself as a multi-dimensional doctor because of his great interest and involvement from the beginning of his profession in medical teaching, research, and writing and his constant activity in community public service. This has included civil rights, aspects of racial problems in public health and medical education, and the African Methodist Episcopal Church. He is a life member of the National Association for the Advancement of Colored People, the Alpha Phi

Alpha fraternity, the Association for the Study of Negro Life and History and many other civic and professional institutions and organizations.

Among titles held are Clinical Associate Professor of Medicine, Emeritus of the University of Illinois, Senior Attending Physician Emeritus of the Cook County Hospital, Trustee of the Cook County Graduate School of Medicine and General Officer, Medical Director, Emeritus of the A. M. E. Church.

He is listed in many biographic registries such as *The American Men and Women of Science, Certified American Medical Specialists, American College of Physicians* and *Who's Who in America.* Dr. Berry believes that an individual reared by religious discipline in a minister's family can become a dedicated scientist, without losing his spirituality.

Introduction

Dr. Leonidas H. Berry, distinguished physician, dedicated churchman and esteemed friend, has written a book that is unique in the literature of African Methodism. This is the first historical work dealing with the African Methodist Episcopal Church from the perspective of a single AME family.

The author traces his family roots back to Nace Jenifer, born in St. Mary's County, Maryland in 1816, the year the AME Church was formally organized.

The chapter on slavery in St. Mary's County describes the first missionary efforts of Richard Allen, founder and first bishop of the AME Church. From Bethel Church, Baltimore, Bishop Allen journeyed into nearby rural districts of Maryland where slave converts held secret meetings with traveling AME preachers in groves near the tobacco plantations.

Early members of the Jenifer and Berry families escaped from slavery in southern Maryland, the second birth place of African Methodism.

My personal satisfaction in writing this introduction is greatly enhanced as I recall the long friendships between the Berry and Morris families. John and Nancy Jenifer Berry, paternal grandparents of the author, were among the founding members of St. John A. M. E. Church, Norfolk, Va., and Bethel AME Church, Hampton, Va. My grandparents were among the founding members of Emanuel A. M. E. Church, Portsmouth, Va. Our fathers, the late Rev. L. L. Berry and the late Rev. S. S. Morris, were consecutive pastors of St. John Church in Norfolk, in whose parsonage I was born. Later they were concurrent AME General Officers, heading the departments of Missions and Christian Education, respectively.

Dr. Berry continues the family tradition of leadership and service to the Church through his concerns for medical missions. At the 1972 General Conference, after establishing and directing medical first aid clinics and health education for over thirty years, he became a general officer by acclamation. He is now General Officer and Medical Director, Emeritus.

I Wouldn't Take Nothin' For My Journey is a fascinating and informative saga of the impact of the AME Church upon the life and destiny of one family. This book is not only of special significance to the AME Church constituency but also to the larger community of those who seek a deeper insight into the meaning of the black experience in American life.

Bishop Samuel S. Morris
Past President, Council of Bishops
African Methodist Episcopal Church

Acknowledgements

Many people have been involved in the research and writing of this book. I have reference to those who have actively assisted and those who have been supportive of my efforts over a period of twenty-five years. Scores of persons, too many to be recorded, have been involved. I am deeply grateful to all of them collectively for their assistance and encouragement. I must acknowledge the help and support of members of my immediate family and dozens of aunts, uncles, cousins, and in-laws of three generations. Most importantly, I am grateful to the memory of my mother who during the last five years of her life gave oral accounts of her family, grandparents and greatgrandparents and wrote definitive descriptions. I had access to her numerous scrapbooks which had been a hobby as well as records from family bibles and other materials in her possession since her early adult life. My brothers and sisters, Richard and Llewellyn, Jr. of precious memory, Gladys, Elbert, and Geraldine gave innumerable interviews and wrote tributes to our parents. My father's death in 1954 gave me the first impetus for writing this book. A prayer of thanksgiving is offered for nearly one hundred individuals, living and deceased, who responded with written tributes in 1955. My wife Emma has been very supportive of my efforts during the entire period of research and writing. She accompanied me on some of the dozens of trips across the states, Canada and the Caribbean. I am very grateful to her for releasing me from many family responsibilities while working on this project. Special gratitude is expressed posthumously for the numerous and valuable interviews and letters from Aunt Lola Berry Annis (1879–1980), Uncles "Gus" (John Augustus Berry, Jr.) (1870–1960), and John S. Harris.

Outside of the family, I am very deeply indebted to my good friend since medical school days in Chicago, Dr. Chester D. Bradley of Hampton, Virginia. He was assigned to Hampton during World War II for army hospital duty, and later became curator of the Fortress Monroe Museum. Being a history hobbyist with special interest in the Civil War, his help and encouragement have been of inestimable value for twenty-five years.

I am grateful for a large number of ministers, members of the Women's Missionary Societies, and Bishops of the A.M.E. Church. Some of the church people interviewed were from the foreign missionary fields during their visits in America or during my visits to these areas. I acknowledge the valuable assistance of Mr. James D. Walker of the National Archives, Washington, D.C. and others at the Federal Archives and Records Centers, for army records, census data and other materials. I acknowledge the assistance and cooperation of librarians. The inter-library services and especially the library of St. Mary's County, Md. and officials of the County Court House of Person County, Roxboro, N.C. and Halifax County, Va. I am indebted to the National Park Service, Milton Wooden of Burrowsville, Va. and Marion V. Taylor, librarian of Pocahontas High School, Powhatan, Va. for help in locating the old battle sites at Wilsons Wharf and Ft. Powhatan. We also wish to thank Mr. Fritz Malval, Archivist, Hampton Institute. I wish to express special thanks for the secretarial services of Juanita Dickson, Ella Scott, Jacqueline Thomas, and Vivian Cochran.

Without the dedicated assistance of Mrs. Doris Saunders, who served as editor and Mr. Norman Hunter, who designed the book and reproduced many photographs, this book could not have been published. Finally, I am deeply grateful for the cooperation and support of Mr. John H. Johnson, publisher, and members of the staff of the Johnson Publishing Company.

Table of Contents

I WOULDN'T TAKE

NOTHIN'
FOR MY
JOURNEY

Prologue

Top: Rev. Llewellyn L. Berry (1876–1954), A.M.E. Pastor, Secretary of Missions; r. Mrs. Llewellyn L. (Beulah Harris) Berry, 1879–1960, wife and mother.

Below: Father and daughter, grandfather and aunt of Mrs. L. L. (Beulah Harris) Berry.

Wiley Jordan (1834–1914) Vinie Jordan Goings (1857–1949)

Above l. John Berry, Sr. (1840–1909), Escaped Slave, Soldier, father of Rev. L. L. Berry; r. Mrs. John (Nancy Jenifer) Berry (1844–1919), Wife and mother, sister of Sam Jenifer (not shown), who was a slave escapee and Civil War Soldier.

Above l. Tobias Harris (1857–1899), Slave in early childhood, son of white master and mulatto slave seamstress. Father of Mrs. L. L. (Beulah Harris) Berry. R. Mrs. Tobias (Elizabeth Jordan) Harris (1860–1898), Slave in early childhood. Mother of Mrs. L. L. Berry.

Above and right: Sons and daughters of Tobias and Elizabeth Jordan Harris (Beulah Harris Berry, oldest child shown elsewhere). Arthur L. Harris (1881–1924); Carrie Harris Brooks (1886–1973); Ursula Harris Clay (1891–); Lula D. Harris Myers (1893–1977); John S. Harris (1895–).

Sons and daughters of John Sr. and Nancy Jenifer Berry, chronologically left to right (Llewellyn L., second child, photo elsewhere), others not shown. John Augustus (Uncle Gus) Berry, Jr. (1870–1960); Lola Berry Annis (1880–1979); Johanna Berry Matthews (1881–1940).

Katherine Berry Barrett (1884–1968); Henry Berry (1886–1907); Arthur Berry (1888–1907); Nace Jenifer Berry (1890–1919).

DECLARATION FOR AN ORIGINAL INVALID PENSION.

☞ **This must be Executed before a Court of Record or some Officer thereof having custody of the Seal.**

State of *Virginia* County of *Elizabeth City*, ss:

ON THIS *16th* day of *April* A. D. one thousand eight hundred and *Ninety*, personally appeared before me *clerk* of the *County Court* a COURT OF RECORD within and for the county and State aforesaid *John Berry, (Colored)* aged *48* years, who, being duly sworn according to law, declares that he is the identical *John Berry (Colored)* who was ENROLLED as a *private* on the *5th* day of *February* 1864 in Company *B* of the *Second* Regiment of *U.S. Colored Artillery*, commanded by *Capt. F. C. Choates* and was honorably DISCHARGED at *Brownsville Texas* on the *17th* day of *March* 1866; that his personal description is a follows: age *48* years; height - *5* feet - *8* - inches; complexion *black* ; hair *black* eyes *black*. That while a member of the organization aforesaid, in the service and in the line of duty, at *Mill Creek + near Norfolk* the State of *Virginia*, on or about the day of *May or June* 18 *64* he *Contracted Varioloid + Rheumatism and + Chronic* (here state the name or nature of disease, or the location of the wound or injury. If disabled by disease state fully its cause, if by wound or injury the precise manner in which received) *Dysentery - through exposure while in Service*

+ The disease Chronic Dysentery may be Hemorage of the Bowels, as claimant says he has frequent passages of blood, + this disease came upon him about the time of his discharge from the army.

That he was treated in hospitals, as follows: (Here state the names or numbers, and the localities of all hospitals in which treated, and the dates of treatment.) *was sent to Small Pox Hospital - Mill Creek near Hampton Va. and Dr. Gross attended me*

That he has *never* been employed in the military or naval service otherwise than as stated above. (Here state what the service was, whether prior or subsequent to that stated above, and the dates at which it began and ended.)

That he has not been in the military or naval service of the United States since the *17th* day of *March* 18 *66*. That since leaving the service this applicant has resided in the *Butler farm Back River near Hampton* in the State of *Virginia*, and that his occupation has been that of a *farmer*. That prior to his entry into the service above named he was a man of good, sound physical health, being when enrolled a *farmer*. That he is now *greatly* disabled from obtaining his subsistence by manual labor by reason of his injuries above described, received in the service of the United States ; and he therefore makes this declaration for the purpose of being placed on the invalid pension roll of the United States. He hereby appoints, with full power of substitution and revocation *James Tanner of Washington D. C.* his true and lawful attorney to prosecute his claim. That he has *never* received *or* applied for a pension ; that his residence is *No Butler Farm Back River 15 miles from Hampton } Virginia*

Official document of John Berry requesting Civil War disability pension indicating date of enlistment, discharge, regiment, company and commanding officer.

DECLARATION FOR ORIGINAL INVALID PENSION.

UNDER AN ACT GRANTING PENSIONS TO SOLDIERS AND SAILORS WHO ARE INCAPACITATED FOR THE PERFORMANCE OF MANUAL LABOR AND PROVIDING FOR PENSIONS TO WIDOWS, MINOR CHILDREN, AND DEPENDENT PARENTS.

State of *Virginia*

County of *Elizabeth City* } ss:

On this *31st* day of *October* A. D. one thousand eight hundred and ninety _____, personally appeared before me, *Clerk* of _____, a *County Court* in and for the County and State aforesaid, *Samuel Jenifer* (Name of Claimant.), aged *51* years, a resident of *Butler Farm* (Give Town, County, and State; and if you reside in a city where streets are named and houses are numbered, give name of street and number of house. If you reside in the country, state about how many miles from nearest Postoffice.), County of *Elizabeth City* State of *Virginia*, who, being duly sworn according to law, declares that he is the identical *Samuel Jenifer* (Name of Claimant), who entered service during the War of the Rebellion under the name of *Samuel Jenifer* (Name under which enlisted.) on or about the *9th* day of *February*, 186 *4*, as *Private* (Give rank.), in company *"B"* (Or vessel, if in the navy.) of the *30"* regiment of *U/Col'd Troops* commanded by *Capt. Andrew Davidson Adjutant or* (Name of company's commander. If upon any General's Staff, state that fact.) and was HONORABLY DISCHARGED at *Roanoke Island, N.C.*, on or about the *10th* day of *December*, 186 *5*, by reason of *S.O. No 249 Hd Qrs Dep* *N.C. 1865* ; that his personal description is as follows: Age, *51* years; height, *5* feet *6* inches; complexion, *Griffs*; hair, *Black*; eyes, *Black*. That he is now suffering from *a continual pain under* (Here state the name and nature of any disease, wound or injury which in *my breast bone, was knocked down in an action by a* any manner disqualifies you for performing full manual labor, no matter when the same originated or developed.) *bullet which struck me on the Buckle of my belt, in the charge at the Crater Explosion before Petersburg Virginia. Dr. Bardelle, of Hampton, Va. operated on me April 6th 1885 for fissure of rectum. Dr. Williams, of Hampton Va. attended me for fissure of the Annus Feb 1885.*

and that the said disability is of a permanent character, and is not the result of vicious habits, and that it incapacitates him from the performance of manual labor in such a degree as to render him unable to earn a support, and that this declaration is made for the purpose of being placed upon the pension roll, under the provisions of the Act of June 27, 1890. That he has *Not* been employed in the military or naval service otherwise than as stated above _____

(Here state what the service was, whether prior or subsequent to that stated above, and the dates at which it began and ended.)

That since the *10th* day of *December*, A. D. 186 *5*, he has not been employed in the (Give date of last discharge from the service.) military or naval service of the United States.

He hereby appoints, with full power of substitution and revocation,

prepared by GEORGE E. LEMON, of Washington, D. C., and is exclusively for his Use.

Request for Civil War invalid pension by Sam Jenifer, describing disability and his action at "Battle of Crater Explosion," before Petersburg, 1964.

Slavery in Old St. Mary's of Maryland

THE "Ark and the Dove" had nothing to do with the Bible story of Noah. It indeed was a ship of sorts—vintage 1634. It was not floated by a flood and moored to a mountain top. It was swept by wind and sail across the turbulent Atlantic and anchored near the shores of Maryland; the first English vessel to make it. The success of the voyage was influenced by the religious faith of Jesuit Father Andrew White, who was courageous, resourceful and practical. His goals were religious freedom, acquisition of land and survival. To wit, his ship log recorded sixty men and women passengers including two "mulatos", indentured servants; Matthias Sousa and Francisco. Leonard Calvert, the proprietary Lord Baltimore, bargained with a certain ship master for the delivery of thirteen 'niggar' slaves at St. Mary's in 1621. Thus, began the nefarious traffic in human cargo and slavery at St. Mary's. From then until now, Maryland, her sister colonies and states have never been free of the burden nor the attributes of the forced immigrants from Black Africa.

It is not known whether Matthias and Francisco were religiously sprinkled with sea water enroute to Maryland. It is known that as the Catholic Jesuits claimed thousands of acres and acquired hundreds of slaves, religious conflicts between the laws of St. Mary's and the English and Roman Catholic church became greater and greater through the years. "To baptise or not to baptise" the slaves and purge them of their heathenism, "that was the question." But once they were purged of their congenital sins, raising the missionary stature and mercifulness of the church wasn't it a "sin-before-God" to keep them enslaved. The very

Reverend Thomas Story reprimanded one of his clergymen at West River in 1699, for baptizing his slaves without conferring their freedom. Whether or not "Matthias, the Mulato" was ever baptized, the record shows him commissioned "skipper and trader" with the "Sesquhanougah" Indians by Father Poulton and in later years a member of the legislature of the Colony of St. Mary's.

Politicians both secular and sacred always come to the rescue where there is a religious dilemma. With the pressure from the tobacco barons, laws were passed denying that Christianizing slaves should make them free. The powerful church of England and their American counterparts fought these colonial laws and the tug of war between business profits and religion went on and on.

Meanwhile, the growth of slavery in this fertile tobacco raising coast line was a gradual but every increasing way of life. Like an octopus, its tentacles stretched, eventually engulfing every activity of the colony. Europe had virtually "gone mad" for the new world tobacco leaf and Indian rum. The barons of Maryland with land confiscated from the Indians and ceded to them by the British crown, were literally "wallowing" in rich flat tobacco land with harbors easily accessible along the Chesapeake Bay, the Potomac and Patuxant Rivers. With thousands of acres out of proportion to manpower, all that was needed for the "bed-rock" of the future American economy were slaves and more slaves.

The flood of manpower from Africa by way of England often included poor whites as indentured servants bonded for seven to ten years. As the exploitation of the slave system continued, Black and white victims found themselves banded together by common interests. For many years political, economic and social status was more important than race. There was free intermarriage between Black and white without regard to free or indentured status. Vigorous proselyting and evangelizing was continuous by the Catholic Jesuits who came to St. Mary's in the first place to establish a religious sanctuary from the British monarchy. They had no hesitancy in bestowing the blessing of marriage or intermarriage upon Black and white. It was good for "sinners" and "heathens" and it enhanced the stature of the church.

Early in the 18th century intermarriage between Black and white, slaves, indentures, and the free and poor posed a serious problem for the ruling class.

So back to the legislature they went with revision of the slave codes. One such revision read; "Divers free born English women forgetful of their condition and to the disgrace of their Nation are intermarrying with Negroes. Such women so marrying must remain slaves; and their children shall serve as endentures for 30 years." Nevertheless, ways were found to evade the law before their severity was eventually reduced. Free born English women continued to be forgetful of their condition and to "disgrace their Nation". Some of the most brilliant men of Maryland's history like Daniel Coker, and Benjamin Benneker were mulattos with Caucasian mothers and Negro fathers—slave and free.

Thus Maryland enacted the first "miscegenation" laws. During two centuries the slave codes were as severe or as moderate as any in the slave states. A Black slave accused of killing his master, had his right hand chopped off; of course without anesthetics in those days. Later he had his head chopped off. Two suspected accomplices were given the leniency of being beheaded without previously cutting off the right hand. When a slave master chopped off both ears of his slave for a minor infraction of his rules, the courts took action. Laws were finally passed at St. Mary's city against branding, chopping off limbs or disfigurement of slaves.

Notwithstanding punitive slave codes, the Black struggle in 18th century Maryland made progress. The census of 1790 showed that fifteen percent of Blacks and mulattos in Maryland were free. Although St. Mary's County remained largely agricultural and land-locked, the Blacks were always in tune with the happenings inside and outside the slave world. There was no grapevine like the Black Dispatch, that word-of-mouth system of communication, from field to kitchen; from plantation to city and vice versa. From the 1831 Nat Turner uprising in Virginia to the first Black convention in Baltimore, the goings-on were narrated, evaluated and acted upon.

St. Mary's County, rich in farmlands, remained agricultural with little industrial development. Many of the free Blacks left St. Mary's County for better opportunities in Baltimore and other cities.

In the early days of the 19th century, circuit riding Black Protestant preachers communicated with slaves with or without sanction of the slave barons.

There were lots of Blacks, free and bonded, who didn't like the

5

Catholic religion with the priest speaking in "unknown tongues" and singing that didn't stir their souls. The Jesuits did much that was good for them, but their ritual of worship failed to excite many of the Blacks.

As it was said, in later years, "they bent their knees a lot, but they didn't stay on 'em long enough."

The slaves of old St. Mary's often sang: "Lord I went into the valley, but I didn't go to stay, my soul got happy, and I stayed all day."

A clergyman in Charles County brought his 25 slaves to Baltimore in 1843, had them "sprinkled into Methodism" and freed under the condition that they would be shipped at once by the Colonization Society to Liberia.

The storytellers of the Jenifer, and Miles-Berry family told their children, the interesting story of Daniel Coker. This religious man was born in Maryland to a white woman slave owner. His father was a slave owned by his mother. He had special opportunities for education, was freed of his slave status, and became an outstanding leader in the Black community. He founded the Bethel A.M.E. Church of Baltimore; and was elected the first Bishop of the African Methodist Episcopal Church, but resigned without serving. Richard Allen became officially the first Bishop of the church. Daniel Coker later sailed to Africa with the first group of Blacks sponsored by the American Colonization Society. A man of exceptional ability he later took charge of the group and led them through a period of severe economic hardships. He organized a nursing unit and supervised the band of colonizers against a yellow fever epidemic which left most of them dead, including the two white agents of the society. In Freetown, Sierra Leone, he organized an A.M.E. church and spent the rest of his life there as a missionary.

At the end of the Revolutionary War the spirit of freedom was very much in the air. Five thousand Blacks fought in the war to win freedom, which applied to slave holders but not to the slaves. About this time an escaped slave named John Kizzel from South Carolina organized a group of Canadian Black escapees and sailed from Nova Scotia to the Isle of Sherbro on the West Coast of Africa. For many years, the colony was prosperous and the Colonization Society selected this spot for their landing nearly 50 years later. The Elders of Maryland knew the story of many escaped slaves who reached Canada and later resettled in Africa.

The Colonization Society, which is said to have originated in Maryland in the early 1800's sponsored the training of many Blacks in the trades and professions for permanent settlement in West Africa. Some of them took advantage of the opportunity for training and then refused to go to Africa. One of these was Dr. James McCune Smith, born in New York City; he received the AB degree from the University of Glasgow Scotland in 1830, AM in 1836, and MD in 1837, and was probably the first American Negro with a degree in medicine. He practiced in New York City, was active as an abolishionist and became well known for a debate against the preachments of Senator John C. Calhoun on the inferiority of the Negro race.

Free blacks in the State of Maryland played an important role in the development of Black American culture and history in the 19th century. Baltimore as a cultural center extended its tentacles out into the surrounding rural counties. It is generally recognized that the Black church has been the principal repository of Black cultural history since very early times.

One of the leading organized Black churches has been the African Methodist Episcopal church. It was founded in Philadelphia, in 1787. During this year, the U.S. Constitutional convention was being held. This was one year before George Washington was elected President. The church was organized as the first non-violent protest against racial segregation, when St. George's Methodist Church attempted to confine its Negro members to the gallery. This Black denomination organized as a national church in 1816, in Baltimore.

From the time of the first A.M.E. General Conference held in Baltimore in 1816, many leaders in the Black church movement including several early Bishops were Marylanders with roots in the outlying agricultural districts of Prince George, Charles, St. Mary's and other counties. Among the leaders were A.M.E. Bishops James A. Handy, Alexander W. Wayman, Thomas M.D. Ward, and Reverend John Thomas Jenifer, who was one of the best educated ministers of the early Black church. He was one of the three members of the first graduating class of Wilberforce University the first Black Church college. This college was established in Ohio by AME Bishop Daniel Payne in 1856 but because of the war and destruction of the first building by fire, the first graduates received their diplomas in 1870. Reverend Jenifer who was born of slave parents in Prince George County, Maryland later acquired his freedom. He served several important commissions of his general church and pastored large churches in Baltimore and California. He

7

pastored the large Quinn Chapel Church in Chicago in the early 1890's. Reverend gave the principal eulogy of Frederick Douglass, a fellow Marylander, as pastor of Metropolitan A.M.E. Church, Washington, D.C. in 1895. Rev. Jenifer was a dynamic speaker and official historian of the A.M.E. Church from 1912–1919. There is no known blood relationship between Rev. J. T. Jenifer and the Berry-Jenifers of Southern Maryland.

Traveling preachers from the Baltimore Bethel A.M.E. Church rode horseback and walked as missionaries in the rural district of St. Mary's and surrounding counties to evangelize Negro slaves and free men. The ancestors of John (Miles) Berry and Sam Jenifer were early converts to the religious and social doctrines of the African Methodist traveling missionaries who preached to them, taught the Lord's Prayer and the Ten Commandments in the groves which had long been the meeting place with or without the blessing of the slave masters.

In 1826 during annual conference of the A.M.E. Church meeting in Bethel Baltimore, Bishop Richard Allen commissioned the Rev. Scipio Beane, a missionary to "preach" the Christian religion to rural districts in the nearby counties of Maryland. These teachings were very compatible with the religious folklore which had evolved since the beginning of the slave trade.

Sam Jenifer had an uncle who became famous around St. Mary's county as "Doc" Henry. When Sam was a young boy his uncle told him many stories of life in earlier times. When his Uncle Henry was between twelve and fourteen years old in 1826, his mother took him to hear Reverend Scipio Beane preach in the grove near Leonardtown.

Henry Jenifer was a slave of Dr. William Thomas whose brother James Thomas also a physician, was the 26th governor of Maryland. Dr. Thomas studied under Dr. Physick in Philadelphia and was graduated from the Philadelphia Medical College in 1814. Along with the practice of medicine, he owned and managed a very large plantation with many slaves. Thomas and his brother were sons of Major William Thomas a celebrated officer of the American Revolutionary. The original Mr. Thomas settled on large acreages at Deep Falls, Maryland ceded to him in 1660. The Thomas family was directly related to Leonard Calvert, the proprietary Lord Baltimore. Young Henry had already taken care of the Doctor's horse and buggy with the prospect of some day becoming the doctor's assistant. The Jenifer family had served the Thomases for two or three previous generations.

"Doc" Henry's younger brother, Nace Jenifer was the father of Sam and Nancy. According to the St. Mary's census of 1870, Nace, then 54 years old, was born in 1816. An official facsimile of John and Nancy Berry's 1867 marriage license in Norfolk County, Va., lists Nace Jenifer of St. Mary's County Md. as Nancy's father. She named her youngest son Nace Berry. Maryland followed the unique custom of giving all slaves and their offsprings the surnames of their first purchaser upon landing in America. These slaves' names were never changed thru the generations of slavery. Maryland's calendar of wills and other documents indicate that one Jenifer family of English and Swedish ancestry immigrated to Maryland in the 17th century. Two grandsons were well known doctors; one was Walter Hanson Jenifer. The other, Dr. Daniel Jenifer had a famous son, Daniel of St. Thomas Jenifer, born in 1723. He was a pre-revolutionary statesman, holder of several provincial offices in St. Mary's, the capital, and had much property and many slaves. In 1776 he was elected a Maryland representative of the Continental Congress and was a signatory of the Constitution of the U.S.A. When members of the slave Jenifers were transferred to the Thomases, or from Charles to St. Mary's County is not known.

Many slaves were attended by old "Doc" Henry who became a skillful practitioner. He could look at your tongue and tell you about chills and fevers, dysentery and the bloody flux. He could go into the woods and come out with just the right roots and herbs, make a stew or poultice and cure constipation, worms, rheumatism or galloping consumption. He once said, "Ever once and agin de best cure fer rumatiz is to thank God it ain't de gout!"

White folks, too, would send for him at night when the master's physician could not be located or when the big boss had failed a cure. Old Doc Henry became a seasoned doctor and a deeply religious man who sometimes preached to the slaves in the grove on Sunday. He would say a prayer and then a few words of voodoo that would work miracles. He could also work black and white magic. Henry Jenifer knew a lot of tricks taught him by his root doctor father Will Jenifer, who drove for the earlier doctors Thomas before the War of 1812. The earliest Thomases were active in the Chesapeake Bay "tea party" equivalent to the one in the Charles River at Boston, which helped to bring on the Revolutionary War in 1776.

On one occasion Dr. Thomas sent his slave apprentice, Henry, to carry out the daily mopping of a large open wound on the foot of a white farmer. The same mop was used each day and the solution was carbolic acid and water. The wound did not heal in several weeks; the patient complained that it was getting worse; Doc Henry agreed and told the patient that he had a better treatment, if he could keep a secret. The patient requested a trial of the slave doctor's remedy. Doc Henry soaked a hunk of wheat bread in water left it in the open air until it was covered with a heavy growth of mold. He applied the molded bread and cured the open wound. Dr. Thomas never knew that his carbolic acid washings did not cure the infection. This crude application of penicillin was a hundred years ahead of its time.

The customs of primitive men involved the search for food among wild animals on land and stream and among growing plants. Wild plants including roots and herbs have also been the source of food and medicines for physical and mental ills for centuries. The slave trade brought root doctors and their practices from Africa to the new world. The slave trade created one of the routes of the spread of "medical culture". The major route leading to modern medicine also had much of its origin in ancient Africa through medieval Europe to America.

Doc Henry, the slave doctor in colonial Maryland had a mixture of talents. First he had the cultural heritage from slave root doctors. He mixed this knowledge with practices of his slave master Dr. William Thomas. Doc Henry used bark of a cinchona like tree similar to trees in Africa in treatment of malaria. Dr. Thomas used the refined quinine made from the real cinchona bark from America and Europe.

Doc Henry learned in his earlier years how to cut for snake bite and suck out the venom. He prescribed the chewing of fern leaves for intestinal worms. The Oleoresin of male fern was listed as aspidium an official drug used by regular doctors many years later for intestinal worms.

Doc Henry also practiced what would now be called psychotherapy and preventive medicine; notably the use of the "Jenifer asafoetida bag" worn around the neck. It had a strong obnoxious odor calculated to drive away the most dreadful of diseases. Regular doctors used it too, but none compared in quality and degree of stench with the "Jenifer variety", nor with Doc Henry's claim of effectiveness. The Jesuits wore charms and figurines of Saints around their necks to protect against disease and the evil One. This practice was far less attractive to most of Doc Henry's patients. Asafoetida after all could attack like the spraying effect of a Maryland skunk and immobilize the victim at 50 paces or could be taken by mouth for its cathartic effects. There were many other preventives of disease and black magic in Doc Henry's "bag of tricks", "Goofer" dust for sprinkling; rabbit's foot for wearing on the person, and the upside down horseshoe for the cabin door. Old Doc Henry was allowed to earn money for night work among the slaves. The money was kept for him by his master Dr. Thomas. In 1848 during an epidemic of yellow fever, Doc Henry Jenifer became one of the great heroes of the County. As the epidemic reached its height, he was taught "bloodletting" and the "cold air" treatment. During the hot summer months the epidemic became widespread and the County officials had to call for help from the surrounding country-side. Almost everybody in the county became deathly afraid of the scorge. Many fled the county to surrounding communities until stopped by gun point. Doc Henry would fearlessly go into a house and treat a semiconscious patient, frequently with family members lying dead or dying on the floor. In one instance he treated a dying mother while the father lay dead on the floor and two small children were the only persons left in the isolated farm house.

He carried his lancet for bleeding and used it often during the plague. The battle cry of Doctor Thomas and the consultants who came to help was "bleed and purge". The blood of bond and free was spilled in front yards and near cabin doors. It dried and putrified, stank and drew flies and mosquitos. The favorite potion for purging was dished out by Dr. Henry and Dr. Thomas' medicine drawer; "ten and ten's" officially ten grains calomel and ten grains of jalop powder. Doc Henry always prayed before administering a treatment. His dedication and fearlessness gained for him a great reputation among black and white. He would stand by his patient, administering and praying, until the last breath was taken. He would then prepare and dispose of the remains with dignity and religious sanctity.

He gathered to work with him a group of black women, whom he helped to train as nurses and black men to do the heavy work. It was remarkable that during many weeks of service only a few of the black nurses had fever attacks; none of them fatal. It was not until the late 19th

11

century that Doctors learned about the parasites of malaria and the virus of yellow fever carried by female mosquitos. It then became clear that these death dealing epidemic fevers began in the swampy lowlands such as existed near the river fronts where there were mosquitos and not because of "eufuvia eminiations" and the "filthy" poor whites and Blacks who lived in these areas.

It was not until the 20th century that the partial immunity of black people to yellow fever and malaria was found to be real. These fevers were brought to the new world for the first time by infested mosquitoes transported with human cargo packed in slave ships. These dreaded fevers were not known to the Western world before the slave trade. Partial immunity was developed after many centuries of exposure to malignant fevers causing the death of millions. Only those developing immunity survived and transmitted immune genes to their offsprings. Sickle red blood cells is a mechanism of immunity to malaria fever. It may be transmitted from parent to children but is not a racial trait.

So much for science and health with key to the "Jenifers". One day at the height of the yellow fever plague of St. Mary's, 'Doc' Henry arose about 4 a.m. to get out the rig for a heavy day with Dr. Thomas. It was a very dark, cold and dreary night when he spotted some moving lights a good distance away in the area of the white folks graveyard. At first he paid little attention, but he began to hear distant noises like the howling of wolves. Suddenly he remembered that on the day before, they had buried "mean massa, Big Jim Milburn" who had dropsy for years and was stricken with the yellow plague. They had given him up for dead when he sat straight up; rolled his yellow eyes and sneezed. It was several hours later that he appeared really dead and he was hauled away for burial. Henry was a deeply religious man and never believed in "haints"—that is, never before this early morning experience. He aroused everybody in the cabin and pointed out the first real "haint" he had ever seen. Big Massa Jim had refused to die and was holding a "pow wow" with the other dead slave masters refusing to stay in hell. Others who had gathered around agreed with Doc Henry that it was time to sing and pray cause "massa Jim" and other "massas" was coming back.

The cabin group was led in prayer by Doc Henry: "Oh God", intoned Brother Henry as he knelt on the dirt floor, "bow our heds belo' our hearts and our hearts belo' our knees, and our knees in some lonesum

12

valley. Dear Lord, please God, tak' away dis plague, but don't bring back dem what's dead. Don't let dem massas stir up no more er dat yella potion." With the aid of the kerosene lamp and with one eye open, Brother Henry looked at his yellow, bile-stained hands as they partially covered his face in prayer. "I smells dat strong bitter gall, Lord, what dey's makin' up over dare, way over here, dear Lord. We have sinned agin you, Lord, but dere's moe sin agin us now dan we can bear. Protect us, your servants, Lord, and when we's dun wit dis world, take us in yo kingdom, massa Lord, where we will praise you name forever, Amen. Amen. Amen."

Up from their knees, the small group began to sing one of "de white folks funeral songs," "Nearer My God To Thee." As they looked outside, they saw the beginning of the break of dawn. The peculiar lights in the graveyard were still moving, but now they could see human forms. They ventured out of the cabin and moved slowly toward the spectacle. Now there was a little more light, and they could see that the lights were coming from lanterns and suddenly beheld not slave masters rising from the dead, but slave workmen digging graves for dozens of slave masters and would-be slave masters. They were piled high in boxes, where they had been deposited the day before. The death toll especially among whites had forced the slave gravediggers to go to the graveyards long before daybreak, after only an hour or two of sleep. "Lawd, dem ain't no haints," cried Sister Matilda, half-joyfully but more relieved. "De Lawd dun killed so many of dem mean white folks wit the plague like it say in the Bible, niggers had to work all night to bury dem." "Lawd have mercy on dey souls."

There were pitiful, sorrowful and fearful episodes in the lives of black and white alike during the long weeks of the summer pestilence of 1848. As the fall winds began to blow north to east and into the ocean currents, the yellow fever epidemic began to tail off in St. Mary's County. The powerful prayers of Brother "Doc" Henry Jenifer, of other slaves and slave masters, white, black, mulatto and red human beings were finally being answered. All of the mortally stricken victims were buried by the first of November, filling all of the graveyards and many corn-fields. The lingering, chronically ill were slowly recuperating and no new cases were being reported.

In order to give thanks to God for preserving the lives of so many, while thousands of others perished, officials of government, merchants, owners of plantations, members of churches of all denominations organized the biggest Thanksgiving in history. On the appointed day, all unnecessary work was stopped. There were no slaves, no masters, no race, no color, no creed. Saints and sinner sat side-by-side in churches. Men, women and children gathered on mansion houses' front lawns, back yards, cabins, open clearings or farmlands, in taverns and river boats. Church bells rang and prayers were offered everywhere mid a mixture of joy and sorrow. Black singers serenaded the people gathered in the big house and churches where they had never entered before with their harmonious religious slave songs. "Nobody knows de trouble I see, Glory Hallelujah!" "There is a balm in Gilead." "I'm so Glad trouble don't las' always, oh my Lawd, oh my Lawd." Hardhearted slavemasters were seen to weep unabashedly. Maids and mistresses embraced their mammies as they listened to the penetrating words set to doleful folk music by their slaves. Jesuit priests and parishioners sang, "Have thine own way, Lord." Songs of praise, resignation and thanksgiving penetrated the air. Young widows and orphans and the newly poor were observed everywhere.

A group of slaves gathered in the large yard in front of Cremona, the Thomases mansion house on the banks of the Patuxent River. They were joined by many white men and women as they sang with bowed, uncovered heads. Their voices reverberated against the water of the famous river nearby. With the precision of a dress rehearsal, their harmony was breath-taking as they sang,

> *"Lord, I want to be a Christian in my heart. Lord, I*
> *want to be more loving, more holy. I don't want to*
> *be like Judas. I want to be like Jesus in my heart."*

This was indeed the long moment of truth and poetic justice when all men, women and children were equal in the sight of an omnipotent and merciful God.

After ten weeks and thousands of deaths in Southern Maryland, Doc Henry Jenifer felt for certain he had at last won the freedom he had prayed for so long. Massa Doctor Thomas had promised that some day he would allow Henry to purchase his freedom if he could save enough money or the equivalent in "good tobacco" from doctoring at night. At a time when Henry was at the height of his fame in religious medical service around the county and as the great calamity was waning,

Henry approached Doctor Thomas with great expectations on the subject of whether he had accumulated enough savings during 12 years to buy his time and freedom. The doctor, who had become quite dependent upon Henry as an assistant and menial servant was reluctant to let him go. "Massa Thomas," said Henry, "I been workin wit you all my life. You sho is a good massa, but I kin care and do jus' as much good workin' fur you after I buy my time as I kin now. You promise' me many years ago, if I could save enough to pay you for yo troubles, I could buy my time. I am gittin' older and my chilluns is grown. I think I give you enuf money for overtime work to buy my time. De plague is 'bout over and I am tired enough to drap right here in my tracks."

Doctor Thomas finally announced that while things were so disorganized during the plague someone had stolen the 12 year savings he had held for Henry and that it might take another 10 or 12 years, if he worked hard enough overtime, to earn enough money to buy his freedom.

Meanwhile, there were many free Negroes and mulattos in St. Mary's, Prince George, and other counties of Maryland, probably more than any other slave state. The population census in 1840 showed that about 20% of all the free people in St. Mary's County were black or mulatto. There were black and mulatto, free and slave Jenifers. Most of Henry's relatives were black and enslaved. Many free blacks were kidnapped and re-sold into slavery in the deep South.

Since the Nat Turner uprising in Virginia in 1831, life for most of the slaves had become increasingly more stringent. Everybody in the slave world was hearing about the activity of the underground railroad escape passage to Canada. This activity was greater during the period of the epidemic. Henry was called old, but really was about 38 to 40 years of age. He suffered deep disappointment and many days of depression because of what he rightfully regarded as an unforgivable betrayal. Slaves were never as dumb as they were supposed to be. Henry had saved some money on his own during the great epidemic, when fever victims were color-blind and money was no object. His many days of depression finally turned into anger, and he made up his mind that he was going to escape by the underground to Canada, following the North Star that he had heard so much about.

One morning when Dr. Thomas was waiting and smoking his

15

after-breakfast cigar, Henry did not show up with a freshly curried horse hitched to a nicely-shining victoria carriage ready for the morning rounds. After waiting and waiting, he took over the reigns himself and rounded up all of the Jenifers to find out about Henry. Nobody knew of the whereabouts of Henry. After several days, the older Jenifers learned by the Black Dispatch what they had suspected all along. "I 'spect Henry dun run away with dat 'Harret' woman," said Matilda to one of her very close friends. "Yeah, she sho is some smart woman". I hear she been hangin' around over to de creek at night." "Dey say if you ain't scared to go, she can take you all de way safe on dat Underground train". "Ain't nobody seed him in two weeks." "Yeah," said Matilda, "I don't believe we's gon ever see him no mo'. "He's mad and ain't scared o' no slave catcher."

Matilda and her friend were dead right. Harriet had contacted Henry through her efficiently working grapevine, although they had never seen each other before. Her Maryland terminal was on the Eastern Shore. Her trail, temporarily interrupted during the epidemic, consisted of a carefully measured system of way stations, a nights run apart. Dozens of people, seen and unseen, were involved on the long route to Canada. White and black, male and female, housewives, businessmen, wagon-drivers, coachmen, riverboat men were involved with signals, code-words, foodstuffs, clothing and camouflage; counter-espionage, base-ments, swamps, attics, cornfields, rivers, churches and schools. Harriett was just as anxious to deliver 'Doc' Henry as Henry was to deliver himself. The time was set, under cover of darkness, the contacts made. The route was eastward from the back roads and fields of Leonardtown, across the Patuxent River to Olivet by rowboat. Then on a fishing boat to Cove Point in the Chesapeake Bay. There, biding his time, following instructions, hiding away in a freight boat for a fee, Doc Henry crossed the Bay into Dorchester County. He had survival rations from the boat. He hid away in the woods until nightfall. Then by foot to Church Creek, and to the outskirts of Cambridge. There he made contact with Harriett, face-to-face for the first time. He had money in his pocket, survival rations in a knapsack, and determination in his heart; but he was far from being out of danger. Like a military picket in a field of battle, this daring young woman continued to blaze the trail. There were other escapees within her range of operation heading northward. Some would falter and need special help, or be lost. But Henry's determination grew stronger as he pushed onward to Smyna, Odessa, and into the outskirts of Wilmington, Delaware and now he could travel by day as well as by night on to the outskirts of Philadelphia and eventually New York and straight upstate to Troy, then westward to Schenectady. All along this northern trail, there were friendly Quakers and friendly blacks commanding way-stations on into Little Falls, Odeida, Syracuse, Rochester and Niagara, and finally across the water into St. Catherine's Ontario. Before he crossed the water he could see the Promised Land in the distance.

As his feet touched the free soil of Canada, he took a deep breath of fresh air. It was as if shackles from a chain gang had suddenly unbound his sore limbs and blistered feet. Suddenly and for a while he thought of his loved ones left in chattel slavery. All were still there. He felt a mixture of joy and sorrow. But, soon he was struck with the reality of survival in a new world. High visibility of Black people was in his favor at this point. He soon found himself in a meeting of the St. Catherine's African Methodist Church, which was founded in 1831 by missionaries from the New York A.M.E. Conference for escapees. Other missions of A.M.E. church were organized by escaped slaves and their offspring at Amertsberg, Chatham, Hamilton, Nova Scotia, Dresden and elsewhere throughout Canada West. One of the most famous escaped slaves was also a former Marylander, Rev. Josiah Henson of Dresden.

Henson was the authentic Uncle Tom of Harriett Beecher Stowe's novel "Uncle Tom's Cabin". He was first an A.M.E. and later a minister of the British Methodist Episcopal (B.M.E.) church an early splinter of the A.M.E. church of Canada. The seeds of liberty were widely sewn in many places.

Slavery in Old St. Mary's had only a decade and half more of official existence. Before many more crops were harvested on the banks of the Potomac, news drifted back to Old St. Mary's. Relatives and friends heard that a Black preachin', medicine man with St. Mary's roots was prosperin mightily with an interracial following among the needy in mind, body and spirit in freedom.

Sam Jenifer, Henry's nephew, and my grandmother's brother along with hundreds like him, waited for their moment to move from slavery to freedom. It is their story and the story of their descendants I tell.

Section One
The
War
of the
Rebellion
(1864-65)

Cremona; Mansion of Slave Plantation on Patuxent River, St. Mary's County, Maryland. Ancestral Home of the Dr. William Thomases where Sam and Nancy Jenifer and some of their ancestors were enslaved.

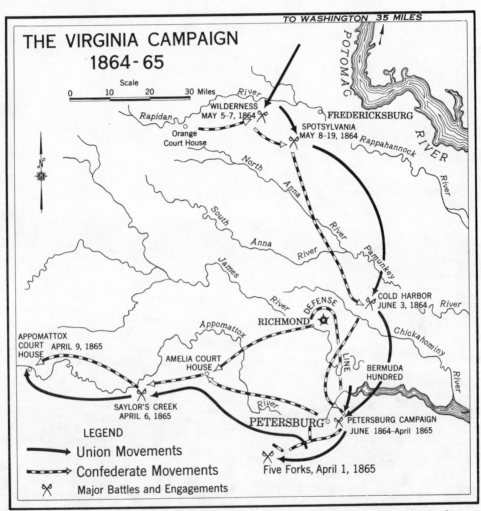

THE VIRGINIA CAMPAIGN 1864-65

TO WASHINGTON 35 MILES

POTOMAC

RIVER

Scale

0   10   20   30 Miles

River

Rapidan

WILDERNESS
MAY 5-7, 1864

FREDERICKSBURG

Orange
Court House

SPOTSYLVANIA
MAY 8-19, 1864

Rappahannock

North

Anna

River

Pamunkey

South

Anna

River

River

COLD HARBOR
JUNE 3, 1864

River

James

River

RICHMOND

DEFENSE

Chickahominy

River

APPOMATTOX
COURT   APRIL 9, 1865
HOUSE

Appomattox

Appomattox

AMELIA COURT
HOUSE

LINE

BERMUDA
HUNDRED

SAYLOR'S CREEK
APRIL 6, 1865

River

PETERSBURG

PETERSBURG CAMPAIGN
JUNE 1864-April 1865

LEGEND

→ Union Movements

⇢ Confederate Movements

✄ Major Battles and Engagements

Five Forks, April 1, 1865

Map of the Virginia Campaign of the Civil War, 1864–65. Unbroken arrows (right), show movements of Army of the Potomac (in which Sam Jenifer fought). Movements of Army of the James (in which John Berry fought), were south of the James River.

Civil War Infantrymen at Fortress Monroe, 1864 (similar to the unit of Sam Jenifer, Infantryman, Army of the Potomac).

Field Cannon Unit of Battery "A" Light Artillery, Second Regiment, U.S. Colored Troops. Similar to Light Artillery field gun piece No. 5, Battery "B" Second Regiment, manned by John Berry's Squad, in Army of the James, Spring, 1864.

Site of the Battle of the Crater Explosion before Petersburg, 1864—Photo circa 1890.

Photo shows three escaped slaves appearing before General Benjamin Butler (seated left), at Fortress Monroe, on May 23, 1861, to aid the Union cause, which was against early war department policy. Butler accepted the escapees and put them to work as "Contraband of War." Butler later commanded Regiments of Black Soldiers. (Photo, courtesy Fortress Monroe Museum.)

Mrs. Leonidas (Emma) Berry in 1970 at the site of the Battle of the Crater Explosion.

"Where Ya Goin' Boy?"

WHERE ya goin' boy?" This was an expression as common as "good morning" in the white man's slave parlance of southern Maryland in 1864. "Yes suh! I goin' after a horse for Massa," was the answer. It was a fact that the white man did not know that "the boy" (getting to be a man) was 10 miles away from the plantation of Tom Gardner where he belonged.

It was near noon on this chilly January morning and there was a bright sun, shining directly overhead. The inquirer was astride a prancing blazed-faced horse with white hoofs; a bag was hanging from each side of his saddle. Protruding from one of them was a bullwhip and from the other a set of leg irons. A pistol protruded from a holster over the rider's left hip and a crude cowboy type lasso was curled around the right front post of the saddle. The rider was unmistakably a roving "slave catcher" on his morning prowl.

However, the twenty-year-old slave "boy" had an effective decoy, that turned the hated hunter of Black humanity, unsuspectingly galloping away. The "boy," not nearly as dumb as the slave hunter thought him to be, had an easily visible horse bridle thrown over his right shoulder. Nor had the white hunter noted the bulging pockets under the ragged overcoat and patched overalls caused by his survival rations. "Praise God, from whom all blessing flow," cried John Berry, for he had just made another hurdle in his plan to break the chains of slavery, escape, find and hopefully join "Massa Linkuns" army, which the Black grapevine had placed several more miles in the woods near Point Lookout, Maryland.

Years later, John Berry told this story many times to his inquisitive young son, Llewellyn, as he relived the dramatic and courageous experience of his escape from slavery; the beginning of his life as John Berry, free man; and the end of his life as Johnny Miles, slave.

"I made my break a little while after New Year's, in 1864. I had been makin' my plans for 'bout two years; I suffered too much myself, seen too much, people bein' whupped and drove like cattle, from sun up to sun down, 'kin to cant,' (can see to can't see); young women bein' forced to white overseers beds to be 'broke' in, to have the white man's chilluns: for him to sell his own flesh and blood at auction. Nearly every day some mother sold away from her chilluns'; sisters, brothers, husbands and wives separated maybe never see'n each other agin'."

"Two years befor' I made my jump, we got a new overseer on Tom Gardner's plantation, where my kinfolks wuz held in slavery as far back as anybody could remember. The new man was to be a 'slave-breaker.' Eve'yday he was beatin' up somebody, a man, woman or child."

"One day I was plowing corn with a fast mule and a rickety plow. I had been hangin' on dat plow all day since sunrise and was wet all over with sweat. Dis overseer saw de plow cut into some stalks of young corn, he come over and say: 'Is that the best you kin do nigger?' and slashed me cross my back six or seven time wid a cat-o-nine tails. It was near sundown, on a hot and sticky day; I wuz already tired and I dragged myself to the cabin, too tired and full 'o pain to eat dat cold slop dey had fer supper. I wuz painful all night and 'fore I could get to sleep dey wuz ringing dat sunrise bell to fall in line and 'hot tail' it to de field."

"A few days later I wasn't plowin fast enough for him and he jumped me agin. This time I was ready for him, I was ti'ed of being jumped when I wuz workin' as hard as I could in the hot broiling sun. I wuz ti'ed of watchin others being 'whupped with cow hide and tree limbs and I had made up my mind. I promised my God dat I would not take another beatin' lying down. When he threw his lash, I grabbed him and rassled him to de ground. He called three husky fellas to double me over and pull down my pants, while the slave driver flogged me until the blood come. He yelled 'goddam you I will kill you nigger.' I resist no more. At that moment when I could hardly stand up, I felt de blood of courage risin' in my veins. I wuz no longer 'fraid to die but I wuz not goin' to give my life for a mess of pottage. When I die I wuz 'termined to carry my share of slave mongers wid me."

22

As a young man, outwardly, John Berry was not a fighter. He was peaceful, quiet, and very religious. There was little joy in his life and rarely was there respite from drudgery and hard labor. At times when he would walk through the woods or near the banks of the Chesapeake, he loved the music of nature, the songs of birds, the whisper of leaves, and the roar of waves on the sandy shores. He had heard about the North star and the path to freedom, he had heard this most of his life from his mother and others on the plantation. He felt that someday, somehow, he would reach that "promised land" of freedom from chattel slavery.

John Berry continued to tell his story of escape to his son Lew. "We kept hearin' 'bout de war and we found out dat the North and the South wuz fightin'. I had several ideas 'bout escapin' to de North. Another year pas' and we started to hear dat soldiers from the North army wuz in Maryland. Soon I heard from de Black dispatch (slave gossip), dat if a slave could escape from de plantation that the North army would take him as a soldier; if he was strong, brave and healthy. We heard de North soldier wuz wearing blue uniforms and we seen soldiers of de South army wearing gray uniforms. De word was dat, it was dangerous to try to reach the North troops and many slaves had been caught by slave catchers turned back to de plantation, tortured and sometimes killed."

"Pop, weren't you 'fraid of being shot with all those slave catchers round that you told me about," Lew asked. "Like I said, my mind wuz made up; I wuzn't 'fraid to die; I wanted a chance to fight fer freedom. I wanted to fight fer myself, my mother and brothers and all de slaves dat had been kidnapped from Africa for 100 years back," the father replied.

"One day I had to ride a two horse team load o' tobacco down to Point Lookout. De overseer took four or five of us fellas to bring back a load o' oyster shells fer de plantation. While we wuz loadin' up, dere wuz other fellas drivin up from other plantations to de market place. De word was passed dat President Linkun's soldiers wuz camped in de woods nearby and dat some slaves had made it into de camp and joined up.

"I went back to de plantation and when I went to bed I prayed all night. I ask God to guide me; I had faith which my mother had taught me from early childhood. De next I had a dream and I woke

23

up wid my plans as plain as day. I told nobody but my own dear mother 'bout my secret. Dis was the last time I ever saw her. She told me to go on and not be 'fraid and fight fer freedom for all of us. Wid tears in her eyes she said, she was leavin' me in the hands of God and she knew everthin' would be alright; she would pray fer my safety and to see me agin someday."

"Pop, you've told me things about slave days and the war before, but you never told me all this before. Tell me some more," Lew asked.

"It was a cold day in St. Mary's County, late January, 1864, I spent most of de night sewin' extra pockets inside my overalls by candlelight to pack in food dat wouldn't give me away and fer some more things I wanted to take. I remember dat my mother give me a little silver cross on a small chain that she had hid away for many years. Co'se it wuzn't real silver. I filled a flat bottle from a jar of apple cider and stuck it in one pocket. I had a small Bible I kept for a long time tryin' to learn to read some words in it. I put de Bible and de cross in another pocket. I wouldn't take a chance on cooked food so I put some raw yams in de other pocket. I put on all de clothes I had; a pair of old patched pants under my overalls and two old shirts and a coat. I had on two pair o' socks and took a pair o' old socks to keep my hands warm. I took a rag to tie over my head and over my ears, if dey get too cold.

"I had a horse's bridle as part o' my plan; I threw it over my shoulder and lit out at 3 o'clock in de morning headin fer Point Lookout 'bout 30 miles away."

On the night that John Berry left his corner on the dirt floor of the slave cabin where he slept, it was blacker than a thousand midnights. When he had fled the first mile, he slowed down to catch his breath and he began to fully realize the awesomeness of a slave making a break for freedom. He began to choke up a bit and he thought of the many religious songs sung by slaves in the shady groves on Sunday afternoons or to steal their strength during long hours of back breaking work. His stirring baritone was well known in these groups but now he could only hum, 'Walk with me Lord, Walk with me, while I'm on my pilgrim journey. I want Jesus to walk with me.'" John Berry remembered these experiences with frightening nostalgia as he told his story to his young son.

"I walked very fast dat first night 'til break of day; after dat I had

24

to be very careful. If I stay along de road-side I be sure to run into slave catchers. If I stay too fer in de woods I might get lost or I look suspicious if I met de wrong folks. Early dat morning I run into a couple of white hunters in de edge of de woods, luckily dey just spotted a squirrel in a hick'ry-nut tree and I moved on payin' dem no 'tention." I had drunk all o' dat bottle o' apple cider de night befor' and now I wuz nibblin' on dem raw yams. In de woods I found a frozen stream; I broke de thin sheet o' ice and fill my stomach and my bottle wid drinkin' water. Twice during dat day I wuz stopp'd by slave catchers. I saw some mo comin' down de road and I had to get over in de woods; I hid behind a tree 'til all was clear. Each time I wuz caught dey said: 'Where ya goin' boy' boy' and each time I said, 'I'm goin after a horse for 'Massa'. My horse's bridle was throw'd over my shoulder to prove de truth, if ever I tole it." Berry said smiling.

He continued the story of his arduous journey to join the Union Army. He got off the course in traveling his roundabout route in search of the encampment of friendly soldiers who would allow him to join up to fight the slave holders. Again it was night fall and after a long cold day on foot, he finally decided to find a spot of relative safety and stop for the night. He found a ditch along the right of way of a farm within sight of the main road. The ditch was about three feet deep, dry and partly flanked by heavy brush and small trees. He made a bed of this brush in the ditch and partly covered himself with the same material. There he stayed until near sunrise of the next day. He knew he was somewhere near Point Lookout and with the aid of the rising sun, and his good sense of direction he again got his bearings and finally made it to the Union camp.

In the early afternoon of that second day John Berry caught sight of a clearing as he came out of the woods. There were tents and soldiers in blue walking around the campground. "Thank God," he cried, and tears welled in his eyes as he shook with a mixture of fright and joy. John Berry was reliving those emotional war years of a quarter of a century before and telling it to his spellbound son. Lew would not let him stop, so his father continued; "All de soldiers I saw wuz white; it was de first time I see soldiers in blue; we all knew dat soldiers in grey wuz 'rednecks,' fightin' fer slave owners.

"I come up close to a soldier standin by his tent. 'How de do boy.'

The soldier said, 'what brings you here?' 'I want to join de North army and fight fer President Linkun,'" the runaway said.

Many slave minds were pretty keen on political issues which they had heard discussed at the dinner table of the big house and in market places. They would pass on this intelligence through the "Black dispatch" or "grapevine" to the slaves in the field. They knew that fighting with the North was no absolute guarantee that freedom would be gained. Moreover, if the South should win it would be hell to pay for soldiers and others guilty of helping the North. They felt that if enough of them joined the North and fought bravely enough their positions as chattel slaves would have to improve. As W. E. B. DuBois said, "They had the good sense to smell freedom in the air." As expressed in the old Negro spiritual, "Over my head I hear music in the air, there must be a God somewhere."

John Berry did not tell the white man, "I want to fight for my freedom or I want to fight for the North," but, "I want to join de North army and fight for President Linkun."

The private on the campground at Point Lookout said with some patronizing in his manner. "Alright sir, I will take you in to see the sergeant." The soldier took John Berry into the Headquarters barracks which was a large one-room office with several windows and one door; a pot belly wood and coal stove and two crude writing desks completed the furnishings. At one of the desks, sat the sergeant.

"Sergeant, this boy says he wants to 'join up.' The sergeant looked up. "Hello, young man; so you wanta be a soldier." "Yes suh, Massa." "From how far away did you come." "Long ways suh! I don't know how many miles." "How long did it take you?" "Two days suh." "Did anybody know you planned to run away from the plantation?" "Nobody but my mama suh." "How old are you?" "I aint fer sure but I think 20 years." "I wuz born five or six crops 'fore the gold rush, my mama said." "Yeh, that would make you about 16 or 17." "What is your name?"

At this point, the new name of the escaped slave was revealed for the first time. Up to that moment he had been called Johnny Miles. An important ingredient in the master plan for escaping slavery and becoming a part of the freedom movement was to change his names and take on a new identity. This was the bridge burning technique that would help to cut Johnny Miles off forever from Tom Gardner's back breaking slave plantation. The answer to the sergeant's question, "What is your name?" came out loud and clear; "John Berry!"

He had said goodby forever to Johnny Miles, son of John and Sarah Miles, and chattel owned by Tom Gardner, at Old St. Mary's, Maryland.

Joining Up

THE sergeant continued his questioning of John Berry, a.k.a. Johnny Miles. "From which plantation did you escape?" John lied and said Milburn Farms. After a few more short questions, the sergeant left the barracks. John Berry was alone.

He was still not sure. His reception so far had been rough and unpredictable. The alert, conditioned mind of a slave was making observations. He saw no Negroes on the compound near the headquarters barracks except a couple of young women washing men's army clothes down near the fence. He noticed that much of the whole area was fenced in and there were guards walking a routine beat with shouldered muskets at all openings to the barricade.

Soon, John's sensitive ears picked up the sound of the rhythmic blowing of bugles, and the rattle of snare drums. He moved closer to a window in the headquarters building and saw a detail of musket-bearing soldiers at drill practice. After awhile the drum and bugle were quiet and the drill master was heard to command in a loud voice, "Compan-n-ny! Halt!—At ease!" A few minutes later, another command, "Compan-n-ny, attention!—Forward march! One-two-three-four. One-two," and the bugle-drum corps picked up the cadence as the proud, erect soldiers continued the precision drill. John Berry thrilled at the anticipation of successfully becoming a soldier, smartly dressed in blue, and marching off to war. With rapt attention to the drill, he moved slowly out of the open door of the headquarters, not wanting to disturb the soldiers working there. He sat on a big boulder close to the building and watched. Four drill teams marched back and forth across the parade grounds and aligned themselves in geometric formation, facing the American flag at the top of a tall pole.

It was near sundown, and after several minutes of silence the bugler stepped forward and as the soldiers stood in position of salute, the bugler blew the call of retreat. The assigned team lowered the flag. John Berry observed and listened to the ceremony for the first time. He realized that there was the hallowed emblem which he was asking to risk his life to defend. What he did not know was that he would be reminded of this again and again at sundown.

John went back into the headquarters room as a mess attendant brought his evening meal. It consisted of a tin plate full of boiled beans with lots of molasses, a hunk of cornbread and a tin cup of water. As the food was put on a small side table, the sergeant returned and barked—"Boy, here's your supper. When you finish, wash your plate at the pump outside. There is a blanket in the corner. You can sleep on the floor for the night. The guard outside will show you the latrine down near the fence." "The la— what's dat?" "There's where you relieve yourself before you lay down to sleep," the sergeant replied brusquely.

The sergeant left for the mess hall and his own barracks, leaving the headquarters under the surveillance of the night guard. The pallet on the floor reminded John Berry of the dirty quilt on the cabin floor where for years he rested his tired body and prayed for freedom. There was a difference. The headquarters' floor was wooden, the cabin floor was hard packed earth.

The twilight air was brisk around the campground. There was a fine sprinkle of snow just barely covering the ground now and shadows were beginning to fall; an orderly came and banked the fires in the coal stove and lit the carbide lamp. The night wore on and all was quiet and motionless except a flickering flame which John could see through the draft window of the coal stove. This would-be soldier, a long way from all the friends he'd known, fumbled with the Holy Testament which he had tucked away in his ragged trouser pocket. Here and there he could pick out a word or two which he had learned at Sunday camp meetings in the grove near the Gardner plantation. He sat at a headquarters table under the dimmed light of the lamp.

He knew the Lord's Prayer which he recited to himself and hummed a few songs he used to sing in the grove as he dreamed of the future while trying to forget the past. There came to his mind the old slave songs of faith and courage, "Lord, I don't feel noways tired. Oh, glory hallelujah! Jesus is a rock in a weary lan', a shelter in the time of storm," and lines from the Methodist hymn, "Through many dangers, toils and snares I have already come." And finally he closed his tear-dimmed eyes and quietly went to sleep.

The next day he was up at daybreak, as was his custom, and went outside to greet the rising sun as it came up over the horizon of the Chesapeake Bay at its junction with the Potomac River. Soon John heard another bugle call—"Reveille;" which he would hear over and over each morning, if he could qualify and successfully enlist into the Army. In mockery, the soldiers added parody to the hated reveille, "You gotta get up, you gotta get up, you're in the Army now; you're not behind a plow; you're up the ditch, you-son-of-a-bitch, you gotta get up this morning."

At 8:30 after a special breakfast in an army tin plate at the headquarters, another sergeant took John two doors down the company street to the dispensary. The dispensary sergeant, reading from a slip of paper, spoke in a loud voice, "You are John Berry." "Yes Suh." "The sheriff was here already this morning with a posse and bloodhounds looking for three escaped slaves. They said they were looking for three burly field niggers, two were jet black and one was griffe. There was six hundred apiece on their heads if captured alive and $50 apiece on a slab." "Your name don't fit—that is if you didn't change your name. Anyhow, we didn't let 'em search the barracks." The sergeant continued, "That don't mean you're in the Army. Some of you slave boys don't know what side you wanna be on. Some o' you all are in the Confederate prison camp three miles down the road cause they wuz waiting on, as body servants, the captured Confederate officers. A lotta white folks in Maryland don't know what side they wanna be on, either. I'm fightin' with the North 'cause I needed a job. The free niggers and the slaves have all the best jobs in St. Mary's County. How would you like to be in that Confederate prison camp down near the water with yo' master?" John Berry was completely speechless.

"Now you gotta be able to pass a stiff examination and then we gotta have a place fer you," the sergeant continued, "Otherwise you don't get in the Army and you can go on back to your plantation." John's heart began to beat very fast but he remained silent. "We'll keep you here and feed you until the doctor comes." Lt. Francis Cox,

31

U. S. Army Medical Corps, was due back from Fortress Monroe, Virginia, with some special supplies on a Navy boat. "The doctor's due back some time today—no tellin' when he'll get here. The water's been rough around the horseshoe curve in the Bay." The sergeant continued. Then, more kindly, "There's another one o' you all down the end of the hall there. You can go over and join him." "Yes suh, Massa," John replied, moving quietly.

At the end of the hallway he found himself face to face with another young man of the same shade of brown complexion, the same height of 5'8", and about the same weight and age. He said he was Sam Jenifer and he had not changed his name. He was also an escaped slave having arrived two days before hiding away in a load of hay. The Jenifer and Gardner plantations were not too far apart in St. Mary's County. Jenifer cautiously admitted that he had jumped from the Thomas' plantation near the Patuxent River. "Dey calls it Cremona," he confided. John and Sam did not remember ever seeing each other before, but they knew many of the same people from adjacent plantations. They figured they may have seen each at one of the Sunday camp meetings in the grove, where John did a lot of singing and leading of the religious slave songs. Slave assembly for religious service, and funerals had not been forbidden in St. Mary's County if they had a white preacher or missionary. They also figured they may have seen each other on the oyster boats in the Bay or the Patuxent or Potomac Rivers, where they both had worked.

They were together all day, in and outside the dispensary, until the company surgeon, Lt. Francis Cox, arrived in the afternoon. They had a lot of time to talk about their aims and aspirations; first, to be successful in getting enlisted, then to become expert with a musket and maybe some day lead a raid on their old plantations and bring their mothers and other family members to freedom. They showed each other scars on their backs from floggings with tree limbs and cowhide whips. Outside the dispensary, they even sang, "Do you think I could make a soldier?" and "Oh, freedom! Before I'll be a slave, I'll be buried in my grave and go home to my Lord and be free." They vowed to keep in touch if possible and pray each night to make the Army and come through the War alive and well.

The lieutenant followed by his sergeant and corporal walked into the examining area; which was a large room with several waist-high wooden examining tables and a dozen low cut benches, six to eight feet long. There were crude weighing scales primarily for freight; a cabinet with glass doors containing doctor's instruments, tinctures, salves and pills.

"John Berry!" the doctor called.

"Yes suh," answered John.

"Sergeant, did you record his weight stripped?"

"Yes sir, Lieutenant."

"His height, waist and leg measurements?"

"Yes sir, Lieutenant."

"Did you find venereal sores? Gonorrhea?"

"No sir."

"Were there any body lice or head or crab lice?"

"No Sir."

"Did you carry out the same test for Sam Jenifer?"

"Yes sir, Lieutenant."

"Call off your findings from your record," the doctor ordered.

The sergeant complied.

"John and Sam, stand over there and start jumping up and down on your toes; keep it up until I tell you to stop—; 1, 2, 3, 4, faster."

While this was going on, the lieutenant inspected more carefully the recordings of his assistant. He continued,

"Sergeant did you find sugar and albumin in the urine?"

"Negative sir."

"Did you send fecal specimens to the laboratory for parasites."

"Yes sir, I did Lieutenant."

"Now you boys stop jumping, hold out your arms for pulse examinations."

"Sergeant, write the following: pulse for John Berry —150 beats per minute and regular; Sam Jenifer— 140 regular."

Now, sergeant take both pulse rates after three minutes and record the figures.

"Give him a hand there, Corporal."

"Yes sir, Lieutenant."

The lieutenant turned again to his candidates and spoke in a loud voice,

> "Now John Berry, if you stepped on a bumble bee
> with the middle of your bare feet, would you kill
> him? or would he sting you?"

John thought for a few seconds and replied,

> "I would kill him sir."
> "You, Jenifer."
> "I would kill him too," said Sam.
> "Let the records show flat feet, sergeant and send both
> of these boys for foot print tests."

Lieutenant Cox medical officer continued with his examination.

> "Now, John look toward the light with your mouth
> open; dental caries, 14, tonsils normal, tongue coated
> $3+$; head and neck-negative; Sam you're next. Open
> your mouth wide, dental caries $3+$, tonsils-normal.
> Tongue coated $2+$; head and neck-negative.
> "Now get buck-naked both of you and lie flat on your
> back on those tables. Bring me my stethoscope,
> Corporal."
> "Here it is, sir."

The doctor examined the heart and lungs of each candidate carefully by palpation, percussion and oscultation.

> "Heart and lungs-negative, no enlargements of the
> liver and spleen," the doctor dictated to his sergeant.
> "Now both of you stand up."

The doctor pressed his right middle finger over the inguinal ring in the groins of each candidate to test for hernia. With each manuever, he commanded,

> "Turn your head to the left and cough! Come on, big
> cough! Try it again. Open your mouth wide, cough
> loud, that's better. Sergeant, you will record inguinal
> rings intact, no hernia. All right, now stand side by
> side, not too close, bend forward at the waist."

The doctor retreated to the rear, parted their gluteusmaximus muscles for inspection and proceeded with a rubber gloved digital examination,

"No hemorrhoids, normal sphincter and prostate." he declared in a loud voice.

"Now stand up, stretch out your arms like this, forward, to the side, and over your head." Commented the lieutenant as he washed his hands.

"Now squat and bend all the joints of your arms and legs."

Both John and Sam passed all of these tests without difficulty.

"Now, get dressed and go to the other end of the room. I want to see you shoulder that hundred pound sack of sand."

That was the easiest part of the examination for John and Sam.

"John, when did you last have chills and fever?"

"Last summer sir."

"Sergeant give John one ounce of castor oil at bedtime and if less than two trips to the latrine, give croton oil, two drops on the tongue in the morning. Begin calomel and rhubarb three times a day tomorrow. Sam, chills and fever?"

"Summer fo' las, suh."

"Same treatment for Sam." "Did you ever have bloody flux, John?"

"Yes suh, Massa, when I was a child."

"None since then?"

"No sir."

"Sam, what about you?"

"Yes suh, Massa, two summers back, mild case, no blood, none after dat."

"Did you or your mother or sisters or brothers that you lived with have consumption? No contact with consumatives? Neither of you?"

"No suh, massa."

"Have John and Sam in the eye, ear and nose and throat infirmary at 9:00 a.m.; that's all today."

The next day at high noon, the post-surgeon announced to John Berry and Sam Jenifer that they had passed the physical and mental tests. They were sworn in with the right hand on the open Bible. Then having had small pox vaccinations and received medications as ordered, the proper tags were attached to their left wrists. Next they were asked to take one step forward over a white line as an act of voluntary enlistment. John Berry and Sam Jenifer gladly complied.

"Congratulations! John, you weigh one hundred and sixty-seven pounds. We are sending you to Fortress Monroe at Old Point Comfort, Virginia, where they are making up a colored battalion of light artillery. With your experience with horses, I think you can make it. Sam, your weight is one hundred and fifty-five pounds. We are sending you to Camp Stanton, near Annapolis in Prince George County, Maryland. They are raising a regiment of colored voluntary infantry there and I think you will make it all right." The sergeant turned from them and said, "Corporal, take these boys to the Supply Sergeant for uniforms and bedding." He then dismissed the two black volunteers, who were about to be outfitted with decent clothing for the first time in their lives. They were each issued two woolen suits, one overcoat, two suits of heavy underwear, one pair of heavy Army shoes and two pairs of socks, towels, soap, two single blankets for Army cots and a back pack or knapsack. They were dumbfounded and overjoyed.

Another corporal then took them to the washhouse and supervised and instructed them in taking a scrubbing bath with the aid of scrubbing brush and Castille soap. No parts of the body were missed. The scrubbing included scalp, feet, finger nails and toe nails, which they had clipped. A kit was issued with verbal instructions and illustrative diagrams for special care of the feet. John and Sam proudly dressed themselves in their new uniforms and took their rags to the incinerator for burning. They were assigned to the colored barracks with attached kitchen and mess hall in the holding area. They strutted around in their new dress, until late in the evening. During the night, as they lay on their new separate folding cots, they reviewed much of their lives on the plantation and contrasted the past with their happy anticipation for the future. They were up early the next morning before reveille and dressed for mess call. After breakfast, they were given written orders confirming the verbal assignments of the day before. Their transportation was made ready and their departure time was announced.

After mid-day, John's instructions were to report to the headquarters barracks. On arrival, he was informed that the ship on which he would travel had blown a piston five hours off shore enroute to Point Lookout and had returned to Old Point Comfort. The ship was heavily loaded with prisoners-of-war and freight. It would be several days before John Berry and the other passengers would leave for Fortress Monroe. John was given a program of calisthenics and jogging to start getting in physical shape for more rigorous activity at the Fort. Sam's date of departure for unexplained reasons was also delayed.

The next morning, John was up before reveille for a jog in cold wintry air around the camp. After morning mess, he and Sam were leaving the cookhouse and headed toward their barracks when they sighted two Black soldiers in a two-wheel horse-drawn cart. The soldiers were seated side by side in battle dress. One had a musket with the butt end on the floor of the cart, nesting between his legs and against his left shoulder; while the other soldier was driving the horse, with a pistol strapped to his hip in a holster. Both men wore ammunition belts. They were well groomed and immaculately dressed. John and Sam saw the driver get out of the cart, which was partly filled with wooden boxes. The driver stopped to talk to a white sergeant whom he obviously knew. John and Sam also recognized the sergeant as their friend from the first day. He called, "Johnny, you and Sam come over here. I want you to meet a friend of mine." They were introduced to Staff Sergeant Tom Jordan, from the nearby camp for Confederate prisoners. "These boys have just joined up and are waiting time for the transfer."

"Think you'll make a good soldier, John?" asked Jordan. "Yes Sir. I'm gonna try real hard, sir."

"How bout you Sam?" "Same fer me too, suh."

"Sergeant McDougal, I'd like to take these boys wid me while we're working our rounds, since they got time on they hands," the Black non-commissioned officer suggested.

"Sure, Sarge. I'll give 'em a pass for the day; maybe they'd like to see the prisoner's camp."

"That suits you, Berry? You, Sam?"

"Yes, Sir, suits me fine." They replied in unison.

They were given passes and then moved on toward the headquarters barracks. The two Black recruits were thrilled to see two experienced Black soldiers in battle dress, one a staff sergeant, the other a private-first class.

"John, this is Private First Class Sam Pindle. He is an infantryman, sharp shooter and an expert marksman."

"Hi dere, John. You look scared. Ain't nobody goin' hurt you— yet!" advised Private Pindle. "No tellin's if you can las' when dem boys git thru fanning yo' tail at de fort."

The errands done, Jordan and Pindle and the new recruits started to tour the campground. The sergeant was a "free issue mulatto" who grew up in Hampton, Virginia where he had attended the earliest free school for Negroes anywhere in the South.

The sergeant inquired, "John, can you read?"

"Little bit. I learn from the Bible."

Pindle interrupted, "Man, how you goin' shoot dem rebels and you can't read? Dey hole up a sign say 'Nigger, drap dat gun or git yo' brains blowed out!' Fo' you know it, you dead."

"Don't believe everything he tells you John," interrupted the sergeant. "That nigger can't read either and he's the best marksman in the prison camp. We'll be driving back soon and takin' you to get yo' first look at what the war is like."

"Dat's good," said John. Sam nodded in agreement.

As their cart pulled up to the entrance gate of the prisoner of war camp two miles away, two colored soldiers on guard with shouldered muskets stepped forward for pass inspection. The passes were made of metal, requiring no reading. The team drove inside, and the new recruits were shown another very large enclosure beginning 50 yards forward. They could see a huge expanse of ground hundreds of yards in length and width surrounded by a thick wall about 20 feet high. Near the top of the wall there was a parapet and a catwalk about five feet wide. John and Sam were startled and almost breathless at what they saw. There were dozens of Black military guards in full Army battle dress, including heavy dark-blue overcoats, walking with shouldered muskets and measured cadance around the entire parapet. Inside the enclosure there were scores of bell-shaped tents housing white Confederate prisoners.

Each tent had one door and an 18-inch opening at the top for ventilation. Very little was needed because of the wintry air blowing through open seams and tears in the tent structure. Officially, each prisoner had one blanket but, in fact, many had none. They slept on the ground. The tents had wood stoves or open fireplaces with a make-shift chimney. Firewood was rationed by the stick with seldom enough for warmth in the freezing Maryland weather of February 1864. Food consisted of hard tack, red beans, molasses, and sometimes thin hot coffee; seldom any meat. When the rebels were weakened and immobilized from malnutrition or stricken with cholera, dysentery, pneumonia, consumption, or gangrenous limbs from frost bite or festered wounds, they were taken to the large prison hospital. Many died there each day and were buried in a common grave.

The party moved from the main prison into the hospital. There John and Sam saw sights, both gruesome and shocking. There were many, many undernourished half-starved human beings in the camp. They saw a man missing both arms and legs; many with his open wounds being mopped with the same carbolic acid solution and mop; they smelled the stench of large open infected wounds with crawling maggots and swarms of buzzing flies. There were men sweating and delirious with high fever, talking irrationally at random. Others were semi-comatose or unconscious. John and Sam were deeply impressed with the horrors of war and wondered if the same could happen to them. The great majority of patients were white "rebs" as they were called, but a few were Black body-servants of rebel officers. Others were slaves cooperating with the secessionists. One Black prisoner was shot and severely wounded while helping a Confederate woman spy escape by rowing her across the Patuxent River. John had mixed emotions when he was told about conditions in the Union prisoner war camp at Andersonville, Georgia. They were much worse.

Sam Jenifer had been around sick people as a boy helping his uncle, the slave doctor, "Doc" Henry Jenifer, as he was called. But neither he nor John had ever seen such horrors before.

Sam had not discussed with John Berry his experiences as part time healer and medicine man or his life back on the Thomas plantation. "I bet if I could be safe and get out in these woods, I could bring out some roots that would cure lotta dis bloody flux what you got here." "My uncle Henry Jenifer, my papa's brother started me off when I was a little boy, hunting roots for de flux, swamp fever, and consumption." "Then I'd hold the lantern for him in de night and watch him break the fever of de farm hand in the cabins. Uncle Henry drove the horse

39

and buggy and helped Dr. Thomas cure the white folks all over the county. Everybody white and Black liked Doc Henry. Dr. Thomas sent him by hisself to cure white folks. Sometimes white folks send for Doc Henry when Dr. Thomas was outa the county." Sam continued. Up until I 'scaped fer de war I wuz part time "medicine man." "My mother always told me to mix healin' with religion—I b'lieve dats right. I always wanted to be a real educated doctor. That's de main reason I came to fight. Someday I spects to be a real doctor and spirit healer."

"Yo' Uncle Henry still doctorin' on the plantation?" John asked.

"No," Sam answered. "One day durin' de fever plague everybody was worried 'cause Uncle Henry, one of the best doctors, went off to the North with a woman name "Harriett. Aint nobody heard from him since, but everybody think he a root doctor up in Canada."

The party moved out of the hospital to the outside camp to prepare to return to Point Lookout. Black soldiers on guard duty seemed to be everywhere.

"Hey, Johnnie Reb," "Get back in that tent! I done tole yu twice, I can't count to three." commanded a Black soldier on guard duty.

The white Southerners, some former slave holders, were "burned up" upon arrival at Point Lookout Prison to find former slaves of the 16th North Carolina Infantry Regiment of U. S. Colored Troops, standing guard duty. They were further chagrined because Gen. Benjamin F. Butler, or "Beast," as they called him and War Secretary Edward M. Stanton had just made an inspection tour of the camp a week before and received a 13-gun salute. The Rebs thought an invasion of blood thirsty Yankees and their "nigger" troops was coming up.

The prisoners who were not too involved with their wounds and ailments, were griping about hunger, freezing temperatures, news of Sherman's March through Georgia, and the possible fall of Atlanta. In the midst of all this, President Lincoln was pushing hard the offer of amnesty for renouncement of the Confederacy and pledging allegiance to the Union. Hundreds of them acquiesed; others preferred continuing to "rot in prison camp." Worse than all else for some of the rebels was the case of a Black guard who shot and killed one of two escaping white prisoners as they went over the wall of the prison camp. Returning to Camp, John and Sam had been impressed. They realized the serious nature of war following their eye-opening visit to the prison camp.

A caravan of double teamed horses and wagons, ready to leave before day, the next morning, for Camp Stanton with soldiers and supplies awaited Sam. John was briefed for sailing time three days later for Old Point Comfort and Fortress Monroe.

Once again, the two new friends John Berry and Sam Jenifer were aware that their parting was a grim reality. Their departure time was firm. At the last minute they shook hands, looked deeply into each others eyes, and choked up as they hugged each other. They were fully prepared to separate with their newly found sense of dignity. With shoulders erect, they went their separate ways into an uncertain future to join "Massa Linkun's" Army and one of the greatest wars of history in search of freedom and their own humanity.

Fortress Monroe and Old Point Comfort Va.

TIME: Three days later, John Berry boarded the Frigate *Annapolis*, for his voyage to Old Point Comfort and Fortress Monroe. As he shouldered his pack and stood in line at the gang plank, words that he would never forget came back to him. "WHERE YA GOIN' BOY?" His silent answer was I'm GOIN' OFF TO WAR! TO BECOME A MAN;" to fight for freedom and to search for the greater destiny of my family and race in the pursuit of happiness. John Berry might have spoken such words but for the compelling illiteracy that his previous condition of chattel slavery had created. He was mute. As his vessel weighed anchor and pulled out into the Chesapeake, her waterline was slightly raised from the heavy cargo of Union soldiers and Confederate prisoners in the hold returning south for exchange.

There were colored sailors aboard ship who pointed out sights of interest to Berry and others during the slow voyage. Waving from the decks of a warship, the *Minnesota*, were Black and white sailors carrying out the friendly "highball" to a sister troop and supply ship flying the Union flag. The *Minnesota* was fresh out of dry dock, where she had been confined for repairs of cannonball holes received in Hampton Roads during the battle of the *Merrimac* and the *Monitor*.

One sailor, whom John Berry would eventually meet in Norfolk after the war, was present on the *Minnesota* as she lay at anchor, with the naval flotilla guarding the captured Confederates at Point Lookout Prison. The sailor was William Benjamin Derrick a former slave from the British Island of Antigua, who was ordained as a minister in St. John's AME

Church at Norfolk while serving in the Navy. He pursued his education vigorously, before and after the War, and became an outstanding bishop in the AME Church. As a local preacher at St. John's AME Church from 1866–1870, he was to become very friendly with John Berry who was a member of the church choir.

After two days and a night of slow and sometimes rough sailing across Chesapeake Bay, John's heavily laden ship docked at Old Point Comfort, Fortress Monroe, Virginia.

The unseasonable weather continued up into March. It was still chilly and flowers were not yet budding. John was not certain whether the rain would interrupt his light artillery field cannon training in its last month. It was no secret that John Berry had better be a fighting man by the end of April. Because he would be off to the wars, fighting white men, men who were staking their lives to keep him enslaved. He would be on his own, using the best skills he had been able to develop in a very short time. The only secret was the day and the hour of departure.

On the 28th of April, Berry knew that four regiments of black troops, including Battery B, his regiment of light artillery, would leave Fortress Monroe for a secret destination. The large number of troop ships gathering in the harbor and the great activity of thousands of white and Black men all over the huge camp told everyone that something big was about to happen. The great Army of the James under orders of the famous Gen. Ben Butler would be moving into action. The high command knew that on May 1, Butler and his division of several thousand men would begin a secret march of approximately 40 miles up the Virginia peninsula. They would go northward following near the course of the James River in the general direction of Petersburg. They would help to establish a foot hold near Wilson's Wharf on the north side of the James, on the outskirts of Charles City.

Throughout the night and day of May 2 and 3, hundreds of "contraband" stevedores and service troops were busy loading dozens of troop and supply ships. Going aboard were heavily armed troops, cavalry horses, light and heavy artillery, with caissons, munitions wagons, mules, quartermaster and commissary wagons, and other heavy equipment for wheelrighting, blacksmithing and carpentry and various other tasks being loaded.

At daybreak on May 4 this huge assemblage convoyed by protective naval vessels steamed out of Hampton Roads into the bay and up the mighty James River. Gen. Edward Hinks of the Third Division with Gen. Edward A. Wild and Col. Elias Wright, Commander of the First Brigade, headquartered on the lead transport ship. Others of John Berry's high command shipped on the transport, *William Small*, while most of the Second Brigade of three Black infantry regiments under the command of Col. Alonzo G. Draper, were transported with two white light artillery batteries, which had been raised in New York. They were all a part of the Eighteenth Army Corps.

The remainder of several thousand Black infantrymen travelled by forced foot march with regimental commanders; Lieutenant Colonels John Holman, Edward Powell and Joseph Kiddoo. These were the first, tenth and twenty-second infantry regiments USCT (United States Colored Troops).

Capt. Francis C. Choate commanding the Second U. S. Colored light artillery of which John Berry was a member proudly marched with his men with their smartly curried mule-drawn wheelcannons glittering in the bright Virginia sunlight. John Berry had already been put in charge of "Cap'n Choate's field gun piece No. 4."

John was ready mentally, physically and spiritually. The night before when he realized that the zero hour was at hand he walked out of his barracks into the darkness. As he walked he sang softly the old Negro spiritual, "Walk with me Lord, walk with me while I'm on dis Pilgrim jou'ney Lord, I want Jesus to walk with me." He had knelt by his cot in the darkness of the barracks and offered a fervent prayer for strength to be a good and brave soldier and to return alive. John had prayed further, "If I must die, Lord, let me die fighting with all my heart and soul and the last breath that is within me for the freedom of my family and my race." Commanding officers soon were impressed with the eagerness and pride with which the black infantrymen marched out of the gate of the fort at precisely the hour that their companions sailed by steamboat. Following the foot soldiers and supporting units came the light artillerymen with their mule-drawn field cannons mounted on caissons and supporting units. Then came an array of contraband workers, the likes of whom deserved a large proportion of the credit for Union successes in the entire War of the Rebellion.

45

A marching drum corps and marching songs could be heard as they passed through known friendly territory in Hampton and Newport News. The contingent had four days' rations and they bivouacked three times before reaching Wilson's Wharf. On the way the forward pickets encountered Confederate sniper's shots, but no real skirmishes occurred.

Certain individuals from each unit were picked for foraging, and there were many stops to graze, water and rest the animals; the mules and the "appropriated Confederate livestock." The animals seemed not to know or care whether the water or food had a Confederate or Union taste or whether the captors wore blue or gray uniforms.

The countryside along the marching route was a series of long crooked historic miles. The James, the York, the Rappahanock, the Chickahominy were not just rivers. They were liquid history. White-educated officers from the North looked, stared, exulted and pointed as they informed their charges of historical sites. Probably the first pitched battle of the Civil War had been that of Big Bethel which occurred just beyond Newport News. It was a Confederate victory as far as overcoming a small contingent of Federal troops was concerned but they failed to reach their goal of capturing Fortress Monroe. John Berry and the great caravan of which he was a part marched just to the West of Jamestown. Capt. John Smith long since lay molding in the clay as were John Rolfe and Pocahontas. A few miles further, the marchers skirted Yorktown. Here, 85 years before, free Black men and French Haitians helped to fight the decisive battle of Yorktown for the promises of freedom, they never received. Many were freed—many more not. But John Berry and other black troops oblivious or unacquainted with disappointments of the past were marching for the future. At many points the marchers could see the mast poles or the ships themselves as they plowed in the same direction up the James River. Signal officers on the march and on board ships were in constant contact. Telescopes, flares, signal flags, rockets and the dot-and-dash telegraphy of that day were the slow but effective methods of communication. The caravan veered a few miles to the East of the river and travelled Northward only a few miles when they caught sight of another town. They were skirting the outer boundaries of historic Williamsburg. The caravan of soldiers was Black and white in pursuit of justice, freedom and the preservation of the Union. Through the trees one could catch a glimpse of the House of Burgesses. This was where Patrick Henry had made his famous "Give me liberty or give me death" speech, setting the tone and expressing the determination of the Colonies suffering under the iron heel of the British monarchy. It is strange how history repeats itself and how often the fate and destiny of an individual or family is but a microcosm of the yearnings and struggles of a nation.

It is stranger yet how often destiny is a paradox.

There were paradoxes in the Berry family as it struggled for freedom, equality and opportunity to make its imprint on American life. There were paradoxes in the life of Thomas Jefferson, the great statesman, as he struggled to defend portions of his famous Declaration among his friends at Williamsburg. Did he not hold slaves at Monticello while he expounded the doctrines that all men are created equal, with inalienable rights to life, liberty and the pursuit of happiness? He was long since buried at his beloved Monticello when John Berry had his first glimpse of the House of Burgessess through the green-leafed elm trees of Virginia's countryside. But the spirit of Jefferson must have hovered over General Butler's marching troops for; paradoxically they were Northern whites en route to fight for a principle not well understood by most; they were marching to kill their Southern brothers primarily defending the right of the rich planters to hold slaves. Even more paradoxically, they were marching with black soldiers, escapees from slavery in double-jeopardy risking greater slavery for half-promises of uncertain freedom.

John Berry and Sam Jenifer fought for the right to fight. They were trained for infantry and light artillery, but often they were assigned to service battalions. They were frequently supplied with inferior fighting equipment, but struggling and determined to be the best at whatever task, to be ready to fight as a soldier believing in destiny; that freedom would be theirs someday.

The marching troops of the Army of the James were growing weary. They were glad to hear bugle calls up ahead followed by company commands of "Halt!" and "Parade rest!" The animals needed watering; the troops needed a rest. Another five miles completed over undeveloped country roads and fields wet with spring rains had brought the long caravan to bivouac at dusk. There were many such stops. Customarily, Black troops built campfires, sang spirituals and other songs, counted out in rhythmic unison the alphabet and "rithmetic table."

47

On the second night of bivouac, some feet were tired and blistered. A few men were felled by the "plague" or overcome by latent malaria, upset stomachs or diarrhea. Some were riding the dispensary wagons. Sam Jenifer sprang into action with first aid. His buddies from Camp Stanton knew he had learned doctorin' from his uncle "Old Doc Henry" Jenifer, a slave doctor in St. Mary's County. The Army doctors, in short supply, accepted his skills and enthusiasm when Sam was not on infantry duty. Some of Sam's famous remedies, as the army moved towards Petersburg, were quinine and castor oil for fever, a charge of gunpowder in milk or mustard in soapsuds for stomachache to induce vomiting, moonshine whiskey pre-mixed with melted tallow for blistered feet, and a spittle of tobacco juice for snakebite. In bad cases, Sam applied hot rocks to the feet.

With evening mess consumed, kitchen areas policed and campfires lit, up stepped Black regimental Sgt. John Richeleau. Addressing the group of black soldiers. "Attention, men!" he spoke with authority. "It's time for us to have a little talk." Richeleau, a free-born, educated Creole, was one of dozens of personnel in small cadres, who were battle-trained, experienced men, assigned to every company. The sergeant continued, "We're marchin' through strange country and enemy territory. We're lucky we ain't run into a strong rebel force. I've already been through the hell of battle, fightin' them gray-bellied rebs. It's alright to sing from them bluebacked spellers. I can read and write a'plenty, but that don't help me a damn bit to fight. Most of Napoleon's soldiers couldn't read. None of Toussaint's slave soldiers in Haiti could read, but they beat the hell out of Napoleon's army. I fought them rebs at Milliken's Bend in Louisiana and got a wounded leg at Port Hudson when Vicksburg fell. A gray-bellied reb don't take no nigger prisoners. You're dead or dying when they leave. Yeah, keep praying, but you gotta keep shooting at them rebs as long as you can see one of them. To you, religious boys, there ain't but one "cheek" to turn in a war, and that's your "behind." And you don't turn that up to no reb. Feel them scars on your back! Look at them brands on your buddy's face and cheeks. Some of you have been baptized with water; you ain't been baptized with fire, yet. And remember, you got a gun in your hands, too!

"Startin' tonight, all the sergeants in the regiment agree with me. You gonna get somethin' new. Silent gun training. Every time we stop and while on the march, you're gonna ram your muskets without the cap and powder. You gonna snap it to your shoulder, aim and trigger double quick. After while, you gonna ram your powder and your ball without the cap. Then you're gonna do it a thousand times standing, running, and on your belly. Always half of you all will stay loaded "on-the-ready" for the rebs. At the same time, silent cannon practice is gonna be in Cap'n Choate's battery. You all got to be understandin' what I say. Do You?"

"Yeah! We hear what you say."

"Is you a fightin' soldier or is you still a slave?"

"No! We soldiers all the way."

"Alright. 'Tention! Unstack your muskets! Fall in! Right shoulders, arms!"

This practice was repeated throughout much of the moonlit nights. The last bivouac found the battle caravan on the plantation near Harrison's landing. They had bypassed Wilson's Wharf by a few miles with oncoming darkness. History in old Virginia was again a part of their fate. By the time they broke camp the next morning to complete the trip to Wilson's Wharf, interesting revelations were abroad. The plantation was Berkeley, the ancestral home of William Henry and the two Benjamin Harrisons, a son and a grandson who became Presidents of the United States.

General McClellan had camped here after failure to take Richmond in the early war days, and Berkeley again had become of historical significance in the war of the insurrection.

At one point, according to the memory of John Berry, contraband workers and army service units laid pontoon bridges and crossed the Chickahominy. As the marching units reached Wilson's Wharf, General Edward Wild and other units of the First Brigade met them. Breastworks were being thrown up by earlier arrivals who came by steamboat. Meanwhile, Butler's major army had landed and captured City Point (Hopewell). Here, Butler set up his headquarters. Other units, including a black cavalry outfit, were landed at Fort Powhatan nearly opposite Wilson's Wharf on the south bank of the James.

General Wild's First Brigade, consisting of the First and Tenth Infantries and John Berry's unit, Battery B of the Second U. S. Colored Light Artillery were stationed at the Wharf. Approximately 1,800 fighting men were held there to rest and later to build earth works.

Soldier-historian George W. Williams recalled, that it was the

intention of the small contingent to remain quiet within the entrenchment, but "a restless and ambitious foe grudged him his quiet and his
(Butler's) northern outposts as Wilson's Wharf were chosen as the point
of attack."

The surprise attack was mounted by a Confederate cavalry outfit of
Virginia "gentlemen," supported with infantry and artillery, some 3,000
to 5,000 strong.[1] It was the first time these Virginia Confederates had
seen Negro soldiers dressed in blue. After an hour of skirmishing against
Black pickets, a message under a flag of truce was sent to Brigadier
General Wild, signed by the famous Confederate, Major General Fitzhugh Lee, nephew of General Robert E. Lee. The note read, "Seeing
that you are outclassed, I offer you the opportunity to surrender with
honor." General Wild returned the answer to the former West Pointer
who seceded from the Union with Virginia, "We didn't come here to
surrender. We came here to fight." Apparently judging the answer to
be arrogance from a troop of Black ex-slaves, Lee ordered a full cavalry
attack against Wild's right flank. Wild ordered his troops to hold their
fire until the enemy was well within the Abatis (entangling tree limbs).
The Black men shouting their approval took all of the firepower the
enemy could give without returning a shot until Lee's forces were at
short range. The order to counterattack was then given.

A war correspondent observing the battle reported in the *New York
Times* that the Confederates on horseback soon abruptly stopped their
charge: "Failing to advance under the powerful counter attack, the
proud Southerners *recoiled* and *sought cover.*" The correspondent's report continued to describe the facial expressions and actions of General
Fitzhugh Lee as he observed them by telescope. Lee showed that he was
deeply chagrined as his "crack" unit retreated from the blazing and ac-
curate gunfire of their former slaves. Lee then ordered a dismounted
attack of General Wild's left flank and personally moved among his men,
urging them forward with loud rebel yells. Again, Wild's Black troops
held their fire for very close range and recounted with such fierceness
that the Confederate "superior race" again recoiled and sought cover.
The battle lasted for about six hours before Fitzhugh Lee retreated in
defeat, leaving behind all their dead and wounded, including Major
Carey Breckenridge, Second Virginia Cavalry, identified by a notebook
in the pocket of his uniform.[2] The rebels fled out of sight with Black

sallying parties in skirmish array hotly pursuing them back into the ravines and scrubbrush for more than an hour. Many official reports from the Battle of Wilson's Wharf were made by Brigadier General Wild, General Hinks of the Third Division, Signal Officers and Commanding Major General Butler to Honorable E. M. Stanton, Secretary of War.[3]

No reports of this battle have been found in official Confederate accounts or in biographies of Maj. Gen. Fitzhugh Lee. Historian George W. Williams said, "... thus the attempt of a division of the enemy's cavalry to turn Butler's flank was a failure. The Negro had fought his first battle in this department, and exhibited a valor which no one disputed."

Years later, John Berry, sitting in front of his fireplace on Butler's farm in Hampton, relived Wilson's Wharf with his war buddies— Robin Carr and John Pie. His son, Llewellyn Berry, then a boy of ten, eyes bright with excitement as his father described Cap'n Choate's field-gun piece #4, "Old Betsy," turning red with heat as he, fighting in charge of the cannon, singlehandedly positioned her on the firing line time and time again. (He didn't have time to wait for the mule.) This was the first important battle by General Butler's troops in the Spring offensive of 1864.

The next morning, Berry recalled, the Black heroes of the day before carrouseled at Wilson's Wharf. He wondered about his new friend, Sam Jenifer. Sam had left Point Lookout for Camp Stanton in Annapolis, but, what then?

Butler's March to Petersburg and
Rapidan to the James

AT the same time, General Butler, commander of the Army of the James, was moving northward up the Virginia peninsula from Fortress Monroe to complete the pincer movement against Richmond. General George Meade stood poised in northern Virginia with the Army of the Potomac at full strength. He was Commander of the Army of the Potomac, Grant's Second Army comprised of 100,000 or more men, some of whom had been raised at Camp Stanton. He rehearsed his grand strategy with his general staff. The salient was identified as "The Rapidan to the James River Campaign."

There were many Negro troops in this powerful unit, which was the main defense of the capitol city of Washington.

Meade, upon receiving orders from his new field general, Ulysses S. Grant, moved his forces of infantry, artillery, cavalry, engineers, contraband workmen, wagon supply trains and other equipment into Northern Virginia.

By laying pontoon bridges and employing small boats, Meade with more than 100,000 men and their supplies and equipment, quickly crossed the Rapidan River at Germania Ford. But from the time they had left Manassas Junction, they had been met with late Spring rains. There was an epidemic of colds from sleeping on the wet ground and in the damp tents.

A division of the Black troops marched through Washington along the way to the major concentration at Manassas. The Black troops were reviewed by President Lincoln and a party of congressmen from the balcony of the Willard Hotel.[1] The troops were all commanded by Black corporals and sergeants. Their division commander was Brigadier General Edward Ferrero of Major General Ambrose Burnsides' Ninth

Corps. During the Washington march, the Black soldiers were informed down the line that President Lincoln would be watching from a high stand at a hotel on the right. They snapped into the most military marching posture that any West Point professor had ever written about in a manual of arms. As they caught sight of their Commander-in-Chief and "emancipator" in review, they executed a shouldered rifle salute with pinpoint accuracy which the smiling President returned again and again.[2] Then, the Black volunteers broke into the famous marching song, "My eyes done seed de glory of de comin' ub de Lawd. Glory! Hallelujah. His troops is marching on."

President Lincoln later received reports that during the Battle of the Wilderness a Confederate surprise attack captured 27 wagon trains. He was informed that the Black division he had recently reviewed staged a counter attack re-capturing all of the wagon trains with no loss of lives, Lincoln sent a message of commendation and stated that he was very pleased, but not surprised after seeing their alert, determined faces and noting their drill and musket handling during the Washington review.

Meade's Army had barely crossed the Rapidan when their pickets encountered rifle fire from Confederate snipers. From May 5 to the 7, the North and South were embroiled in heavy fighting in the Wilderness, a cruel battleground of tree stumps, virgin pine saplings and thick underbrush. The battle was bitterly fought with heavy losses on both sides. While the black troops were involved in skirmishes, they were not a part of the main fighting force. Meade continued on southward with various encounters near important plank roads, churches and taverns which were used as barricades for small Confederate groups.

The northern troops encountered a strong rebel force at Spotsylvania Courthouse, which lasted from May 8 to 19. Again, Jenifer's infantry and other units of his division were part of the overall stalemate— neither North nor South were clear victors. General Meade assigned Ferrero's anxious Fourth Division of nine Black regiments, including Sam Jenifer's Thirtieth Infantry, to the inglorious duty of directing and guarding supply trains for the most part along the old plank roads. During the lull of battle, the Black soldiers practiced silent "sham battles" and gun maneuvers and drill formations so as to be ready for the big battle when given the chance.

Failing to decisively defeat the Confederates, Grant ordered Meade on a wide southeastward sweep, hoping to outflank the Confederates. They arrived at Cold Harbor on June 3, 1864 just eight miles from Richmond, where they found Lee with a small army entrenched and ready to defend to the death the Confederate's capital city.

Thousands of Black troops with blood in their eyes, pleading to get into the fray in large numbers, continued to be relegated to their "proper places"—guarding supply trains and along with contraband servicing their white brothers in blue. At other times, they assembled around campfires and prayed for a face-to-face engagement with their former enslavers. But, the facts were simple. Their white brothers in blue were slow to accept the Black soldiers as social equals, even in battle with a common enemy against whom they were making slow progress.

Cold Harbor turned out to be quite "frigid" for the northern forces, Lee successfully defended the Confederate flag, which still waved over Richmond. A disappointed Gen. Ulysses S. Grant, called a strategy meeting which included Meade, Burnsides and his other generals. Sitting on a tree stump, leaning against an adjacent oak, puffing his cigar and whittling one green twig after another while looking into the distance as was his custom; he discussed the new strategy, listened to a few opinions, and issued his orders for the month of June.

"You will separate your divisions with good military maneuvering space; set up necessary pickets; outposts; reconnaissance and news-walkers. We will bivouac for two days in preparation and be on-the-ready southward to move at dusk to join with Butler's Army of the James. Together we will surround the enemy at Petersburg and cut off his lifeline to Richmond and starve him out of his entrenchment. Expedite regular reports to my headquarters at all times. Meeting dismissed!"

Grant's reconnaissance had determined that the enemy was entrenched as a defense arm and would not expose his thinned-out flanks in an offensive move.

Receiving orders down the line that after a two day rest all units would move into battle, the Black non-commissioned officers and corporals held a night-time pow-wow around a campfire. Many units were represented. Sam Jenifer of the 30th Infantry, was asked by his sergeant-major, "Little Doc, did you git dat keg 'er moonshine and tallow from de dispensary wagon for our tired feet?"

55

"Yes sir," replied Sam. "Everything's all fixed."

"Did you melt de tallow and mix it in de moonshine?"

"No, sir, sergeant." Loud laughter came from all around the campfire. The soldiers, in a good mood, began to clap hands and break into rhythmic chants as they pulled out tin cups to be served the moonshine without the tallow.

"Clap hands, here come Sammy."

"Der ain't much to go around. You ain't gon to get but a little bit. Ain't nobody goin' to get drunk here" were the commanding words from the regimental sergeant-major.

The hand-clapping and happy songs led to other songs like "Old Joshua fit the battle ub Jericho, and the walls came tumblin' down." Sam Jenifer, who sang in religious meetings back home, led the verse. The group got larger with privates and contraband workers in the rear. Many couldn't read or write, but their premonition pointed to some kind of a victory not far ahead, and they were preparing for it. A young private with a fine singing voice rose and led a song, "Do you think I could make a soldier, soldier, soldier in the year of Jubilee." The answer in song was,

"Yes, I know I be a soldier fer de year ub Jubilee
befor' I be 'er slave I be buried in my grave and go
home to my Lord and be free."

Frivolity and the feast continued. All soldiers, when chance permitted, foraged on nearby farms. Blacks, very frequently, found house and plantation slaves eager to secretly give help. There was barbecued pig, fresh milk direct from the cow's udder, cured ham, food staples and souvenirs.

"Say, Steeplehead," said one soldier to another, "How you doin'?"

"Um doin' good, 'Fat Butt. My head may be steeple, but I got mo brains in it dan you."

"You got to prove dat."

"Alright, when de las' time you had some lovin'? I bet it be 'Napolis."

"Yeah! So you ain't got nuttin' on me."

"Oh, yeah?" Pointing in the distance, Steeplehead said, "See dat dar barn behind dat plantation big house?"

56

"Yeah."

"Well, how you think I got der Massa's sugar cured hams you been eatin'."

Fathead, with a glint in his eye, replied, "You lucky dawg."

After much frivolity the meeting got serious. The boys pulled out their blue-backed spellers. They ran out the alphabet and arithmetic tables in rhythmic unison before going to bed, never forgetting their hunger for book learning and the approaching year of Jubilee.

The next day after the big campfire, postal wagons, couriers, week-before-last's newspapers and *Harper's Weekly* caught up with Brigadier Gen. Edward Ferrero's Black Fourth Division. The big news: Commendation from President Lincoln straight through the chain of command of Generals Grant, Meade and Burnsides for "courageous, alert and swift action on re-capturing 27 supply wagons at the Battle of the Wilderness; only two men wounded, one missing."

One newspaper read by the sergeant-major quoted an African Methodist *Christian Recorder*'s story, dated May 9, 1864.[3] "During the Quadrennial General Conference of the African Methodist Episcopal Church, convened in Philadelphia, news was received of the victories of Black troops in the Union Army of the Potomac down in Virginia. The conference stood and led by Bishop Daniel A. Payne sang *Praise God From Whom All Blessings Flow*. Bishop Payne then offered a prayer for the success of the Negro soldiers and the Union Army."[*]

Following this, according to the *Christian Recorder* story, the conference was addressed by an honored guest, Capt. Robert Smalls. This officer of *The Planter*, a converted gun boat, was a former slave and expert ships pilot in South Carolina. He stole the Confederate steamer while it was anchored in Charleston Harbor, with the help of a slave crew, and surrendered it to the Union Navy. He was highly decorated and served as official captain of the ship through the war.

At mess time on the second bivouac night, all nine regiments of the Black Fourth Division of General Meade's Army of the Potomac received news of the Battle of Wilson's Wharf and the great victory of General Butler's Black soldiers in the Army of James. Sam Jenifer knew his buddy John Berry went to Fortress Monroe to join an artillery unit in General Butler's Army of the James. He prayed often for his buddy's safety and that they might meet again.

While some of Butler's troops were tied up by the Confederates at Bermuda Hundred, Butler's 18th Army Corps under Gen. W. F. "Baldy" Smith crossed the Appomattox River on pontoon bridges at Broadway Landing, on June 15, 1864 and ordered an assault against Petersburg. Among his troops was General Edward W. Hinks' Third Division. This Division consisted of two brigades of Black infantrymen and one artillery brigade of three batteries, one of which was Capt. Francis C. Choate's Second U. S. Colored Light Artillery with John Berry in charge of Field Cannon No. 4; the position he had held at the Battle of Wilson's Wharf. This was indeed a major offensive, with more than 10,000 men, which occurred at a place called Baylor's farm on Three Points-Petersburg Turnpike.

As the charge was mounted, John Berry recalled years later, he was "rough and ready." The job of his battery was to drop cannon fire into Confederate trenches. Captain Choate and his lieutenants barked out the command: "Order your piece to load! Search your piece! Sponge and fill your ladle! Put in your powder and thrust home your wad!" As the battle got hot, the orders were "Load! Ready! Fire!"

Confederate fire was returned with a vengeance, especially when they saw the mass of Black faces among the enemy troops. Soon the battle lit up the countryside. The Black squadrons manning field cannons in Battery B raced with each other in the rapidity of their fire.

Berry said that after an hour and a half of continuous firing, he was drenched in sweat; the water in his sponge bucket had turned black as the sizzling hot tubes were sponged between firing rounds; "Old Betsy" turned a dull red with heat, and his leather thumbguard smoked and blistered his thumb. In the midst of battle and stiffling smoke, one of his men was hit squarely in the head with a missle fragment. He fell across the cannon and a mixture of brains and blood spattered the face and chest of Gunner Robin Carr. Without flinching, Carr wiped the bloody mess from his face, lifted the body from the cannon, placed it far in the rear near a tree. He then returned to his post, helping to fire Captain Choate's No. 4 and to repay the rebels fire for fire.

The Black troops pushed their charge up a slope and captured the enemy stronghold at Baylor's farm. Near nightfall, General "Baldy" Smith called off his attack for the night.

Historians retracing the battle of the 15th of June, have said that Petersburg was ready to fall. The decision to relax the pressure overnight gave the Confederates time to dig more entrenchments and bring up supporting troops, thus prolonging the war ten more long months before the final fall of Petersburg and Richmond. The Black troops were personally complimented by their commander, General Smith but failure to follow through and capture Petersburg necessitated a long siege operation.

The next day, Gen. Ambrose Burnside's Ninth Corps of Meade's Army of the Potomac arrived at the salient, having crossed the James the day before. Included in the corps was General Edward Ferrero's Fourth Division, comprising eight regiments of Black troops. Among them was the 30th Infantry, U. S. Colored Troops, of which Sam Jenifer was a member. On the night of June 16, while giving first aid behind the lines of his regiment, Sam Jenifer sighted a Black artillery unit of the Army of the James. He busied himself among the resting troops and found John Berry.

"My God," he cried, "there is John!"

"Doggone if it ain't Sam."

They hugged and leaped for joy. They briefly reviewed their battle actions and spoke of their grim determination to fight the rebels to the death. They spoke of their belief in an eventual victory and a hard earned life of freedom. They committed to memory the names of their respective units and vowed to keep up with news of their locations and to hope and pray that they would survive and meet again after the war.

Soon there was a bugle call to assemble with their units and bivouac for the night. Sam and John had to part, to continue in their separate actions in the siege against Petersburg.

On the 7th of July, 1864, Berry's unit was ordered to Portsmouth, Virginia, with a contingent of troops to guard the Norfolk area from which supplies had been slipping through to the embattled Confederates around Richmond. Meanwhile, Meade's Army had tried unsuccessfully several times to encircle Petersburg. As the month of July wore on, the entire command from the war department and President Lincoln to Grant and on down were concerned about the slow progress of the Virginia campaign to capture Petersburg. Burnside's Ninth Army Corps moved slowly over the ravines and gulleys toward a Confederate fort protecting Petersburg on Cemetery Hill. He advanced to a distance of not more than 150 yards from the hill. The Yanks were seemingly unable to move any further against the Confederate rifle and cannon fire.

Finally, men of the 48th Pennsylvania Volunteers, many of whom were coal miners, conceived the idea of tunneling and dynamiting Cemetery Hill on the top of which was the strong Confederate fort. The high command first rejected, then accepted, the idea. General Burnside was enthusiastic as he studied a plan of attack. He considered that his three white divisions had been continuously involved during the Battle of the Wilderness, Cold Harbor and other skirmishes during the previous weeks. He therefore decided on the selection of General Ferrero's Fourth Division of Black troops to be specially trained and lead the attack of the entire operation, after the planned massive blasting of Cemetery Hill.

The Black troops had seen the least amount of fighting up to this point. They underwent a special plan of training devised by Generals Burnside and Ferrero behind the lines for several weeks. There were shouts of joy among the Black troops and their fighting blood boiled with anxious anticipation, when word came down that they would lead the offensive. Of all the Union troops, they had a score to settle. They had heard of the massacre of captured Black soldiers at Fort Pillow in April. They practiced an answer to the rebel yell, which was "Remember Fort Pillow." There would be several thousand troops of infantry, heavy artillery and cavalry, and this Black division was being trained for the honor of leading the attack after the dynamiting of Cemetery Hill.

But, unfortunately such recognition of black power was not to come to pass. General Meade of the Army of the Potomac, described by some historians in later years as having strong racial feelings, countermanded the order at virtually the last minute. Undoubtedly, this was one of the most significant military decisions of the war; for it probably made certain the Union's failure and prolongation of the Virginia campaign. After this important battle, when the facts were brought out in an investigation, it was the opinion of some members of the high command, including General Grant, that if Meade had allowed the Black Fourth Division to lead the attack, The Battle of the Crater Explosion would have been successful. This division was the largest and the troops were fresher. They were best prepared psychologically and tactically by weeks of special simulated training to go swiftly through the Crater.

The weary white Massachusetts division, mostly cavalry, was ordered with one day's preparation to lead the attack, without rest and by drawing of straws which ruled out the two remaining white divisions.

The secret tunnel, 500 feet long, required the removal of 18,000 cubic feet of earth which was covered with tree limbs to avoid Confederate's spyglasses. Eight hundred pounds of dynamite were placed in four magazines in the Y-shaped terminal of the tunnel under Cemetery Hill. The magazines were connected to a long fuse traversing the entire length of the tunnel. At the appointed time, the fuse was lighted and the estimated time of the explosion was 3:00 a.m. Saturday, July 30.

As the minutes ticked away, there was no explosion at 3:00 a.m., the fuse had burned out mid-way the tunnel. Two brave soldiers, Sgt. A. Reese and Lt. Jacob Doty, of the 48th Pennsylvania Volunteers entered the tunnel, repaired and relit the fuse, and scampered to safety. It was 16 minutes to five o'clock, near daybreak when it was said that all Hell broke loose with the explosion under the Confederate fort. Tons of earth were blown skyward, more than 100 feet above the hill. Through the gray dawn, flashes of fire permeated the sky bringing into view cannon wheels, fragmented caissons, and portions of torn bodies of horses and men which were hurled skyward. The huge mass of debris fell back into the huge Crater which became a valley of death and destruction.

The Union advance which followed was slow. The rebel survivors and reinforcements had time to advance to the edge of the crater and gun down the first Union troops who tried to cross the rubble-covered ditches in the floor of the crater. Some of them tried to scale the steep sides of the 50-foot wide ditch which was 25 feet deep and 200 feet long.

With the slowly rising sun and increasing daylight, General Ferrero received orders to advance with his Black division of 10,000 infantry men to the rescue and support of their white comrades bogged down in the mud, water and rubble under continuous fire from the rebels. Ferrero, unlike General Meade who stayed far in the rear issuing orders by telegraph, was at the vanguard with drawn sword, pointing his troops toward the right flank and the broad edge of the smoking crater. The rebels, sighting the Black horde of blue-clad fighting men with barking and smoking field pieces and flashes of musket fire, met the charging Blacks with destructive force; with chagrin for their northern enemy brothers and hatred of the fierce fire power of their former slaves.

61

Sam Jenifer, one of those former slaves, now a tough and hardened sharpshooter with the 30th Infantry USCT, was only a private first-class, but as he told the story years later, he found himself leading a squad of riflemen.

"Follow me, boys," he cried. "Shoot, kill! Leave 'em dead." he yelled as he rapidly loaded and reloaded his musket giving his ramrod an extra twist for better impaction of powder, cartridge and fireball.

The Black division, charging without prelaid defensive obstacles, overran many of their advanced white troops and falling before superior positioned rebel fire mixed blood and limb with their northern comrades. But, they pressed on, finally pushing back their former captors. Confederate cannonballs continued to explode here and there over the heads of the advancing Black 30th Regiment, digging nasty holes beyond range. Rifleballs whistled past the ear of Sam Jenifer, as he described it years on end after the war. He was no longer afraid of death.

An occasional Black comrade fell by his side; here and there a blue-clad Black and bleeding arm fell off or Sam would stumble over a severed, bloody leg. Once in a while, a rebel cannonball would find the range and blot out a nest of advancing Blacks. Others were being bayoneted as they climbed the steep walls of the Crater, implanting their own detached bayonets as make-shift ladder rungs. The "rebel yell" could be heard here and there above the sound of gunfire. The Confederates could not fail to hear the answering yell of thousands of Blacks, "Remember Fort Pillow." As the hours wore on, the Black infantrymen succeeded in advancing around the edge of the Crater.

"Dey's fallin' back!" "Dey's runnin'!" cried Sam Jenifer and the men of the surrounding squadrons. There were cries of joy muffled with cries of pain, their uniforms torn, their bodies drenched in sweat and blood and mud under a glaring sun. But they were getting their second wind, enraged and encouraged by retreating and falling rebels.

Sam was temporarily knocked to the ground by a bullet which caught him in the buckle of his belt, thus saving his life. He was soon crawling again and shifting his trusted musket. Back on his feet, choking with thirst, his canteen dry, he crashed forward with a dozen Black men engaged in hand-to-hand combat with the rebels. They captured a standard of Confederate colors as it fell from insurgent hands to the ground. Amid yells of victory from Black and White, they evacuated the captured colors to a rear position. Black troops later received the Congressional Medal of Honor for bravery out and beyond the call of duty for this mission.

The record of the Crater battle shows that the Fourth Division of U. S. Colored Troops put up the most effective assault of the Union offensive. They lost about "250 out of 600 wounded men," wrote Christian A. Fleetwood, a company sergeant.[4] Appomattox was yet to come, but the rebel troops and all the world knew that Black troops, backing up their white comrades would fight to the bitter end in the face of death to make their proclamation of freedom become a reality.

Destiny at the Crossroads

THE destiny of America was at the crossroads during the first two weeks of April, 1865. The future of a downtrodden race was inseparably involved in that destiny. John Berry and Sam Jenifer were members of that race. As April 1 approached there was excitement in the Union forces. The rebel defenses were breaking down. Richmond, the Confederate capitol was almost completely surrounded. The rebel Northern army of Virginia was foot weary, hungry and bedraggled.

On Sunday, April 2, Jeff Davis president of the confederacy received a cryptic telegram while at worship at St. Paul's church. The message came from General Lee announcing the fall of Petersburg to the Union forces and advising the immediate evacuation of all citizens from the city of Richmond. Word traveled like wildfire. Confederates fled in all directions, setting fires and blowing up the 14th Street Bridge as they fled. Government officials escaped to Danville. The hope of military officials was to leave only scorched earth for the advancing Union army. Some 900 buildings were destroyed before Union troops could control the fire. Through the smoke and blazing fire confederate guns barked as they made their token last stand.

John Berry and Sam Jenifer had fought bitterly for long hours under continuous fire against the defenses of Petersburg and Richmond. When these two strongholds finally fell, John and Sam had been deployed with their units for duty elsewhere. They regretted very deeply not to have the honor of marching into Richmond.

By Monday morning, thousands of people were trying to escape by all possible means. One slave broker moved up to the crowded railroad station with a coffle of fifty handcuffed chattled slaves, chained together two by two, worth $50,000. He was met by rifle-bearing black soldiers with fixed bayonets. He was ordered to unleash his property and watched the ex-slaves flee to freedom. On the third day of April the first Union soldiers entered Richmond. They were the Fifth Massachusetts Cavalry, a black regiment under Col. Charles Francis Adams, grandson of Pres. John Quincy Adams with two white regiments. Gen. Godfrey Weitzel's black troops marched down the main street to the Confederate White House, hauled down the red stars and bars, hoisted the stars and stripes over the dome and established General Weitzel's headquarters in the principal sanctuary.

Other black troops triumphantly marching into Richmond that day were companies 'C' and 'G' of the 29th Connecticut Colored Volunteers and the 9th U. S. Colored troops. As a large portion of Richmond's population fled, nearly 5,000 blacks remained or crowded into the city during the first week of April, 1865. They greeted with tears and shouts of joy the smartly dressed black foot soldiers and cavalry men standing high in their saddles. They had heard the news and were crowding into the city in all directions from the outlining country side.

On the fourth day of April, President Lincoln decided to make an unannounced visit to the capitol city. He left City Point where he had held a summit meeting with Grant, Sec. of War Edwin M. Stanton and others. He traveled up the James on the "River Queen" which met enemy placed obstacles in the river. He completed the trip by twelve-oared barge. Negroes working around the wharf recognized him. He was accompanied by Admiral David Porter with guards carrying rifles and fixed bayonets in front and behind the President. During the mile-and-half walk to the Confederate white house and General Weitzel's headquarters, the crowd of jubilant Negroes increased, and at one point the President was nearly mobbed by them, as they temporarily obstructed his march. Lincoln thought it best to say a few words to the cheering throng. He took off his hat, patting some of them on the shoulder and urging the former slaves to live up to the laws, obey the commandments and prove themselves worthy of the boon of liberty. Thereupon his Negro orderly shouted and cheered in approval.

Paradoxically similar words had been spoken to Negroes by George Washington and Lafayette at the surrender of Cornwallis at Yorktown to end the Revolutionary War. Negroes had played a crucial role as spies and messengers role in the decisive battle and victory at Yorktown. They had asked the generals if victory meant freedom from slavery for them. Finally, now it did.

During that fateful week, fragmented rebel troops attempted to escape toward the North Carolina border to join other comrades. Union troops, white and black, followed in hot pursuit. On April 7 Grant sent a message from Farmville to General Lee requesting a surrender to put an end to further useless bloodshed. The fleeing rebel troops were finally caught and surrounded near Appomattox on Palm Sunday, April 9. The surrender of Lee to Grant in the McLean House at the little city of Appomattox followed.

At one point in the ceremony Grant and Lee met under a famous apple tree doffed their hats and shook hands, in full view of several hundred weary blue and grey clad soldiers standing in an open field. As they stood there gazing at the two generals a curious mystical silence came over them. The Union soldiers on one side observed on the opposite side their bitter white enemies in grey. Their hilarious shouts of victory suddenly diminished; an air of quiet respect developed for the bravery of their brothers in grey. There was intermingling and congratulatory shaking of hands where blue and grey front lines faced each other. Bruce Catton captured the spirit of this occasion in his *Stillness at Appomattox*." Who knows but what the fate of their black comrades in arms and all other Blacks were sealed for another hundred years in the spirit of the "stillness" at Appomattox. They were joyful but subconsciously concerned about their future. A large number of them stood on the sidelines watching the ceremonies. One of them, interviewed at a Virginia WPA project in the 1930's, said she was present and witnessed the ceremony. Her memory was that the two generals hugged and kissed and as she put it, "Cullud folks have been sold in slavery ever since."

Section Two
Ain't Goin'
Study War
No More
(1865-95)

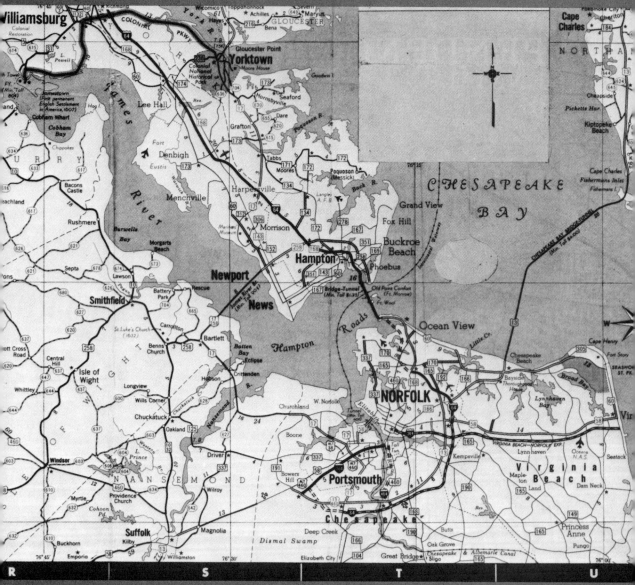

Map of Virginia showing: Site of "Taylor's Farm" near Ocean View. Site of "Butler's Farm" near Hampton, Back River and today's Langley Field. The water route of John Berry, Sam Jenifer and other war veterans in their "Raft" project, Taylor's Farm to Butler's Farm in 1870.

Marriage License.

STATE OF VIRGINIA, } To-Wit:
COUNTY OF NORFOLK,

TO ANY PERSON LICENSED TO CELEBRATE MARRIAGE.

You are hereby authorized to join together in the Holy State of Matrimony, according to the rites and ceremonies of your Church or Religious Denomination, and the Laws of the Commonwealth of Virginia,

John Berry

and *Nancy Jennifer*

Given under my hand, as Clerk of the Circuit Court of said County, this _7th_

day of *November* 1867. *G. F. Edwards* Clerk.

CERTIFICATE TO OBTAIN A MARRIAGE LICENSE.

Time of Marriage, *November 14th 1867.*   Place of Husband's Birth, *St. Mary's Co. Md.*

Place of Marriage, *Norfolk City Va.*   Place of Wife's Birth, *" " " "*

FULL NAMES OF PARTIES MARRIED   Place of Husband's Residence. *Norfolk Co. Va.*

John Berry & Nancy Jennifer   Place of Wife's Residence, *" " "*

Color. *Colored*   **NAMES OF HUSBAND'S PARENTS** *John & Sarah Berry*

Age of Husband, *27 years*

Age of Wife, *23 years*   **NAMES OF WIFE'S PARENTS** *Nace & Easter Jennifer*

Condition of Husband: Widower, Single or Divorced

Condition of Wife: Widowed, Single or Divorced   Occupation of Husband, *Laborer*

Given under my hand this _17th_ day of *November* 1867

G. F. Edwards Clerk

MINISTER'S RETURN OF MARRIAGE.

I Certify, That on the _14th_ day of *November* 1867

at *Norfolk Co. Va.*, I united in marriage the above named and described parties under authority of the annexed license.

No tax on seal

R. H. Parker

☞ The minister celebrating a marriage is required, within two months thereafter, to return the license to the office of the Clerk who issued the same, with an endorsement thereon of the FACT of such marriage, and of the TIME and PLACE of celebrating the same, and for failure to comply with this law is liable to a fine.

A Copy, Teste: Alvah H. Martin, C.C.
Per: Cora P. Parker, D.C.

Copy of Marriage License of John Berry and Nancy Jenifer, November 14, 1867. They remained married 42 years until death of John Berry in 1909. The name of Nace Berry, father of Nancy is listed here and in the St. Mary's County, Md. Census Record of 1870 at age 54, born 1816. Nace Jenifer Berry, youngest son of Nancy was named for his grandfather, Nace Jenifer.

Present day site of Butler's Farm,
reached by way of Butler Farm Road.
(photographed in 1955)

Types of first cabins built on Butler's Farm by Black Civil War veterans and other freedmen, immediately after the Civil War.

Virginia State Legislators, elected during and after Reconstruction Period. Honorable John H. Robinson (back row, left), represented Elizabeth City County, which included Butler's Farm and Hampton. The John Berry and Sam Jenifer families were politically active through Bethel A.M.E. Church and The Prince Hall Masonic Lodge.

Below: Bethel A.M.E. Church, Hampton, showing burial church yard. (photograph by the author in June 1950) The buiding was constructed in the 1880's. Rev. Llewellyn L. Berry attended Sunday School and entered the Ministry from this church. The tall weeping willow tree was planted as a sprig by Nancy Jenifer Berry to mark the grave of her daughter, Florence, who died at age 16 years in 1890. Mother Berry whose headstone is hidden in the shadows close to the church nurtured the willow tree and watched its growth until her death in 1919. The U.S. War Veterans stone in the foreground is that of Civil War Infantryman, Sam Jenifer (brother of Nancy Jenifer Berry), who died in 1907. Cited for "Distinquished Courage" before Richmond.

Back To Ole Virginny
To Study War No More

SAM Jenifer got out of the Army at Roanoke Island, N.C. near Christmas time, 1865, four months earlier than John Berry's discharge at Brownsville, Texas. Sam received a free pass to return to the old plantation in Old St. Mary's County, Maryland, with 30 days rations and terminal leave. Such a joyful reunion! Members of his family had discussed his whereabouts even with their master and had prayed for his safe return. They assumed that he had been accepted as a soldier. There had been various versions of his whereabouts on the grapevine, which had filtered back to the plantation, including information that he and other escaped slaves were fighting with the Union Army.

Joy was mixed with sorrow when Sam Jenifer learned that his mother had passed away a few months before his return. "What caused her to die?" he asked his younger sister, Nancy.

"She'd been getting thin, her clothes were loose on her and she couldn't eat much. And then she caught a bad cold and had to stay in the cabin. She slept on de same pallet on the floor she had when you run to the War. She had hot fever and the slave doctor saw her and gave her herb tea and give us grease to rub her and put a hot red flannel on her chest to break up the congestion. Massa sent an old bed from the big house for her to sleep on. But she kept getting worse and the doctor come agin. He put on a flax seed poultice and we put on hot mutton suet and she slept with the flannel on her chest all night," Nancy recounted. Then she began to sniffle and the tears that welled in her eyes slipped down her cheeks. She hesitated for a minute and then said, "The next day she coughed up a pot full of blood and then she died."

"Where is she buried?" Sam wanted to know.

"In the slave grave yard near the magnolia tree," Nancy responded. "All the men in our family hunted for a big grey and black rock and they put it on the grave to mark the place. It's near where Grandma is buried. Somebody took Grandma's rock away, so they put another one there for her, too."

"Let's go over to her grave." Sam said, quietly. As they walked, Nancy continued, "Mama prayed to live till you come from the War. She say God told her you would come and we would all be free at last. I wish she could see your soldier suit. You look so good in it." His sister smiled with pride.

At the grave site they prayed and Nancy cried some more as they stood by the rock on their mother's burial place. There were other slave relatives buried there going back two or three generations. Sam straightened up his soldier suit and said, "I'm so sorry she could not live for me to see her agin, but I believe she is looking down at us from heaven."

And removing his Army cap, he continued, "I promise you, Mama, I will help Nancy get book learnin' and your chilluns will live the free life, that you prayed for and I fought for."

As they walked away, Sam was now choking up a bit, but he composed himself, and said, "Nancy, I've got 30 days rations. I'm goin' to take you back with me to Norfolk. There is lots of plantations around there and all the Massa's either killed or they run away and leave everything. They is given acres to black soldiers to farm and make their own livin' like real freefolks."

The next day they were on their way on a return boat trip to the Norfolk-Hampton area where there were hundreds of ex-soldiers and thousands of refugees coming into the so-called contraband camps to be taken care of by the newly established Freedmen's Bureau, which had been established by Congress in 1865 to protect the interests of the former slaves. It was under the direction of Gen. Oliver O. Howard, later the first president of Howard University.

Sam and Nancy went to St. John's AME Church which had just been organized in 1863, by a preacher from the Baltimore Conference. The former white Methodist Episcopal church, now had a congregation of both free Blacks and freedmen. They met Rev. Richard Parker, who had been preaching to the refugees on Taylor's Farm, as well as assisting at St. John's. Sam was still wearing his uniform and receiving courtesies on every hand. Happily, he had some savings from his war pay, although for most of his service, he had been paid only half of the pay of a white soldier, eight dollars a month, instead of fifteen.

On the second Sunday at St. John's, Sam and Nancy spoke to Rev. and Mrs. Parker after the service. "Reverend, I got some land on de Taylor plantation, given to soldiers by the Freedmen's Bureau, but my sister don't have no good place to stay. Too many sinful men and women everywhere she go."

"Yes," said Nancy, "I don't know anybody here. I don't want to live with bad people. Maybe Mrs. Parker and you could help me find a nice place. I can do any kind of work and I want to get an education."

Mrs. Parker smiled at the anxious young man and woman, and said, "We'll be glad to do all we can to help. Give us a few days. Will you be coming back to church next Sunday?"

"Yes, M'am," responded Nancy. "Every Sunday, if I can. Thank you very much, if you can help me."

As they parted, Mrs. Parker said to her husband, "I like her very much. She seems to be a good young Christian woman. She sat near me in church. She enjoyed the sermon, and joined in all the singing. I was surprised, but she told me that preachers came out regularly to their plantation from Baltimore, and that she always sang when the slaves got together for church meetings."

The Parker's were free-born Blacks, had received some schooling, and the minister worked as a carpenter when he was not preaching.

Mrs. Parker continued, "She is getting rations from the Freedmen's Bureau, and she could help me with the housework and the children. I would like to have her live with us for a while and see how it works out. She seems ambitious and I think we could help her."

Reverend Parker agreed, and Nancy moved into the Parker's modest home. Almost immediately she was being taught the alphabet and was learning to read and write. Nancy was very happy, and the Parker's were very satisfied with the arrangement. Sam continued on the huge Taylor plantation, where he had been allowed to stake out two acres for farming, and with the help of other freedmen, to build a shack.

It was many months before Sam and John met again. But one day, near Norfolk, in the Freedmen's Bureau Camp, the two veterans met once again. There at mess time, in a reconstructed barracks, John and Sam relived their war experiences well into the night.

"Boy, them rednecks can sure fight," said Sam.

"You should have seen them at the "Crater Battle," they gave us hell! But the white Army from the North, we fight like brothers. Men were dropping dead all around me."

It was hot, my soldier suit wet to the skin; I walk in mud and blood but I keep my powder dry. After a while I catch a hot bullet in my belt buckle. I fall to the ground and don't know nothin'. Two boys snatch me up; I catch my wind; then I rams my musket and keeps up with the charge.

"When the Crater fight stopped I look at my buckle; it was bent all out of shape. I pray to God. I cut the buckle off with my jack knife and save it, 'cause it save me. Here 'tis, I keep it in my pocket all the time."

"My God, man," said John, "that buckle didn't save you, the Lord did."

Observers reported that "Ferrero's colored division dashed forward gallantly toward the Crater, although the approach was swept by a heavy cross-fire right and left. A part of these troops rushed straight for the chasm and rushed into it, filling it so that there was barely standing room. Some of them pressed through the troops near the Crater, partially formed, and charged toward the crest, capturing two or three hundred prisoners—the only success on this fatal day."[1]

John continued, "My worse fight was at the Wilson's Wharf; three miles from Charles City, close to the James River. Them Rebs laugh when they see us and they say we can give up if we want to and they could let us off easy. "We tell 'em we come here to fight!" They get mad and charge us with fast horses. They holler with that Rebel yell trying to scare us. We hold back; take all their shots 'til they come up real close. Den we cut loose. They thought hell done busted. I was in charge of Cap'n Choate's field piece #4 I call her "Betsy." We shoot 'em up so fast that ole Betsy turned almost red from the heat: them Rebels lose their horses and they run like hell on foot. Way late in the afternoon they raise the white flag. We took some prisoners and had to bury their dead 'cause they was takin' no chances. So we pack up and stay ready. Then we follow the advance pickets; Hell bent for Petersburg.

Sam picked up the narrative, anxious to tell his exploits. His 30th Regiment was involved in the skirmishes around the Weldon Railroad in August, between the 18th and the 23rd; they fought at Poplar Grove from September 29 to October 1, and at Boydton Plank Road near Hatcher's Run in late October. The outfit was then sent to North Carolina, where they were deployed in the second attack against Fort Fisher and Sugar Loaf Hill in January of 1865. The Carolina campaign of the 30th Regiment Fourth Division continued around Goldsboro and Raleigh. They were attached to General Sherman's Army Corps and helped to defeat and bring about the complete surrender of Confederate Gen. Joseph Johnston near Bennett's House on April 26, 1865.

After prolonged occupational duty in the area of Raleigh, Sam Jenifer was mustered out with his regiment at Roanoke Island, North Carolina, on December 10, 1865, by General Order No. 249, Headquarters Department.

Then John traced for Sam the movement of his light artillery unit after the Old Plank Road Battle near Boydton and recounted many experiences for his unit fought on the front lines for many weeks, before being sent to Portsmouth to guard the Confederate Supply Lines to Richmond and protect the war base at Norfolk. After Appomattox fell, John was ordered on the troop ship *Illinois* with a large contingent of Negro troops down the Southern Atlantic, through the Gulf of Mexico to Texas and the Rio Grande River. By an interesting turn of fate Gen. Samuel Chapman Armstrong commanding the 25th Division of Negro troops was aboard this same troop ship *Illinois* for the trip to the Rio Grande. Little did it occur to John Berry that this General, who showed so much interest in Black troops would be the founder of Hampton Institute immediately after he returned to the Hampton area from duty on the Rio Grande.

Within the first weeks on Taylor's Farm with the help of his war buddy, Sam Jenifer, John Berry became rather well acquainted with the lay of the land around Norfolk. On the first Sunday, John accompanied Sam to the St. John's AME church where he met Nancy Jenifer, Sam's sister.

John Berry's baritone voice made him a candidate for the young choir and before very long he was singing with this group where Nancy Jenifer also lent her lovely soprano voice to the choir.

75

It wasn't long before John Berry too had staked out a claim of land on the Taylor's Farm.

Meanwhile, he was becoming more and more attracted to Nancy Jenifer as he met her at choir rehearsals and at the Sunday services. John began to dream of a house with a vegetable garden under the supervision of Nancy as Mrs. John Berry.

On September 26, 1867, Rev. Richard Parker united John Berry and Nancy Jenifer in marriage at the St. John's church. By this time they were both getting help from the Freedmen's Bureau. The Black veterans in the community combined their efforts in cutting down trees, obtaining slabs made either by their own hands or obtained from a nearby sawmill and built one room cabins on this plantation which had been confiscated by Federal authorities.

By a system of underground communication and word-of-mouth, many Marylanders from Old St. Mary's County drifted into the Norfolk area and John Berry was reunited with some members of his family. Between 1866 and '69, Daniel and William Miles, half-brothers of John Berry, also staked out small farms on the old Taylor's Plantation.

For two or three years, things went rather well with these veterans and the aggressive men with their families from the group of contraband. But rumors began to spread that President Andrew Johnson, who had succeeded the assassinated Abraham Lincoln, would return the confiscated land to their original owners. In due time it happened by Executive Order of the President. The sheriffs of Norfolk County and other counties throughout the South ordered the Blacks off the land. John Berry and the other veterans had improved their cabins, cultivated the land and were growing crops, raising chickens and hogs to supply food for their families. They decided to resist the take over. Many of the veterans had guns and ammunition which they had managed to hide away in gunny sacks upon being mustered out of the service. There had been no bloodshed when the sheriff finally gave them forty-eight hours to get off the land or be taken prisoners by Federal Troops. There was a feeling of hopelessness among this band of refugees and veterans. The sheriff's men showed they meant business by breaking down all unoccupied shacks and sheds. But the Blacks held them off their homes for two weeks with their firepower.

Finally, they called a special meeting in a large barn which had been used as a gathering place usually for religious worship. Nearly all night they sang their songs of bondage which they knew so well. They had volunteered to fight the confederacy at the Call of Lincoln; they had tipped the balance of victory in war for the Union and now they faced the stark reality that the Rebels, their former masters were winning the peace. The older members of the band prayed in monotonous unison, "Oh Lord send us a miracle," while the younger men grouped on the outside to vent their rage against the assassins of Abraham Lincoln and the Yankees that were betraying them. Ironically, Taylor's Farm was near the historic James along whose shores many of the veterans had fought on their way to Petersburg and Richmond. Taylor's Farm was at a place called Ocean View where the Elizabeth and the Nansemond Rivers converged with the wider James to form a broad inlet of waterways known as Hampton Roads which emptied into the Chesapeake Bay then the Atlantic Ocean. These were the famous waters where the Naval battle between the *Merrimac* and the *Monitor* had taken place and through which large ocean-going steamers entered the harbor at Norfolk.

However, two years before the showdown at Taylor's Farm Gen. Benjamin Butler had acquired 115 acres of land a few miles north of Hampton to be broken up into seven-acre plots and made available for purchase by Freedmen. Some of the people on the Taylor's Plantation had heard about the Butler's Farm but they had no previous need to consider its availability to them.

Late one evening while praying and singing could be heard inside the assembly barn a heated argument was going on outside. There was serious talk of hiding out in the woods and taking on a last ditch skirmish with the law.

At this point up came a squarely built young veteran who stood 5'9" and weighed 175 lbs. with broad shoulders and muscular arms. This was John Berry, age 25, who had grown long sideburns reaching a heavy mustache. With an air of quiet sagacity for his young years he spoke to the group in a firm voice, 'Just a minute fellows, these angry speeches won't get us anywhere. I got an idea that I think will work. I was in General Butler's Army and I hear that he has a farm for veterans back of Hampton. They are selling a few acres on easy terms for each family. Now I know that country from the war days; it is near Back River,

77

which flows into Hampton Roads a few miles above Old Point Comfort. How come we can't go down to the river, build two or three rafts, then pull down our houses, load up the lumber and all our belongings, row cross Hampton Roads towing some of the lumber and come into Back River right next to the new Butler Plantation. We built the pontoons and took an army across the James and across the Rappahannock and we forded the Chickahominy River and by God, if we pull together, we can cross Hampton Roads to the Butler's Farm. Soon there were words of agreement. The men vowed to pitch in and build their houses. This seemed to be the miracle that many had been praying for night after night.

Crossing Hampton Roads

WHEN the big meeting closed that night the men went to their cabins lit their kerosene lamps, turned them down low and spent most of the night discussing with their wives what they had to do. These farm women were as rugged as the men. They knew how to roll logs with can-hooks and chop down small trees. Early the next morning the men and some of the women met at the waterfront. John said, "How many men and families can we depend on." John Pie said, "there are seven of us here." Dick Miles spoke up—"what you think we're here fo." They all chimed in "we got muscle, we got de nerve, we ain't 'fraid of de water and by God we can fight if anybody mess with us on land or sea." John Berry spoke again, "dey say de land is cheap, no money down. We is buyin' from General Butler, he was my General in the war. We all like him. He was always fair wid the Black man. Dere's room enuf here on this waterfront and the bank is high enuf to float a raft close to the shore."

The men spent a half day discussing and laying out the plan for pulling down their houses, building a strong raft and loading up their belongings and lumber. Some of the lumber would be towed attached to the raft. They had one mule between them and a broke down two-wheel cart, for which would come in handy. They would sell the cart and mule before leaving Taylor's Farm. They knew it would be necessary for some of them to go to Hampton and see the Butler's Farm that they had heard about, check on the size of each farm, how close it was to the landing place and other details. Only Oscar Carr and Berry had a vague idea. Carr spoke up saying "Berry trained at Fortress Monroe and we know something about the land around there." Pie said, "You all should go over by ferry and find out how we can reach the shore." Dick

79

Miles spoke up and said, "yea and I'll go wid you and pay my own way." The others chipped in the fare. The party of three; Berry, Miles and Carr, caught the early morning ferry the next day from Willoughby Spit cross Hampton Roads to Old Point Comfort about a 45 minute ride. They walked the mile and a half through the edge of Phoebus to Soldiers' Home in Hampton where the news of Butler's Farm came from first.

Arriving at Soldiers Home they were ushered in to see Colonel Raymond. "Howdy do men. I'm glad to see you. I had hoped you'd come." "Yes sir, Colonel," spoke John Berry, "we saved some money from the war and the Freedmen's Bureau helped us with rations. We think we can buy the land and we have a plan to tear down our houses, bring the logs and lumber 'cross Hampton Roads to the farms." "What!" said Colonel Raymond, "that sounds impossible." Miles and Berry responded, "we worked around Potomac and Patuxent Rivers all our lives and the Chesapeake Bay too." Carr said, "we build rafts and floating bridges in the war and dey drivin' us off the Taylor Farm: we got to do sumptin." "If you think you can do it," said Colonel, "I'll give all the help I can, and General Butler wants to help his boys. Rev. L. L. Lively will show you all the available land out there." "It's already surveyed into seven-acre plots. Some families have built already, there are 110 acres in all and part of it borders near Back River." "Yes," said Berry, "and that river connects with Hampton Roads." The men asked the Colonel if they could talk with him after they saw the land. "Yes," he replied, "I want to, this sounds like a very risky project." "But I am willing to listen."

The trio took the horse car from Old Point Comfort to Newport News; it travelled through Hampton on King Street. Just beyond the city limits they came to Back River Road. They got off there and walked to Reverend Lively's house on Butler's Farm. The Reverend welcomed them with a glad handshake. I have been expecting to hear from the Taylor Farm folks. "We got seven families who want to live near each other," said John Berry, "we all kinfolks, and we got the down payment if the agreement is like Colonel Raymond said." "Yes," said Reverend Lively, "I am the agent here for General Butler. Understand we ain't talkin' 'bout nothin' but lan'. You have to build your own houses." "Show us lan', not too far from Back River." "Alright sir, let me hitch up the horse and cart and drive you'll over the whol' lan'." "Why you

80

want to be close to Back River?" "Well not too close, but if we like the lan', we goin' pull down our houses and tow them over here across Hampton Roads on a raft." "You mean you want to paddle a raft by all them big ships across Hampton Roads?" After seeing the Back River front and the large acreage, tall timbers and cleared land, they were sure they wanted it. "You see, Reverend," said Oscar Carr, "we built pontoon bridges during the war and we know how to cross rivers."

John Berry thanked Reverend Lively, and said, "we be goin' to make the Soldiers Home now, befor' it gets too dark. We be back soon to bind the bargain for six or seven families." The veterans spent late afternoon and the night at Soldiers Home and had a long talk with Colonel Raymond about helping them bring their families and rebuild on Butler's Farm. Before returning to Taylor's Farm the next morning, they had a firm arrangement for the very young wives and children and elderly women to stay at Soldiers Home after crossing by Ferry from Taylor's Farm. The men would paddle their raft past Old Point Comfort north and eastward up Back River to Butler's Farm.

Seven families began immediately in June, 1870, to assemble work tools, of wooden mallets, sledge hammers, axes, hoes, hammers, single-hand saws, two-men saws, and large quantities of heavy rope from the nearby shipyard salvage. They found two leaky rowboats and recorked their seams with "okum," (a caulking substance) to serve as life boats. They found some discarded cork filled life jackets. Using a mule and a two-wheel cart which some families owned together, they gathered logs and slabs around the plantation and cut some new ones to build their large raft.

Meanwhile, old man Taylor, the former rebel plantation owner, had returned to his old mansion following President Johnson's Executive Order. He found it partly in shambles and was trying to rebuild and take over his former property. He approached the Black vets packing to leave. "What you boys doin," said Taylor. "We leaving this land 'cause you called the sheriff and we ti'ed 'er fightin'. It really don't b'long to you. You run when the Yankees come. We fought for it, some give up their lives, we won't. We built these houses, cut these logs, raised these crops, they belong to us. Since yo' folks 'sassinate President Lincun, the Army forced us to leave but we taking all our belongings." Taylor said, "I am not goin' to try to stop you. Remember, I suffered too, all this land was mine,

81

but I am nearly broke. You take all the lumber you need, I can't use it. Some of you folks want to work for me on shares it will be good for both of us. "We wouldn't work for you 'cause we don't believe you would treat us man-to-man."

After about a month the seven families had pulled down their houses, dragged and hauled the lumber and much of their belongings, crates of chickens and pigs, they were ready to sail with the tide and sunrise to the shores of Hampton Roads. They built a substantial raft of logs, slabs, lumber tied together with Navy rope, wooden pegs, rail spikes, and a large canvas movable sail to take advantage of tail winds. They took lanterns in case of darkness or heavy fog; took signal flags which they learned to use in the war. They figured to make the 15 mile trip between sun up and sun down.

So on an appointed day at sunrise, they said a prayer with joined hands, and sailed with the morning tide. The trips were made one week apart. They built three rafts one at a time out of the lumber from their cabins, dismantling each raft on the banks of Back River on Butler's Farm. They returned by ferry between each trip. The families doubled up in the remaining cabins and finally lived in tents made of quilts and old canvas and young tree stoves. The backbreaking trip across Hampton Roads was a rough experience as everybody knew it would be. On the first crossing they had to find the bell buoys to avoid the lanes of the big Old Dominion and Merchant Miners ships, Philadelphia, New York and Boston. They were sighted by a commercial tug boat which steamed over out of curosity, and asked if they were in trouble. Nearing Old Point Comfort, another boat blew a distress whistle to see if they were what was left of a sunken ship. Finally these water vagabonds pulled into Back River where there was no traffic. On the second crossing a police boat asked if they were sure they could make it and trailed them for a few miles to be sure the raft was under control. On the last crossing they were caught in a squall, and high waves from an Old Dominion Passenger liner enroute to Norfolk, swept the raft off course. One of their main sweeps was broken and they had to use over-sized oars from the two life saver rowboats, attached to the main raft. While Pie was bailing out water from the rowboats he fell into the water. He was a good swimmer and found the cork filled life jacket a handicap. He removed the cork filled life jacket and swam back to the main raft, climbing over some of the logs and lumber being towed along. Many years later, he was kidded about his experience. The tales had it that he was trying to be sporty walking the logs and fell in the high waves, and they all had to jump in and save him when he was going down for the third time.

While their cabins were being rebuilt, mattresses were made of straw stuffed in bags, flattened and spread on the ground. When the last raft with house furnishings and farm utensils were landed, cabins were already being rebuilt.

By the first frost in the fall of 1870, the Berry, Jenifer, Miles and Garner families had completed their crude cabins, launched out on their undeveloped but independent farm life to rear their children and serve their God.

Butler's Farm

THE band of seven families which crossed Hampton Roads by rowing their crude raft and towing their lumber across 15 miles of water, were finally settled in their slab cabins on Butler's Farm. Because the men and working women had to travel back and forth between Soldiers Home near the campus of the New Hampton Institute and the Butler's Farm they became very much acquainted with general conditions in the area.

There were contraband camps everywhere. The town of Hampton had been burned by the Confederates during the war and abandoned by the white population. Slabtown was still present, it consisted of a group of cabins built from slabs made by sawing logs lengthwise at a local sawmill. There were abandoned houses which were still filled with contrabands, sometimes an entire family in one room. In some places chimneys were still standing after the houses had been destroyed by fire. The former slaves constructed cabins which included the old chimneys and fireplaces. At one time there had been an estimated ten thousand refugees within a radius of five miles of the Hampton Freedmen's Bureau headquarters. They came with their wives and children by foot, on mule back, on wagons, two-wheel carts bringing such meager belongings as they had on their old plantation. Gen. Samuel Chapman Armstrong seeing and observing the activities of escaped slaves and Freedmen remarked that, "a Negro in a tight spot is a genius." He said that "We issue 18,000 rations a day to those who would die of starvation if it were not for this." * In modern times it has been said that Negroes can do more with less, and less with more than any group on earth. In the midst of this squalor and crude refugee camps around Hampton there was a center of culture developing around Hampton Institute. The members of the group on Butler's Farm learned of the development of the learning centers slowly being developed. The American Missionary Association from the North had sent missionaries to the area from the first year of the war to teach the Christian religion to escaping slaves. The Freedmen's Bureau was organized during the war and played an important role in helping to provide material means to the refugees.

Even before the war there emerged a Black woman who would become a great heroine and benefactor and the history of the race. Her name was Mary Peake. She was born free and received some education in the District of Columbia, before the schools there were closed to Blacks. This remarkable woman later moved to Hampton and taught many slaves, children and adults as well as free Blacks in her home, after dark, at great personal risks. When the war broke out she continued her activity and established a school for contraband children under a large oak tree near the modern campus of Hampton Institute.

This tree became legendary and is known as "Emancipation Oak." It still stands as a sentinel of ages as a monument to the Black struggle for continuing education. The eagerness of blacks for "book learnin'" was greatly manifest here, as children begged to join her school under the tree. Soon there were more than fifty in each session. This school continued for many months as the first public school for Negroes in the United States. In spite of failing health, Mrs. Peake carried on with the support of her husband, Thomas, who acquired his freedom during slavery until Rev. H. H. Lockwood representing the American Missionary Association provided an indoor school which opened on September 17, 1861, in a little brown cottage. Mrs. Peake died late in 1862 during the battle of the *Monitor* and the *Merrimac*. The ships were seen and the cannon fire heard from her bedroom as she breathed her last.

In 1866, under Gen. Samuel Chapman Armstrong, director of the Eastern district of the Freedmen's Bureau, Hampton was envisaged as the strategic spot "for a permanent and great educational works," and he suggested to the American Missionary Association that a school for Freedmen be established. The Butler's Farm School was there for some of the community school children, but the new Hampton Institute was modeled after the kinds of institutions that General Armstrong had seen his father establish on the Hawaiian Islands where he was Minister of Education. In April, 1868 classes began at Hampton Institute.

By 1872 many of the Butler's Farm families had their crude houses built or in the process of being completed. While things were looking up because they were purchasing their own land and homes, they faced conditions more primitive than it is possible to imagine. In spite of these crude beginnings the Hampton area was already a resource of great potential for the future development of the Negro race.

On one sunny Sunday afternoon, John Berry and Sam Jenifer, Oscar Carr and John Pie were sitting in their rustic hand made chairs and rockers in the front yard of the Berry home. They had returned from the Sunday prayer band services at their newly started AME church. "Well," said Berry, puffing on his clay pipe, "I think things look pretty good here, for all er us, on dis here farm." "Why you think it so good," said John Pie: "we ain't got but one mule betwix all fo' of us, and what we plan for summer, vegetable, for de mule and raisin' a few chickens, ain't hodly goin' be enuf to git thru the winter." "Yea, said Oscar Carr, older than the rest, "Iffin it don't be fer de Freedmen's Bureau we couldn't be makin' it now, and your family an' my family would be workin' hard and hungry jest like slavery time." Sam Jenifer who had weathered more hell-fire in the war than the rest spoke up saying: "My God, we all got some land and wid papers to prove it." "We made the down payment wid the war money and General Butler done made it easy to keep up the payments." John Berry spoke up again: "Dats what I'm talkin' bout. We livin' mongst the folks we fought against. We killed some of ther kinfolks. We don't know how long de North soldiers at the fote and Yankees goin' protect us from the Rebs. He continued "I know one thing we gotta lotta educated Negroes around the fote. Some from de North and dey talkin' bout education and politics all de time. Besides that, all us can vote. When I say things look pretty good, I mean up de road: if we vote fer our people, git mo book learning fo us and chullins, den freedom will mean sumpin. Outside of dat it won't mean nothin." John pulled on his pipe. During the brief period of the Reconstruction years Blacks in Hampton were successful in electing to office Rufus Jones, a storekeeper who served in the Virginia House of Delegates from 1871–1875; Alexander G. Lee, who was in the House of Delegates from 1877–78, and Luke B. Phillips who was a member of Hampton's first City Council after the War and was, for a time, acting Mayor.

The Butler's Farm people gradually strengthened their friendship and cooperation. They purchased farm animals including oxen, mules and horses jointly until they could become more independent. Many of them raised crops jointly. They felled trees and sold timber buildings and small trees for pulpwood to make paper all from their land. The Berry's had been on Butler's Farm nearly six years. In 1876 their second child that lived, was born. This was Llewellyn Longfellow, "L. L." as he was frequently called. Their first child John Augustus Berry, Jr. was born on Taylor's Farm the year they moved away.

The year 1876 stood out in American history in the destiny of the nation, of the future of the Negro race and the destiny of the Berry family. In February the country was well along in its preparation for the centennial celebration of its birth as a nation. During this year of campaigning for a fall election of the President, it was obvious to political observers that the South was growing tired of their struggle for dominance against newly freed Negroes and the white Republicans, within southern borders. Likewise, Northern industrialists were growing weary of supporting the "Negro cause." The presidential election of 1876 ended in a virtual tie between Republican Rutherford B. Hayes and Democrat Samuel J. Tilden. The matter came to the House of Representatives and a special commission for settlement. A "compromise" resulted after much uproar, in fighting and filibustering. Hayes and the Republican party were "awarded" the presidency for which they paid in a manner destined to undo the Civil War, and virtually re-enslaved the Negroes for another hundred years. This reversal of history as far as the Black struggle is concerned was called by the Southerners; "Home Rule." This meant withdrawal of federal troops of occupation which guarded Negro constitutional rights; such as voting, office holding, equality before the courts, freedom of speech and assembly, including freedom from re-enslavement. The Berry family and the struggling dirt farmers on Butler's Farm, many of them veterans, like Blacks all over the South were turned over to a merciless revengeful South. There was an immediate increase and development of new organizations like the Ku Klux Klan, and the establishment by state action of such laws as the "Black Code," "Grandfather Clauses" and Poll Tax which kept black citizens largely re-enslaved for a hundred years.

On May 1, 1876 the fifteen quadrennial General Conference of the AME church was convened in Atlanta, Georgia with Bishop Daniel A. Payne presiding. At this session he resigned the presidency of Wilberforce University which he had founded in 1856. His purpose of resigning was to give full time, he said, to the writing of the history of the AME church which he subsequently published. By previous selection Bishop Payne preached a Centennial sermon, in which he reviewed the long hard past of the Negro, his present accomplishments and his God ordained promise of continued success for the future. Arrangements were made for a Centennial Exhibition by the entire church connection commemorating the founding of the nation, and the birth of American Democracy.

Shortly before the General Conference met in Atlanta, the AME Bishop's Council had met in Washington, D. C. It organized the agenda for the General Conference including a plan to build a Metropolitan Church in Washington, D. C. While in session the Council received an invitation to have lunch with the Honorable James G. Blaine at his residence. They accepted and enjoyed informal discussions with other guests, including the Honorable George Hoar of Massachusetts and the Honorable James A. Garfield of Ohio. This meeting was probably more political than social. Negroes still had the vote in the North and many continued to vote at the risk of their lives in the South. No one there could have known that destiny would put James A. Garfield in the White House, four years later, but the politicians "smelled" success and they wanted the Negro vote even while they were plotting "Home Rule" for the South and virtual re-enslavement for the Negro.

As "Home Rule" became more and more a reality in the years between 1876 and 1895, gradually and sometimes by intimidation, Blacks were gotten out of political office and ultimately because of harassment and fear, Blacks stayed away from the polls and their voting strength declined. In 1888, The Fourth Congressional District sent a Negro, John Mercer Langston to Congress, but he was not permitted to take the oath of office and his seat until September 23, 1890. He would be the only Negro representative in Congress from Virginia. Violence and intimidation accelerated, and when John R. Holmes, a Negro candidate for State Senator in 1892, was shot to death by a white man in Charlotte County, no other Negro candidates presented themselves for election to State or Federal office.

The Post War Struggle

As the years passed the family of Nancy Jenifer Berry and John Berry grew until it included, in addition to John, Jr. (Gus), and Llewellyn L., Lola, Johanna, Katherine, Henry, Arthur and Nace Jenifer.

Life on Butler's Farm was not easy. Earning a living and keeping a roof overhead was the chief concern of most of the small farmers and laborers like John Berry and Sam Jenifer. Wages were low, and while Negro laborers were without work, a State commission was set up in 1869 to encourage foreign white labor to migrate to Virginia.*

While life was difficult for the grown folks, for the children growing up this first generation born out of slavery, it was the best of times. The children went to the Farm School and after that there was the Whittier School, which was the practice school for the students in teacher training at Hampton Institute. The Whittier School had a very high rating.

But the Church was the center of life for the people on Butler's Farm. As the children grew up they were all required to go to Sunday School, to church and to class meetings like their parents. Lew and his sister, Katherine, were special buddies. They both had religious leanings and enjoyed playing "church." They would even preach the funerals of chickens which had been killed for the dinner table.

One of Lew's best friends was William Johnson Miller, "W. J." as he was called. They were near the same age and practiced "preaching" in the woods. Each one monitoring the other's sermons. Each one would pick out a well-known pastor who preached in their community to imitate. One of Lew's favorite was Rev. James Garner, a distant cousin of the Berry's who was known for his eloquence in the Tidewater section of Virginia.

91

"W. J." and Lew also attended the same class meeting at Bethel Church in Hampton. John Berry, Sr., now heavy-set, with long side-burns that reached into his full mustache was the leader of the class. The class meeting was a gathering of members who "testified" to their Christian experience, praying openly for the forgiveness of sins and asking for the help of fellow class members in walking the "straight and narrow" path of righteousness. Between testimonies, John, Sr., would lead the group in his strong baritone voice in singing the spirituals and AME hymns.

Lew and "W. J." didn't spend all of their time studying "preach-ing." They ran rabbits together all over the Butler's Farm countryside. They even looked at the girls once in a while. And some time it was the same young lady that caught their eyes. One particularly pretty brownskin miss whom they both liked to walk home from The Christian Endeavor church meetings on Sunday afternoon was Mollie Melvin. She was very popular and very active in church work. Lew said to "W. J." one time, "Find yourself another girl to walk home from Christian Endeavor, I saw Mollie first," but W. J., not to be outdone, said, "Oh, no, I like her, too. We'll both go for ourselves and see who wins." And apparently neither did. Lew also liked listening to his father and the other male neighbors get together and talk about the old times. They were frequently joined by veterans who came from the Soldiers Home, which had become a national home for Black soldiers who had sustained injuries in the War. From them Lew learned about the massacre of Black soldiers at Fort Pillow and the brave stand of the 54th Massachu-setts regiment at Fort Wagner.

One day Lew asked his father if any one had written about the things they had accomplished as soldiers. His father had answered, "No, nothing." History was added to preaching, as one of Lew's challenges.

His father also told his sons about growing up in the days of slavery, and how as a young teen-ager, he would go to the water's edge in Old St. Mary's County, looking toward the distant horizon and imagining that he could see Africa, the home of his ancestors, just beyond. As he would think of the cruelties of slavery and how some of his forebears were brought to this country in chains, he knew that conditions must be better in the Africa that he knew nothing of, than the land to which they had been brought. He craved to learn about Africa and to touch its soil. And he told his sons, that often as he stood and gazed and dreamed, tears rolled down his cheeks as he turned back to a day of drudgery as a slave. He prayed and knew intuitively that there was a better world coming for Black people, and he wanted to live and experience the reality of his dreams.

Lew, knowing of his father's dream, used to go down to the shore of Back River, and think of his father and his father's father and pray that it could be made better for his people someday.

One evening after supper, Nancy Berry held son, Lew, in the kitchen when the others had left the table. She told him that the Lord had directed her to ask Lew to find someone who would advise him on his life's work. Lew was surprised at what his mother was telling him and confided in her that he had had a dream the night before. He had dreamed that the Lord was calling him to preach and he was told to talk with Reverend Lively about it.

The next day, he spoke to Reverend Lively revealing his and his mother's dreams and their conversation. Reverend Lively was encouraging and told the young man, "Son, you are called to preach."

From that day on Llewellyn was convinced that some day he would be a great preacher. When he told his mother of his decision to follow the ministry, she broke down weeping on his shoulders, and said, "This is what I have prayed for since long before you were born." Her tears were of thanksgiving.

As the children grew up they were all required to go to Sunday school, to church and class meetings like their parents. Katherine, Llewellyn were buddies. They both had special religious learnings. Katherine wrote in later years that she and her brother "Lew" enjoyed "playing" church. They would preach the funeral of chickens when they were killed for food. Katherine also wrote that her mother told of talking to her son Llewellyn in the kitchen one evening after supper, telling him that the Lord directed her to ask Lew to find someone who would advise him on a life's vocation. Lew was surprised and revealed to his mother that he had a dream the night before. The Lord was calling him to preach and he was told to talk with Rev. L. L. Lively. This he did the very next day. Rev. Lively encouraged him and said, "Son, you are called to preach." From that day on Llewellyn was convinced that some day he would be a great preacher. When he told his mother

93

of this decision, she broke down and wept on his shoulder and said, "This is what I have prayed for since long before you were born." One of Levi's friends was ("W. J.") William Johnson Miller. The two boys practiced preaching in the woods while monitoring each other's "sermon." They each picked out a well known preacher to imitate. One that "Lew" patterned his preaching style after was Rev. James Garner, a celebrated eloquent preacher in Tidewater, Virginia, a distant cousin of the Berry's.

W. J. and Lew attended the same class meeting at Bethel Church. Their leader was Lew's father, John Sr., he was heavy set, about 5′8″, wore long sideburns reaching a full mustache. The class meeting was a gathering of members who testified to their "Christian experience," prayed openly for the forgiving of sins and asked for the help of fellow class members to walk the straight and narrow path. John Sr., the leader would intersperse between testimonies by his strong baritone voice leading spirituals and A. M. E. hymns. These stories were told many years later by the Rev. "WJ" William Johnson Miller, who left the "work-year" at Hampton Institute and Shellbanks farm to become a minister.

John and WJ didn't spend all of their time studying to preach. They ran rabbits together all over the Butler's Farm countryside. They even looked at the girls once in a while. According to WJ there was a particular pretty brown young lady whom they both liked to escort home from the Christian Endeavor Church meetings on Sunday afternoons. Her name was Mollie Melvin. She was very active as a church worker and very popular. Lew said, "WJ, find yourself another girl to walk home from the Christian Endeavor. I saw Mollie first." WJ said, "Oh, no, I like her too, we will both go for ourselves and see who wins." Apparently neither one got very far with Miss Melvin.

As a pre-teen and teenager Lew had quite a companionship with his father who told him many stories about the war and the slavery days back in Maryland. On occasions veterans from the Soldiers Home would visit John Berry and sit around the fireplace reminiscing about their experiences in the war. He met veterans of the Battle of Wilson's Wharf, Hatcher's Run, Deep Bottom, the Crater Explosion before Petersburg, New Market Heights, Milliken's Bend. Other veterans came from the Soldiers Home, which had become a national rest haven, especially for black soldiers, including many who sustained injuries in the war. Lew heard about the black massacre at Fort Pillow and the brave stand of the 54th Massachusetts regiment at Fort Wagner. He met veteran sailors who were involved in the battle of the *Monitor* and *Merrimac*, in Mobile Bay.

Many years later when Rev. Berry's career was at an end, there was found among the papers left in his library a typed statement titled "My Challenge" which read in part as follows: "As a child before I reached the teen age my father who had served as a volunteer soldier in the Civil War, used to thrill my young life with stories of his experiences in army life. A mear boy he escaped slavery and joined the union army near his home town in St. Mary's County Maryland. My father was an artilleryman and drove the horse or mules which drew the carriage, carrying Capt. Choate's field gun piece #4. My father was my hero in all these matters. As a child I saw many of the soldiers visiting my father's home, and I was allowed to sit in their midst while they related their experiences of life as a soldier. One day I asked my father if anyone wrote about these things. They did as soldiers. He answered, "no." I said, "Nothing at all?" He, "No nothing we ever heard about black soldiers. So through the years I think about what told me by this parent, the hardship, exposure to death and witnessing their buddies die beside them. Yet when I asked for written history, my father said no. So from that time until now history has been my challenge."

John Berry Jr. did not entirely escape the ever present atmosphere of "becoming-a-preacher." John Jr. became an exhorter for awhile. Two other brothers escaped "scott free" and worked in hotels, including the Hygeia in Hampton, others in New Port News, Philadelphia, and points in the North East. Arthur married and reared two sons in Philadelphia. Nat was called the "ramblin man," because he like to travel. He was expelled from Hampton Institute during his work-year because he ate a forbidden apple from a tree on the shellbanks student farm. He died as a young man without having married.

Many years later Mrs. Louise Garner Perry at the age of seventy-four told many stories of growing up on Butler's Farm with the Berry boys and girls. Her stories were corroborated by Lola Berry Innis about the same age. They both knew that their parents were in slavery as teenagers at St. Mary's County, Maryland, near Leonardtown. Mrs. Perry's mother's name was Katherine Miles Garner who told her daughter about being a slave as a teenager at St. Mary's County, working in the big house of a plantation owner, Henry Milburn. Her mother told her of watching the slave master read in the newspaper when war clouds were gathering. And how he would slam the paper to the floor in disgust. This made Katherine Miles grieve because she was unable to read and understand accurately what she knew intuitively to be bad news for the confederacy. Lola's parents had told her that her mother Nancy Jenifer Berry had been a slave by the John Thomas' and her father by Tom Garner, all of St. Mary's County. Her father had been born Richard Brown, he became the stepson of George Miles who married his mother Sarah. He had many half brothers and sisters whose names were Miles. Her father had changed his name to John Berry as a technique of escape from slavery to join the Union army. Many of the Garners, Miles had John Berry and Jenifer families came to the Taylor's Farm and were part of the Hampton Roads project. These stories were further confirmed by John Augustus Berry, Jr. who remembered being carried by his mother when he was about seven years old, back to the farm of her former enslavers in St. Mary's county near Leonardtown. It was near a body of water and I met my mother's former young mistress and master, as she called them. The man took John on a sleigh pulled by a horse and the woman played the piano for him. The plantation owners were the John Henry Thomas' and the body of water was the Patuxent River. The plantation house that still stands is called Cremona. Mrs. Perry furnished the writer with a long list of farmers, their wives and children and their approximate ages as she remembers them from her childhood on Butler's Farm (see Appendix.) An article appeared in the journal called the Southern Workman published by Hampton Institute, Feb. 1905. The article by J. E. Davis, entitled "The Old Butler Farm" with some of the houses as they appeared then and a story of an interview with Mrs. Catherine Miles Garner, the mother of Mrs. Perry. In the interview, Mrs. Catherine Miles Garner spoke of being a member of the party that crossed Hampton Roads on a raft in 1870.

How fortunate the writer was to get Louise Garner Perry and Lola Berry Innis reminiscing about their childhood on old Butler's Farm. It was on a Sunday afternoon in the summer of 1955. John Augustus Jr. who lived in the Bronx later joined the women in the interview and reminiscing stories of the old days down in Virginia. John Jr. recalled the yearning desire of his father to visit Africa. He said that his father told him of these journeys as a young teenager and the days of slavery. He would go to the water front during a quiet period frequent in the early morning and look over the distant horizon and imagine he was looking over toward Africa, the home of his ancestors. As he would think of the cruelties of slavery and how some of his forebearers were brought to this country in chains he knew that conditions must be better in the homeland that he knew nothing about, but whose history he craved to learn and whose soil yearned to touch. As he stood and gazed and dreamed, tears rolled down his cheeks as he would turn back to a day of drudgery as a slave. He prayed and knew intuitively that there was a better world coming, for Black people, and he wanted to live and experience the reality of his dreams.

Lola spoke up and said, "Well you know your brother, Lew, he used to do the same thing on the shores of Hampton Roads. He knew of his father's dreams about Africa and apparently became obsessed with the same idea. At one time after he became licensed as an exhorter, all he could talk about was preaching and going to Africa." They all smiled and Mrs. Perry said, "that was not all he talked about I remember that he had a sense of humor. And, to some degree, he liked the girls."

"What about non-religious life on Butler's Farm and Hampton in the days of your childhood?" the Butler's Farm folk were asked. John Jr. responded by saying, "The educational life of Negroes became a very important thing and one of the leading activities of the South when Hampton Institute was a center of learning. Not only did Negroes come there to study as teachers and to learn the trades, but Indian students also came from Oklahoma and other places in fairly large numbers at one time. As you all know I stayed there until I reached medical school age and saw a very interesting development around Hampton Institute. It became a kind of oasis and a desert. It had an outreach program into the community especially to Negroes. Their football kick games and other attractions such as Broadway stars in music and the theatre were brought to the Hampton Campus. Sometimes they were people who had never played in local theatres at Norfolk or anywhere in Tidewater. Local white people would clamor to attend these affairs wanting to sit up front but never were permitted by Hampton's white president and faculty to sit in front of the students. The local whites became jealous and accused Hampton of practicing "social equality" and generating miscegenation. Hampton which would spring from Northern liberals, during and post Civil War, maintained its independence and frequently described itself in bulletins and other publications as an institution where three races of men worked at the problems of everyday life without friction. That, of course, was a white lie but they got away with it."

"What about voting and the Ku Klux Klan after the Reconstruction," Mrs. Perry was asked. She answered saying, "I remember we were all worried about the Ku Klux Klan but I don't remember any of their activities around Hampton. We all knew about the lynchings all over the South every year. And when I was an adult, before moving North, we used to read in the Norfolk *Journal and Guide* and Richmond *Planet* about these terrible lynchings and burnings at the stake, and that there were protests from Washington by Negro leaders and the whites in the North and even some whites in the South." The interviewer asked Mrs. Innis, "What about Negroes in Politics as you grew up in Virginia." "I don't remember any Negroes holding office. I remember Poppa paying his poll taxes but most people said the vote wouldn't count anyway, so they didn't bother." John Jr. spoke up and said "Negroes achieved their greatest success politically during the Reconstruction period, that is from the end of the war until about 1876. They still had political battles during this period but with the help of Northern whites and some Northern Negroes with superior education. More Negroes were elected to high office than has occurred at any time since then. There would have been undoubtedly much more bloodshed except for the Northern army of occupation, which manned polling places, political meetings and other areas where people gathered to talk politics. Some of the soldiers serving as guards were Negroes. The Southern whites or ex-Conferedates, if you will, were burned up at the sight of a Negro in uniform with a gun on his shoulder guarding them at the polls. Negroes everywhere were anxious to vote as they were anxious to learn, so my father used to tell us."

In Elizabeth County, where Hampton was located there was a Negro sheriff by the name of Andrew Williams. When I was six or seven years, we had black assembly men elected to the states assembly in Richmond. As I recall, there were two, John Robinson, and Robert Smith. We learned from Black History from lectures at the church and in the Masonic lodge that these assembly men played an important role in establishing public school system of Virginia and setting up the state school, which turned out to be all Negro called Virginia Normal and Industrial at Petersburg. I learned back in those days that there were more than a hundred elected Black officials in the state of Virginia during this period of so called Reconstruction. At one time there was an acting mayor for the city of Hampton. I knew Luke Phillips who was a Hampton graduate a well-known merchant who had served as a member of the city council and also at one time justice of the peace for the city of Hampton. I remember hearing that Tom Peake who was the husband of Mary Peake, the famous woman that established the first Black school under Emancipation Oak, held the office of Supt. of the Poor. I did not know him personally, I think he must have died before I grew up.

John Jr. said, "Our school books taught us that all Negroes were ignorant and were pushed down the throats of white Southerners by the victorious Northerners after the war. As I grew up to manhood we learned from Black sources and especially by lecturers at Hampton Institute that this was not true. The criteria established for qualifications to run for office was that the candidate must own some property, must have a minimal education and to have had some experience as a business man, running a farm, etc. It is often forgotten that all the white folks that ran for office in that period were not college graduates by any means. Generally speaking there is proof that these Black office holders for the most part measured up in everyway with white candidates and in some instances were superior. Our parents and yours, too, Louise, were active as we grew up in community affairs. Most everything for the betterment of the community carried on between the church, or lodges. Our parents were among those who sometimes went from house to house to get people to come out to vote, so I was told. Now by the time that I became a pre-teen and older all of the political advantages changed. That is when the South obtained what they called "Home Rule." Gradually, and sometime abruptly by intimidation, Blacks were gotten out of office. There was all kinds of harrassment around Hampton to keep Negroes away from the polls, so their voting strength gradually decreased."

"What about entertainment for young people," they were asked.

Gus spoke up and said, "Oh we had fun alright, we sang shout songs, like "put on skillet, put on the lead mammy's goin to cook some shortenin bread." They all laughed and Louise said, "Don't forget KC Jones," "That's right" said Gus, "we wore that one out." "We made up our own words, like,"

> *"come all er round us if you want to flirt,*
> *here comes a gal with a hobble skirt,*
> *you can hug er and kiss her as much as you please,*
> *but never get that hobble above her knees"*

They all laughed and Gus continued, there was another versus,

> *"When I die bury me deep,*
> *put a jug of molasses at my feet,*
> *put a pone of cornbread in my hand,*
> *I'm goina sop black lasses to the promised land."*

Lola chimed in "don't forget 'Shine on harvest moon,' and 'Peg o' my heart.' I am sure that you have not forgotten that we could cut quite a rug in the school house when we had a young teacher after school and the old folk weren't around."

Section Three
John Berry's Son Goes to College
(1895-1899)

Special railroad car
furnished Kittrell
music department
for Cantata in Ra-
leigh; Allen Build-
ing, Girl's Dormi-
tory.   Graduation
Invitation and Class
Day Program of
Beulah Anne Har-
ris, 1897. Gradua-
tion Invitation and
Class Day Program
of Llewellyn L.
Berry, 1899.

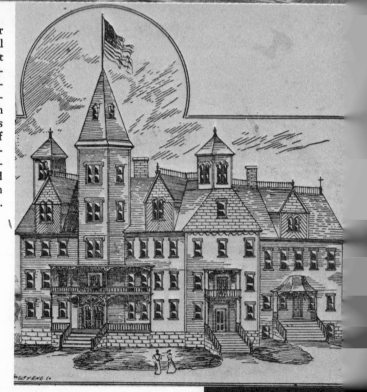

Motto: *Finis Nodum Est.*
Colors: *Blue and White.*

The Graduating Class of '97,
Kittrell Institute,
request your presence at the
Closing Exercises.

Class Day:
Tuesday, May 25, at 10:30 A. M.
Graduating Exercises:
Wednesday, May 26, at 10:30 A. M.

CLASS DAY PROGRAMME.

Tuesday, May 25, at 10:30 A. M.

PRAYER.

1. March Song.
2. Salutatory, ... BEULAH A. HARRIS
3. Class History, . . . SALLIE W. WARD
4. Vocal Duet, ... { BEULAH HARRIS / FANNIE TELFAIR
5. ORATION—"Power of Man," PARIS P. BRYAN
6. Pantomime, ... FANNIE TELFAIR
7. Class Prophecy, . . . GEORGE W. TAYLOR
8. Class Poem, ... BESSIE I. BOONE
9. Vocal Quartette.
10. Valedictory, ... WILLIAM A. PEELE
11. ANNUAL ADDRESS—"What to Do" C. H. JOHNSON
12. Class Song—Words by { F. E. TELFAIR / G. W. TAYLOR

The Graduating Class of 1899,
Kittrell College,
request your presence at their
Closing Exercises,
Class Day,
Wednesday, May 24th, at 10:30 A. M.
Graduating Exercises,
Thursday, May 25th, at 12:00 M.

CLASS DAY PROGRAMME,
Wednesday, May 24th, at 10:30 A. M.

MARCH SONG.
INVOCATION.

Salutatory, ... Miss Maggie W. Leak
WELCOME SONG.
Class History, ... Miss Lona L. Clay
Psychological Oration, . . . Miss Mamie A. Lee
INFLUENCE OF THE MIND.
Vocal Duet, ... Misses Broadfield and Leak
Oration on Civil Government, . Mr. James E. Sanford
Mathematical Oration, . Miss Adeline V. Broadfield
SONG OF ADVICE.
Historical Oration, . . . Mr. Pompey L. Hawkins
GROWTH OF CIVILIZATION.
Class Prophecy, . . . Miss Melinda B. Cowan
BOARDING HOUSE SONG.
Arbor Oration, . . . Miss Maggie A. Wethington
Ivy Oration, ... Miss Corinna C. Fountain
CLASS SONG.
(Words by Miss Melinda B. Cowan.)
Valedictory, ... Mr. Lewellyn L. Berry
AFTER THE DAWN OF MORNING COMES THE DAY.
PARTING SONG.

Left: Llewellyn L. Berry—Kittrell graduate, 1899; below, Beulah Anne Harris—Kittrell graduate, 1897; across, Certificate of Marriage of Llewellyn and Beulah, at Woodsdale, N.C., September 26, 1900.

For me and my house, we serve the Lord. Josh. 24:15.

This Certifies That

Mr. Lewellyn L. Berry

of Hampton, Va.

Miss Beulah A. Harris

of Woodsdale N.C.

Were by me united in

Holy Matrimony

according to the ordinance of God and the

Laws of North Carolina

at Woodsdale N.C. on the

26th day of September

in the year of our Lord

Nineteen Hundred and 1900

Witnesses:

Mrs. Lucy A. Foster
Mr. A. L. Harris
Miss Lona L. Clay

Rev. L. E. Edwards
Pastor Roxboro Circuit
Roxboro N.C.
Minister

Mt. Zion A.M.E. Church, Woodsdale, North Carolina, where Llewellyn Berry and Beulah Harris were married, September 26, 1900. Below, Beulah, age three years, taken on a trip to Danville with her father. Across, Boys Literary Society at Kittrell, Arthur Harris, brother of Beulah (extreme left, middle row).

Copy of Deed to 304 acres of farm land in Person County, North Carolina. Purchased by ex-slave, Tobias (Tobie) Harris for $1,880. Cash dated February 11, 1898. Harris already owned an adjoining 60 acres and a house, totaling 364 acres. He was father of Beulah Harris Berry and father-in-law of Rev. L. L. Berry. Document obtained from Registry of Deeds, Person County Court House, Roxboro, N.C., December, 1978.

Journey to Kittrell

IT was a crisp September morning in 1895, just after daybreak, and Llewellyn Berry awoke in his bed at home on Butler's Farm, Virginia. "Get up Lew," said his father, and help me get the horse curried and fed while your mother is cooking breakfast." "Yes sir, Pop, I'm half dressed, my trunk was completely packed last night." Nancy, was kindling a fire in the wood burning kitchen stove with a pine knot for fast burning.

"Get up yo' all," she yelled to the rest of the household. "You know we got to get Lew and your papa off to catch that Baltimore boat for Norfolk." "Yes, Mama" came a voice from the girls' room. It was Lola's morning to milk the cows, Kate would feed the chickens and do the cleaning. Gus, the eldest, named John Augustus, Jr., and Arthur would be off to the field after breakfast.

There was lots of scurrying around in the John Berry house that morning for Lew, the second eldest of eight children, was going off to college. John Berry wanted at least one of his five sons to become an educated minister; to pastor a big church and to be looked up to as a community leader.

Lew had accepted this challenge, though his father was a poor farmer, barely able to read and write, with a big family. Lew had completed the work year at Hampton Normal and Industrial Institute for Negroes and Indians. He had not wanted to continue the four years for a trade since he preferred the ministry, but training for this field was not then on his horizon. It had been a year of hard work, farming days at Shell Bank near his home on Back River, taking night cultural classes over the Normal School taught by white teachers from the North.

There was great rejoicing in the Berry household when the Virginia Conference of the African Methodist Episcopal Church meeting in Roanoke in May of 1895 had awarded a scholarship to Llewellyn L. Berry for Kittrell College in North Carolina where psychology and theological studies were taught.

Lew was soon out in the barnyard with his Father. "Well Pop, I'm happy to be going off to Kittrell to study for the ministry, but I am sorry I'll be gone for such a long time and won't be here to pitch in with the boys to help you with the fall harvest."

"Don't you worry about that, son, remember what I have always tried to teach all of you, as your class leader both at church and at home. God will take care of those who serve him. I am sorry that I cannot see a way of sending my other children off to boarding school after they finish Phoenix here on Butler's Farm or Whittier in town. Your scholarship is a Godsend and as long as you get your lessons, I will do all I can to encourage you; your brothers and sisters are also happy for you." The elder Berry smiled and continued, "They said so when you went away last weekend to speak at the Sunday School Convention in Newport News. You know your mother and I will be praying for you each night, as well as all our friends here on the farm and in the church. Your mother is already planning to send you a shoe box of good food once in a while." John Berry spoke formally, but kindly to his second son.

As the stable door was opened old "Nell" was the first to get up from her straw bedded floor, she shook herself and started. Lew began pulling hay out of the barn loft, while his father bridled the horse to lead her outside to be watered, fed and curried. The harness had been tested out the night before and hung on the walls on either side of the four wheel wagon in the shed. The Berry's also had a wide two-seated buggy with fringe around the top. This carried some prestige on the 700 acre Butler' Farm which had been divided into seven acre family sized plots and acquired for veterans and free men by Gen. Benjamin F. Butler, former commander Major of the Army of the James in which John Berry had fought.

Sam Jenifer, Nancy Berry's brother, lived with his family on the adjoining plot to the east. As the bright sun rose on a clear sky on this auspicious morning, Lew and his father looked over toward the Jenifer house of rough hewn oak and gum slabs, they could see the barnyard through a clearing in a small thicket of pine, oak and elm trees. At the distant end of a broad field of rich looking wheat, oats and corn nearing the time of the harvest, Uncle Sam Jenifer could be seen scurrying around in his yard. He and the other Butler farm community, all veterans of the War. John Pie, Oscar Carr and their wives would all be coming over to the Berry farm to say a fond farewell to young Lew. John Berry asked Llewellyn "Do you see your Uncle Sam stirring around his yard, yet? He promised to come over after breakfast to see us off.

"Now let's set your trunk, and all your other things in the cart so when breakfast is done we can hitch up and take off for Old Point." "Yes sir, Papa." Nell was eating her hay—The elder Berry was currying her and Lew was drawing water from the well for Nell to drink.

Mother Nancy, as she was affectionately known at Bethel AME Church on Lincoln Street in the nearby town of Hampton, had breakfast about ready and the family table was set with the help of her three older daughters, Lola, Johanna and Kate, as Katherine was called.

Gus and Arthur were dressed in their overalls for the field. The call for breakfast was made and they all gathered around the dining table with Father Berry at the head and Mother Nancy at the foot. John Berry could do very little reading, but he had memorized many passages of the Bible. He led the prayers on this Friday morning in mid-September in a manner usually reserved for Sunday mornings.

But this was a very special occasion. "Bow your heads please." "Heavenly Father, we thank thee for this food and we ask a special blessing for our Son, Llewellyn, who is going off to school. Guide and protect him from hurt, harm and danger. Help him to learn his lessons well and bring him safely back to his family when school is over." The family repeated the Lord's prayer in unison and began to serve a delicious Sunday morning type breakfast. There were hot rolls which had been set to rise the night before. There was a choice of ocean trout and flounder, perch from Chesapeake Bay the day before, all cleaned and iced and kept in the yard ice box for Llewellyn's sending off breakfast on this Friday morning. "Butter your rolls while they're hot. And you can have molasses or maple syrup." announced Nancy Berry. There

were also grits and Virginia ham gravy. And there was plenty of everything because the Berry's raised their own pork and cured their own
hams. There was also milk served hot with water and sassafras tea. "Hand
me another roll, Kate and some sugar to go with these grits. From what
I hear about boarding schools, the boarding at Kittrell ain't going to be
like this." Lew grinned between mouthfuls. The other children were
too busy with this Sunday morning breakfast on Friday to do much
talking. The boarding house reach was truly in effect and their mother
smiled with loving approval of the family's enjoyment of her, special
"sending-off" breakfast.

Everyone had a second helping and was nearly filled to the gills
when Gus with a grin, broke his silence—"Well, Lew, we'll think about
you when you study Bible and public speaking and we'll be eating wild
turkey and partridge from Quail Hollow and Virginia ham. You sure
goin' miss the hunting season. I've seen a few rabbits hopping out in
the potato patch already and before you know it the squirrels, will be
jumping from the hickory nut limbs to the walnut trees storing away
their food for the winter and shooting oughta be good this Fall."

"Stop teasing him, Gus," cried Lola, wiping a tear with her apron.
"It's going to be a long time before we see him again." "That's right,"
shouted sister Kate, "You just mad you don't have a scholarship. Don't
forget that you been around exhorting and trying to preach yourself."

Nancy Berry was suddenly quiet. She moved away from the table
when she felt a choking in her throat, hoping to hide the tears which
were forming in her eyes.

She loved her brood of eight, and had never been separated from
them for longer than a day and a very occasional night. Only when
Lew or Gus or Papa John were away at a distant church conference
or when she or the girls would attend a Sunday School picnic at Cornwallis Cave in Yorktown or other nearby places. Papa and Gus got up
from the table and announced, "Well, we'd better be loading up. We
got to have plenty of time to get to Hampton and on into Old Point to
catch that steamer coming from Baltimore. It docks at 8 o'clock and we
got to be ready, check the trunk and get Lew on that boat on time.
It don't stay there long."

At this point, W. J. Miller knocked on the back door. "How's
everybody? I told Lew I'd come over and ride with them to Old Point

and help him and Mr. Berry with the trunk and satchel." "W. J." and "Dan" Austin were Lew's best buddies. "W. J." was enrolled over at the Normal School and working on the nearby Student Agriculture Farm known as Shell Banks. He had gotten excused for the morning to accompany his buddy off to Kittrell. "W. J." himself had a secret, or not-so-secret desire to preach like his friend Lew.

"You're a little ahead of us, but I'm glad, "W. J.," you could get away from Shell Banks—make yourself comfortable, we'll soon be ready. The girls had the breakfast dishes cleared away. The scraps from the table except the fish bones were thrown into the swill barrel with the dish water for the pigs. They were making ready to receive other neighbors who were expected to drop by before going about their usual early morning farm duties.

At this point, Lew's father called him upstairs for a private word. "Son, I am proud and happy that you are going off to college to be an educated preacher. Your Mama and I prayed for the son who would be an educated preacher and leader of our people. Without the scholarship from the AME Conference, it would not be possible. I know you will have to work besides to make enough money like you did this summer, but, with eight children, I don't know if another one will get to college. I hope so. Maybe your Mama's second dream will come true, that one of you boys will be a doctor like her uncle, "Doc" Henry Jenifer—but with much more education."

"You work hard in school, as I believe you will. Your Mama and I will pray, and if there is anything more I can do, anytime, let me know and I will do my best to help." With this, John Berry gave his son a hug, and patted him on the back before hurrying outside for the horse and cart ride to Old Point Comfort.

All the other morning farm chores were interrupted for, as the girls and Mother Nancy came out of the kitchen into the yard, there stood her brother, Sam Jenifer and his wife, the Oscar Carrs, the John Pies, and Reverend L. L. Lively, who collected everybody's monthly farm payments for the Butler Farm trust, i.e., from all those that had it. All the women kissed Lew, the men shook his hand, Lew and "W. J." loaded the trunk and a bag on the wagon and Lew with his light overcoat on his arm climbed in with his father, his friend sitting on the same long wooden seat. Off they went to Butler's Farm Road which would lead into Hampton, past the Normal School, the old Soldiers Home and Federal and County jail on into Phoebus and finally to Old Point Comfort. The distance was negotiated in a little less than two hours in spite of the slow down by horse-drawn streetcars, horse-drawn drays and buggies on cobblestoned streets in the center of Hampton.

Lew and "W. J." began to sing to break the journey. "W. J." who was a big lively fellow led off with "Joshua fit the Battle of Jericho-Jericho-Jericho repeat and the walls came a tumblin' down!" Lew joined in, putting his feet on the wagon but soon said, "Let's sing somethin' with harmony in it." "Here goes, "Sweet Adeline" worded by "W. J." and Pop sang bass. "Let's try another one" and "W. J." led off with "In the evening by the moonlight you can hear those darkies singing. And then down in the cornfield hear that lonesome sound all the darkies are sleeping Massa's in de cold, cold ground." They didn't like the words much but it was folklore and the harmony was good so John Sr. who had a good singing voice joined in with bass. Soon, however, he changed the tune to "Amazing Grace, how sweet that sound that saved a wretch like me." All three finished the last verse in a lusty chorus as they pulled up near the wharf at Old Point Comfort Ground. Papa Berry hitched old Nell and summoned a stevedore to check the trunk and satchel Lew had on the wagon for loading.

The ticket to Kittrell had been purchased several days before and the trunk would be checked straight through from the Old Bay Line steamer at Norfolk and transferred to the Seaboard line train to Kittrell, North Carolina. Lew went to the edge of the pier and could almost see in the far distance the white smoke of the steamboat but the contour of the ship itself had not yet come over the horizon. Lew's knowledge of the waterfront told him that the Old Bay Liner steamer was about 45 minutes away. Lew and "W. J." removed themselves several yards from father, having a final conversation. Odds were they were talking and kidding about the girlfriends that Lew was leaving behind in the care and keeping of his buddy, "W. J."

Lew's father turned and looked a couple of hundred feet away to view the familiar and picturesque grass covered mounds, which covered Fortress Monroe, housing the underground, 12-inch disappearing gates which guarded the entrance to the important Norfolk Harbor since the War of 1812.

John Berry never passed in view of this unique and majestic fort without remembering that it sheltered the huge parade grounds where he had learned the drill and discipline of a soldier and mostly how to handle the light artillery cannon that carried him unscathed through the seige of Petersburg and Richmond before the surrender at Appomattox.

He had often thought how he entered this historic fort, a ragged escaped slave and came out a courageous, confident, disciplined soldier in charge of Captain Choates' Field gun piece #5 ready to fight for freedom.

The huge white majestic steamer of the Old Bay Line docked, unloaded and reloaded and steamed away to weigh anchor. Lew had left home. He was now a man.

At Norfolk harbor a half hour later, the passengers, mail bags and express baggage were transferred by horse drawn drays, hocks and carriages to the Seaboard line train to continue its route from New York, Baltimore, Norfolk, Raleigh and Atlanta.

Lew understood well that an under mounted horse pulling a weather beaten, open shay driven by an unkempt colored driver wearing a tall tattered out-of-shape top hat would be his transportation from boat to train. Hopefully, this four-seated vehicle and another similar one would carry all the colored passengers or one would have to double back for several colored passengers. If they were lucky, no one would miss the train.

Old number #49, Norfolk to Atlanta section, was puffing away with a new head of steam ready to complete the final route of the New York/Atlanta Seaboard Line, when they arrived.

Lew entered, with the other colored passengers, into the very smelly waiting room where only colored passengers sat. It had its own bituminous coal stove; small and smoky, a scuttle for coal and wastepaper, brass spittoons, hard bench seats, and male and female unkempt "Colored" toilets.

Kittrell Days
—Becoming a Minister

The month was September and the year 1895. It was a propitious year in the history of the country and particularly in the direction of the lives of its Negro citizens. Llewellyn Berry was alert and a well-read young man. While he was deeply concerned with a religious life and future, he was interested in the politics and the economics of the country, and especially the future of the Negro.

As the train picked up speed in the southern suburbs of Norfolk and toward the northern border of the state of North Carolina, Lew pulled out his Bible but instead of reading it, he relaxed in a state of intense thought. The country was in a poor economic state. It had not recovered from the stock market crash and the panic of 1893. Political analysts were already predicting the election of William McKinley in '96. There were rumblings in the Caribbean waters and America was having disputes with Spain. This was the year that Alexander Graham Bell sent his crude voice transmitter, the telephone, to Queen Victoria and had it rejected with the quip, "Why talk to an infernal machine?" This was the year that Koch discovered the causative germ in Tuberculosis, the Tubercle bacillus. Roentgen was shooting electric currents into tungsten targets to produce the magic x-ray. These discoveries revolutionized the practice of medicine. Closer to the interest of the 19 year old Lew Berry, away from home and family, on his way to college, were events more directly affecting the Negro race.* Lew was really asking himself, what about my future? What are the real limitations and directions of members of the Negro race?*

The U. S. Supreme Court was considering the momentous decision which they rendered the following year in the case of Plessy vs Ferguson. The decision modified to some extent the previous decision in the Dred Scott Case, which held that there are virtually not any rights that

111

a Black person inherently has, which a white man is bound to respect. The decision in Plessy vs Ferguson, established and enabled states to codify legal segregation under the "separate but equal" philosophy.

The great Frederick Douglass died in February of 1895, and before long, the man who was to become his successor as the "spokesman" for the Black Race, had made his famous speech relating to racial equality.

Douglass' funeral which was held at the magnificent Metropolitan AME Church in Washington D. C. was conducted by the nationally known Reverend John T. Jenifer, the pastor of Metropolitan Church. Rev. Jenifer and Lew's mother and Uncle Sam were all from the same section of Southern Maryland, and could have been related, for all they knew.

Booker T. Washington's speech had everybody, black and white, talking about it. It became known as the "Let Down Your Buckets where you are" speech, and was given by Washington at the Cotton States Exposition in Atlanta in the late summer of '95.

In his speech, Washington held up his hand with fingers spread and proclaimed that, "In all things social, Negroes and whites should remain separate as the fingers, but in all other matters, solid as the hand."

One aspect of the Booker Washington philosophy that interested Lew most, was the philosophy that Negroes should look to a future of the skilled use of the hands. The inference of course being that they should not seek the professions. As Lew's train was speeding toward Weldon, North Carolina, he was reviewing in his own mind and heart the determination to become a professionally educated minister, Booker T. Washington, notwithstanding. He suddenly realized that it was near lunchtime and that he had eaten a very early breakfast. He opened up his shoe box which his mother had given him and proceeded to eat chicken drumsticks, wings and other goodies which he washed down with a cup of water from the cooler at the end of the car. A couple of young ladies had boarded the train in Norfolk who appeared to Lew to be students. As the train moved into Henderson, made its stop and loaded new passengers, there were a half dozen or more young people who entered the same car, obviously students, some of whom knew each other. Finally Lew introduced himself to a young man who said he really boarded the train in Norfolk. He had already spent a couple years at Kittrell, and his name was Poole.

The train pulled into the station at Kittrell around 2 o'clock in the afternoon. There was a dray being drawn by two horses. The driver assisted the students to transfer their trunks and bags to the campus, but the students walked the one mile distance to the school.

The young ladies reported to Allen Building and the young men to South Hall. The new students went to the registration office next door to the office of President John R. Hawkins. Lew was wearing his derby and hoping to look like a preacher. This attracted the attention of President Hawkins. Lew immediately introduced himself and mentioned that he was there on a scholarship received at the Virginia Annual Conference several months before. President Hawkins was present at that conference and remembered the announcement of the scholarship.

Lew spent the next few days going through the orientation period, meeting new students and acquaintances and registering for classes.

Llewellyn had his spirits uplifted when the President of the college, John Hawkins recognized him. This was not to be compared, however, with the spiritual and romantic lift he got when he first saw a modest looking, fair-complexioned, girl with the curly black hair on his first evening in the dining room. This was Beulah Harris of Woodsdale sitting with her cousin, Lona Clay. The girl's attention was attracted to table #4 where there was a new student sitting with Sam Davis of Eastern Shore Virginia. They commented on his formal-appearing suit. This was Llewellyn Berry who would later meet Beulah Harris at a social. He lost no time on that occasion in asking her to be his girl. She modestly responded in the negative saying that her parents did not allow her to keep company with boys. With this rebuff, Lew put all serious thoughts of girls out of his mind, and got down to the serious business of study.

Within the first few days Lew had the opportunity to walk around the campus and its immediate environs within a half mile radius. He admired the beauty of the rolling hills in the area, and the red and gold leaves of the elm, oak and maple trees. The fall leaves kept the work-students busy raking them from pathways and lawns. Earlier in the 19th century, Kittrell was known as Kittrell Springs, famous for its mineral waters and health resort for white people. It gradually lost its popularity and was purchased for the school by the Reverend R. H. W. Leake and the North Carolina Conferences of the African Methodist Episcopal Church.

Lew had some lonesome days during the first months at Kittrell. He would walk down the hill toward the old spring by himself and think about his mother and father, brothers and sisters back at Hampton. He never dreamed that he loved them so much. When these thoughts would come, he would realize that it would be a whole year before he would see them again. He would then say a silent prayer and vow to make them proud of his development at Kittrell.

Lew soon became a popular leader at the Wednesday night prayer meetings and his resonant voice could be heard over the rest during group singing. He was so much in love with Beulah, it was said that the song he led most was "Sweet Beulah Land."

He gradually attracted the attention of faculty members, among them were C. P. O. Kelley, Joe Wales, C. H. Johnson, and others. Two of his teachers were women, Adella Ruffin and Lula Norris of Norfolk.

One of his best friends and roommate at Kittrell was John Avery who became one of the founders and vice president of the North Carolina Mutual Insurance Company. Another was Joseph Mills, who became a physician and practiced in Durham for many years. And still another, Wade Hammond, who directed the band and was a band leader in the Army, remained friendly with the Berry's for the rest of their lives.

Many years later, Dr. Mills reminiscing about the days at Kittrell, said that Llewellyn Berry became a student leader. He was particularly trusted and respected by President Hawkins. The boys all knew this and when they got into trouble, they would call upon Lew Berry to intercede in their behalf with the President. He recalled an incident in which the kerosene lamps were burning much too long into the night. The matter was reported and brought to the attention of President Hawkins. Lew stepped forward to take the blame explaining how he was talking to fellows about black history and a very interesting discussion developed about their African Ancestry causing the time to slip away. Dr. Mills said that the truth of the matter was, the boys had a little pennyante game going on in one part of the room and a game of 'Rise and Fly' whist in the other. Lew had the smallest audience.

Lew's experiences at Kittrell prepared him for the ministry and community leadership in many ways. He heard sermons and lectures by Bishops and high-ranking officers of the AME church as they visited Kittrell. One of them was the outstanding minister and pastor of the

Metropolitan Church in Washington, The Reverend John T. Jenifer. Another was Bishop Henry MacNeil Turner, an ex-slave and former member of the GA legislature during reconstruction.

Lew's extra-curricular activities included playing the Alto horn in the band and umpiring baseball games. He soon gained a reputation for telling the tallest tales at social events. In his senior year, he very often preached in small churches in the area around Henderson and Raleigh. One of the years at Kittrell was as a work student in which he attended school only in the evenings.

Beulah Harris

ONE of the first persons that Lew saw when he went to supper the first evening after he arrived at Kittrell was Beulah Harris of Woodsdale, North Carolina.

Beulah remembered the first time she saw Llewellyn L. Berry, and she later recounted those days. "In 1893 when I was between thirteen and fourteen years of age, my parents sent me to, what was then known as, Kittrell Normal and Industrial Institute. At the opening of the school term in 1895, my friend and roommate, Lona L. Clay, and I entered the dining hall for supper. It consisted of homemade loaf bread, syrup and tea, and while looking around before the blessing was asked, I happened to see at the second table from me two strange young men. I said to my friend, "Look Lona, there are two new students at table No. 4." We looked at them and thought no more of it. One of these young men, as I learned later, happened to be Mr. Llewellyn L. Berry of Hampton, Virginia, the other was Stephen Davis of Eastern Shore, Virginia.

After orientation and classification, Llewellyn became a classmate of my friend Lona Clay. We were allowed monthly socials in the chapel where the girls and boys would meet and chat together, being sure not to talk to one special person too long. We were to change around among several students then, at intervals, there would be joke telling, riddles, the grand march, and so on. When someone would play the piano, one couple would lead and the other would team up and follow. When we tired of that we would start again these conversations. I do not remember just when I was introduced to this Virginia gentleman but somehow we began talking at one of these socials early in the fall term of 1895. When he asked me, as was a custom in these days, to become his friend, my reply was, "My papa does not allow me to go with boys." He took it seriously, I guess, for he waited a year.

117

I learned later he had inquired of the little girl who wore the red dress and walked so spryly. She was me. I was nearly 16 years old, then.

The next term at a social he asked the same question. This was my last year at Kittrell. I was a senior and expecting to leave there to enter Wilberforce University the next year. Also most of the girls had boyfriends, so, when he asked then, I shyly and embarrassingly answered in the affirmative. I don't remember the exact words but I told my roommate what had happened, feeling that I had really committed a crime. The girls all yelled, 'Hurrah for Beulah. Make time with him,' they said. They had lots of fun over it. Some of the boys afterwards hearing it remarked, 'I thought Miss Harris hated young men, until Old Berry came along.' The first note I received from him was brought by a friend of mine, then Annie Norris of Norfolk, who was his tablemate. I was really afraid to answer it knowing it was against the rules of the school which I dared not disobey. Later, encouraged by my roommates, Leah Fitzgerald and Lona Clay, I began to answer the notes signing my middle name, Annie, instead of Beulah Harris. Anna Brooks who laughed at Longfellow's (Lew's middle name) signature asked, 'Who is this hick with a name like that?' I was 17 and he was 20. Then May 1897, Commencement Day arrived. I was salutatorian for Class Day. George Taylor of Raleigh, North Carolina wrote and read the Class Prophecy. He prophesied how some day I would live in some parsonage with its brick walls and stone steps and how happy I would make it. Some of the boys remarked how very serious Berry tried to look and how my father blushed. During the years of our courtship I was impressed by his genteel Christian-like manners and thinking 'He is just such a young man as my parents would appreciate.' Leaving school I was afraid to receive letters at first. My father asked me to read my first one to him. My mother said, 'What do you want her to read it for, it wasn't written to you.' 'I want to hear what he is talking about,' said my father. After that I didn't have to read them though my father mostly brought the mail from the Post Office.

Commencement Day was a sad day, saying goodbye to all the girls, boys and teachers. Prof. John R. Hawkins was principal and Miss Lovey A. Mayo, Lady Principal. There were, during my time, as teachers Prof. C. G. O'Kelly (Music, Band), Joseph Williams, James Wilson, C. H. Johnson (Art and Latin), Misses Adela Ruffin (English teacher),

Lula Norris (Music), Corinne Gibson, Adeline Williams, Rose Alexander, Mrs. Lillian Hawkins (Music teacher), and Mrs. Margaret Davis, matron. We corresponded for three years.

Lew graduated in 1899 as the valedictorian of his class. He was highly commended and congratulated by his teachers and President, John R. Hawkins, who predicted for him an outstanding career as a minister and community leader. He received his first charge as a minister, a small circuit at Pope, Virginia."

War clouds were precipitously condensed into windblown rainclouds when the Spanish Man of War blew up the Battleship Maine in February 1898. Then the threatened Spanish-American War became a reality. Llewellyn Berry, finishing his theological courses at Kittrell was turned down for Chaplaincy Service with the Negro U. S. 9th and 10th Cavalry. His interest was aided by friends at Negro colleges in the Raleigh-Durham area. Prominent among them was Wade Hammond, one year ahead of Berry at Kittrell. Hammond was successful in getting an assignment to the 24th Infantry Band. The very young Reverend Berry totally lost no tears about the Army, but began in earnest his real and deepseated interest in a battle offensive against every obstacle for the love of, and marriage to Beulah Harris. She was now in her second year of teaching for North Carolina's Person County. Second to this was his dedicated concern for a successful career in the Christian Ministry. On the homefront. December, 1898 the war was ended.

At school's end, Llewellyn had saved enough money to pay his first visit to Beulah's home at Woodsdale. He had not seen her since her graduation from Kittrell, two years earlier, when her father had fetched her away in a covered wagon. Now, he was to see the one girl in all the world who would bring happiness and success into his life no matter how long he lived. But, as the N. & W. milk train rattled along to Woodsdale, there was a lump in his throat because the beautiful girl of his dreams had lost both her mother, and her father.

They died just one year apart, the mother, Elizabeth first, probably of a pulmonary disorder at the young age of 38. The father, Tobias, was 42 when he died one year later. His family felt he had probably been poisoned by jealous whites, who resented his acquisition of an additional piece of prime farm land and buildings in the lush Woodsdale area.

Beulah, the eldest of their eight children was teaching, and with the help of Uncle Joe and Aunt Ida Jordan, who lived in a small farm house about a hundred yards away from the Harris homestead, she supervised her younger brothers and sisters without too much difficulty.

Beulah recalled Llewellyn Berry's first visit to her family home.

"During the summer he came up to Woodsdale, making his first visit with me. He had been pastor for a month. My parents had both passed. While there, he attended the wedding of my cousin, Bettie Drumwright and Charles Royster who had also attended and graduated from Kittrell College. My girlfriends in school had written me how he had developed as a speaker and became a fine young minister. When I was still in school we used to remark about his frock coat, derby hat and sharp toed shoes and how he tried to look like a young minister. I was not one hundred percent in favor of that. I remarked to my friends how I would never marry a preacher because, I thought they only had what people gave them and they were to me the most pitiful people in the world. I was judging from what I saw as a young child when I used to go with my mother to the parsonage to take baskets of food, butter, eggs and vegetables and my father would give the pastor a ham now and then. Ministers families had to have charity to survive.

On his first visit to the farm we walked, one very warm day, down the hill to the large running brook in a grove of large oaks edged with pine trees and during that conversation he asked me to marry him. My answer then, was, 'I can not leave my sisters and brothers, especially the younger ones.' His reply was he would not take me away. I could stay at home until the next oldest sister was able to take over. I asked him to wait awhile."

But the young, sedate Reverend Berry was an immediate hit with the surrounding countryfolk at Woodsdale, especially with his occasional flash of humor. He was impressive as he carried out an invitation to preach at Mt. Zion AME Church, and wagging tongue's began to express approval of the young man so obviously in serious pursuit of poor Tobe and Bette Harris' beautiful and oldest daughter. The wagging tongues belonged to a community both black and white, still shocked and saddened by the tragic death of both parents. The deceased Harris' were head of the Negro family which may have been the most determined and best able in the Woodsdale area to educate their children.

Beulah's ambition to enter Wilberforce immediately after her Kittrell graduation already had her father's approval after Reverend L. E. Edwards, pastor of Mt. Zion said "Brother Tobe, Wilberforce in Ohio is as far above Kittrell as Kittrell is above Rogers' little one-room red schoolhouse on the Woodsdale-Halifax Road."

"Tobe will own half of Person County." The gossip was that when Tobe Harris bought the last increment of land he had been poisoned by drink administered by his vengeful and envious white neighbors. Tobe Harris had purchased the plantation from the heirs of former slaveowners some 100 yards east of the one-room Rogers School on the Woodsdale-Halifax Road and five miles from the Hyco River.

Beside Beulah, the newly appointed teacher in charge of Rogers school, there were two brothers, Arthur and Irving, in their late teens, two younger teenage sisters, Carrie June and Ursula, and the three youngest children, Lula, Elbert and Johnnie. The two older boys, under the supervision of Uncle Joe Jordan and some hired hands, operated the farm; cultivating, curing and marketing the fine tobacco Tobe had developed at the auctions in South Boston, Durham and at Danville, Virginia. The girls, attending their older sister's school, took care of the other farm chores, characteristically handled by the women folk.

Lew Berry, the budding, young minister, from Hampton's by way of Kittrell, was intrigued by the contrasts encountered at Woodsdale. His own father's spread at Butler's Farm was strikingly different from the 365-acre former slave plantation that Beulah's father had acquired at Woodsdale.

Beulah remembered that "It was Christmas of '99 when Lew returned to my home and asked my uncle and aunt's permission to marry me. They finally agreed and on his return to his charge he sent me the ring. I always looked forward, happily, to receiving a letter every Tuesday. An old friend of the family whom we called "Uncle" asked him about taking me away. His answer was 'My religion would not allow me to.' "Well, so you have religion, then," "Uncle" said. Family and friends were very anxious to hear him preach, so on Sunday night they arranged for him to preach in the little schoolhouse where I taught. His text, as I remember, was in Revelations. I cannot remember the text now but everyone enjoyed the sermon and from then on whenever he was there long enough he would be asked to preach in the churches, both AME

121

and Baptist. He became a great favorite in the neighborhood among relatives and friends of both races of the Harris family. As one of the country merchants remarked, "Parson, you are getting one of the finest young girls in our vicinity and Person County and I hope you will treat her right.

At commencement of 1900 we met again at Kittrell. I was then Alumni Secretary and had gotten together a short program. One day during the commencement week, Prof. C. H. Johnson came to Allen Building, the girls' dormitory, asked me to take a little walk with him out behind the dormitory. We sat on a large rock, I felt so embarrassed, but sat there beside him while he talked about how the faculty had known of the friendship of Mr. Berry and myself and how they approved of it but could not let it be known; how they felt about it when we were in school. Still he was very much impressed with Mr. Berry and felt that he was just the right person for me. I almost fell off the rock but managed to listen 'til he finished talking and we returned down the hill to the building, with girls all staring and whispering "Eh? Professor Johnson, a bachelor, and Beulah." I, at once, had to explain.

Many of the students going to Virginia and North Carolina left together. We, "L. L." and I, both had to lay-over in Durham. I was wearing the ring. I stopped with my aunt, Sue Warren, whom he visited, and Lew stayed with Rev. W. E. Walker, pastor of St. Joseph's AME Church. He came with his friend, John M. Avery, who was a schoolmate and lifelong friend. Mr. Avery married my class and roommate, Lulu L. Aiken. The Durham Kittrellites had a party for me and they danced but didn't invite "L. L." since he was a minister, and Avery. After they ate dinner and left, they danced. I didn't dance. I didn't know how. My Durham cousins, Sallie and Annie Warren, Will Fouchee, Nannie O'Daniel, John Allen, and many others, were at the party. We rode on the same train the next day part of the way enroute home. I got off at Woodsdale and he kept on to his home in Hampton, Virginia."

Family and Race

WITHIN the context of this narrative, family and race have a special meaning. With wide variations, stories of family and race extending back before the Civil War may arouse pleasant or very unhappy emotions. Tobe Harris, a central figure in this story, was enslaved by Drew Harris of Halifax County, Virginia. He was born of Jane Harris, a mulatto slave seamstress in 1857. This was the year of the great Cog's snow in North Carolina. His real father was also a slave owner whose name was Tom Faulker. He also lived in Halifax County, Virginia near Harmony. Tobe's mother had several mulatto and other children of darker complexion. Among them were Richard, Susie, Stephen and others; they were all children during the Civil War. After the war they remained a very close and loving family.

Tobe, whose complexion was very Caucasian, grew up and had early schooling with his father's white children. At about 12 or 14 years, just after the war (he left to be on his own) went across the Virginia state line into North Carolina, some five miles away and found work on the plantation of Mose Jones. This white planter was the owner of a 1,000 or more acres of tobacco land, yet he couldn't write his name. (See deed signed by his "X" in Appendix.) Tobe had learned how to write and figure very well and learned tobacco farming very fast for his age. As a young farm hand he soon attracted the attention of his employer as a dedicated worker with unusual interest in learning at every opportunity. After a few years the planter found Tobe's knowledge of farming and grading tobacco very useful. Beginning as a hired hand Tobe within a relatively few years, was allowed to work on shares sufficient to make a living and save some of his earnings.

123

When Tobe reached the age of twenty, about 1877, Mr. Jones said "Tobe, you doin' a mighty heap of courtin' these days." I speck you goin' to be thinkin' of marriage pretty soon." "Yessir Mr. Jones," Tobe responded, "I' been thinkin about it for some time. I been savin' for that all along. If I get married, I' got to have a house. I been wantin' to ask if I could give you more of my shares on the year and move in the little house down by the orchard. I believe that with a wife I could bring in much more each year." "Let me think about that Tobe, you are one of my best hands." Jones answered.

In June of 1877, Tobe married Betty Jordan, daughter of Wiley and Ann Jordan from McGeehee's Mill up around the Mt. Zion Church area. Betty was a pretty, light-brown girl whose parents had Indian, Caucasian and Negro blood. Like her new husband she also came from a very large family. Both were children during the Civil War. They were born into the racial culture of the times. Betty was very well liked because of her soft-spoken sweet disposition. She attended Sunday-school regularly at Mt. Zion Baptist Church. One of the lady church members had a private school which Betty attended in the evenings. The announcement of her marriage took the white folks that Betty worked for by surprise. They hated to lose her general house work and care of their children. Betty's relatives and friends around Mt. Zion had met Tobe on visits, when he was not in attendance at his own church; Bailey's Chapel of the A.M.E. denomination. Everyone predicted a good marriage.

Tobe and Betty moved into the little house near Mose Jones' orchard. They talked of a future, educating a family, owning some land of their own, and having a big house like the successful white farmers in Person County. They worked very hard during the first years. Betty raised chickens, sold eggs on the local market and attended a kitchen garden. Tobe farmed and cured tobacco, raised hogs and a cow. His friend Mr. Jones was proud of Tobe's earnings the first year after marriage, and allowed Tobe to hire his own extra farm hand, at harvest time. There was never any question about dividing the shares of the farm products and sales at the end of the year. When Tobe was short of cash he could always quietly borrow from Mr. Jones at harvest time. It was more like a Negro part-ownership of a white man's plantation. A most unusual arrangement in those times, Mr. Jones' was also increasingly dependent upon Tobe's figuring ability and honesty in tobacco trading.

Betty soon learned of Tobe's white father who lived a few miles away in Halifax. She learned that Tobe had been brought up in the household of his father with his white half-brothers and sisters until he reached the age of 12. It was here that he had unusual opportunities for early schooling. Betty met Tobe's father, Tom Faulkner and his white son Tom Faulkner, Jr. in a semi-social relationship and occasionally visited the Faulkners with her husband. She became acquainted with one or two of her husband's white half-sisters, who admired the beauty of Tobe's wife.

On December 12, 1879, two years after their marriage, Tobe and Betty had their first child whom they named Beulah Ann. The name Ann was given by one of Tobe's half sisters, who wanted the child named after her. Tobe Harris had several half-brothers and sisters of many complexions working as farmers and farmwives around the country-side. They were always in close touch and saw each other frequently at Bailey's or Allen Chapel, the A.M.E. churches of the area. These churches came together at a great revival meeting in August of each year. This was a great family reunion time.

Betty Jordan Harris also had a number of brothers and sisters; Vinnie, Eliza, Joe, Bullock, Garner and others. In fact, "old man" Wiley Jordan as he was called had had three wives and nearly 20 children. All, or most, of the Jordans met and had a great family get-together during revival time at their Mt. Zion Baptist Church. The Harrises and Jordans became a close knit and loving family clan, especially as the next generation came along. They were all complexions of the rainbow. They had no particular pride in the mixture of Caucasian, Indian and African blood, which flowed through their veins. It had nothing to do with the love that developed between these kinfolks; it was an accepted inheritance from the old slave culture. When Negro marriages became legal as well as "ordained-in-heaven" during the previous generation there was a great acceptance of legal marriages especially among church folks. The "glue" that had held Negro families together for survival without benefit of legal sanction, continued to hold together groups of legally married families in a unique multinuclear family kinship.

After Beulah, Tobe and Betty Harris were parents of two more children Arthur and Carrie, each born two years apart. By this time Tobe had saved enough money to purchase a large house and farm of

60 acres. He quietly made a deal to purchase the Chisolm Farm with an option to buy the adjoining acres. It had been the old Rogers plantation in days of slavery. This deal was to take place when Tobe became financially able. But for now Tobe and Betty had made a great stride which attracted much attention in the neighborhood. Here the younger children of Tobe and Betty were born.

At one time the big house of seven rooms with two picturesque outside chimneys, one at each end, had been the big house, with some 500 to 600 acres of tobacco land tilled by slaves in the old days. There were six large tobacco curing barns on the farm, of which three were included in Tobe's purchase. There was also an orchard, one mule and some necessary farm equipment. Soon Tobe bought more farm animals which included a few pigs, chickens, some cattle and another mule. During these years, Tobe continued to work very hard and his white friend, Mr. Jones, continued to encourage him. Tobe's tobacco leaves were of especially fine quality. He developed a reputation among buyers and auctioneers for the high market value of his tobacco in Danville and South Boston.

The elegant home and farm of Tobe Harris was virtually a reproduction of a pre-Civil War slave plantation. The big difference, of course, in 1890 was that instead of slaves, there were hired farm workers. Instead of a white slave owner of black slaves, there was a prosperous Black owner of a tobacco plantation with hired farm hands, organized in the spirit of America's "free enterprise system."

By 1895 Tobe began thinking of purchasing more tobacco land. His family had now increased to eight children and he was generally regarded as a very successful and prosperous Negro farmer. One of the younger Harris daughters had been named Rosa at the request of another one of Tobe's half-sisters in Halifax who wanted a namesake in Tobe's family.

Tobe's opportunity to make his big purchase came when he learned that a member of the Rogers family had made a big loan mortgaging his farm of many acres adjacent to Tobe's sixty-acre holdings. The farmer who loaned the money had threatened foreclosure over a period of two years and there had been considerable misunderstanding and threats. Finally the property had to be sold to prevent further lawsuits and increasing interest payment. Tobe, who now had a very good standing in the county, was accepted as a purchaser to clear up the legal problem between the two white farm owners. Deeds recorded in the Person County Court House at Roxsboro, state that Tobe Harris purchased 304 acres of the Rogers farm land for $1,800 cash in 1897, bringing his total holdings to about 365 acres.

In order to perfect the deal, Tobe traveled to Baltimore and slept on the floor of the rooming house bedroom where the Rogers owner was then living. When the deal was all settled and the land surveyed it was discovered that Tobe Harris had purchased a good portion of the front yard of the seller's sister, a member of a large well-known family of former slave-owning tobacco farmers. The news of the new ownership by the Negro farmer, Tobe Harris travelled like brush fire around the county. The Black farmers could hardly hold back their happiness and quiet elation at Tobe's success. Many whites became upset and angry with the Rogers. The Rogers family members and their heirs were angry with each other for making the sale to a Negro. Even more anger was generated by inadvertantly selling a portion of the front yard being used, and presumably owned, by the sister of the seller. Tobe Harris was now the most prosperous financially of any black farmer in Person County as far as anyone knew. Apparently few, if any, realized that his worth with the exception of two or three was greater than that of any other black farmer in the state of North Carolina. F. Logan in his study and publication on the "Negro in North Carolina (1876–1895)" records finding only three black farmers in the state owning more than 300 acres. Tobe's property was not included. The largest farm consisted of 500 acres.

As the discussion of the Tobe Harris transaction increased among white and Black throughout Person County, Tobe decided to accept a second deal to put things at ease. He agreed to have the land re-surveyed and to deed back the portion of the land which consisted of the Roger's sister's front yard. In exchange for this, he was given a set of "barn logs." These logs were not used for many years. Tobe's youngest son, John Slyvester Harris recalls that as a little boy he had lots of fun climbing up and down this pile of logs, which remained for quite a time near the house on the Harris property. The logs stood as a symbolic reminder of a never-before heard-of Black-white real estate transaction and the commotion it caused in Person County. However, the Rogers family re-established their front yard and the matter was thought to be settled with no permanent damage.

Tobe Harris and his family of wife and eight children were the possessors of a recorded 365 acres of land, 6 tobacco curing barns, 2 mules; "Pete" the slow-draught animal and "Rody" the fast and spirited one. The Harris holdings also included a fine chestnut colored riding horse, buggy, surrey, a regular wagon, a special covered wagon for transporting tobacco to the markets. There were the other usual farm animals, some acres of wheat, oats, corn, other garden vegetables and a fruit orchard on rich low grounds.

As was the architectural fashion on the larger farms of Person and other counties in North Carolina, there was a detached house several yards in front of the main building of the Harris estate. This was known as the summer kitchen. There was an area for cooking; a larger area with an appropriate long table for dining and another area which, in modern parlance, might be called a family lounge. The chairs for the most part were hard seated, with hard backs and a few wicker pieces.

The main house which might have had an exotic name in the old days was a two-story oblong structure with an outside picturesque chimney at each end. During pre-Civil War days in North Carolina and other southern rural areas, the number of such chimneys on an elegant mansion constituted a social-status symbol. Two chimneys were high on the totem pole and four chimneys signified the very highest status in the slave culture. Tobe Harris refurbished the outside and inside of his house, including new paint. Off to the center of the front yard there was a tall pole with a bell at its top which could be rung by pulling an attached rope. This was for the purpose of summoning the farm hands for lunch and to indicate starting and knocking-off time. In another corner of the large front yard there was an area which might have been appropriately called "the Harris' Medical Marsh." There was a closed-off area about fifteen feet square which contained transplanted medical roots and plants, known to be good for medicinal purposes. From this vegetation, teas, brews and other forms of medical concoctions good for malaria, typhoid malaria, rheumatism, locked bowels, the flux and other ailments were made. Uncle Joe, who lived with his family in one of the small houses on the plantation, was a kind of foreman for the necessarily increased number of workers on the Harris plantation. Peculiarly, there were always a few poor, white farm-hands applying for jobs. Some of them were kept as regular workers.

128

The elegantly rehabilitated former slave owner's mansion completed and Tobe Harris' fine tobacco bringing in a good return, some of the dreams of Betty and Tobe for which they had prayed were coming to pass. Beulah had graduated from Kittrell College and was nearly completing her first year as teacher at the one-room Rogers School on the Woodsdale Road. Arthur knew that he was to be the next one off to boarding school some place. This was discussed during the previous year with his parents.

One day in the fall when all the crops were in, Tobe, his wife Betty, and all their children went to church at Bailey's Chapel, specifically to give thanks to the Lord for His many blessings. Not many days thereafter, Betty Harris developed a severe cold. It rapidly developed into pneumonia, or so it was diagnosed. In spite of all the available doctors' care she grew rapidly worse and died after a relatively short illness. All of the available members of the Harris-Jordan clan in Person County and other nearby towns gathered to express their love and sympathy to the Harrises. The shock of this fine young woman's passing at the young age of 38 and leaving eight children traumatized the entire community. Tobe was completely in a daze for many weeks and only slightly better as the months passed.

Meanwhile mixed with this sadness for many people there was still ugly talk among the white people about the prosperous Harrises. Negro farm hands and women domestics heard many unpleasant comments by the white folks. Many of the whites didn't think it was right that a Negro should own so much property. Soon it was being heard that "If he keeps on, pretty soon Tobe Harris will own half of Person County."

According to Uncle Joe Jordan, Betty's older brother and foreman for the Harris farm, the next episode in this story is as follows: The account as told has passed down through the generations of the Harris-Jordan and later the Berry related family clan to the present time.

A group of two or three white men became very friendly with Tobe shortly after the death of his wife. They had known Tobe for a long time and occasionally appeared to recognize a certain closeness short of equality but apparently due to the fact that they could hardly tell any difference between their skin color and features and those of Tobe Harris. One night two of these white men came down to see Tobe, explained how sorry they were because he had lost his wife and spoke of how well everybody liked him around the county. They wanted to come back the next night and take Tobe out to a private social hangout of white farmers, to cheer him up and have a few drinks to show how much they appreciated him.

Tobe took these white men at their word and on the next night he shaved and mounted his fine chestnut-colored riding horse and went off to the appointed place where there was a known private liquor still in "dry" North Carolina. He returned home after having his "social" engagement and a few drinks which they insisted that he should have with them. He reached his home, got off of his horse and took him to the stable. He was feeling sick most of the way home, but now was getting very sick. He began to vomit and to have chills and fever and became very weak. He managed to get out to the yard and pull the bell used to call the farm hands. While Beulah and the other children in the house were trying home remedies, Uncle Joe finally located a root doctor who came to see him. The next morning Tobe Harris, formerly in good health, was dead at the age of 42, almost exactly one year after the death of his wife Betty. Needless to say the generations of the Harris-Jordan-Berry clan have felt quite certain that Tobe Harris was poisoned by jealous sons and grandsons of former slave holders, because, "If he keeps on, pretty soon Tobe Harris will own half of Person County."

Tobe Harris was given an appropriate burial beside his recently deceased wife in the "garden" behind the Harris house. The little cemetery was enclosed by heavy briar trees and each burial was marked by a heavy selected boulder from the Harris plantation. Many years later at last count, nineteen of the Harris-Jordan clan members had been laid to rest in this private cemetery.

Ironically, some of the men in the Harris family had occasionally prowled thru the brush and unkept land some fifty or more yards behind the big house. There they had seen flat stone like covers almost completely submerged by soil. When the soil was removed engraved names and dates back to the 1830's were revealed. There was one clearly visible smooth granite grave cover bearing dates only 30 or 40 years before. John Harris, Tobe's youngest son remembered that as a little boy he and his little sister Lula played "bob jacks" on one of these smooth granite covers, not realizing the significance of this convenient spot.

As the years and generations have passed Tobe Harris' stately mansion and prosperous plantation have deteriorated; have been broken into smaller units, divided by marriages, the times and white intrigue. Two burial areas remain but the Harris-Jordan burial place remains encircled by the briar bushes planted generations ago. While the larger boulder markers are no longer accurately in place. The white slave barons preceeded the Harris' in life and death. They were separated and racially segregated in life but they lay silently and equal in death. Dust thou art, to dust returneth was not spoken of the "soul." But how truly it is spoken of the mortal frames of those who inherited the earth. Here in this lonely place there is neither time nor distance, rich nor poor, race nor creed, bond nor free, where at last these mortals lie in the coldness of mother earth.

Section Four
Traveling A.M.E. Minister
and Young Family
(1899-1917)

Family of Reverend and Mrs. L. L. Berry with their first two children. Left, Leonidas, age 3 years, and Richard, age 18 months, Winston-Salem, 1905.

St. James A.M.E. Church, Winston-Salem,
built during the pastorate of Rev. Berry,
1905–1907.

Home of J. W. Jones, M.D., with his family in Winston-Salem, 1907. Dr. Jones inspired Leonidas to announce his intention at age 5 years to become "A Dr. Jones."

L.: Rev. and Mrs. L. L. Berry with family of four children. L. to R.: Richard, Gladys, Llewellyn, Jr., and Leonidas in front of the parsonage of St. Paul's Church, Chapel Hill, N.C., 1908. Below: "Baseball Team" at Sister Caroline Jones' private school in Chapel Hill, N.C., 1910. Sitting from right: Richard and Leonidas Berry. Standing, from right: Milton Campbell and Teddy Stroud. Some teammates are "smoking" candy cigarettes. (Photo by teacher, Sister Jones.)

LEE and OTis - 1908
HAMPTON Va to visit GRAND PARENTS

Above l.: Leonidas and Richard Berry, ages 7 and 5½ years, in Hampton, Va. to visit grandfather, John Berry, during his final illness, 1909. Above r.: Mt. Zion A.M.E. Church, Princess Anne Court House, Va. Photograph taken during pastorate of Rev. L. L. Berry, 1912. Right: Family of Rev. and Mrs. L. L. Berry during Presiding Elder-ship years, Norfolk (1916–1921). Photo taken on day Leonidas (standing, l.) entered high school (1916). Standing, rear r.: Mrs. Berry's youngest sister, Lula Harris, student at Hampton Inst. Front row, l. to r.: Elbert, Llewellyn, Jr., Richard, and Gladys.

A Family Man

WHEN Beulah Ann Harris of Woodsdale, North Carolina and Llewellyn L. Berry of Hampton, Virginia were united in marriage at Mt. Zion AME Church in Roxboro, North Carolina, on September 26, 1900, by the Rev. L. E. Edwards, it was not thought to be the beginning of an era. It was a country church wedding, and as Beulah remembered, "When Lew came he stopped in the home of my friend and his classmate, Lona L. Clay. Uncle Joe took him to get the license which cost one dollar and fifty cents. We were married on September 26, 1900 by the Reverend L. E. Edwards, pastor at Allen Chapel A.M.E. Church, Roxboro Circuit. Lew was then pastoring Drakes Branch near Circuit, Virginia, a small church there, and one at Charlotte Courthouse, Virginia." Uncle Joe gave Beulah away. Relatives and friends of Beulah's parents attended the wedding, mostly families of tobacco farmers in Person County." Steve Drumwright and others of considerable blood from Drumwright township. They all knew that Beulah was a pretty girl, upright, intelligent, and of good character. They knew that the young preacher she was marrying pastored a little country church in Virginia and that he was intelligent, affable and apparently very much in love with one of the nicest girls in that farm community. They wished them well and prayed that Beulah's life would be happy.

"Now Reverend," said Aunt Ida, Uncle Joe Jordan's wife, "You are now a member of our family. Don't forget your promise that you would not take Beulah away until the younger children are better adjusted to the loss of both of their parents." "From now on, you are Aunt Ida and Uncle Joe to me and I will prove to you my loyalty to my new family" the new husband said. Aunt Ida continued, "You know Joe and I have moved into Tobe and Betty's home with their children for good, and if we all pull together, we'll make it."

135

Following the ceremony and all the good wishes and the punch and cake, the new Reverend and Mrs. Llewellyn L. Berry rode off in a horse-drawn buggy to begin their new life as man and wife. Beulah recalled, "We went on a short honeymoon to Bedford, Virginia, where my Aunt Julia Allen gave us a reception. Then we came back to Woodsdale, where Lew spent a week getting acquainted with the farm. During that first week, my brother, Arthur and Uncle Joe took him on a tour of the farm. He was already familiar with one part of the farm, the long gradually sloping hill, where the spring was nestled in the grove of tall trees. This is where he had proposed marriage to me. Much of the tillable land was planted with tobacco which was our main crop, but there was also wheat, corn, sugarcane, vegetables and a sizeable orchard of apples, peaches and pears. There were also the usual number of farm animals, including pigs, cows, a horse and two mules."

The following week Berry took his bride to visit his little church near Danville, Virginia. They would have to return promptly to Woodsdale where Beulah would resume her teaching job at the one-room Rogers School.

During the train ride, the new Mrs. Berry told her bridegroom the history of her father's farm. "Did you say you were born in the farm, house where we now live?" he asked. "No, only my younger sisters and brothers were born there. I was born, as you know, in '79. While we were always in this house and farmed some of the land, the actual purchase of the larger acreage did not occur until about 1890." "Was it always a single unit farm," he wanted to know. "No, the original plantation was operating long before the Civil War, and as Papa used to say, was twice as large as it is now. So I suppose it was 600 or 700 acres." Lew commented. "I was deeply impressed with the business-like attitude of your father on the three occasions that I met him, when he would drive up to bring you back to school at Kittrell. The faculty folks held him in very high regard."

"Yes, I know. You remember how I would get teased when Papa would bring those sugar-cured hams to President John R. Hawkins, while we were eating beans and fatback in the Allen Hall student dining room."

"My Lord, what a great success he would have been had he not passed away so early in his life."

"Yes, he talked success all the time for himself and his children. As you know, he was a young child in slavery time and never had a chance for much education, but was taught in the 'big house' during and after the Civil War. He wanted much more for us, and said all of us had to go to college. He had all the arrangements made for me to go to Wilberforce to continue my music the next year after graduating from Kittrell. And Arthur would have been next. But, that was the year he died."

"That would have been great for you, but how in the world would I have seen you again, way out in Ohio?" The young husband asked. Then taking her hands in his, he said, "Well hon, I will do all I can to lessen the burden of our young family, and make up as far as I can for your great loss. It must have been part of God's plan. We can still plan." And plan they did.

Life for the young bride-school teacher and foster mother and her minister husband, was not easy and for the next six years, L. L. Berry commuted to Woodsdale from his various charges. He used foot, horseback and Jim Crow railroad cars. Each year, he had a different church, and none offered sufficient income to keep a family.

Beulah's teaching and the farm contributed to the upkeep of what became one big family. L. L. Berry became "Brother" to the younger sisters and brothers and "Hon" to his wife. She said, in recalling those early years. "During the summer I was active in preparing food for winter. My father's farm had orchards of apples, pears, plums and berries but no peaches. The friends and relatives were always free in sharing with each other. During one of his visits to North Carolina after I had made my visit with him on his little circuit, he and I drove a horse and buggy across the border over on the Virginia side to my uncle's home to can some peaches. After filling a dozen jars and elated with the job we started home. We had a river to cross, whose bridge was washed away by a recent heavy rain so we had to ford the stream. On our way back it had swollen and water was higher. My husband, not realizing it, drove in. In the middle of the stream the buggy struck a stump. He was driving one of the high spirited mules from the farm. When he began to rear up on his hind legs and my husband stood up trying to hold him and began to yell for help. A little ways uphill a family of cousins, young men and friends came running to the scene imagining what had happened. One waded in and unhitched the mule, both getting on his back and rode to land, leaving me and the hot canned peaches in the buggy in the middle of the stream. Some of them waded back and pulled the buggy out. There I sat with my feet propped up on the spatterboard, hoping the jars of peaches would not break. It was a great tease with the friends for a long time, 'Well, you left Beulah for once didn't you?'

"The next spring at the Virginia Conference in 1901 he was sent to the North Danville Circuit, Virginia. After my school closed in March I went there for awhile and was taken very sick. When I was better I left for home. My brother failed to meet me and I walked to a friend's home who gave me dinner and got a friend of ours, a local preacher, to take me home several miles on horseback. I sat behind him riding side-saddle.

"I then began the regular routine of summer canning of fruits and vegetables and making preserves and pickles, drying apples, sewing for my sisters and baby brother, getting ready for the opening of school.

"The next conference year, April 1902, he was sent to Harris Creek Circuit, Virginia, near Lynchburg, Virginia. I was six months pregnant. On July 20th of this year, our first baby arrived. Leonidas Harris. He was born on a Sunday morning at my family home in Woodsdale, North Carolina with the help of a midwife 'Aunt' Lizza Duke and 'Ma' Brooks.

"I taught at my same school that winter. In the spring of 1903 after school closed and the baby was nine months old I took him to Lynchburg, Virginia, Harris Creek Circuit, to join my husband. Then to Hampton to visit and meet his parents for the first time.

"They graciously received their new daughter-in-law and grandson. Mr. Berry met us at the C & O Railroad station in Newport News with horses and carriage. We had taken the trip by Pullman sleeper because of the baby and the increasing segregation. I liked my new mother and father, Pa and Ma (Nancy and John) Berry very much. Pa Berry was a big tease. He kidded Lew because the creditors had taken away the mattress where he roomed while he was at the Harris Creek Circuit. He referred to our firstborn child as the "Little It." They had been the parents of twelve children, living and dead. Nancy Berry ran a little store on their farm. I stayed with them while Lew went to the Conference. Lew attended the Annual Conference which was held at Trinity,

Berkeley-Norfolk. At this conference he was asked by Bishop B. F. Lee to preach at the Sunday morning service. The bishop and officers were so pleased with the sermon that they asked that he be assigned to Trinity as pastor but the Presiding Elder, Rev. J. C. Williams, would not agree to it.

"In those days a young minister did not have a chance and was only given missions and small circuits. In six years, my husband had six charges. From Trinity that year he was sent to Campbell Chapel, Portsmouth. In a most impossible appointment of about a half dozen members. His mother gave us underwear. After he took us home to North Carolina, he returned to Portsmouth but decided to return to North Carolina where we attended summer school and taught school in adjoining districts. We rode ten miles by mule and buggy to buy Christmas gifts. I nearly froze. At this conference he was ordained Elder. Anxious to consecrate the elements for his first service, he arranged for communion that Sunday morning at Campbell Chapel. Just a few but very small membership. We stopped with a former schoolmate, Mrs. Mamie Manning, in Portsmouth. We went to her home for dinner and came back to church at night. Probably a half dozen came out and had given their offering in the morning so the offering at night amounted to ten cents."

"Fully realizing that we could not exist at this charge is the reason he came to North Carolina and taught that winter. It was good in two ways for us, to have a place to live, as well as care for my sisters and brothers. The terms were very short and salary very meager, thirty dollars per month, for four or five months. In the spring of 1903, the conference met at Roanoke, Virginia. My husband, with what we both had saved, attended the conference, where he was transferred to North Carolina Conference at Rocky Mount, Church-Chapel Circuit, four or five months of that conference year had passed and he remained there seven months until conference in November, scarcely making a living, even for himself. Mrs. M. C. Henderson, a member of his church, took much interest in him, helping him all along thru those seven months. She instigated his securing a young man, James Dean, to bring the farm to help my brother Irvin, who was an old bachelor then.

"Following Aunt Ida's death, Uncle Joe had married again, my husband performing the ceremony. During his visits to the farm from which we secured our board, he always fell in line and helped the boys in the tobacco and cornfields the few days he would spend there. While I prepared the big vegetable dinners, also consisting of apple and berry pies and buttermilk. When it was very hot sometimes the table would be placed in the yard under a large pear tree where we served dinner. Everyone was happier when Lew came. A cousin would send the largest and choicest watermelon to be found in his patch for the young Reverend Berry but he did not like them.

I was not able to visit him until conference time when he was sent to Laurinburg Circuit, Scotland County. Reverend J. E. Holt also had charge of a circuit in the county and lived in a three-room house used for a parsonage. He and his wife shared this house. After the closing of my school in Person County, I took my two little boys, Leonidas, three and now Richard eighteen months to spend a month or two at this charge. There were three bedrooms, one a guest room and a kitchen shared between the families. Rev. and Mrs. Holt had one little girl, Esther Mae. There was an epidemic in town and country called the "bumps," a somewhat mild form of small-pox. In visiting his members my husband contracted it, after which Leonidas and I were sick but Richard seemed immune and escaped it. Before this we shared the same cooking stove and table as one family and enjoyed the fellowship. After this epidemic broke out, Mrs. Holt with her daughter, left for her home in Raleigh, North Carolina.

"I'll never forget the 4th of July. The weather was very hot. I tried to keep cool. It was pretty hard with me as I was expecting the third baby and the doctor wasn't sure it would survive. Leonidas kept busy with his itching bumps. When I would call and ask if he were scratching his answer, 'No m'am, mama, I am just rubbing.' My husband would get to his church out on circuit by bicycle. When we were sufficiently cured the doctor allowed us to return to Woodsdale. I did not teach there any more, as Irma, our first daughter was born in September.

"In November 1905 at the Conference my husband was transferred to St. James, Winston-Salem, in the Western North Carolina conference. At Christmastime he came for the family and I went with the two boys and our three-months-old infant daughter to really live in our first parsonage. It was sad to say goodbye to my sisters and brothers and the old farm where we had obtained most of our food and which my husband had learned to love. He was devoted to my family, as they were to

"Brother," as they called him, always glad to see him come and happily receive whatever he was able to bring them, no matter how small. He was like a father to them, the three sisters and baby brother, and like a brother to the two oldest brothers. He so often referred to his first visit when my third brother, Elbert, then 12 years old, became so attached to him, taking his hand and directing him over the fields where he attended the cows, over hills and valleys of tobacco and corn. My uncle Joe Jordan was overseer. A farmhand, Joshua Carrington and family and my second brother Irvin, Arthur the oldest brother worked in hotels and at resorts. Later in the summer, Elbert was accidentally thrown from a mule and received injuries which caused his death, so he never saw him again. At this time Johnny, my baby brother, was three years old. When we married he was four years old and cried to go with us on our short honeymoon. From then until my husband's death (54 years later), there was a strong tie of close relationship between the two always and Johnny along with our four sons was a pallbearer at LL's funeral.

"At St. James Church, Winston-Salem, North Carolina, he followed Rev. J. W. Walker who was made Presiding Elder. We were happily received and welcomed by the officers and members. The church was just a hull outside and Bishop W. J. Gaines expected him to finish it and entertain the Annual Conference the next November. This was his first charge with a parsonage, a nice Sunday School and choir, and with a membership of about 400 people. With all the past Missions and Circuits he never gave up hope and ambition that it was better farther on though the way seemed very dark."

Early One Year Circuits
(1899–1905)

THE youthful Rev. Llewellyn L. Berry had entered his professional career upon receiving an appointment to his first pastorate at the hands of Bishop James A. Handy, during the 33rd Session of the Virginia Annual Conference of the African Methodist Episcopal Church. Bishop Handy was a distinguished African Methodist Bishop who had just written a book which later became a classic in A.M.E. history. The title was "Scraps of African Methodist Episcopal History." The bishop held the conference at Emanuel Church, Portsmouth, Virginia from April 25th to May 2nd, 1899.

At the end of the Sunday night session, Reverend Berry extended a hand shake to the Bishop and expressed his gratitude for the conference scholarship which had helped him to study for the ministry at Kittrell. The Bishop accepted the hand shake with congratulations and said "You have a great challenge out there, son, go forth in the name of the Lord." Berry would hear similar words for a long, long time. He was given his first pastoral appointment which read "Yales Mission, Pope, Virginia." Llewellyn Berry had never heard of the church and he soon found out why. It was so far back in the Virginia thickets and woodlands that one really needed a compass to find it. He had been given his first charge in the Virginia circuit.

The term "circuits" refers to the stopping places of the travelling minister, and the real meaning of the circuits was soon understood by Rev. Berry. His early appointments were certainly in the best tradition of travelling "round and round" from one little mission to another on an annual basis. In fact he was sent to six different pastorates of mission churches in six years. None of them could possibly sustain a pastor and there was no subsidy from the general church. It was said in those days that the young minister was expected to "live on earth and board in heaven." Fortunately, he was able to teach county school near some of the church appointments. The average rural school term for Negro children at that time in Virginia and North Carolina was about five months or until the money ran out. Teachers were so scarce and the pay so low that new appointments each year were more often the rule rather than the exception. The bicycle was the most convenient and economic mode of travel between church and school and back again.

After Llewellyn and Beulah married on September 26, 1900, he commuted from pastorate to Woodsdale in the middle of the week when he was not teaching. There he would help with general farm duties and serve as a father figure and brother to his wife's orphaned sisters and brothers. The farm also served as an important food source for the Harris-Berry family.

After the pastorate at Pope, Virginia in 1899, there followed a pair of missionary charges at Drake's Branch, Virginia and Charlotte Court House, Virginia. In the spring of 1901, the young reverend was sent to North Danville, Virginia Circuit. He was enjoying the Christian ministry and appreciated the need of his services in these mission churches, although the difficulties in giving these services were almost unsurmountable. He began to realize that preaching every Sunday was a method of growth in spirituality and pulpit eloquence, in which he felt so deeply the desire to excel. He read fervently the few classical books in his possession during spare time and lonely hours by kerosene lamp in his single room dwelling places, far from the bride he loved so dearly. These were disappointing times and the future frequently looked very dark for this young minister of great ambition who had taken on the responsibility of rearing a family.

Shortly after his arrival at the mission on the outskirts of Danville, he viewed the very small attendance at his Sunday morning service. He had surveyed the rural environs and knew that the sparsely populated area would offer very little from which to build a supporting church. He opened his worship service in the usual manner and searched for an appropriate hymn. He stopped at a familiar page and led the congregation in singing an old Methodist favorite; "A Charge To Keep I Have A God To Glorify." With great power and emotion he led the second stanza; "To Serve The Present Age, My Calling To Fulfill; Oh May It All My Powers Engage, To Do My Master's Will."

He chose as a text for his sermon; "I Will Lift Of Mine Eyes Unto The Hills, From Which Cometh My Strength. My Strength Cometh From The Lord Who Made Heaven And Earth." He was given encouragement by his small congregation, "to keep the faith and carry on in building the kingdom here on earth."

The annual conference of 1902 was convened in April at St. Paul's Church Danville, Virginia under Bishop Benjamin F. Lee. This conference produced "more of the same" for Rev. Berry. He was sent to Harris Creek Circuit in the Blue Ridge Mountains near Lynchburg, Virginia. The six months pregnancy of his wife had no effect upon the episcopacy.

After a short visit, Berry left his wife and baby with his parents while he attended the Annual Conference of 1903 at Trinity A.M.E. Church in Norfolk, Virginia. He was jubilant at this time because he would be eligible for ordination to the status of Elder if he passed the examinations. In this he expected no difficulty because he was one of the best trained young ministers in the conference. For certain, he felt that this would be a time of advancement. At this 37th Annual Session of the Virginia Conference, 'Rev. Llewellyn' arrived, wearing his spoon-tail coat; stuffed shirt with English break back collar; sharp toed black patent leather shoes and homburg hat. Friends and acquaintances among the ministers and laity gave him the glad hand and remarked about his fine appearance. They did not know that his farmer father and his grocery store keeping mother had contributed to this fine wardrobe.

In due time, the young "ministerial dignitary" passed his examinations and was ordained elder at the hands of the Right Reverend Benjamin F. Lee presiding Prelate of the conference. This ceremony authorized the minister to perform marriages and baptisms and to administer the Lord's Supper. The Bishop knew of Berry's preparation at the A.M.E. Church School at Kittrell and had heard high praises of his pulpit eloquence. After the ordination was assured, he called the candidate aside; "Berry, I continue to hear fine things about you. I'm asking you now to prepare to preach the morning sermon for the Sunday service on the closing day of the conference. It was indeed a great honor and Rev. Berry thanked the bishop profusely as he received a firm hand shake. "I will prepare to do my very best, Bishop;" replied the startled but grateful young minister.

At the appointed time, Reverend Berry was introduced and presented to the "packed house," the usually large congregation was assembled from all over the state. Out-of-state visiting ministers, an occasional guest general officer, college president and associate bishops were
present. The young minister had never previously stood before an
audience of this size and ecclesiastical importance to preach a sermon.
He began with a short public prayer and announced his text as follows:

"Go ye into all the earth and preach my gospel sayeth the Lord." He
held the rapt attention of his audience throughout the sermon as he
presented a scholarly and historical analysis of the meaning of this portion of the scriptures. He led them to an emotional climax and had them
"talking back," as the saying goes, with Amen's from the congregation
and encouragements from the dignitaries in the pulpit. He closed his
bible in exactly twenty minutes. He had already set the course of his
preaching style which would never go beyond fifteen or twenty minutes. At the close of this sermon, an unusual number of new member-
ships were received. At the end of the service, there was a profusion of
back-slapping from the preachers and hand shaking from the members
at the altar.

The minister of the host Trinity church was finishing his five year
limit annual appointment and could no longer succeed himself at that
church. A committee of officers of the church, one of the largest stations
of the conference, had a closed meeting immediately after the morning
service. In the afternoon, they waited on the bishop and reported that
they had been authorized in an official general church meeting to eval-
uate, choose and recommend to the bishop the best available minister
for appointment as the new pastor of Trinity. After much consideration,
they said, "Bishop, we have unanimously chosen and beg your decision
to appoint Rev. Llewellyn L. Berry as the next pastor of Trinity A.M.E.
Church."

Many leading members of the church had buttonholed the committee, whipping up the enthusiasm for Berry to be the next minister.
Rumors were spread like wildfire all the afternoon on the church
grounds, in the sanctuary, and eating places, anticipating the bishop's
young "dark horse" appointment. They had noted the bishop's glowing
introduction, the standing congratulations and fervent hand shake given
Berry as he finished his sermon. Members were all aglow and still talking

about the electrifying sermon. Some members were saying, "At last the talk about the educated ministry is coming through." Ministers were whispering, "Berry, I think you've got it in the bag." By the time of the 7 P.M. opening of the final session where the bishop would read his appointments, Rev. Berry had grown a full twelve inches taller and he was ecstatic with anticipation. He had knelt in secret prayer and thanks to his Lord and Master before leaving his stopping place for the church. He had sat quietly for a few minutes thinking about his wife and baby with his parents back on Butler's Farm. He was thinking what a pity they couldn't be there with his pretty, young wife sharing the accolade of his finest hour. "It is too bad," he said to himself, "that funds and facilities were not available to have her here to witness at last the fine appointment which I think I deserve with the great help of my dear wife."

The usual preliminaries, introductions, and order of services were carried out. The climactic, zero hour was delayed; but it inevitably arrived. A few expected appointments were read followed by predictable applause. Then the bishop called in the usual loud voice without modern day acoustical amplifiers; "the Rev. Llewellyn L. Berry will approach the altar." The audience began to buzz with excitement as the young reverend walked forward with squared, erect shoulders, appropriately dressed, and wearing an expression of confident dignity on his face. The bishop reached for the minister's hand and repeated, "Rev. Berry-, he paused and the audience became deathly silent to hear every word of the good news. The bishop continued, "Rev. Berry, I'm sending you to a charge of great challenge and unusual opportunity. "You are assigned to the pastorate"—and the audience could hardly wait for the burst of applause. The bishop continued, "to the pastorate of County Street Mission in Portsmouth, VA. The young minister's shoulders suddenly drooped; a vacant stare came over his face; he appeared to be in a state of shock; his appointment scroll fell from his hands to the floor; he quickly and embarrassingly retrieved it as the audience murmured loudly in concerted disappointment. The bishop finally had to call for order as the young, saddened Rev. Berry returned slowly to his seat. The bishop continued with the reading of his next appointment over the ceaseless buzzing of the audience. Rev. Berry pulled a handkerchief from the pocket of his swallow-tailed coat to mop his moist brow. As he turned he saw women wiping away tears from their eyes.

Reverend Berry's new church at last count had about a half a dozen members. The sanctuary was a made over store front building at the lower end of the County Street slum area.

At the close of the service, people crowded around Rev. Berry offering sympathetic support and expression of their mutual disappointment, but assuring him that things would get better. Ministers were now conspicuously absent from this group. Llewellyn Berry had, inherited or early acquired spunk from his Civil War veteran father. He rarely had the occasion to use it. He was thinking strongly about demonstrating it again at this point. He waited in the pastor's study for the bishop long after most of the crowd had departed. The long waiting served to settle his tensions to some degree. Yet, he stood there remembering that he had not felt such deep resentment since a white boy slapped his face and called him a nigger when he was working after school at the Chamberlain Hotel. The bishop finally appeared and closed the door and without waiting for a statement from Rev. Berry the bishop said, "I know how you feel son, but that was the best that I could reasonably do. I had a lot of requests for you from Trinity members but the Senior Presiding Elder, Rev. J. C. Williams objected very strongly and he had the unexpressed backing of all of the other presiding elders."

Bishop Lee was formerly a president of Wilberforce University and professor in the Theological School. He continued, "Berry I understand the temporary disappointment that you feel at this time. I have nothing with greater development potential to offer you at this time. I will say to you that you are well prepared and that you have a great future in the church. I advise you to work hard this year on your new assignment, and sooner or later something better will turn up for you."

With a stiff upper lip and with a slight bow he said, "Thank you, good-bye," and departed the presence of his lordship, the presiding prelate of the 2nd Episcopal district. He sent a hurried letter to his wife on the next day by the returning minister to Hampton. He explained part of the story and instructed her to borrow money from his mother and meet him with the baby and all belongings at the home of their friend and former schoolmate, Mrs. Mammie Manning in Portsmouth.

The Berrys reported to their 6th consecutive annual mission in time to administer his first communion as an ordained Elder. "Ye that do truly and earnestly repent of your sins and are in love and charity with your neighbors and intend to lead a new life, following the commandments of God and walking from henceforth in his holy ways, draw near with faith and take this holy sacrament to your comfort; and make your humble confession to almighty God meekly kneeling upon your knees."

As Rev. Berry spoke these words with great pathos and emotional feeling, his wife and seven members came to the altar to receive the Lord's Supper. At an earlier point in the service, a total of ten cents had been received in the collection plate.

Rev. and Mrs. Berry prayed together and separately daily for a week while they contemplated momentous decisions. At stake was Llewellyn Berry's dilemma, he considered giving up his career as a minister and seeking a better livelihood for his family. He would lie awake at night reviewing his life back to childhood. He remembered his "getting religion" and feeling "the call" to preach while sitting in the family kitchen with his sister Kate and his mother. He recalled his mother directing him to Rev. L. L. Lively on Butler's Farm for discussion and direction regarding his life's career. He recalled the tears of joy in his mother's eyes when he announced his decision to preach and her tearful response, "I've prayed all my life for this."

"How can I give up my life as a minister, he said to himself, "but I must do just that. I have a family and I love them more than anything else." He had discussed many pro's and con's with his wife, who was wise enough to let him make his own decisions. She only assured him that she had taken her marriage vows and would be with him to the end. She went into the next room and sat in a chair, with a book in hand, pretending to be reading. As her eyes became moist with tears she repeated silently, as she had done many times before; "I Beulah take thee Llewellyn to be my wedded husband, to have and to hold, from this day forward, for better, for worse, for richer, for poorer, in sickness and in health; to love, cherish and to obey till death do us part, according to God's holy ordinance; and thereto I plight thee my faith."

Two days later, her husband whom she called "Hon" announced that he had bought a cap to substitute for his homburg hat. He had reported to the employment office of the Seaboard Line Railroad and

149

applied for a job as railway mail clerk. He had a pass to go to Raleigh to take the examination. "Hon," she replied, "I have nothing to say except I will abide by your decision. Think out everything carefully and prayerfully. I will be praying for you the whole time you are away." The wavering Rev. Berry, with his cap pulled down toward his eyes entered the day coach of the Seaboard train, next to the engine. He put his satchel in the rack above his head and slouched into his seat. As the "All Aboard!" signal was called and the engine puffed away, he was alone with his thoughts. The train picked up speed and rattled away in unison with the puffing coal-burner. He raised the window to relieve the summer heat in the stuffy car; cinders and soot from the engine blew into his face; he pulled his cap further over his eyes and continued to think far away thoughts. He remembered a favorite poem from his studies in literature. It was William Cullen Bryants' "To a Waterfowl". The poem was now reassuring to the wavering young minister as it was to the young author who wrote it. The climactic verse, as he remembered it, was repeated aloud over and over again. No one else would here it in the noisy train.

> "HE, who from zone to zone guides through the
> boundless skies, thy certain flight; in this long path-
> way that I must tread alone, will guide my steps
> aright."

Llewellyn Berry took the examination, passed and was soon called to work. While in the presence of his wife, he opened and read his letter of appointment as a railway mail clerk. He took off his cap and for the first time broke down in tears. He tried to leave the room. His wife held him back. He proclaimed softly, "I don't see how I can do this." At this point his wife came through with all the strength she had developed in facing the great tragedies of her early life. "Listen Hon," she said, "Please go in there and get your homburg and throw that cap away." I will not allow you to quit the ministry. There is no room for a mail clerk in this family." I have shown you many times Hon that I love you. We have made it so far and we will continue to make it together." The quivering voice of his wife gave him the confidence that he needed.

With this support from his wife, he made a firm decision. He notified his presiding elder that he was leaving the impossible mission and moving to North Carolina where he and his wife could teach County School to make a living for his family. He expressed grave doubt that anyone in authority could have believed it possible to develop a sustaining church in the slums of Portsmouth with Emanuel Church not far away. The Berrys attended a summer Institute for teachers and received appointments to schools in Person and adjoining Orange County for the 1903–1904 session. They lived at the Woodsdale house, saved their little earnings, and enjoyed living with their younger brothers and sisters and their own young family.

At Christmas time their schools competed in a literary contest; Mrs. Berry and her students "picked up all the marbles."

Richard, their second child was born on Jan. 19, 1904 in the Woodsdale House. He was delivered by the family midwives (Ma Dukes and Ma Brooks), who had served the Harrises since the early 1890's. Rev. Berry reported to their Annual Conference at St. John's Church, Norfolk, April, 1904. He explained the necessity of his move but was chastised in open conference by the bishop and transferred to another mission in North Carolina. He served an abbreviated seven months term at Rocky Mount, N.C., and another full year at Laurinburg, North Carolina, where the third child, Erma Elizabeth was born.

St. James, Winston-Salem (1905–1907)

NOT until the Fall of 1905, did Rev. Berry receive his first sustaining ministerial appointment. He was sent to St. James Church in Winston-Salem, North Carolina by Bishop Wesley J. Gaines. There was a membership of over 400, a choir, and a Sunday School. There they had started to build a new church building on a pay-as-you-go basis. The pastor, Rev. J. W. Walker, had been promoted to an opening as presiding Elder. With Lew's assignment came the challenge to construct a church on the foundation already laid, in time to keep a commitment to entertain the next Annual Conference. There was very little time, but the young minister accepted the challenge joyfully. It would give him the chance to show what he could do... how capable and devoted he was to his service. The Berrys, with two vigorous little boys and a 3 month old baby girl, bade a sorrowful farewell to Woodsdale. They left Beulah's two weeping young sisters, Ursula and Lulu and a younger brother, Johnnie, in care of Aunt Ida and Uncle Joe Jordan. Carrie married Gibbons Brooks in 1905. Arthur was a head waiter in Newport News and Irving, still a bachelor, worked the farm. Beulah and Llewellyn had kept their vow not to leave while the children were young. But it was sad for him, leaving the farm and the children who had devotedly called him "brother." All of the Harris brothers and sisters called him "Brother" to the end of their lives. Beulah and Lew Berry never gave up their Woodsdale "children", married or unmarried, returning there once or twice each year for reunions. The move to Winston-Salem provided Beulah Berry with her first private family home, a beautiful two-story parsonage at 639 E. 7th Street, next door to the still unfinished church. She thrilled at being the minister's wife, working with the Missionary Society, which was composed of a fine group of cooperative ladies, and singing in the enthusiastic choir. Most of all she enjoyed being the mother of her *own*-children. Her happiness was short-lived, however.

A scant three months after the Berry family moved to Winston-Salem, the baby Erma Elizabeth was stricken with whooping cough, which developed quickly into bronchial pneumonia and after only six months of life, the lovely little girl was dead. It was the first heartbreak that Beulah and Lew had shared, even though the going had not been that easy for them, but the loss of the little daughter seemed to bind them closer to each other. Before too many more months passed Beulah was expecting another child, and while she asked God to give her a healthy baby, she and Lew were both delighted when the infant born to them in the parsonage at St. James was another little girl, whom they christened Gladys.

The Berrys soon became a significant part of the community life of Winston-Salem. There were former Kittrellites and other previous acquaintances in the city. Among them was Professor C. G. O'Kelly, teaching at Slater Normal School. He had taught Llewellyn Berry and Beulah Harris at Kittrell. Thru the friendship of Prof. O'Kelly there developed a very cordial and mutually supportive friendship between Prof. Simon G. Atkins, founder of Slater Normal School and the new vigorous Pastor of St. James and their families.

There were well known citizens in the Negro community, who were members of St. James. There were those who were not so well known except as church going Christians, interested in a family life of high moral standards, and honest living and a better future for their children. They demonstrated their dedication to progress by sacrificial hard work in completing the functionally new church structure in one year sufficiently to entertain the next Annual Conference. Some of the more ardent workers and loyal members were William and Alice Mendenhall; Edward and Jencey Penn; Rebecca Jones; George Williams; John and Susan Harge; I. B. and Minnie Scales; Cora Harroway; Dr. and Mrs. W. E. Hayley; Dr. W. A. Jones and Lawyer and Mrs. J. S. Lanier.

When the Western North Carolina annual Conference of the A.M.E. Church convened at St. James, as the host pastor Rev. L. L. Berry had the finest hour of his career up to that time. Bishop Gaines and Professor John R. Hawkins, Commissioner of Education and former

Kittrell President, during the years when Lew was a student, stayed at the Parsonage as the Berry's guest. St. James reported the largest amount of monies raised of all the churches in the Conference, including the special finances for constructing the church building. There was an appreciable attendance of visiting ministers from other conferences, including general officer, Rev. John H. Collette, manager of the A.M.E. Book Concern. One of the very active and supportive lay delegate's at the conference was John M. Avery, Lew's Kittrell College roommate and ranking officer of the N.C. Mutual Life Insurance Company of Durham.

For the opening session of the conference, the host pastor had arranged the program. In the temporary absence of the Bishop, who had missed his train, the program was conducted by presiding elders R. H. W. Leake and J. W. Walker. The welcome address on behalf of the citizens of Winston-Salem was delivered by Mayor O. B. Eaton after being introduced by Rev. Berry. A solo was rendered by Mrs. C. G. O'Kelly accompanied by her husband at the organ. A welcome address on behalf of the city ministry was given by Rev. J. C. Alston, followed by a vocal duet featuring Mesdames Scales and Walker. There was then a welcome on behalf of the church by Professor C. G. O'Kelly.

On the third day, the Conference was assembled for an evening, "educational mass meeting." Appearing with Bishop Gaines on the rostrum was Prof. Simon G. Atkins, founder of Slater Normal and Industrial Institute, Prof. C. G. O'Kelly and Prof. John Hawkins, Commissioner of Education of the General Church. Prof. Hawkins gave a one hour long principal address on "The Importance of Higher Education To The Negro Race and The Role Of The A.M.E. Church." An offering for Kittrell was lifted bringing the total contributions from all churches of the Conference, during the year, to more than $16,000.00.

Rev. Berry was highly visible as host minister and was clearly the most active member of the conference. This was indicated by his appointment or election to the following committees: "Public Worship", "Judiciary", Chairman, "Finance". The "Fourth Studies committee", carrying the function of presenting the successful candidates for ordination to the status of elder. He was also elected trustee of Kittrell College; to The Conference Missions Board and Post Office Messenger for the Conference.

He was publicly commended by Bishop Gaines along with his presiding Elder Reverend W. Walker and the members of St. James Church, "For providing this beautiful edifice for the worship of God." [1]

On Sunday evening, near the close of the last session a complimentary resolution was read and approved by the Conference commending Rev. L. L. Berry, the host pastor and members of St. James Church. The resolution read: "Whereas, the Pastor Reverend L. L. Berry has labored so hard to get the church ready for the reception of the conference and has made untold sacrifices to accomplish this noble work and whereas, he has provided so carefully for the comfort and convenience of the brotheren, and whereas all have had the services of Brother Berry in looking after mail and doing everything possible for the success of the conference. Therefore, be it resolved that we the members of this Conference do acknowledge the same and thank Reverend Berry for his untiring service and pray God's blessings upon him and his. Respectfully submitted." Separate resolutions were presented and approved, commending the choir, the Church members and friends and Mayor O. B. Eaton. The Conference closed with benediction by Bishop Wesley J. Gaines to meet again in April, 1907.

With the Conference over, the Berry family settled into a less hectic routine, broken by birthday parties and accidents. I was given a party on my fourth birthday. It must have been a gala affair, because my mother described it over and over until I went to college. There were many little children there from all over town. Among them was Jack Atkins, the Professors' son and Sidney Lanier, son of Winston-Salem's only Negro lawyer, according to mom, the family historian. Both boys grew up to be nationally known adults. Jack in the legal field and Sidney in education, becoming president of Hampton Institute. When I was at Wilberforce University in Ohio, Sidney arrived as the captain of the debating team from Lincoln University of Pennsylvania. He did not remember ever hearing of Leonidas, but the name Sidney Lanier rang a bell with me. A confirming letter dispatched from his mother in Norfolk, Virginia placed little Sidney, age four, attending a momentous birthday party at 639 East 7th Street, Winston-Salem, N.C., on July 20th, 1906.

The next significant episode in the lives of Mrs. Berrys' children again involved me. At age five years, I ran across the floor in my bare feet and stuck a long needle in my heel. Dr. John W. Jones, Leonard School of Medicine of Shaw University, class 1891, arrived in his shiny, well kept buggy drawn by two beautiful black horses. I alarmed the neighborhood and attracted many children to the front gate to witness the scene of the crime on the front porch. The operation without anesthesia but with the patients' feet restrained between the doctor's thighs was successful. After the third visit, the wound was healed and I had an announcement. I said, "Mama, When I grow up, I'm going to be a Dr. Jones."

For one thing, Rev. Berry served his second year as St. James Pastor and completed building the church in 1907. His popularity in the church and city continued to grow. This was also the year that Richard J. Reynolds introduced Prince Albert Pipe Tobacco in a flat tin box for five cents. It sold like hotcakes. It exceeded in sales the popular Reynolds plug tobacco of many flavors for chewing. This era was long before, "I'd walk a mile for a Camel" or "Winston tastes good like a cigarette should." The Reynolds tobacco company made Winston-Salem become world famous and made billions of dollars. Its founder had little formal education but he was unquestionably a "card carrying" genius. Many of the members of St. James Church earned their livelihood with the Reynolds Tobacco Industries. It is said also that Mr. Reynolds made a charitable contribution to the Slater school when he really couldn't afford it.

In 1907 word came that the beloved Sam Jenifer had died quietly in his sleep, at Butler's Farm.

At the Western N.C. A.M.E. Annual Conference of 1907, Pop reported the completion of the new St. James Church at Winston-Salem. The church membership had increased considerably and the indebtedness on the building was being met promptly and satisfactorily.

St. Paul, Chapel Hill
(1907–11)

THE exigencies of church politics are often unpredictable. The message from the "Holy Spirit" to the bishop seems at times unsupported by logic or metaphysics. Lew Berry completed plans and built a beautiful church and successfully hosted the state conference two years. The good Bishop Gaines apparently with another plan in mind sent Pop to Chapel Hill, a quaint little university town and the center of North Carolina culture. Many Negroes went there to the college, through one door and out the other, only as janitors. They were not admitted. The young Berry family left an entirely adequate parsonage at St. James in Winston-Salem, for a smaller one and lower financial income at St. Paul's, Chapel Hill.

The church was smaller in membership and was heralded by the bishop as another great challenge and opportunity for service, earned by proving unusual ability of leadership at the previous charge. Reverend Berry's successor at St. James was his good friend, Reverend T. W. Cotton, who had pastored a smaller church at Lenoir, N.C. and served as the bishop's chief secretary for a few years.

With two little boys and a baby girl Gladys, Reverend and Mrs. Berry moved into a parsonage which was a 3½ room cottage, with an open wood burning fireplace. Officers and church members received the new minister and family very cordially in a warm and very clean parsonage and served them a well prepared and enjoyable dinner.

When the reception committee departed, leaving the family alone in their new quarters, Richard Otis age 3½ broke the silence. He said "Mama, whose house is this." Being informed that this was his new home, he cried to go back to his Winston house. This was the temporary feeling of the entire family, but the atmosphere soon changed. The

159

people in this little university town were very warm and friendly. The church people were happy to receive their new pastor and were very cooperative from the start. Some of the veneer of the college intelligensia had apparently rubbed off on members of St. Paul's church and others in the town. Most of St. Paul's members earned their livelihood directly or indirectly in the university community.

Dear to my heart are the scenes of my childhood, but dearer are the events that made the scenes. They all seem to have begun in Chapel Hill, a lazy little college town, or so it seemed to me. Nothing much was going on beyond "Front" Street and "Back" Street. Yes, there was a church on a street, on the way to a railroad station. It was a passage-way connecting "Front" Street and "Back" Street. It had no name. The church was on this street and next door was my house, the parsonage. On the other side there was a large play lot. I thought it was large. I played baseball on it. It was bare; no grass. There was lots of gravel on it. I know because it skinned my legs and arms when I tackled "the man with the football." Just beyond the lot was a school with three rooms. At one time I went there, when my father was principal. My first school had one room joined to the house of Sister Caroline Jones. She sang in the choir. She opened her school with church songs and prayer. I remember one song very well. We sang it every day when school closed. "God be with you til we meet again."

When I began school I was six-going on seven. I was left-handed; they made me write with my right hand, like I had to eat at home with my right hand.

I liked school; I grew up fast; I made friends. We had a baseball team. "Teddy" Stroud was the best player. He was a runt but he could catch a ball. He owned the catcher's mitt. Milton Campbell owned the first baseman's glove. My little brother Richard Otis and I owned a bat. I seem to remember, they took up collection in church to buy it.

Our teacher 'Sister' Jones took a picture of our team. We had cigarettes in our mouths; some of us did. You bet they were made of candy; not tobacco. I remember a tobacco experience. Somebody gave me a "chaw" of "peach" tobacco. The smell and taste were fine at first. I must have swallowed the juice. I had a terrible stomach ache and vomiting spell which I never forgot. I needed a stomach doctor; but I didn't dare tell Mama and Papa about my sickness.

I had a happy time in Chapel Hill, playing baseball after school and at recess. Sometimes I had to stay in the house and rock the baby in a cradle and sing a lullaby until the baby went to sleep. I could hear the boys outside playing baseball. Home it! Home it! they would yell. I would rock the cradle faster; I would sing louder; "Go to sleep little b-a-b-y." Tears ran down my cheeks. I would sing louder and faster and the baby would wake up and cry. And then the game would be over. It was too dark to play.

Most of the time I was allowed to play; especially as I grew older. I remember the lopsided ball. Somebody had a "Louisville slugger." If you didn't hold the trade mark up it was bad luck. If you hit the ball too hard it would come apart. The cotton seeds would fly all over the lot. We got a new ball; I was at bat. Teddy Stroud called for a drop. Jimmie Atwater threw a straight; I struck out. Herbert McMaster was big and strong. We called him "Herbert Black-Master" because he was really black. He would hit a home run if the ball didn't come apart.

We saved pictures of baseball players, that were thrown away by cigarette smokers. The pictures came in packs of cigarettes. I remember "Home Run" Baker and "Three-Finger" Brown and "Barefoot" Jackson in color on cards. I kept them in a cigar box.

Other things happened on our street. There was an older boy named Bruce Stroud. He was white; his papa was rich. He rode along the street at high speed in a "toy" automobile. It was not much bigger than a little boy's wagon. He made it by himself, I think. It made a loud noise and would scare the horses. We would run out and watch him go. In later years, I understand he became an expert mechanic and Ford dealer.

Horses and carriages passed down our street. What I remembered most was the little children in wicker carriages drawn by Shetland ponies, driven by one of the children. I learned their parents were rich. Gee! how I wanted a Shetland pony and carriage.

I remember lots of men passing by our house going to the station. There was only one walk way. It was across the street from my house. The men were dressed like they were going to church, with hats on. They didn't look like our church people. I learned they were called "White." We were "Colored." They were students from the university. "Will I go to their school, when I grow up," I asked Mama. "No child, you're not white." "I saw some 'gray' men with them yesterday," said I.

161

"Not gray," she said. "They were brown like us but they are not Americans like us; so they can go to the university." Little did she realize that the destiny of her inquisitive young son would have him attending the University of Chicago's Rush Medical School in 1925 instead of the University of North Carolina.

In Chapel Hill I called my father, "papa." It was here that I began to learn that he was a very special person. On weekends he brought a box of candy, "chocolate drops" to our mother whom we called "mama." He brought the weekend *Raleigh News and Observer* and read the funnies, Mutt and Jeff and the Katzenjammer kids to the older children. The income from the church was very small. I remember that papa soon had a bicycle and was riding to his job as county school teacher to supplement his income. I later learned that he sold insurance from day to day for the Negro North Carolina Mutual Insurance Company of Durham. The bicycle was also handy for his insurance route. By the end of the second year at Chapel Hill, Llewellyn Jr. and Elbert were born and there were five children. The Berry family already had the family doctor services of Dr. E. A. Abernathy, whom I believe delivered "Lew" and Elbert. Mama's sister Ursula, a teenager came from Woodsdale and lived with the family for about a year. Plans were being made for her further education after helping with the children. But there was a fellow named Tommy Clay for whom Ursula already had heart throbs. She returned to Woodsdale in 1909 and married him. Mama's youngest sister Lula then joined the Berry family. She was offered a "bill of goods" which she liked, or maybe it was the best she could do. I'm sure I was happy to be relieved of rocking baby cradles while ball games were going on in the next lot. Lula became a lovable permanent member of the Berry family, until she graduated as a home economics teacher from Hampton Institute and taught in the Norfolk public schools.

Meanwhile, Papa's financial load became heavier. The insurance route increased and his bicycle became less adequate. Very soon his father, John Berry must have received a message, more or less of Divine origin. Grandpa wrote; "Dear 'Lew', as you know, we have moved from Butler's farm into the city of Hampton for good. I have a young horse named Nellie. Your mother and I would like to give the horse and the buggy to you, if you will come to Hampton to receive the horse and rig." "Love your Mother and Daddy."

162

Needless to say, Papa went and brought home the chestnut brown horse, Nellie, and the buggy. The buggy was shiny black and in a good state of repair. This raised the stature of Reverend Berry in Chapel Hill. It was more appropriate for a community leader to travel around with horse and buggy than riding a bicycle. The well constructed buggy was wide enough to transport his wife and some of his children. The trip to Hampton had provided the first opportunity to see his mother and father for two or three years. They were proud to see him looking so well. They had heard and read many reports of his successful pastorate. His uncle Sam Jenifer, who always encouraged him and predicted great success for his nephew in the ministry had died two years earlier. Papa visited his uncle's grave, in the church yard of Bethel church on Lincoln street. He noted an army veterans headstone furnished by the government, it bore the epitaph; "Private 1st Class, 30th Infantry Regiment U.S.C.T. (U.S. Colored troops) Civil War 1864–65. (1849–1907) Papa had a nice long talk with his father. This was the last time he would hear his father's voice. A year later in the summer 1909, Grandpa Berry had a stroke paralyzing his left side and rendering him unable to speak.

Papa returned to Hampton carrying my brother Richard Otis and me. I remember riding in a large boat. It was the first time I had ever seen a ship. There was lots of water. I learned in later years that we crossed Hampton Roads from Norfolk to Old Point Comfort, enroute to Hampton. It was approximately the same route traveled by Grandpa Berry, Uncle Sam Jenifer with other veterans and their families on the "famous raft" to settle on Butlers farm in 1870.

During our trip to Hampton, my brother and I had the enjoyable experience of meeting Aunt Kate, Mrs. Katherine Barrett, the sister of our father. She had come down to Hampton from New York, to visit her ill father. She entertained us with stories of the big city. She said, "One of these days when you grow up, you can visit New York where I live. The traffic there is so thick that you have to push a horse's nose out of the way to cross the street." This dramatic picture stuck in my memory. Years later when I confronted her with this story, she would laugh and say "I don't remember telling you any such tale." She enjoyed her visit with us during the several days we were together in Hampton. She sang with the Clef Club in New York; she taught us current songs

163

of the day. One was "Peg O' My Heart." She applied this song to her young nephews. She took us to a photographic studio and had pictures made.

We returned with Papa back to Chapel Hill. But unfortunately, we never saw Grandpa Berry again. He died two months later on September 4, 1909. Papa returned to Hampton for the sad task of attending his father's funeral. This ended a career which began with the courageous escape of John Berry from slavery and service in the Union Army for the freedom of himself, his family, and his race. His courage and far-sightedness had been a great inspiration for his minister son. He was buried in the National Veterans' Cemetery Section B. Grave number 9790 near Old Soldiers' Home, in Hampton where he had spent many happy hours with his Union Army buddies. His epitaph reads, "John Berry Private 1st Class, Battery B., 2nd Regiment, Light Artillery, U.S.C.T. (U.S. Colored Troops) (1844–1909).

Shortly after Papa's return to Chapel Hill, a new teaching job came through. He was appointed teacher and principal of the three-room school on the far side of the church and parsonage. There were two other teachers, Mrs. Mittie Kirkland and Mrs. Estella Oldham. Papa had a brass bell with a black handle, something like the bell around the neck of the lead cow at Woodsdale. He used that bell to call children in from play and for the beginning and dismissal time of the school day. I, now, have that bell, as a precious possession. It is seventy or more years old. It was used by both parents throughout their school teaching days.

Papa believed that "reading, writing and 'rithmetic should be taught to the tune of a hickory stick." As a widely known minister, he chose to temper his beliefs with diplomacy. Discipline was enforced by so many strikes to the palm of the out-stretched hand with a ruler. It seemed that when other children were paddled, so was I; whether I deserved it or not. I think I was the victim of pastoral diplomacy. In addition to the "three R's" papa's students always got a full measure of training in self expression, literary performance and religion. They all learned the meaning of punctuality, perserverance and accomplishments. "Go onto college; raise a family; acquire your own home and go to church." These were resounding commands frequently heard as the children stood assembled in the hallways for morning devotionals.

Somewhere along the line of the Berry activities, Mama got into the act or should I say, she increased the act she was in already. She began teaching a group of older boys at night, who had to work during the day. She taught them around her kitchen table a few nights a week for twenty-five cents per person on a weekly basis. With all of Mama's chores, with a large family, missionary work (or wasn't it all missionary work) and choir duty she took on the night class because she really enjoyed teaching, and of course the money came in handy.

There came a time in 1910 when all of Chapel Hill and the nation were talking about "Haley's Comet." I remember well some of the excitement. It would appear in the sky like a large bright star with a tail. "It might strike the earth and destroy it by fire and fulfill the prophesy in the bible," they said. It would be the end of time. The rich jumped out of windows to their death; the poor watched and prayed. In later years, Mama told and retold the story of the comet; how she and Papa watched for days, far into the night. The comet finally came as a bright red streak across the sky but without catastrophe. "The comet appears every 76 years or 77 years," the astronomers say. It is expected again in 1986. It will soon be time again in Chapel Hill and elsewhere to watch and pray.

The North Carolina university and university students were always in the spot light at Chapel Hill. Well remembered are some of the stories of the awful pranks of hazing circulated through the Negro community. "Freshmen," they would say, "Lecture on, 'the which-ness of thus,' or the is-ness of the not yet." Student athletics interested the whole town. Football teams were transported to and from the railroad station in large horse-drawn "drummer's hacks," the equivalent of a modern small bus. When the team returned victorious from an out-of-town game, the joyful students would un-hitch the horses and they themselves would pull the hack load of players back to the campus. I remember; they passed my house cheering loudly enroute from "Back" Street to "Front" Street.

Two favorite Negro janitors would sometime walk with the cheering crowd of students back to the campus, or so I am told. I knew these well known "custodians," they were members of St. Paul's church. They were called "Short" Bill Jones and "Long" Bill Jones. "Short" Bill Jones had a son named Sam who caught the "college spirit" vicariously and dreamed the impossible dream of playing football at the university. He was crazy about the game. He stood 6 feet 2 inches; weighed 240 lbs and played vacant lot football. Nobody ever stopped him short of the goal line. He attended Shaw University, a Baptist school for Negroes in Raleigh, N.C. and graduated as a doctor of medicine at its Leonard School of Medicine and Pharmacy. He was their all-time-great football player. He played 'center' to make holes for the quarter-back. When that didn't work, he would go to the back field; put the quarter-back over the ball and run for a touchdown. On defense, he was wherever the opposing team ran a play to make the tackle. They sang school songs that rang around the state in the tune of the song, "Casey Jones," quote, "Big Sam Jones made another touchdown, made another touchdown and we're abound to win."

Papa attended the 18th Annual Session of the Western North Carolina Conference held at Bethel A.M.E. Church, in Greensboro beginning November 23, 1910. There he greeted many of his old North Carolina Conference friends. Among them were Reverends K. C. Holt; J. W. Walker; A. J. Wilson; T. W. Cotton; R. L. Tillery; W. T. Carnish; J. D. Cowan; W. H. Pearson; A. D. Avery and Professor D. J. Jordan, President of Kittrell College.

Bishop Levi Coppin presiding bishop opened the conference by leading the congregation in singing "And are we yet alive." Papa was again chosen as the statistical secretary, he was also appointed to the Committee on Children's Day and one committee on Temperance. On the morning of the fourth day, Reverend R. H. W. Leake made a motion as the presiding elder to excuse Reverend L. L. Berry from the conference in order to attend the funeral of his brother in Hampton, Virginia. The motion was passed with expressions of sympathy. Papa attended the funeral of his 24 year old brother, Henry, whose death was rather sudden and of unknown causes. On this short visit the life of Papa's brother Henry was discussed and reviewed with his mother. Henry was named for grandma Berry's favorite uncle, Henry Jenifer, who was widely known in St. Mary's county of Maryland, in the days of slavery as "Doc." Henry. It had long been known that Grandma had hoped and prayed that there would be a regular, educated doctor in the Berry family. She was now certain that her uncle's namesake would not be that doctor. I later learned that she was very happy when Papa told her that I had announced to the family at the age of five that I was going to be a doctor.

At the 19th Annual Session of the Western North Carolina Conference which was held at St. Joseph's A.M.E. Church in Durham, November 23–26, 1911, Bishop Levi J. Coppin, presided in accordance with his appointment for the quadrennium, 1908–1912. Papa was again selected as the statistical secretary and as trustee of Kittrell College and of the missionary board. On the evening of the first day of the conference, the bishop spoke of the time honored annual sermon which opens the annual conference. He introduced and presented Papa, who had been selected for the honor at this time. He read the scripture lesson from the 27th Psalm. "The Lord is my light and my salvation: whom shall I fear? the LORD is the strength of my life; of whom shall I be afraid? The text of this sermon was taken from the 62nd chapter of Isaiah, a portion of the first verse; "For Zion's sake, will I not hold my peace, and for Jerusalem's sake, I will not rest."

The minutes state that Reverend Berry preached a very helpful and inspiring sermon. This was a very auspicious occasion for Papa. It was the first time he had been chosen to preach an Annual Sermon. Bishop Coppin gave him quite an introduction, and commendation after the sermon. This was the beginning of an important turning point in Papa's career which he did not realize at the time. I heard him say in later years that Bishop J. Albert Johnson came late at this session because of poor train connections. Arriving as the sermon was beginning he remained in the pastor's study and heard Papa's sermon. It was a great surprise when after the doxology and benediction by Reverend Berry he observed Bishop Johnson coming from the pastor's study to the pulpit. Papa was overjoyed. Bishop Johnson gave him a firm handshake and complimented him highly on his sermon. This was the beginning of the long friendship between the two. Papa always said that his real climb up the ladder of success in the church was due largely to the friendship and high regard that Bishop J. Albert Johnson had for him.

As the Conference opened on the next morning, Bishop Johnson was escorted down the aisle (amid cheers and applause) to the pulpit by a special committee. The group consisted of the host presiding elder, Rev. R. H. W. Leake, the host pastor Rev. J. E. Jackson and a layman of the host church, John Merrick president, N.C. Mutual Life Insurance Company. Bishop Johnson was presented and spoke briefly at this time of his work in South Africa.

Later three visiting general officers were introduced, namely; Ira T. Bryant, secretary Sunday School union, Julian C. Caldwell, secretary Allen Christian Endeavor League and John R. Hawkins, Commissioner of Education. The introductions were followed by two old A.M.E. favorites "Oh For a Thousand Tongues to Sing My Great Redeemers Praise," and "Amazing Grace How Sweet the Sound that Saved a Wretch Like Me."

At the end of the conference session, Papa received his fifth and last annual appointment to St. Paul's in Chapel Hill. He knew this when Bishop Coppin re-appointed him because of the five year limit of service at a given church. Returning home, he had the first of a series of discussions with Mama about their future. Papa had always returned annually to visit the Virginia conference where his roots were. His friends in the Virginia ministry were constantly begging him to return to his home conference over the years. Papa re-evaluated his past services at Chapel Hill and determined to end his pastorage there in a blaze of glory.

On the first Sunday beginning the new conference year, Papa was met with an unusually large turnout of members. They welcomed him back with obvious enthusiasm. Papa was prepared for the occasion, he preached one of his favorite sermons from the text taken from the 127th Psalm. "Except the Lord build the house, they labor in vain that build it: except the Lord keep the city, the watchman waketh but in vain." At the close of the service, he greeted many people at the altar and among them were L. R. Hargreves; William J. Jones; Mittie Kirkland; Bruce Caldwell; Viola Brooks; H. C. and Susie Merritt; Dr. D. E. Caldwell; E. T. and Golda Sellars; Jess Kirkland; T. H. McDade; Will and Maggie Morphies; Martha Whitted and Oscar Pindle.

Perhaps the principal accomplishment at Chapel Hill was the Berry's involvement in the community. They became very active with young people through the public schools, by attracting them to church activities and encouraging the older ones to go off to school for higher education. Papa encouraged many young people to go to Kittrell where he was trustee and Professor J. D. Jordan, father of the late Bishop Frederick Jordan was the president. The Berry's had a wide acquaintance in Durham, through earlier Kittrell friendships, through relatives of the Harrisses and Jordans, and through church circles. Negro business people in Durham were widely known as being among the most progressive of any Negro community in the country. Especially well known was the N.C. Mutual Life Insurance Company the largest owned by Negroes in the United States which was held up as a beacon light to Negro youth.

Many people of the Durham business community were members of the St. Joseph A.M.E. Church. Among the friends and acquaintances of the Berrys in Durham were John and Lula Avery; John L. and Mary Wheeler; C. C. Spaulding; John and Martha Merrick; John W. O'Daniel; J. C. Scarborough; W. G. Pearson; and Dr. J. M. Mills. Relatives of Mama's included Susan Warren Jones, (Aunt Suzie) Sally Warren, Ed Warren and others.

In April 10–14, 1912, when Papa attended the Virginia Annual Conference held at the Bethel Church, in Hampton, he requested of Bishop Coppin a transfer back to the Virginia Conference. This is the church in which he grew up as a boy and from which he went into the ministry.

The bishop stated that there was one appointment which would be available at this time. It was in a rural area, but there was a nice large two-story parsonage and a fine group of people there. He said he "felt sure that a very fine church in the city would be available to you in a short time." The charge was the Mt. Zion A.M.E. Church in Princess Anne Courthouse, Virginia, twenty miles outside of Norfolk.

Papa had informed Mama that he would accept a transfer back to the Virginia Conference if there were a reasonable appointment available. This was thought to be better for the future education of the children, and in light of predictable prospects in the North Carolina Conference.

At the appropriate time, Papa preached his farewell sermon to the congregation of St. Paul's Church. Not only was there widespread disappointment and regret among the members that the final year was not completed at the church but there was widespread disappointment and regret throughout the city. In addition, members of the Berry family were saddened to have to leave their many friends. The Berry's always remembered Chapel Hill through some of these friendships which lasted throughout their lives. Especially dear to the Berry's are the memories of the long friendship with the late Mrs. Maggie Morphies and the Morphies-Jones-Atwater family.

Looking back and noting the progress at Chapel Hill, the Berry's were pleased with the coming of two liberal educators to the University of North Carolina. They became national leaders in the field of human rights. They were President Frank Porter Graham and professor of sociology Dr. Howard Odom. These men boldly spoke out as white Southerners deploring the ill-treatment of Negroes and urging better race relations in the South. This was before the Martin Luther King era of the 1960's. Several years later the citizens of Chapel Hill were to attract national acclaim for electing the first Black mayor of a southern city since the Reconstruction Period following the Civil War. The honorable Howard Lee served with outstanding success in this post.

Mt. Zion:
Princess Anne Court House
(1912–14)

AFTER a sojourn of seven years in the Western North Carolina conference Pop finally yielded to many old friends in the ministry to return to his native Virginia, and an A.M.E. pastorate. He had visited all of the Virginia sessions while carrying on his work in North Carolina. He went to Princess Anne from a five-year pastorate in Chapel Hill, N.C.

This was Pop's first appointment to an entirely rural area, which he disliked but he was expected to get "back in line," as they called it in the Virginia Conference. As it turned out the two years in Princess Anne were very enjoyable for Pop and the rest of his family.

Princess Anne Courthouse was only about 20 miles from Norfolk. Situated in the southeast portion of this state the county was formed in 1691 and named after Princess Anne, the daughter of the English king, James II. The Princess later became the Queen. Princess Anne's history-minded citizens are proud that the first English settlers in Virginia landed at Cape Henry, which is a part of the county, in April 1607 and then sailed to Jamestown which historically has the credit for being the first such settlement. They are proud of the Old Cape Henry Light House which is still present having been built in 1791 to guide ships through the very treacherous waters off the Cape. The county in more recent years has been incorporated into the division known as Virginia Beach.

In our day there was rich farm land which yielded fine strawberries as well as many other vegetables. The county was famous also for its easy accessibility for personal and commercial fishing. I remember the sandy undeveloped beaches not far away from our church and the next door parsonage. In the winter months or in the stormy weather, one could hear the constant roar of the ocean. At the shoreline and in the proper season, schools of fish could be seen swimming together and changing the color of the ocean almost as far as the eye could see, especially if you had little eyes like the young Berry children. I remember enjoying bird watching as large flocks of ducks and geese would fly through the rural skies day-after-day to their appropriate seasonal feeding grounds.

In addition to the chores as the minister, Pop enjoyed hunting, especially birds, rabbits and squirrels as I recall. Also, included in those days were partridges and wild turkeys which have by now become either extinct or forbidden to the hunters. I remember Pop's double barreled shot gun and his canvas hunting belt and as he returned from the fields with a hunting partner. I was happy to see the bulging game which he brought back in the pockets of the vest. My brother Dick and I, at the age of 7 and 9, were allowed to learn how to trap small animals, especially rabbits. Early in the morning before leaving for school, we would go out to the woods and underbrush to inspect our traps and to see if we had had any luck. When we made a catch, there was great childish joy and equal disappointment when the animals avoided our best efforts.

We had brought from Chapel Hill our horse Nellie and the buggy which had been given to Pop by his father a couple of years before. In Princess Anne we added a surrey, the popular two-seated carriage of those days with the fringe around the top. We all piled into this contraption for trips which I remember fondly. Those were the days of the Christmas season when the minister and his family were invited by many of the parishioners for breakfast, lunch or dinner. The unique and very special Princess Anne cuisine will never be forgotten.

There were always plenty of fresh fish from Ocean View and, in season, the famous Lynhaven Bay oysters. George Washington Carver must have gotten some of his ideas from Princess Anne County. The dishes which could be prepared from Virginia yams were almost innumerable. There was the Nancy Hall variety which was roasted to a soft consistency and served with natural syrup seeping through the hulls. The potato inside was a reddish brown color, apparently achieved today only by artificial additives. The Nancy Hall Virginia yam could be fried or baked into pies or biscuits and other delicious dishes. The delectable meals served to the parson and his family always included three or four meats, three or four different desserts and brother Dick and I always sampled them all, and usually went home with a bellyache. But the next day, as soon as Pop could get old Nell curried and fed we were off on the country roads in our rubbered tired surrey covered with lap robes to keep out of some of the cold winds blowing in from the ocean.

I remember my childish pride when I was allowed to drive Nell hitched to the buggy to take Pop to and from the railroad station on his trips to Norfolk and elsewhere. The mile-and-a-half trip from our house to the station required traveling over Dozier's bridges. This was a two-way crossing over a narrow extension of the Virginia Dismal Swamp. Each bridge consisted of long wooden square shaped logs across the stagnant stream. These were covered crosswise with wooden slabs and loose planks which rattled as if they were going to fall apart as you drove across them. In the summertime with no windows in the buggy that you could raise, you were immediately attacked at the bridge by thousands of huge Virginia mosquitos that could cover nearly every uncovered spot on the horse or the passengers, singing, biting and stinging before you could finish crossing the bridge. If this did not take too much of your attention, you could look at either side at the cypress trees and stumps growing in the swamp with hungry looking water moccasin snakes curled and sunning themselves, near the surface of the water. I never heard of anybody falling through but I was always happy to get across the bridge with Nell hooked to the rig.

During the two years, Pop also taught in the local colored school and Mom had the job of occasionally teaching cooking and sewing. Mom, of course, with five children, 4 young boys and a girl was always kept quite busy as a cook, housekeeper, seamstress, disciplinarian and missionary worker. There were some very pleasant times with her which I still remember. Through the years I have discussed them with my brothers and sisters. It was on the quiet Sunday afternoons when nothing was happening in the country very much, except the singing of birds and the distant roaring of the Atlantic Ocean. Mom would assemble us around her Kimball foot-pedaled organ, which her father bought her as a young girl at Woodsdale in the early 1890's. The organ had been hauled across two states to every Berry pastorate; repaired when needed, but it was still capable of beautiful music in Princess Anne. As the children grew older, they often smiled as they reminisced about standing by Mom's side in unison joined her as she played and we sang, *Sweet Alice Benbolt, Annie Laurie, Amazing Grace, How Sweet the Sound, Loves Old Sweet Song*, and *Bringing in the Sheaves*.

Dick and I had a little dog named Rover. We were always trying to train Rover to hunt. I wanted a 22 rifle to try my luck at shooting birds but Pop would not go for that. I finally got a BB gun and time-and-time and time again I tried to shoot a bird on the wing, with predictably, no success.

I think I probably had my first lesson in sex and reproduction when a local farmer rode a big healthy looking male horse neighing and foaming at the mouth, across our front yard into a nearby woods. I soon noticed that Pop took Nell by another route into the same wooded area. They stayed for quite a while. Meanwhile, Dick and I noted that the neighing continued from the big horse who was out of our sight. We later learned a male horse was called a stud. Some months later Nellie had a colt whom we named Prince.

It was then that Dick and I began to put one-and-one together to make three. Prince was quite a lively little colt and we enjoyed seeing him racing around the yard, nursing and wallowing around in the grass.

Pop's preaching must have been good there. The members all seemed to like him and they especially enjoyed his "August meeting." This was a full week of revival services, when young people and hardened sinners got religion. Many old friends came from miles around and migrants to the eastern big cities came back home for a great reunion on these occasions. At last check "August meetings" are still being held at Princess Anne, now Virginia Beach.

One of the strangest practices of "racial social equality" which I have ever seen or heard about occurred at Pop's church in Princess Anne. On some Sundays, white folks would drive up in horse and buggy or horse and carts to the side of the church building where the windows were raised high for ventilation and cooling. They would sit there until the sermons were over so that they could enjoy some good preaching. I understand that this practice began long before our time. One preacher who attracted quite a few such worshippers was the Rev. James Garner, an older and distant cousin of my father, who had a reputation in the

174

Tidewater area as a great preacher. My father is said to have followed the style of this older cousin who went to the Hampton Institute for a trade and basic cultural studies and then went into the ministry. A dramatic bit of history of that period includes the true story that Rev. Garner dropped to his death in this church while preaching a sermon.

As far as the Berry family is concerned one of the greatest rewards of this pastorate was the forming of the friendship with the Sawyer family, Father Willis, Mother Henrietta, and their four daughters, Bertha, Nannie, Sadie and Odell. The children all went off to college and later married and made their homes in New York City. The friendship between the Berrys and the Sawyers continued throughout the lives of the older members and the younger generations still feel as close as natural brothers and sisters.

Personally I still feel that the two years spent in the wilds of rural Virginia with all of the attributes of nature were probably the two most enjoyable years of my childhood.

Section Five
The
Metropolitan
Ministry
and Older
Family
(1914-1933)

Wilberforce University—Ohio (1920–24)

Galloway Hall and Chapel, above; Carnegie Library, below.

Relay Track Team (l. to r.: Otis Freeman, Leonidas Berry, John Clark, Gaston Lewis, Charles Sedgwick). University Quartette (Homer Smith, L. H. Berry, Charles Williams, Homer Williams).

Metropolitan Ministry of Rev. L. L. Berry in Virginia

Right: Pastor and Official Board, Emanuel A.M.E. Church, Portsmouth, Va., 1924. Below, l.: St. John's A.M.E. Church and Parsonage, Norfolk, Va., 1927. Center: Home of Rev. L. L. Berry and Family, Presiding Elder Years (1916–1921), Norfolk, Va. R.: Emanuel A.M.E. Church and Parsonage (1921–1926).

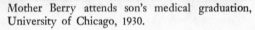

Mother Berry attends son's medical graduation, University of Chicago, 1930.

Late Dr. Sidney A. Portis, Professor, Rush Medical College, sponsored the author's specialty training at Cook County Hospital and Courtesy Staff at Michael Reese Hospital. On campus of Hospital St. Antoine, Paris, after observing famous professor, Francois Montier (center), perform gastroscopic examinations, 1954.

My great teacher and "father" of gastroscopy, Professor Rudolf Schindler (r.), expatriated from Germany to University of Chicago during affiliation with Provident Hospital, 1936. Also, Mrs. Schindler, his constant assistant. L.: Dr. Angelo Dagrati (photo: at Longbeach, Va. Hospital, 1964); below: 1st Lieutenant Berry (center), U.S. Army Medical Reserves, on active duty, Civilian Conservation Corps, 1935.

605th Co. CCC Camp Deer Grove SP

St. James-Norfolk Va. (1914–17)

REV. L. L. Berry had attended the 48th session of the Virginia Annual Conference, April 22 to 26, 1914, at Mt. Zion AME Church in Roanoke. He had received his appointment from Bishop Levi J. Coppin for the St. James Church in South Norfolk. This town was an extended community of Berkeley, the eighth ward of the City of Norfolk. The church was located just at the dividing line between Norfolk and South Norfolk. The line extended along the right-of-way of the Norfolk-Portsmouth Belt Line railroad. The parsonage faced the railroad tracks.

He spent two nights and a day at the parsonage with the retiring minister, whose family was in preparation for moving to another Charge. I shall never forget Pops graphic description of his dramatic and startling experience during this visit. After he had been asleep for about an hour on the first night there, he heard a sudden loud and jolting noise. He jumped out of the bed in his flannel nightgown and dashed toward the door. The whole house was trembling. The noise was deafening, and lightning-like flashes of light lit up the room. Through his frightened mind ran the thought, "This must be a hurricane! A tropical storm with overtones of thundering and lightning or more likely, this was suddenly "Judgment Day" that I have been reading and preaching about so fervently for years!"

The five long frightful minutes seemed like several years Pop told us. Finally, the long and short whistle overtones revealed the truth of the maddening experience—a passing freight train. This could have literally been the setting which had inspired the song entitled, "The Railroad Ran Thru the Middle of the House." Pop vowed he would never move his family into this parsonage.

He met his official board that next night and described his experiences. He announced that his wife and family were all packed and ready to move, but . . .

"Gentlemen," stated Reverend Berry prophetically, "I have five young and vigorous children, who are so active that I am afraid they would never survive so close to that railroad track."

J. E. Fulford, a mailcarrier and young trustee in the church, rose and concurred.

"Brethren, some of us have known for a long time that the kind of minister that St. James wants to develop her potentialities probably would not accept graciously the parsonage which we now own. You all heard the Reverend Berry preach when he visited our church a couple of months before the Annual Conference. I headed your committee that waited on Bishop Coppin to ask for him. We like his vigor and progressive spirit. I believe that with his leadership St. James can do anything it wants to do."

This was followed by "Amen" from several members.

"It is true that the church owns the old Bray school lot on St. James Street just beyond the park?" Reverend Berry inquired.

"Yes," said Brother Miles Simmons. "It is bought and paid for. We burned the mortgage on that lot four years ago, and the plan is to tear down the unused wooden school building and erect a church there some day."

"The lot is really big enough for a church and a parsonage," chimed in Brother Noah Painter.

The next week the Berry family unloaded their hugh packing crates, which had become a standard fixture in the itinerant family of Reverend L. L. Berry, follower of John Wesley and Richard Allen. The new address was Todd Street, South Norfolk, Virginia. Shade trees lined the walk in front of #32—a two story, eight-room house about six blocks from the church. This was the rented parsonage, where we lived for nine months until we moved into the new parsonage, which had been built on the old Bray school. The newly built parsonage was located at #46 St. James Street.

War clouds were forming in Europe but most people in the Berry-Harris clan were not concerned with the goings on in the far away world. Some prince or other was killed in Prussia but that was royal business. Much more important in the fall of 1914, was that Mama Beulah had the grippe according to South Norfolk man of magic, Dr. G. Hamilton Francis. With five children ages four to twelve and Reverend Papa Llewellyn trying to establish a high level of leadership at St. James all thoughts turned to the old family standby Aunt Suzie Warren in Durham. She was Mama's father's sister. On time "Aunt Suzie" arrived first by sitting in a one horse hack driven by a friend then by Northwestern "Jim Crow" coach (meaning the converted rear end of the baggage car.)

As was her custom when the Berry's needed her, Aunt Suzie took complete charge on arrival. All the children were quickly conscious of her benevolent discipline. But they loved her and the younger ones were around her neck as soon as she hung up her light fall coat on the hall tree. Then upstairs she went to the front bedroom where her favorite niece lay covered with a goose down comfort and a crazy quilt. Mama had been having chills off-and-on all day. "How are you, Beulah, my dear?" "I have been quite poorly, Aunt Suz'; I sure am glad to see you. Now I won't have to worry about these children while I'm sick. My, my," Mama continued, "I feel better just seeing you. How have you been?" "Fine, just like the Rock of Gibraltar; you know, I know how to take care of myself. Now, are you running a fever?" Mama smiled weakly "Dr. Francis says that I have fever; I have chills once in awhile, too, but I just can't get strength enough to get out of this bed." "You will soon be alright, Beulah. When I heard you had chills I brought along "Three 666," I know your doctor has prescribed quinine but you need a poultice to your back; a hot iron wrapped in a towel at your feet, and an ice bag to your head." Mama interrupted "I'll tell you what I would like first, Aunt Suz; help me with a warm sponge bath and we can phone Dr. Francis when he finishes his house calls tonight." "Alright, Aunt Suzie was positive I will give him two more days! Just two!!"

The sponge bath and the fresh nightgown were soon out of the way and Aunt Suz had taken over in the kitchen preparing dinner for Rev. Berry and his children who were accustomed to having dinner not long after arriving from school.

Aunt Suz had on her familiar blouse ruffled up at the shoulder; her long apron tied in a big bowknot behind her back and a neatly cut sprig from a gum tree protruding from her mouth like a cigarette.

The older children learned that the business end of that stick sprayed out into spicules to form a brush. Once in awhile she would turn her back, dip the brush into a small can of snuff carried in her apron pocket and brush her front teeth leaving the sprig sportily protruding from the corner of her mouth. Aunt Suz would appropriately remove the brush when the spirit moved her to plaster a kiss on the cheek of her adopted brood of Beulah's children.

In later years when all were adults, brother Lew, would recall with laughter that he discovered Aunt Suz's sneaking a small flask of bourbon from a secret pocket built in behind her long flowing apron gathered at the top. She would take a small swiggle about three times a day and pretend it was medicine if anyone saw her.

By eight or nine o'clock that night, Aunt Suz had all chores for the day under control. The older children were ordered to quit their studying, go to bed and finish getting their lessons by rising early in the morning.

Within a week or so, whether by Dr. Francis' magic or Aunt Suzie's Three 666's, Mama was back on her feet and Aunt Suz had returned to Durham, but she left a feeling of warmth and good cheer behind her.

It was a pretty, two-story, seven-room, white house with green trim and outside window blinds called shutters. The living room, dining room, kitchen, and front and rear porches made up the first floor. Three bedrooms, a study, a bathroom, and a rear porch were on the second floor. There was running cold water only, which had to be cut off below the ground level on winter nights to keep it from freezing. The rooms were heated by coal stoves, which Dick and I polished every Saturday afternoon. I remember the convenient scuttle of anthracite coal and small shovel behind the stove because it was the daily chore of the two older boys to keep up the supply of hard fuel from the storage bin outside. Ashes had to be sifted on weekends. The coke which was left was used in banking the fires at night.

The new parsonage at #46 St. James Street was a block and a half beyond the limits of Norfolk's eighth ward community known as Berkeley and within the township of South Norfolk. Because of this, we had to attend the inferior Waterford Elementary School two miles away rather than the sixteen-room Abraham Lincoln School of the Norfolk system only one-half mile to the North.

182

South Norfolk was a tough little town in 1914, with streets of cobblestones or tar and gravel. Twenty percent of the population were Negroes, who lived mostly in the Northern end toward Norfolk. Eighty percent were mostly the type known by Negroes and whites alike as "poor white trash." Consequently, there always seemed to be an abundance of vagrant, loud talking, poorly dressed white men standing or sitting in front of the little business places along the principal thoroughfare, Liberty street. Their chief occupation, other than drawling chatter which we never stopped long enough to understand, was to whittle bits of wood with long pocket knives and to spit tobacco juice out on the sidewalk.

Here and there along Liberty Street, there were barrooms, as they were called then, with swinging half doors. As those doors swung, in or out, to admit a customer, one could catch a fleeting glimpse of men standing with one foot on a rail. Sawdust was scattered on the floor. Here and there strategically placed shining brass spittoons were seen being attended by a Negro handyman. Occasionally, a man would reel out of the barroom, stepping high and without coordination, as though he were walking in a darkened room and could not find the door. The most conspicuous evidence of work among these white citizens would be seen when the six o'clock mill whistle blew and dozens of women and a few men rushed out of the door of a cotton textile factory and were homeward bound. The men usually carried dinner pails, and the women workers were unmistakable because of the white lint that littered their brown stringly hair and clung to their thick brown cotton stockings.

One day when Pop had walked half way to school to meet us, he ran into Professor A. J. Sykes, Principal of Waterford School.

"Hello, Reverend Berry. If I had known you were going to meet your children today, I would have gone directly to Camp Stello."

"Good afternoon, Professor Sykes. It is good to see you. I have been meeting the children everyday this week. However, getting to school in the mornings seems to be the problem now."

Our father was referring to the fact that we often had to fight our way through the poor white neighborhood to get to the colored Waterford school. A favorite pastime of some of the young adult white males was to detain the white boys enroute to their school and have them block the sidewalk as the colored children attempted to pass. We could either force ourselves past the blockade and be pounced upon by a platoon of adult exponents of southern chivalry or we could walk out in the street to the tune of their jeers and shouts of laughter and thus establish an admission of the so-called "Negro's place."

"We have had trouble, Reverend, off-and-on during the entire five years that I have been principal. It used to be that several men and older boys would gang one of our children, tear their clothes and throw their books out into the street, slap their faces, call them 'black niggers,' and send them to school crying—often with a bloody nose or a swollen face. These incidents have been reported to the sheriff's office, but they have steadfastly refused to interfere. Since the beginning of this term the colored children have been meeting before they reach Rodgers store on Liberty Street Extended, where they are usually molested. I have only heard of one group free-for-all this year."

"Yes," Reverend Berry concurred, I know the pattern. Those ruffians rarely attack man-for-man. It is usually a group assault on one lone boy or girl. It is the same story, many against one, whether it is a school fight in Virginia, a lynching in Mississippi, or Ku Klux Klan maneuver in Georgia."

"I suppose you have already heard about the colored girl who stabbed the white boy a few days ago?" inquired Principal Sykes.

"Yes," said Reverend Berry, "What about that?"

"Well, the girl came dashing into the school all out of breath and almost hysterical, having run a distance of three or four blocks. She showed me a bloodstained half of a four-inch pair of seamstress' shears. She admitted that she had stabbed the hand of a white boy, who had molested her, and that she had been carrying the instrument in her coat pocket all of the term to protect herself."

"The victim's father came to the school later with the boy's hand conspicuously bandaged and carried in a sling. The father demanded to see the girl. We produced her, and had the two explain what had happened. The girl told her story straight. The boy, however, had obviously gone out of his way to molest the girl and told a confused and inconsistent tale of woe. The father became disgusted with his son, and chastised him, then took him home."

A few weeks later Dick and I were pushed off the sidewalk, and our books were scattered on the ground. My prize geography with its colored maps was smeared in the mud. Since parents purchased school books in that day, I knew I could not expect to get another one. There was no fight, not because we were preacher's kids, because as a matter of fact, we had been known to tackle our weight with reputable fierceness when belligerently molested, but we didn't fight back when the opposition was a platoon of boys and men outnumbering us five-to-one whether they were black, white or "yellow." We did, however, report the incident to Father. We had not learned yet of the courage of our Dad except in a pulpit fight against the devil or in spanking us when we were wrong, or seemed to be, but we were about to witness the righteous indignation of the Reverend Berry reaching the boiling point and to see a man of God who never picked a fight but who during fifty-five years of life in the ministry never ran from one.

The next morning, bright and early Pop escorted us to school past the white gang in front of Rodgers' store without incident and went directly to the office of the Justice of the Peace.

"Mr. Cuthrell, your Honor, I am Reverend Berry, the minister of St. James Church."

"Yes, Parson, What do you need?"

"What I need, and all of the Negro citizens of this community need, is better protection by law enforcement officials. We are repeatedly plagued by the ganging of our school children by large white boys and men. Little girls have been slapped. Boys have had their noses bloodied while white men dared them to retaliate. They are forced to get off the sidewalk and walk in the street. I personally have protested this, and others have reported these instances of mob violence against school children.

"Yesterday my own children were pushed into the street, and their books scattered on the ground. Today I had to escort them to school."

"You may be taking your life in your own hands out there, Parson!"

"I have one life and one time to give it up. I know of no higher motive than to risk it while protecting my family."

Pop could always be depended upon to meet the challenge that interfered with the welfare of his family and the people of his church community. People came to admire that quality in him.

Reverend Berry never told his congregation the extent of his protest to the legal authorities about the school fights. However, in an Educational Day sermon with a large audience of children he took

185

his text from the passage of scripture which says "Wisdom is the principal thing, therefore, get wisdom." He said: "When the noise of battle gradually ceased at the close of day the Black troops of the Civil War laid down their arms. They gathered around camp fires, not only to rest from battle fatigue, but to turn their thoughts to 'book learnin'. For the first time in the weary lives of most of them they could then hope to read and write.

"My father often told me that he and his buddies of Battery B of the 2nd Volunteer Regiment of Colored Light artillery often carried their blue back spellers in their packs as they went into battle. As they sat around their camp fires they would "sound off" in rhythmic cadance the alphabet or the 'rithmetic tables. Then they would sing a song, perhaps of deliverance or of faith and hope or of joy. "Did my Lord Deliver Daniel" or "Joshua Fit the Battle of Jericho and The Walls Came Tumbling Down" would resound through the countryside, lifting the spirits of their white officers and filling their Confederate foe with amazement and consternation. Later in the war they would sing *Mine eyes have seen the glory of the coming of the Lord . . . His truth is marching on. Glory, glory, hallelujah . . . In the beauty of the lilies Christ was born across the sea . . . As He died to make men holy, let us die to make men free, While God is marching on.* Yes, our fathers fought a quarter a million of the enemy in the great war of the rebellion. Thousands of them did die to make men free and that you and your children and that I and my children might have the right to "Book Learnin'."

"I have been greatly disturbed because many of you young people have continuously had to fight your way to school and back to obtain that 'book learnin'. The offspring of some of those who could not keep you physically enslaved are determined to keep you ignorant and economically enslaved. Thank God, they cannot spiritually enslave you. That is, if you have been born of the Spirit of the Redeemer. You must know and believe that the death and suffering of Christ on the Cross established for all time, the freedom of the spirit and the human dignity and equality of all men. As long as the spirit is free, you can attain intellectual freedom. When the intellect is free, you can attain wisdom. The teachings of God say 'Wisdom is the principal thing, therefore get wisdom.' Christianity and ignorance are incongruous. The hope of the race lies in the attainment of Christian brotherhood, knowledge and understanding of people and things in the world about you. You must love your enemy as Jesus taught us. Ask God to forgive them, for they know not what they do, but never, no *never*, let them stop your determined search for knowledge and understanding of people and the world about you. We call this attainment "education". Our forefathers called it "book learnin'."

"Victory in the Civil War brought certain constitutional guarantees of Negroes' civil rights. Among them is the right to a common school education. The Fourteenth and Fifteenth Amendments were ratified fifty years ago, but it is still necessary to struggle for the educational opportunities which are rightfully yours. During the days of slavery, laws were passed making it a crime to teach a slave to read. These "laws" were inspired by the slave uprising such as Nat Turner's insurrection in South Hampton County, Virginia just twenty-five miles from here and the freedom break led by the African Methodist minister, Denmark Vesey, in South Carolina. It is thought that these laws against learning to read would doubtless prevent the spread of news of slave uprisings, but the so-called masters were not sufficiently acquainted with the news agency that were better than the newspapers and the wireless of that day. It was called *The Black Dispatch* the word-of-mouth messenger. And so the uprisings continued, and the yearning for learning increased.

Those of us who are your parents have watched these episodes year-after-year. We know, by now, that these attacks upon you are more than boyish pranks. They are instigated and promoted by adults. They are practical exercises in the philosophy of racial hate. The motive and the acts are a sin in the sight of God and a crime against humanity. These white children do not represent the better class of their race but they are being taught the doctrine of inherited racial superiority, rather than Christianity and brotherly love. They are taught to manifest their feeling of superiority by brutality. They will grow up to be the hooded Klansmen and self-appointed posse's that engage in man hunting their underprivileged neighbors with bloodhounds and to respect only the lynch law. Negro children will be inclined to grow up with bitterness in their hearts. But we must be bigger than they. We must turn the other cheek and continue your courageous trek to school. I have faith. You must have faith like our God-fearing fathers and mothers who sang, *There's a better day a comin', Hallelujah!*

187

"We must carry on the struggle for liberty and enlightenment in our day and time. You are not going to be stopped in elementary school by ruffians along the roadway to school nor the politicians who incite them. God being your Helper, you are aiming for normal and industrial training and education in our colleges. You must not stop now! You are the future skilled craftsmen, teachers, doctors and ministers of our race and country! If you will trust the Lord and fight for your rights, recognize and grasp the educational opportunities provided, you will grow and prosper and further the kingdom of God here on earth.

I have no fear for the future if you can learn and know the meaning of faith in yourselves. You need have no fears for your future education if you have courage and ambition and if you can learn to fight for your rights.

And so I say to you as you go forth like Christian soldiers marching off to war and see the cross of Jesus going on before. You must hold your heads high with boldness and courage as you walk to school, even out in the street, things will get better as we continue to fight. As you believe and know in your hearts that God has made of one blood all nations of men to dwell together on the face of the earth."

Following Pop's visit to the sheriff's office, the protest blossomed into a community effort. Tensions were somewhat relieved, but in all essentials, the problem still remained. His interests did not stop with personal problems and civil rights. Any type of movement that seemed to point toward progress of the oppressed people of his race could count on him to join up.

The Berkeley Building and Loan Association interested him. He joined himself and then championed the cause of the organization from his pulpit on many occasions.

One day after a Building and Loan Meeting, he struck up a conversation with his old friend, Atty. R. G. L. Paige, Jr., one of the officers of the Building and Loan. Atty. Paige was not only an astute lawyer but a dedicated person in the common struggle toward greater participation in the benefits of democracy and against second-class citizenship. His interests had begun back in his childhood days, for Atty. R. G. L. Paige, Sr., his father, had been a member of the Virginia Legislature during Reconstruction and assisted in the reorganization of the Virginia state government following the Civil War.

"Rev. Berry, how is the Waterford school problem coming along?"

"Well, I think there has been some improvement, but progress is very slow. I have been planning to seek your advice, "Judge," on trying to get my children transferred to the Abraham Lincoln School. This school was much closer to the Berry home. It was a new two-story brick plant with 16 classrooms and in many ways a better school than Waterford.

"I think it can be arranged, Rev. Berry. We'll think about it for a while, and if I can work out something, I'll give you a ring."

"Thank you, Judge. I'll expect to hear from you. Something just must be done, if possible, before the beginning of the next term."

A few days later "Judge" Paige called Rev. Berry and told him that he knew of a small, frame house on Eleventh Street, which was to be sold at auction. There were relatively few bidders, and he felt that he could buy it up for a very small amount.

"If you can close a deal on the purchase of a small piece of real estate, Reverend, anywhere North of the Belt Line railroad tracks," the "Judge" advised, "you will immediately become a Norfolk taxpayer, and your children will be eligible to attend the Abraham Lincoln School."

"That sounds fine, Judge, but what will we use for money."

"Well, don't worry too much about that, Reverend."

Judge Paige appeared at the auction and opened the bidding very low and finally closed the bid for $350, the final purchase price, for a little house which was really a tumble-down shack.

Judge Paige arranged a mortgage through the Berkeley Building and Loan Association which incidentally is still operating 50 years later at the Berkeley Federal Savings & Loan Co. Pop became a taxpayer, and when school opened in September of 1915, his school age children were duly enrolled by Principal John Riley Dungee, away from the firing line of racial tension. This was another step forward toward Pop's perpetual goal of a broader and better life for his offsprings.

During the second year at St. James, Dick had suffered from malaria; I had come down with the measles; and Elbert, who was an infant then, had been troubled with summer diarrhea, which Dr. C. Hamilton Francis feared would "go into typhoid." Those were rugged days, when children were expected to have childhood diseases. Most mothers, black and white, thought that they were inevitable, and the sooner the children had them and got over them, the better.

The memories of fighting a race-conscious mob in order to get to school were soon pushed into our subconscious mind. With a new school and activities for young people around the church, we were soon involved in a wholesome childhood development under the strict religious discipline of Rev. L. L. Berry, our father and aggressive religious leader of the St. James community.

There were now five Berry children separated in age by one and a half to two years. I, Leonidas was the eldest. Elbert had been born while we were still at Chapel Hill. To the North of the parsonage there was an enclosed grove of tall trees covering perhaps half an acre of ground. It was entirely surrounded by a heavy tall wooden fence and known as St. James' Park. It was the property, of course, of the church and had been set aside for picnics, church parties, and general recreation for the young people. In it were swings, slides, a horseshoe court, a barbecue pit and a clearing where children could play games. Here on a moonlight night a favorite affair was a colorful Japanese lantern party with music furnished by the Sunday School orchestra. We took full advantage of the swings in the shady park between well-organized household chores which were necessary in a big family operating on the tight budget of a minister's salary in those days.

St. James was a very interesting church founded just after the Civil War. It was 50 years old. Its members included schoolteachers, mail carriers, Navy yard workers, small businessmen, skilled and unskilled laborers, housewives and school children. The majority of 200-300 persons on its rolls were blood kin or related by marriage. It was best known around town for its excellent singers. The choir director, Hiram Simmons, taught piano and voice, trained quintettes and choir. He tuned and repaired pianos and composed several songs.

Professor Simmons as he was called, operated a hand printing press in a letter shop behind his home. He printed his own musical arrangements, handbills, announcements and tickets for church affairs. He was an excellent organist and widely known for his book of "Sacred Anthem" and his "Last Supper" Oratorio.

I remember the sound of church bells simultaneously ringing from all around the town—some far, some near, some muffled, some clear.

Here and there we heard a chime which played a familiar sacred tune which the other accompanying chimes nearby emphasized as if in counterpoint. It all created an atmosphere of serenity throughout the community.

At our house, however, it was a signal to get on a little faster with the dressing for Sunday School and the preparation for Sunday morning breakfast and family worship at the table, a ritual which was never omitted in Reverend Berry's household. As a matter of fact, preparation for the Sabbath had really begun on Saturday with special house cleaning and the performance of all routine daily tasks so that only the chores of absolute necessity would have to be carried out on Sunday.

Meanwhile, father had spent Saturday afternoon in the quietude of his study preparing his sermon, or to use his own words "Getting myself together." This was a familiar phrase which meant to us come anything short of fire or high water, he was not to be disturbed. The last things for us at night were likely to be polishing five or six pairs of shoes, a bath in a zinc tub, water having been drawn from a cold water faucet and heated on a coal stove. Alternately we made glances at the Sunday School lesson, the funnies, (Mutt and Jeff, The Katzenjammer Kids, Bringing Up Father, and Happy Hoolligan).

Mother was the first to rise on Sunday mornings as on other mornings. Hers was the responsibility of completing Sunday dinner, which had already been started the night before, with the setting of rolls to rise. Breakfast for eight had to be prepared before Lula went off to Hampton Institute. Then there were only seven but Lula's departure relieved mother of a strong right arm. Lula was mother's youngest sister who was now a member of the Berry family. Usually it was a matter of all hands on deck to make up beds, set the dining room table and get dressed. After all, four boys had individual four-in-hand knots to tie; in winter, four pairs of high shoes to lace, four pairs of black ribbed stocking to pull up to the knee while eight legs of shrunken white union suits were pushed down to the ankles. If we were lucky, there were unbroken straps to anchor them underfoot and eight elastic garters to hold stockings above the knees. We could then don our smart suits in time to answer the first call to breakfast.

We all assembled together, father, dressed in ministerial attire with his Bible in hand, sat at the head of the table, and Mother, the only one not dressed for church, sat at the opposite end. Then followed Scripture reading, prayer and breakfast, and we were off to Sunday School at nine-fifteen. By eleven o'clock, Mother had joined us at church for the adult services.

Father, in dramatic and reverent tones announced the hymn, "Praise God From whom all blessings flow" and conducted the customary Methodist morning Prayer.

Before the morning church service began, the Berry children had joined many others in Sunday School. There were always mischievous boys that found occasions to get their minds off the Bible lessons.

All the sheep in the Berry family were black, but one of us came powerfully near being the "*white* sheep of the family" in spite of the very well laid plans of Pop and Mom to the contrary. Dick for many years now has been an Administrative Officer as a civilian in the U. S. Department of Defense. It is now agreed that in the interests of historical fact it should now be truthfully admitted that Dick's ambitions for the business world were far in advance of his years. Also, at an early age he frowned on "free schools," that is public ones, being much more strongly attracted to private boarding schools, if one, he reasoned, just had to be "schooled" in order to succeed in life.

This aberrant philosophy functioning at such an early age caused Pop much concern and eventually some consternation. The family Bible records that Dick's ripple in the otherwise rigidly disciplined and stable lives of the Berry quartet of boys came somewhere near his fourteenth birthday. Jim Charity, later an affluent Harlem businessman and proprietor of the Swank Sunset Barber Shop on Seventh Avenue, told it like this:

"We were about thirteen. I was a bootblack and an apprentice barber at Welch's Barber Shop on Liberty Street. I had to quit school to help the family. One day when Dick, my former classmate and buddy was supposed to be in school, he came by the shop.

"Jim," he said, "You know I've been doing some thinking: Why should a man have to go to school all his life to succeed? Abraham Lincoln didn't do it, and I'll betcha Mr. Welch didn't fool around a lot of years in school. And he owns this shop, ain't that right? Man, you know what? We've always been buddies; we could hide away in a ship to Baltimore. We could both get jobs shining shoes and learn the barber trade and see some of the world at the same time. It wouldn't be long before we could have our own shop and then a chain of shops like Woolworth's."

Jim says he fell for Dick's scheme hook, line, and sinker. Dick maintains that it was Jim's idea. But at any rate, some time later Pop fished both of them off the Baltimore Pier hiding behind crates of freight which they had been watching the stevedores load into the ship's hull all afternoon. It seems that one of the stevedores was a member of St. James Church and had spotted them with small bundles of clothing under their arms trying to pick their chance to sneak aboard ship. So that was that.

This became a very difficult period for Pop, for he was having to learn for the first time that while the razor strap ranked high as the proper instrument of discipline of the day it was not always an unfailing persuader in the field of education for boys.

Dick finally learned the hard way a trial at persuasion by counseling—thanks to Mom's prayers and tacit suggestions.

He finally agreed and seemed enthusiastic at the suggestion of going off to Boarding School at Thyne Institute, Chase City, Virginia. Reverend Jones of Suffolk had a boy enrolled there, and the adventure seemed inviting. Pop would now have to figure out how to get the tuition and board with Lula already at Hampton Institute. We now know that Pop made his first acquaintance with the loan shark's about this time.

So Dick came home at Christmastime sporting a beaver hat, a crease in his knickers, and his hair neatly combed and brushed with pomade. He already had a budding interest in the track team for the spring, and all-in-all this matter of education of questionable necessity to him was being moved along.

Several years and three boarding schools later, Dick finished high school at Kittrell, North Carolina, by way of Hampton Institute with academic diploma and athletic letter for service as a broken field halfback. By now coeducational boarding school had become a way of life with Dick. So he went on to receive the baccalaureate degree in business at Wilberforce University, having stayed out only one year to help finance Lew's graduation during the economic Depression of the early 30's.

Presiding Elder Years
Norfolk
(1917–21)

MY mother's voice called, "Leonidas, why don't you stop nodding over that Latin and get up and go to bed? Early in the morning while you are wide awake and rested you can learn much—that's the way I did it in my school days." "OK Mom, I am taking Caesar across the Rubicon. I know Professor will call on me. I have just a little more tonight"—this type of dialogue would occur every week or two. Finally after a few good nods with study in-between, I would go to bed. One evening, while I was nodding, probably over geometry, I felt a light backhand slap against my right cheek. "It's 12 o'clock Leonidas, everybody else is asleep, you've got to put out that light and go to bed."

Mom never realized the joy of slouching down in a comfortable chair and nodding. I always learned something in between and getting up very early in the morning, getting an important chore done before launching out on the days program was always a difficult task.

Years later after medical school I took unto myself a bride. After about three weeks on the marital voyage, around about 11 p.m. one night, I heard a sweet feminine voice saying, "Leonidas, why do you nod like that, why don't you go to bed and get a good nights rest." A few weeks later the episode was repeated. At this point, I sat up in my chair, silently for a few seconds while remembering the old legend that a young man unwittingly looks for his mother's personality in choosing a wife. Then in a crisp firm voice, I said "Listen Honey, one of the main reasons that I grew up to become a man was to be able to sit up and nod unmolested. This privilege you may not be able to take from me, so please try to get used to it."

There was no period in my life, more zestful, more romantic than my teen years. High School was an exciting experience of learning and curiosity about every facet of life past, present and future. These years happened to be synonomous with World War I. My home town of Norfolk, Virginia bristled with war activities. It was one of the largest Naval Training Centers. It was a port of embarkation for soldiers and the shipment of war material for the European theater of war. In addition, nearby army camps made Norfolk a great hub of wartime excitement.

I sold the afternoon Norfolk *Ledger Dispatch*, read news of every fighting front from the Hindenberg Line to the Soissons Sector, Chauteau-Thierry, and the battles at sea. I went to the waterfront to see the German battleship, *Prince Eitel Frederick* captured and interned near the Norfolk port. The streets of Norfolk were crowded day and night with soldiers and sailors wearing the uniforms of all the American Allies; France, and the British Commonwealth from Canada to New Zealand and the British Isles.

The American Contingencies had a unique interest for me. Before the war when I was a preteen, I had noticed that I never saw a Negro sailor wearing a commissioned officer's uniform, or even the boxed shaped blue coat of the petty officer. Ninety-nine percent of Negro sailors wore bell bottom trousers and a middy blouse. Even when a black sailor's hair was turning gray and his service hash marks extended from the chevron encircled half moon (meaning 'mess' department) to the dog tag on his wrist, he was still wearing that middy blouse.

I learned to recognize departmental insignia on the sleeves of the sailors uniform. Crossed feathers meant yeoman, crossed anchors, machinists, crossed cannon barrels, gunners mates, etc. One day I saw a Negro sailor dressed in a chief petty officer's 'garb' with crossed anchors within his chevron and service stripes to his wrist all in gold braids, meaning good conduct. I followed him for two blocks just to look at his insignia. At first, I thought he had to be a Philippino, but a closer look left no doubt; he was a gray-haired Negro chief machinist in the U.S. Navy. This one Black man among many thousands had somehow broken all precedents and taken many long years to achieve it.

I observed thousands of Black soldiers who passed through Norfolk during the war years. I soon learned that the Black Buffalo insignia on the khaki uniforms of some of them indicated the Black 92nd Division of Infantrymen. Members of this Unit had seen action in the Spanish-American war and Mexican border conflicts. They were enroute to Europe where they were attached to French army units to fight the Germans. These units were the only Black soldiers allowed to go into battle alongside white American fighting men. There were other Black soldiers in stevedore and service units whose commissioned officers were all white. I remembered the thrill of seeing Black commissioned officers wearing Lieutenant and Captain's shoulder bars as commanders of the Black Buffalo infantrymen, some returning from France with decorations for bravery.

These experiences buoyed my spirits as a young boy and filled my heart with pride. This was good as a character builder for me because I was studying the history of great achievers in America and Europe, even back to ancient times. My official text book taught me that there were no Black achievers worthy of history. This was difficult for me to accept. The Berry children were able to reject the racist attitude of public school historians because of the teachings of Black history by our parents and Negro orators who visited our churches and told with great emotion of the valiant Black soldiers in all America's wars.

Visiting ministers and their wives turned our dinner table into a virtual forum platform, as they analyzed war strategies, war politics, predictable war aftermaths and Black heroes. The essence of such discussions were woven into gospel sermons on Sunday mornings. I was most impressed by the stories of Colonel Charles Young, the second and most celebrated Negro graduate of West Point. He survived ostracism and physical harassment in the academy, fought valiantly with cavalry in Spanish American and Mexican border encounters, with General Funston and Pershing. There was much Black clamor to assign him to the command of the Black Buffalo Div., as Brigadier General, but instead he was retired for "physical disability" one day before a large number of white colonels, many of them with lower military records than Young's, were promoted to Brigadier General. He protested courageously but unsuccessfully by riding horse back nearly 1,000 miles from his home at Wilberforce, Ohio to the war department in Washington. During the war, I had one chance to see Colonel Young when he appeared in a lecture at St. John's Church, Norfolk. I was deeply disappointed when he appeared in civilian clothes. I left before the end of the lecture.

197

While horse cavalrymen saw little or no actual service in World War I, I recall the neatly fitting khaki riding breeches and leather boots or puttes and the campaign hats with leather chin straps worn by the Black 9th and 10th cavalrymen. These soldiers evoked a special thrill because I had heard Black orators describe with great emotion how the tenth cavalry had rescued Teddy Roosevelt's "lily white" "Rough Riders" from the Spanish at San Juan Hill during the Spanish-American War.

One of the most talked about Black soldier units to pass through the Norfolk area was the 370th Infantry/93rd Division, converted from the 8th Infantry Chicago, Illinois National Guard. This was the only Black fighting unit which went to France with a complete complement of commissioned officers from second lieutenant to colonel.

During the war years Pop was Presiding Elder of the Portsmouth district of the A.M.E. Church. He visited each of his churches quarterly. Some of these churches figuratively required most of the quarter to reach, partly by a slow railroad train, T-Model Ford, horse and buggy or horse and wagon. He visited and preached at Emanuel Portsmouth, visited other pastorates at Suffolk, Great Bridge, other rural churches and Smithfield. The latter, famous for its special brand of Virginia hams. Brother Walter Shivers was one of Pop's very good friends. He was one of the largest processors of Smithfield hams and raised the special bred, peanut fed razor back hogs which produced the hams. From the rural districts "Pop" brought parcels of vegetables, fruits, Virginia yams, etc. for his large family. Brother Shivers furnished Pop with delicious smoked Smithfield hams. I remember that Brother Shivers had seven beautiful daughters trying to get a son as heir to his business. One of the younger daughters' had my heart going "pitta patta" in my senior year in high school. A beautiful, lovely older Shivers' daughter was one of my teachers in grammar school. One of the reasons I sold newspapers, was to buy apples for her.

As Presiding Elder, Pop helped to arrange a parade by the 370th Infantry through the main streets of Portsmouth, Virginia, shortly before embarkation from Newport News, Virginia to the fighting front in France. Flowers were thrown on the streets with pitch forks for the Black soldiers to walk on. They were loudly applauded and cheered by black and white citizens as they marched with military precision in full battle dress through the main streets of the town.

The rise of joyful emotion and pride in the Berry family and others of that day were often dampened by news from France that Black soldiers were often refused the purchase of cigarettes and other courtesies at white American army canteens. There was evidence of American intelligence officers and others spreading propaganda among white French citizens against extending social equality to Black soldiers. To a great extent the propaganda backfired as many hundreds of Black soldiers bouvacked in the homes of French families during the war. Some Black soldiers married French girls but were given the options of remaining in France with no war records or benefits or returning to the states without their wives.

Dr. Robert R. Moton, President of Tuskegee Institute in Alabama was sent by the war department to France for the purpose of lecturing to thousands of Black troops advising them not to seek social equality which they had not had in America but to fight hard, to hold high the brave tradition of America and that they would enjoy all the blessings after helping to make the world safe for democracy and returning home. Dr. Moton was thoroughly repudiated by Black soldiers and was very ineffective because of the treatment of equality by the French people and the news of increased lynchings and race riots in many cities of America.

This kind of news was very depressing for me, but it never daunted my determination to attain high personal goals in spite of racial obstacle. I sang and enjoyed war songs, listened to phonograph recordings like everybody else. I remember them now: "The Rose of No Man's Land," "The Yanks Are Coming," "Over There," etc. White parade bands played "Stars and Stripes Forever;" Black bands "Bringing Up the Rear" turned the towns upside down with "Alexander's Rag Time Band" and "Dark Town Strutters Ball."

Pop was much more serious and concerned about the ultimate fate of Black people, than with many other aspects of the war. The continuing lynchings and torture of Negroes even as they returned from fighting fronts decorated for bravery, stirred resentment and anger. For Pop, the way was dark and more unpredictable than ever before in history. He preached fervently to his congregation about the meaning of faith in God. I remember that at the end of one sermon, he led a fervent hymn that expressed the fears and faltering hopes of our people for the fruits of democracy in America. Pop and his congregation sang "Guide

Us Oh Thou Great Jehovah, Pilgrims through this barren land, We are weak but Thou art mighty; hold us with thy powerful hand."

As a minister's son, I joined in singing the meaningful words of the beautiful old hymn. But as a teenager my mind turned quickly to more mundane things. I quit selling the afternoon paper for an after school job of shining white sailors shoes in Patsi's Italian Barber Shop near the entrance to St. Helena's Naval Training Station. This wasn't bad; I got tips and brushed my hair with "Wild Root" Tonic for school each day. Later, I delivered packages from Nusbaum's Art and Gift Shop on Granby Street after school. One day as I walked into the lobby of the elegant Monticello Hotel, a loud voice yelled "take yo hat off boy!" During one summer I worked at Cuthrell's box factory for sixty cents per ten hour day.

As I appear with my old school clothes I met a youngster about my age wearing overalls. He looked me over and said, "You'se a school boy ain't yer." I admitted that I was. "Well," he said, "you stick wid me and I'll show you how to use yo head and save yo behind." I wasn't sure of his meaning at first but I had an idea. He explained how to lift leg instead of with hands only. He explained how to work fast then sit down for a rest. One day while on our unofficial rest period up came the boss. He looked at me and said "What you doing?" I answered, "Nothing right now." Then he asked my teaching buddy, "What you doin'." My friend pointed at me and answered, "I am helpin' him."

In the summer of 1918 when I was sixteen years old I had an insatiable desire to work to make some of that good war time money. I caught the Berkley to Portsmouth Ferry and then a street car arriving at the Navy Yard in less than an hours time. For days I had seen screaming want ads in the Norfolk *Virginian Pilot* morning newspaper and *Ledger Dispatch* afternoon papers. Wanted! $5.50 per day, Ship Caulkers, Carpenters, Cement Workers, Shipping Clerks, Colored Men, Laborers, lowest pay $5.50 per 10 hour day. I had replaced my short pants for an old pair of Pop's long pants. In I walked following signs that said Employment Office carrying all of my 120 lbs. on a 5'7" frame. I picked up a federal government job application for laborer which, even then, was a long complicated document. "Answer the following in legible handwriting" Race, Religion, Age, Height, Wt., Marital Status, Place of Birth, Naturalized, Unnaturalized, Number of children, etc.

After a long wait of several hours it was lunch time. I am hungry. I have no extra money. It was a long distance to a Greek restaurant in the colored neighborhood so I bought some *Tootsie Rolls* and drank some water from my hands taken from the faucet in the Colored Men's restroom. I waited around until 2:00 p.m., my number was finally called.

"Come over here, boy!" "Did you ever have measles," answer "No sir," "Whooping Cough," "No sir." Is there any tuberculosis in your family?" "No sir," "Is sixteen years your right age?" "Yessir." "When did you have yo las dose o' clap?" "Never sir." "Alright shoulder that 100 lb. sack er sand." I got it ⅔ of the way up and dropped it. "Is that the best you can do?" "You want to try it again." "Yessir." My score was the same. "Alright step on the scales, now pick up a bottle and write your name on the label go in the toilet and leave your specimen of urine on the bench."

Around about 4:00 p.m. my number was called again. "OK, boy, you hired—here's your slip. Report to work at the Carroll Electric Company shack at Dry Dock #5. Report to work Monday morning 6:45 ready to go to work at 7:00." I went home happy and joyfully reporting the good news to the family.

I found I could take a short cut across a narrow point in the eastern branch of the Elizabeth River. Workmen rowed across in rowboats for $1.00 a week. I reported to work on time and was given a wheel barrel to haul sand and gravel to the cement mixer. Later I was a carpenter's helper for six weeks of the summer season. In those days the Berry's managed two to three weeks to go with Mom for summer time rest and family reunions at Woodsdale.

Later I worked up to delivery boy and clerk at the "colored" Progressive Drug Store on Liberty Street. Between those chores, I helped as assistant "soda jerker" and alternated with janitorial arts. I had the inside track for once—Pop was a member of the corporation contributing the church congregation in lieu of much hard cash. The job was educational and it motivated my ambitions which were probably already out of proportion to reasonable probability in a white world.

Upstairs over the drug store there were offices of corporation owners, G. Hamilton Francis, M.D., Dr. Mosley, the Dentist and Attorney R. G. L. Paige, Jr. The attorney's father had been a Virginia state legislator during Reconstruction. Between hours, they would come down the back stairs and engage in "bull sessions;" "the strategy of the war," "the flu epidemic," "Black theatricals," Bert Williams and Charles Gilpin on Broadway, Abbie Mitchell and Andrew Bishop with the Black Lafayette Players. They talked of their professors at Howard University. Dr. Francis, who trained at MeHarry held us spell bound time-and-again about his professor of surgery, Dr. Daniel Hale Williams, who performed the first successful human heart operation, commuting from Provident and St. Luke's Hospitals in Chicago to MeHarry in Nashville.

I could not have known that it was in my destiny to one day meet Dr. Dan Williams in his declining years, and to become chairman of a department at the Provident Hospital which he founded. Neither could I have dreamed that destiny would have me go to National Guard Camp twelve years after the war as a first lieutenant army medical reserve with some of the veterans whom I had seen in their triumphant march in the streets of Portsmouth. I met Captain Jimmy Smith who was wearing his "Croix de Guerre" the highest French decoration for bravery. He and his entire Company "B" of several hundred officers and men were decorated in battle at the same time with the "Croix de Guerre" for their valiant stand in the bitter Meuse-Argonne Forest in France. When I revealed that as a young boy I had seen them on the march near their port of embarkation, they flooded me with such expressions as "Doc, you didn't see nothin in Norfolk. You should've seen us shootin' up them krauts, after we got in a fightin' mood in the French trenches." Their tales were punctuated by demonstration of battle scars, citation ribbons, a captured German pistol and other relics. At officers' mess, these veterans continued with unbelievable tales between "shots" of bourbon.

Returning to my teenage stories in Norfolk, I would cross town to Booker T. Washington High with prospective college days and medical school training of the highest order tingling in my head, always with the encouragement of Mom and Pop. I dreamed of attending medical school at the University of Virginia at Charlottesville; my friends smiled at my naivete and wondered at times about my sanity. Neither they nor I could have known that there was in my destiny medical training at Rush Medical College of the University of Chicago. It was not until I was enrolled there did I realize that in the world of medical achievements and stature, the University of Virginia was dwarfed by comparison with the medical school that would become my alma mater.

Yet, as a teenager in Norfolk, I was a long way from where the destiny of the Berry family would carry me. Reminiscing back to those days I must have learned a great deal of substance in my "separate-but-equal" high school. Some of my teachers compared favorably with the best of those in big universities in later years. The classes were smaller and the teachers were dedicated. Bertha and Fannie Jones were excellent teachers. Another very good one was Professor Curtis, always dead serious and "straight laced." Occasionally, he would gather a group of boys on Friday afternoon for lectures on good manners and morals. One of his preachments was quote: "Learn to look at the young lady from her head down rather than from feet up." Those were the days of course of short skirts. Years later on a visit back to Norfolk, I asked "How and where is Professor Curtis?" The answer was "He's retired now, and just a little flighty. He still lives near the school, sits on his front porch in his rocking chair and when the school girls pass, he whistles."

I participated in debating and with choral groups. I did not always win in debating nearby high schools, but we did receive some accolades for singing, which I learned while hand pumping the pipe organ in the back of the choir at St. James. I recall that our high school chorus gave a command performance of Negro spirituals for the white faculty and students at Maury High School. The memory is still fresh in my mind of the smiling enthusiastic applause of the white faculty and comments to our director and chaperones quote, "Aren't their voices wonderful and so natural—just think, we have to study to learn how to sing."

As America entered the war I was 14 going on 15, Dick was 13, Gladys was 11 and Lew, Jr. and Elbert were preteens. Lula, previously mentioned as Mom's youngest sister, being reared as a member of our family, was a student in home economics at Hampton Institute. Need I say, Mom's hands were full as a mother and housewife. However, she found time to be active with the missionary society and other chores at St. James, where all the family worshiped and Pop had pastored just before becoming Presiding Elder.

One of Mom's roles in holding the family together was "saving up" whippings for the boys, which Pop would administer upon returning from his long weekends quarterly meetings and sermons at various churches on his district. One of his methods was to have two of us kneel side by side with arms folded and heads bowed, resting on a bed as if in the act of prayer. With razor strap in hand he administered his strokes alternately to each buttocks, preaching a sermonette between strokes. I believe he would read from Mom's written list, each alleged crime allowing a few seconds for repentence just before and just after each lick. Whether the plea was guilty or not guilty, apparently made no difference in the rhythmic frequency of the application. If one "criminal" would hear and not feel an impact, the anticipation of knowing he was next was worse than the stroke. Mom was usually in the next room or somewhere out of hearing range probably with tear dimmed eyes, feeling like a young prosecuting attorney listening to the sentence of a "runaway child" whose prosecution he had just won.

Many years later, as I walked arm-and-arm with Mom across the University of Chicago campus, wearing my medical school graduation cap and gown, we reminisced about my childhood. I said "Mom, you may not believe this, but I never had a 'paddling' that did me any good. It only made me mad." I looked at her out of the corner of my eye and found her with a smile looking like the cat who had just swallowed the canary as she replied, "Well, Leonidas, you didn't have many spankings." I then said to her, "That ain't the way I remember it."

With all the activity in the Berry household during the war years, Mom and the children always managed summer vacation days at the old farm in Woodsdale, North Carolina and/or visiting our cousins in the home of Pop's oldest brother, John Augustus, Jr. in Hampton. "Uncle Gus" as we called him had a little neighborhood general store and doubled as an iceman. Ice delivery occurred usually early in the morning while someone else would mind the store.

During the Hampton visits, I was sometimes happily pressed into service by my cousin John III to help deliver parcels of ice, using ice tongs. We found that pulling the ice on the steel railing of a freight train right-of-way was a fast and thrilling experience. By the time the ice was delivered the customer had only about one half of the ice she paid for. Between chores of helping Uncle Gus, the older boys visited Buckroe Beach for surf bathing and playing in the sand by street car with open sides instead of windows. This was okay with our parents but one day John and I slipped away from the waters edge at Hampton Roads where there was no beach in North Hampton. John convinced me that a certain delapidated rowboat, tied to a stave had belonged to Grandpa John Berry, who had died several years before. We climbed into the boat and bailed out the small amount of water it contained with a leaky rusty bucket. We than paddled off shore for about twenty yards until the boat was filling with water faster than we could bail it out with out leaky bucket.

Finally, the boat sank in what must have been six or eight feet of water. I could not swim at all. John could swim a little bit, but he was no expert. I managed to scrabble toward land with an occasional push or pull from John. At long last, I could feel the bottom with the water line no higher than my chin. I remember strangling and swallowing dirty salty water. We finally reached shore, hid behind some nearby box cars, disrobed completely, wrung out our clothes and hung them up and waited until they were nearly dry in the hot summer sun. After what appeared to have been several hours, we returned home and met two mothers, greatly disturbed and wondering where we had been so long. John explained that we went over to the "dike," got lost and were caught in a terrible rain storm. At any rate John and I were grounded for the next few days and for recreation had to settle for racing with my brother Dick and John's brother Tom down the block to the corner gas light at sunset.

During alternate summers my brothers and I had just as much fun or more down on Grandpa Tobe Harris' old tobacco farm in Woodsdale, North Carolina. There, we could run around barefooted and help with all the farm activities. This included minding the cows, helping to harvest tobacco and occasionally spending the night sleeping in a tobacco curing barn, monitoring the fires with the farmers. Our family always managed two or three weeks vacation even when the older boys were working in the early weeks of the summer. These were times for happy reunions of the large interrelated families on Mother Berry's side. These included the Marrises, Jordans, Drumwrights, etc. These reunions were not stopped by the great battles in Europe involving principal nations of the world.

In our young adult years, Pop became sort of a "brother" unleashing all of his wit and humor with his sons and daughters. Dick was especially vulnerable as a child, because he rejected school. He was sent to three boarding schools before he finally finished high school at Kittrell.

At that period, his point of view began to change, probably finessed by his interest in athletics. He began to make up for lost time, finishing college with a bachelor's degree in business administration. He had a splendid career as an administrative officer for the U.S. Dept. of Defense and with his school teacher wife Maryland Hall (Berry), reared a lovely family.

The war was still on but moving swiftly toward the armistice in the fall of 1919. People at home were digging in for a long winter of shortages and high prices. During the winter before, the entire country, even the southland had experienced heavy snow storms and one of the coldest winters in recorded weather history. Hampton Roads the Elizabeth and James Rivers in the Norfolk area were filled with ice, broken into huge hunks by steel hull ships. Wooden bottom boats had to be tied up in docks. Pop had laid in the family food staples from his rural church connections during the summer. We were anticipating a possible repetition of the winter before. A full barrel of Virginia yams was stored snuggly in the closet under the stairs to the second floor at the Berry house on Berkley Ave. Near the potato barrel, there was a half filled barrel of flour. Outside in an abbreviated cellar there were a couple of kegs of salted mackerel and other processed fish.

All was quiet in the Berry household, with children in school and Pop traveling his district when tragedy struck, bringing turmoil and racial confrontation. Mom was up and around, but not feeling well. Doctor Francis had attended her two or three times in the past several weeks. Early on a Friday morning, Pop had boarded a Norfolk and Western local train at the Union Station, in route to a rural church several miles beyond the little town of Ivor. All the children had left for school and Mom was all alone. She was reclining on a couch upstairs resting from the morning "hustle and bustle," when the doorbell rang. Down the steps she walked, slowly opened the door and there stood a young white boy dressed in an olive green uniform with his bicycle leaning against the front gate. It was a Western Union delivery boy with a telegram. Mom could not get it open fast enough, because there were two stars stamped on the envelope. The familiar half sheet was unfolded; the place of origin of the telegram was Hampton. The message was addressed to Rev. L. L. Berry and read: "Mother is dead. Contact your brother Gus at once."

Mom immediately realized that Pop would be met at Ivor and then would be transported several miles back into the country. It would then be next to impossible to contact him for three days when he would return home on Monday. She looked at the clock and realized that Pop's train would be arriving at Ivor in about one and half hours. She began to pray and said to herself, I must stop that train before it reaches Ivor. The thought came her to call the passenger agent. She went to the telephone, mounted on the wall in the front hallway and contacted the agent's office. "Whose calling please," said a woman's voice on the other end. "I'm Mrs. Berry, wife of Rev. L. L. Berry. I would like to speak to the agent." The agent came to the phone. "What can I do for you Madam," said he. Mom excitedly explained her problem. She wanted the message of the death of her husband's mother delivered to him on that Richmond bound train before it reached Ivor. The agent said, "The time is short Madam, but I think maybe I can reach him. Do you happen to know what car he is riding in?" "Yes, I do." "He is a colored minister and he is riding in the Jim Crow car." "Ah—what is your first name?" My name is Mrs. Berry. "Well 'aintie' we do have communication for railroad business, but otherwise it would have to be something very important." "Yes," said Mom, "He is only a law abiding citizen, paying his fare on your train, who needs to be informed of the death of his mother. This may not be of special importance to you because he is a Negro, but if he were a Negro accused of a crime, this would be of very special importance and you would find a way to reach him." The end of the story is that Pop was reached thru the conductor on the train who informed him of the passing of his mother. Pop got off the train at Ivor and returned to Norfolk the same day.

The passing of Nancy Jenifer Berry, my beloved grandmother, marked the end of an era. She was the last of the Berry-Jenifers who lived during the days of slavery. As a teenager with freedom on her horizon, she dreamed of being a wife and mother in a loving family. This dream became a reality. She reared a son who became a religious community leader, this was the answer to her most fervent prayers. She lived out her destiny and made her honorable contribution to life. She lived to witness the commitment of a teenage grandson to be that educated leader in medicine that here Uncle "Doc" Henry, the medicine man, could not achieve.

Leonidas to
Become a Doctor

THE spring of 1920 was a time for welcoming in a new decade of the 20th Century and time for the relaxation of national tensions. A great war has been won and the country was "back to normalcy" and experiencing an economic recession. The Berry family had been too concerned with child rearing and the launching off to college of their first born of five children to be concerned with such matters which were largely out of their hands anyhow. Leonidas must have his chance at life.

I was president of my class at Norfolk's Booker T. Washington High and thinking hard about college and medical school. I knew that my father was a successful pastor and preacher of renown, but that gave him little rating in the financial world.

"If I am going to be an outstanding doctor, I've got to get the best education," I told my history teacher, Lillie Reid.

"Yes, Leonidas, I agree," the understanding teacher said. "There are good doctors around town, but you must be better than any of them because you are of a younger generation and you want better opportunities."

In high school, except for mathematics I was mostly involved with literary classes primarily because my high school had few science courses. I knew all about Ralph Waldo Emerson's essays, his "Hitch your wagon to a star," and "the better mouse-trap," and I took them seriously, but my science background was separate and unequal. The best colleges and medical schools had to be in the North, I reasoned. Certainly, the better ones in the South were not available to me.

In the summer of 1919, Dr. George Russell, dental surgeon of Boston, visited my family. The family attended Papa's church. Learning of my interest in medicine, Dr. Russell offered me encouragement. He was a graduate of Boston University and spoke glowingly of the academic excellence and stature of "B. U." I knew that scanty family finances and the problem of my separate but unequal high school education were formidable obstacles to college and medical school in Boston. The Russell home was purposely subdued on the outside but elegant and impressive on the interior. My sharp eyes had seen the Russell home. There I caught my first glimpse of the famous seven-foot shelf of Harvard classics edged in gold leaf. I was fascinated by the mahogany plate railing around the upper walls of the dining room and the elegant multi-patterned china dinner plates resting there. Oriental rugs adorned the floors. A hugh colorful bell-shaped chandelier hung over the heavy mahogany dining room table. The chandelier consisted of glass figurines of fruits held in place by leaded border strippings. When the electric light was turned on by pushing a loud sounding button on the wall, the chandelier presented a beautifully colored translucency. All of this produced for me a fleeting dream of post-medical school affluence too distant to-be-but briefly entertained. The study of medicine at Boston University was one of my earliest impossible dreams. It hung in the back of my consciousness, but was never within the realm of immediate retrieval.

In May, 1920, just 30 days from my high school graduation, my Dad led the Virginia delegation to the A.M.E. quadrennial general conference in St. Louis. There, he surprisingly ran into Prof. C. H. Johnson of Wilberforce (Ohio) University. Affectionately known (behind his back) as "Pussyfoot, the Second." Professor Johnson, a graduate of Chicago's Art Institute, taught art and had been the teacher of both Lew and Beulah, at Kittrell at the turn of the century 23 years before.

"I have just the solution to your son's problem, Berry. Send him to Wilberforce, our fine A.M.E. school," Prof. Johnson said. "Wilberforce has a combination premedical program with Ohio State University. After two or three years at Wilberforce, he can enter Ohio State University to study medicine, taking his B.S. degree from Wilberforce and his M.D. from Ohio State."

The lower tuition and campus expenses at Wilberforce would be the springboard to launch me into the ocean of my ultimate dreams. Pop returned from the general conference bringing the good news, with exciting approval at home.

But there was much for me to do before the fall opening at Wilberforce. I was class president, member of the debating team, supervisor on Class Day exercises and editor of the class book. There were final exams, and other incidentals like my after-school job, violin lessons, choir practice, and occasional vocal solo at school or church, and visits to my girlfriend on Sunday afternoons. I helped out with household chores, too. Mama saw to that.

Dear Old Wilberforce
(1920–24)

I went off to Wilberforce when I knew that University of Virginia and Boston University were out of the question. Besides, Professor "Pussy Foot" Johnson who taught "Mom" and "Pop" Art at Kittrell, had convinced Pop that Wilberforce and Ohio State University had a joint curriculum for pre-med and medical students. At the appropriate time I boarded the Norfolk and Western crack train "The Cannonball," for the 1,000 mile trip to Columbus, Ohio then to Xenia and Wilberforce. The scenery was beautiful through the western parts of Virginia, portions of the Shenandoah Valley, the Apple Blossom country, around Roanoke and then into the hills of West Virginia.

I was not riding a sleeper, but I curled up on the seat of the day coach, covered with my overcoat. At daybreak, I was in beautiful Ohio and seeing the evidence through windows in the early morning light. I began to sing a song, which was popular at that time, "Beautiful Ohio."

Reuben Tynes, another A. M. E. preacher's son rode with me, also enroute to becoming a freshman at Wilberforce. We transfer to a Pennsylvania R. R. train at Columbus for the 50 mile trip southward to Xenia. As we got off the train, we saw other students, who had been on other coaches coming from the east not previously recognized by us. There were cabs waiting marked "to Wilberforce," which was 3 miles away. While we checked our baggage, another Pennsylvania train loaded with students arrived from Cincinnati going northward. At the Xenia station I had my first look at beautiful co-eds and intelligent looking young men who were upper class students returning to a Black college.

I happen to get into a cab with other students, driven by Guy Leach. Soon we arrived on the campus of the much heralded Wilberforce. Enroute I had met Tommy Mitchell, from Philadelphia. We exchanged pleasantries. I learned that he hoped to make the football squad. He smiled when I said I had the same ambition at 136 pounds. He didn't know how many other ambitions I had or he would have cackled. I knew a few upper classmen but there was a hometown sophomore, whom I felt would show me around fast. I soon located this friend who had begun high school one year ahead of me in Norfolk. "Well Claude," said I, "Your sister Maxine told me to look you up on arrival and give you her love." I knew I would find you so I didn't bother to write. "Glad you came to Wilberforce Leonidas, I am sure you will like it. You didn't really need to write. In fact I would not have received it, I just arrived yesterday from Cedar Point, Ohio where I had a summer job at a resort hotel." "Have you been assigned a room?" "Yes, but only temporarily in Shorter Hall." "How's Norfolk, you know, I haven't been there for 2 years to see my folks. I attended the academy here and I've worked hotels every summer in these parts." "Yes I have heard." "You are a sophomore, now aren't you?" "Yes, that's right, following the pre-med route and like the rest of the men in my class I've sworn to be rough on freshies." As we both laughed, I said "Gee, I've got to find out quick who's organizing the freshmen defense." "Well," said Claude, with a snicker, "can't be too rough on your home town boy, besides I was once a freshie too. With that, Claude announced that he had a registration appointment in 15 minutes. "Say Leonidas, let's have dinner together tonight around 4:30. I've been eating over there at the "Greasy Spoon," pointing across the edge of the campus to the main street. Maybe I can help you cut some red tape around here." "That's fine, Claude, meet you there on time."

Feeling a bit relieved at meeting a home town boy on this big beautiful college campus, 1,000 miles from home, I hurried off to follow some registration directions of my own. I passed the beautiful fountain constructed into a picturesque 30 feet monument; to the loving memory of the wife of a Bishop, a former president of the university. I soon learned that it was near the center of the campus and served as a meeting place for outdoor oratory; a trysting place for lovers; a viewing stand for girl watchers; a guide post for new arrivals and a water spraying spot for first quarter freshmen caught out of bounds by sophomores. I hesitated for awhile to observe the elegant fountain with its streams of water trickling from its 4 rectangular sides as it rose majestically like an oblisk between the nearby elm and maple trees.

My musing was interrupted by a strong articulate voice coming from a rather compact short man who qualified for a Mr. "5 by 5." He was not a fraction over 5 ft. and weighed an estimated 170 lbs. He wore a fluffy gold and green sweater with the letters 1923 across the chest. Loudly and authoritatively he said, "How do you do, sir? Pardon me, but you look like a freshman; might there be something I can do for you?" Nonplused, I replied hesitatingly "Not that I can think of, but thank you just the same." "Fare thee well, young man, our paths undubitably, will cross again," said Mr. 5 by 5.

At 4:30 dinner, I described my interrogator and quoted him to my friend Claude Ferebee. "Gee whiz man, that sounds like W. D. ("Lump") Johnson, Jr. Why he is a sophomore; in fact, president of the class. Hope you didn't get fresh with him. He is a smart guy, from Plains, Ga., I think they call it. Any rate, his old man's an A.M.E. preacher and they say he's sitting on a sack; peanuts farms, I believe." "Lump" or rather "WD" (only a few close friends call him Lump) changes his sweaters and slacks every day. Never seen him in a suit—don't know how he'd look in one; but he's got plenty of everything else.

"Berry, you've got to be careful around here. Don't be so wrapped up in books that you don't watch the sophomores during this quarter. The first 3 months is hazing season. No freshman is allowed out of the dormitory after dinner time, around 5 p.m., without an excuse. Otherwise you can get your "hide" tanned. Sometimes during earlier hours, if you are too far off base you can get your "rump roasted"; but if you can beat it to a building on a dead run, you're home free." "Freshman curfew" is approaching now. I'll escort you to the Shorter Hall door. With 1923 across his sweater the sophs won't bother him."

As we walked across the campus, I noticed an occasional young man streaking toward a building with several others in hot pursuit, removing their belts from their pants and yelling F-A-C-Q! Claude said, "You don't want to get caught in a chase like that." "Look, they are closing in on a freshman and strapping him into the dormitory with their belts." "I am glad you're with me tonite." "I don't go for that kind of stuff even if I am a freshman." "Why are they yelling F-A-C-Q?, what does that mean"—Claude laughed and said, "Man that's a "code," always keep your ears pricked up to hear it, it means *Fresh A—Come Quick.*" I managed a laugh but not too happily. I was glad to escape; having observed my first college lesson unscathed.

Three days later I chanced to meet Ferebee again at dinner time, at the "Greasy Spoon." I had been reminded that I had only 2 days left in which to choose a roommate or have one selected for a mutual conference on rooming together. Claude was having a somewhat similar problem. He and Lucien Dunlap of Paducah, Ky. a sophomore had planned to room together, but Lucien was being delayed and uncertain for the Fall Quarter. Claude said, with a smile, "How would a freshman like the honor of rooming with a sophomore." "Sir," I replied, "If that's an invitation, I will gladly accept the honor." "Well it will be quite an intellectual atmosphere for you. You see, there would be sophomore visitors on off hours and you would have to be on your P's and Q's, if that's possible." "OK, fine, I'll be glad to take the chance." "So let's settle the matter now and I can concentrate on trying to eventually become a sophomore." At that point we shook hands; closed the agreement with the business office and moved into a nice second floor room in Shorter Hall, already selected by "Mr." Sophomore Ferebee.

There were 2 army-type cots with a comfortable mattress, sheets, blanket, and pillows. A sturdy table with a local goose neck lamp and 2 chairs graced the center of the room. There was a closet; room for 2 wardrobe trunks and a couple extra chairs, and a couple of highboys with small mirrors.

I had to get used to sophomore visitors during off hours and their kidding remarks like "How are you making out, Mr. Ferebee with a freshman roommate. Isn't he stunned into embarrassing silence, when sophomore visitors engage in weighty discussions of science and philosophy?" "Yes, but he is doing pretty well; making haste slowly. He has just about covered the first 25 pages of freshman chemistry and they say he has spilled only one bottle of hydrochloric acid on the laboratory floor during the first month. Besides, he has gone out for football; he has made the college glee club, and he made A's and B's on mid-quarter finals.

"That's enough! Sounds like he is on a 'boom-bust' course." "No," wait, a minute," said Mr. Ferebee, "All of you may not have heard that he made the Sphinx Club and is now pledged for Alpha Phi Alpha fraternity." "Oh yea!' Bully for him." "Well, as a freshman we would say he's making some kind of start."

My ambitions were in no way stymied by the ribbing of the sophomore buddies of Claude Ferebee, most of whom were Alpha fraternity men. In the winter quarter, I joined the society debating team; won a place on the two man freshman team for the annual freshmen-sophomore debate. My friendly detractors were confounded. On the night of confrontation, they watched me dress in "tails," standing white butterfly tie and patent leather slippers. I remember taking my seat with my teammate at a table on the platform in Galloway Hall Auditorium. The sophomore team, similarly dressed, sat at a table at the opposite end of the platform. Each of us paraded onto the platform, brief case in hand, amid much applause from the respective class audiences and their sympathizers. Dutifully and customarily we each drank a few sips of water from a crystal clear glass poured from equally crystal clear water pitchers. We then very confidently pulled out our notes and our pens and were ready to go.

The master of ceremonies announced the subject for debate. It was a "capital and labor question" involving whether labor should "share" in the profits of industry. The judges took their places. The affirmative and negative speeches and rebuttals developed into considerable emotional fervor. When it was all over the judges ruled in favor of the freshman team for the first time in several years. I proudly left the auditorium amid loud cheers, shaking hands with freshmen and other well wishers and made it to my room across campus in Shorter Hall where I knew the sophomores would be waiting for me.

In contrast to the usual depreciatory greetings there was a warm gesture and of hand shaking and back-slapping for this freshman. I was addressed with some degree of pride as a young Alpha-to-be Freshman who had won his spurs.

What they didn't know was that I had had plenty of time to do library research at the Carnegie Library on the campus and libraries in Dayton during the Christmas holidays. This was the saddest Christmas I think I ever experienced. It was the first holiday, a 1,000 miles from home. Because I knew the financial circumstances I made no request to spend the holidays (2,000 round trip railroad miles away) with my family. Near the end of the quarter as the holidays approached a song began buzzing in my musical ears that could have been, "I'll be home for Xmas if only in my mind." A white Xmas at college in Ohio was pretty to look at, but without my brothers and sister, Mom and Pop and the family tree—Xmas had little meaning for me. After all I was a freshie six months out of high school. I must have looked like lonesome Joe from Kokomo. The Delta Sigma Theta Sorority was holding its national convention on campus. There was a shortage of upper classmen for social affairs. Probably with grave reluctance their social committee offered this freshie a blind date with a soror from Columbia University, New York. At least this freshie had a new 3-piece suit and wistful smile for pretty girls. I exulted with joy upon receiving the bid. (At an introductory affair I had a chance to meet my blind date.) I never heard but I am sure that the Delta soror was valedictorian at Columbia; for certain she could never have been a part of the daisy chain at Vassar. Following the introduction to my blind date-to-be, I had a sudden violent attack of chicken pox with high fever. I assured the committee that even if my date could physically support me to the dance, I would get off an epidemic which could get the whole convention quarantined. Don't get me wrong, I appreciate female intellect in its place and of course I know that beauty is only skin deep—but I had known a few lady intellectuals who would have been more attractive without skin.

The Social Committee chairman sensing the cause of my acute affliction came to the rescue. "Leonidas, we find that some sorors' will not have male escorts. After meeting the Sister with whom you were matched, we are sure she has a understanding heart. So if you can patch yourself up we have a fine substitute for you from the University of Pennsylvania."

True to my freshman ambitions, I went out for the track team in the spring of my freshman year. Having had some experience in high school, it turned out that I had only one real challenger in running the mile. The track was mostly an intramural sport at Wilberforce in those days. I was always concerned with scholastic responsibilities. I had always enjoyed singing since early childhood and with some training I had tried my hand as a tenor soloist, in high school.

At the beginning of my sophomore year, four of us who were male singers in the glee club organized into a male quartet. After much practice we impressed the music world on campus as we harmonized. I was a member of a student critical group mostly male, which maintained a highly critical standard for every activity on the campus. Homer Smith, who died only a few years before this writing, sang first tenor and became a lifetime friend. After college he organized the famous "Southernaires" which was the first black singing group to broadcast nationally on radio.

They sang Negro spirituals and religious or semi-religious songs on radio every Sunday morning for many years. They were a widely travelled group just before World War II, and became the Mariners of the Coast Guard and for some time thereafter a feature of the Arthur Godfrey Show. I sang 2nd tenor and became manager of the group. Homer Williams sang bass and later became a public school teacher and principal down in Florida. Charles Williams was baritone and became the center of one of our funniest quartet experiences. On a certain Friday afternoon Charles, who was a sophomore, was "whipping it up" at a freshman-sophomore football game. He was yelling for the sophs louder than anybody else on the field. I came by and said, "Listen young man don't forget we've got a concert tonight in Chillicothe." His reply was, Mr. Senior, "You just take care of the second tenor and I'll take care of the baritone." With that he continued to yell, cheering the sophomores who were barely hanging on against the onslaught of the freshmen.

At the appointed time, Guy Leach was ready with his Hudson super six, to drive us the forty miles for the church concert. When we arrived, the church was packed. We decided to find a room in the church basement to "tune-up" before going upstairs for the concert. Lo, and behold, Charlie Williams, our baritone, could not sing a note. The audience had to wait an additional thirty to forty-five minutes while we rearranged a concert for three voices. Meanwhile, Charlie with his hoarse voice said, "I remember a couple of recitations from Paul Lawrence Dunbar written in, 'before the war Negro dialect.'" We then marched into the main sanctuary, took our seats on the platform feeling a little doubtful that we could live up to our reputation as a quartet with three voices. After the first group of songs we put Charlie on with his hoarse, squeaky voice in Negro dialect from Paul Lawrence Dunbar. He broke up the audience and in between our group effort and solos by each of the other three, we interspersed Charlie with his recitations in dialects. We made a great hit and we were never sure that the audience realized that Charlie's squeaky, hoarse voice was not a part of his purposeful act.

My years at Wilberforce became more rewarding and joyful as the years passed by. If I had it to do all over again, I would always want to go first to a Black college. In a so called "separate but equal" institution in America always reveals that "whites are more equal than the Negroes." But by contrast with integrated schools while they usually have integrated advantages, the black student in America's black colleges is not only at the college but it can also be in the college.

Among the interesting experiences at Wilberforce was the opportunity to learn about the black founding of the school in 1856 before the Civil War, entirely as an African Methodist effort and the long history of its outstanding and successful black graduates of the institution. It was a revealing and enjoyable experience to meet so many "colored" young people representing all of the hues of the rainbow from every state in the union where Negroes lived and from Africa and the isles of seas. Some were exceptionally brilliant talented in music and athletics, some were exceptionally brilliant and came from middle class Black families especially from the larger cities of the South. The parentage of some included physicians, lawyers, teachers, ministers, businessmen and civil servants of the federal government, in my day.

In my description of the finer things of life on a Black college campus by no means would I leave out the beautiful co-eds whose delightful skins ranged from the smooth Black ebony of Benin quality to the medium brown sweetness of unrefined sugar to the cafe sole of coffee and cream to the pinkness of rosebuds and peonies in Wilberforce's sunken garden. Yes there was one that made my heart beat in a special and different kind of way for the first time. I think they called it the first blush of love. Her name was "Gerty," she came from Oklahoma. She was a mixture of American Indian, Louisiana Creole with a touch of African.

Yet you guessed it, romance and the struggle to study medicine did not mix in those days. Gertie married a lawyer and later a minister. She reared two fine children, sent them to college and one of them, now holds a high position in the diplomatic service of the United States Government.

There were many interesting people at Wilberforce in my day, before, and afterwards. Lifetime friendships were formed there, my buddie Claude Ferebee graduated in dentistry at Columbia and taught at Howard University for many years. I was godfather for his daughter. Homer Smith's story has been mentioned. We were friends until his passing a few years ago. He was godfather for my daughter Judy.

While Homer and I participated in choral music lyrics and classics there were others who were talented in popular music, including jazz. Like Homer, some of them became outstanding professionals. Leon and Otis Renee left Wilberforce the year I came. They were well known music composers and publishers and were responsible for "Sleepy Time Down South," "When the Swallows Come Back to Capistrano" and others. Henderson's Collegians were formed there in my day and other jazz greats were affiliated with the Cab Calloways and the Duke Ellingtons. The university community was proud of an ex-president still living near the campus, Dr. William Saunders Scarbrough, the classic authority whose published version of ancient Greek grammar was used in several major universities. After my day the university was proud to mention such former students and graduates as Bayard Rustin, Leontyne Price, William Grant Still, the famed composer and symphony orchestra director and others.

Wilberforce University was undoubtedly in the destiny of the Berrys. Following my graduation, brothers Dick and Lew earned their degrees at this institution. Dick received a Bachelor of Business Administration and Lew, a Bachelor of Science, with a Chemistry major. While they were at Wilberforce and I was at the University of Chicago, sister Gladys was pursuing a bachelors degree in elementary education at Virginia State College. With four of us in college and the "depression" getting no better, Dick decided to leave school, and continue his job as a waiter for a year. This was done to support his roommate and brother Lew, through his senior year. Dick then returned to Wilberforce to complete requirements for his degree.

Somewhere along the line, Pop received an honorary Doctor of Divinity from Payne Theological Seminary of Wilberforce.

Many years into my career in medicine, I received an honorary Doctor of Science as the fifth degree, three of them earned, received by the Berry family from "the Noble Alma Mater." For my senior year I was fortunate to be selected as student instructor in zoology. This strengthened my experience in this field. I graduated from Wilberforce and was off to the next stop on my long trail for the study of medicine.

221

In the summer of 1924 on my way from Wilberforce to a summer job, I stopped by home in Portsmouth with a diploma in my bag which read Bachelor of Science. I only have one vivid memory of this two-day visit with the family. Pop took me out for a ride in his Haynes automobile. I presumed that it was for some fresh air and to show me some spots in the city which I had not seen. He continued to drive almost to Truxton as we discussed various subjects. Then came the bomb shell. "Well Leonidas, so you have finished college: that's fine." "You know, sometimes when people finish college, they succeed in life" (period of silence). It was like sticking a pin in my ballooned ego. But before I could recover, Pop was pointing toward the big ships getting repairs in the Portsmouth Navy yards.

I spent the summer as a waiter at the Belvedere Hotel, Larchmont, New York on Long Island Sound. I had been refused entrance to the Ohio State Medical School. This inspite of a "theoretical" statement in the Wilberforce catalogue describing a pre-med-med arrangement between the two institutions. I had considerable anxiety and at times depression not knowing where I would study medicine. I worked hard, made tips as a waiter, organized a quartet of Black college boys including myself, "working our way through college." I induced the manager to allow me to clean and press men's clothing in the basement quarters. Only occasionally did I ride the Boston-Westchester Suburban train for a little respite, such as one could have without spending money in glamorous Harlem. My brother Dick had just finished the academy at Kittrell and joined me for a job at Larchmont when no guests turned up at his Asbury Park hotel because of cold weather. We had a talk and he decided to go to Wilberforce in the fall to study business administration.

My letters to a couple other medical schools either bore no fruit or were not to my liking. I had a friend and fraternity brother formerly of Wilberforce, Ralph Scull whom I heard was studying medicine at the University of Chicago. A letter of reply from him made me think quite seriously of attempting admission there, in spite of his description of great difficulties which I would encounter. I returned home at the end of the season pondering the scholastic and economic difficulties if I went to Chicago to attempt entrance into the medical school. As I talked to Pop, he took me on another long ride in the "Haynes." Again, I was not ready for a bombshell which in no way had I anticipated. I explained that the University of Chicago only recognized two Black colleges and their students had to present very high grades. The University of Chicago was one of only two medical schools with the highest entrance requirements in the country. One of the two recognized Black schools was run by the federal government, the other organized and run by white Presbyterians to keep Negroes from applying to Princeton U. The University of Chicago was willing on the basis of my grades to accept me as an unclassified student to see if the standard of my scholarship under their supervision earning one of their bachelors degrees would earn my acceptance as an applicant. Meanwhile, where would I get the money? Then came Pop's devastating "Leonidas, I think I understand your dilemma, my advice to you is regardless how the difficulties, if that's where you want to go. Pack your bag and go on to Chicago. Work hard and as long as you do the best you can I will do all I can to encourage you." I felt like Atlas, just after the world had toppled off his shoulders. There would be four Berry children in college at the same time.

University of Chicago
and Medical Training
(1924–29)

I arrived in Chicago during the last week of September, 1924. I was met at the train by Ralph Scull, a medical student at Univ. of Chicago, a former schoolmate at Wilberforce and fraternity brother. He was responsible for my coming to Chicago to try to get into the medical school. I spent the first night in the Alpha Phi Alpha fraternity house. On the second morning I reported to the registration office on the campus of the University and started to look for the job I would need immediately thereafter. The medical department was set up as a graduate school requiring an acceptable bachelor's degree with other stipulations for entrance. I knew before arriving that my bachelor's degree was not acceptable but that I would be given a chance as an unclassified student to prove my scholastic ability under university supervision. If satisfactory, I was told that it would be possible to receive a University of Chicago bachelor's degree in one additional year.

I was successful in satisfying all requirements by taking examinations in chemistry and physics and by making superior grades in graduate subjects. However, I encountered overtones of racial attitudes at my very first stop, namely the admissions office. This was consistent with the times and of course would have been found in practically every medical school in the country. I did not have to arrive on the campus to realize that I would have to work exceptionally hard to get into and graduate from an exclusive and highly rated medical school. The first racial encounter was very discouraging and came near being a catastrophe for me. Then came the first paradox which I encountered in medical school. The dean of unclassified students and chairman of the department of philosophy came to my rescue. He was Caucasian of course and had a distinct Southern accent. When he offered to carry a petition to the faculty to straighten out the unfairness I was definitely surprised. I was beginning to learn that not all white Southerners are racist. I would learn later that not all white Northerners are non-racists.

Professor Thomas Vernon Smith had grown up in western Texas, was distinguished in his field at that time and became even more so in later years by the several books which he published; by becoming a state senator and later a congressman. He then returned as a college professor to continue his writings with philosophical and political overtones. Following his career in later years I knew of his special consideration for Negro students. Interestingly, I was involved during my second year out of medical school in helping him to get elected to the state legislature from a district had become about 40 percent Negro. His political opponent accused him of having been a member of the Ku Klux Klan in former years. Negro students whom he had befriended or who knew about his liberal attitudes joined his campaign for election. Literature was printed of a man wearing a white hood, face mask and dress of a Ku Kluxer with the name Professor T. V. Smith as the caption. Counter literature was gotten out by Negro students. On the night before election I joined others who went from door to door removing the Klan literature which had been stuffed into mail boxes and replaced it with out counter leaflets.

I must hasten to state however that T. V. Smith was a professor of philosophy and not a professor in the medical school. With a four quarter system there was often much overlapping between sophomores and freshmen. There were two other Negro medical students, at least one of whom was in the same class section with me in some instances. When this occurred we were expected to be partners. When it did not work out that way a Negro student might find himself having to choose another minority as lab partner, a white girl. In one such instance a southern white boy kept his eyes glued on us much of the time in the laboratory as we dissected the human cadaver. My girl partner noticed this and became quite annoyed by it. However, this young man flunked out by the end of the year and that solved one of his problems.

226

On another occasion my partner in physiology was a rather attractive white girl. She was not a medical student but a candidate for a Ph.D. in nutrition. Our laboratory work involved a lot of small live laboratory animals, such as white mice and kicking frogs. I had never known a female who was not afraid of live mice and my lab partner was no exception. Nor did she enjoy handling live frogs. Furthermore, she did not have the mechanical expertise of setting up laboratory equipment for our experiments. In the third place she did not have the background in science to be a superior student in advanced physiology. It fell my chore to do at least 80 percent of the work and as we quizzed each other on theory, I had the feeling that she was not going to lead the class scholastically. In this laboratory we had a European with a foreign accent as a laboratory assistant, who gave us a lot of attention. Not with a "jaundiced" eye as the previous detractor but rather he was always in a helpful mood as he came around.

At the end of our final examinations in which this instructor was responsible for the grades, I received the first "D" in my entire school career before that time or afterwards. My laboratory partner received an "A." This annoyed her very much, accrediting me with being responsible for getting her through the course to a great extent. She further admitted the social approaches of this instructor on occasions outside of the laboratory. The instructor was a youngish-man with premature baldness, a protruding abdomen who wore thick glasses and walked with a slue-footed gait. He did not qualify as a "handsome dude" in my opinion and my partner apparently had a worse opinion. My protest took me to the chief of the department. I was informed that papers were destroyed immediately and that grades could not be changed anyhow. I replied, "even so I want you to give me an examination in this course!" "Well," he replied in his Swedish accent, "if you just want to write I will give you an examination in the course." "When would you like to take such an examination?" My reply was "Right now." "I am busy with my research," he replied, "I can't stop everything and give you an examination now." My answer was "What about tomorrow?" "Well," he replied, "if you are so anxious, come back in two days and I will give you an examination." When he had corrected my written answers to his questions, his statement was "This is quite a good paper, why didn't you write such a good paper in your final examinations?"

227

I was allowed to take the lectures all over again which the chairman was giving during the next quarter, with exemption from the laboratory work. The professor stated, "We will record whatever grade you make in the final examination in my course." I received a "B+," but the "D" (a low passing grade) also remained on my record.

Before leaving the basic sciences, I had another interesting experience in physiology. I deciced to take a nonrequired advanced course, called the "special physiology of mammals." The underground gossip was that this course was very difficult and usually taken by students with advanced experience often working on an M.D. Ph.D. program. However, I liked physiology and decided to take the course. Another Negro student whom I knew very well also registered for the course. He happened to have been married and lived with his family in a house with a basement. We of course became lab partners. We knew we had gone out of our way to risk "flunking" or getting a low grade in a subject which inspite of its attractiveness might jeopardize the required overall average in each department. It is said that necessity is the mother of invention. All experiments in this course were done on dogs and cats under anesthesia. We decided to "borrow" the laboratory equipment (when no one was looking) and transported it to my buddy's basement. We knew that we could catch enough stray dogs and cats in our neighborhood alleys to do the experiments ahead of the appointed laboratory time. This was quite a successful move. When the other lab teams were doing the experiments for the first time we were doing the same experiments for the second time. On about the third laboratory period we had observed that the instructor, a brilliant physiologist, would visit the other five teams for discussion and come to us last. We had a particularly difficult experiment, technically, on an anesthetized cat. My partner and I had already done the experiment a couple nights before on a cat which we caught in the alley. The professor came to our table with impatience written all over his face and said "Alright give me your scalpel and your dissecting forceps and I will isolate the *corda tympani* nerve for you." We informed him that we had long since isolated the nerve and were at the end of our experiment. The nerve was very fragile, difficult to identify, being about the diameter of a hair. It had to be stimulated with just the right amount of electric current to produce secretion of the salivary gland at a measured rate. The instructor continued "You have isolated the corda tympani nerve? This I've got to see." He picked up our preparation with delicate forceps, stimulated the nerve and duplicated our results on a revolving drum, which was identical with our recordings. We received a fairly decent grade perhaps because we always finished our experiments ahead of the other teams. This was very good for our ego and for racial sensitivities which we never had to look very hard to find.

At the end of the sophomore year each Negro student was called by Dean Harvey into his office and given a suggestion. He said to me, "Mr. Berry, your grades have been satisfactory, but next year as you know you will be handling patients. You will be running into some problems. (with white patients) I would suggest that you transfer to Howard or MeHarry. "You see you would lead your class there." I, of course, declined his offer and stated that I felt I would get along alright for the last two years. Other Negro students had always reacted the same way as far as I was able to determine. At Wilberforce I did not graduate, "Magna Cum Laude" nor did I graduate "Thank You Laude." I suppose I was a "gentleman" student, too proud to make a "C" but unwilling to stop everything else and work hard enough to make all "A's."

Incidentally having gone to Wilberforce, a Black college where I did not lead my class, I knew that I would not necessarily achieve this at Howard or MeHarry. True to the warning of the dean, I ran smack into the next racial problem, which would challenge my ingenuity to solve. The catalog listed the requirements of each medical student to spend 3 months at least wearing a white suit as an intern's assistant in a hospital. I soon learned via the grapevine from Negro upperclassmen that "we boys" were exempt from the requirement of a clerkship." In my junior year I had an experience in the office of another dean in charge of upperclassmen which I think I will never forget. He was Dean Ernest Irons. He had an unsavory racial attitude by reputation among Negro students present and past. Having been admitted to his private office which was not the easiest accomplishment, I was allowed to stand in front of his desk "cooling my heels" for about 3 minutes before he decided to look up. His greeting was a firm "name please." I answered, "Leonidas Berry." He then pulled a pad in front of him and wrote, Berry—negro with a small "n." "You may proceed," the dean continued. I stated that I had come in to see about arranging for a hospital and the schedule for the required clerkship. "Negros don't get clerkships," he replied. "Yes," I answered, "I had heard that by the grapevine but no one has told me this officially and I didn't think it was a closed matter." "I came to suggest that perhaps the tax supported public hospital, Cook County across the street could be a place where the clerkship might be provided." The dean answered, "No that cannot be arranged and yes it is a closed issue." He appeared to dismiss me, but I was not quite ready to go. I continued, "Dean, there is a course in intravenous medications which I understand is quite popular and is assigned to applicants alphabetically. Since my name begins with a 'B' and since I cannot have a clerkship, could I be registered for this course?" The dean replied in a stern voice, "Of course not, that course is in great demand and if I registered you over everybody else that would be giving you special privileges." At that point, I thanked the dean, did an about face and went out to look for my own clerkship.

I discovered that Dr. U. G. Dailey, graduate of Northwestern U. Medical School in 1907, a Negro surgeon, during the last few years had established a private hospital and "sanitarium" of twenty beds at 37th Pl. and Mich. Ave. He rented several offices to doctors on the first floor. A high level of medical and surgical practice was carried out there. Dr. Dailey had his basic surgical training with Dr. Dan Williams, the Negro doctor who was credited with doing the first successful heart operation in the early 1890's. Dr. Williams had graduated at Northwestern Medical College in 1883 and later established Provident Hospital on the southside, a bi-racial venture with practically all Negro patients at that time. Dr. Dailey after some years separated from Provident to establish his own private hospital. I sold Dr. Dailey the idea of allowing me to live in the hospital to take clinical histories and to carry out physical examinations and perhaps some minor laboratory work, all in the evenings after school for board and keep. I remained there for two years with considerably more experience than the three months requirement for white students only, would have afforded me. The experience was great, the "keep" was an important plus, the board was "for the birds," mostly intravenous post or pre-operative glucose and recuperating soups. Eventually I found a solution for that problem also. I got a job preparing and serving sandwiches and coffee to poker players in a private club all-night on Saturdays. The job included tips and I could catch up sleep on Sunday mornings. It might be asked "Where did you go from there? Mr. Doctor to be?"

At this point I want to say that not all of my time was consumed with racial incidents although too much of it was. On the other hand I had very excellent teachers throughout the four years. Many of them were internationally known and some of them were authors of textbooks or contributors to textbooks and systems of medicine and they were well trained and experienced in a great majority of cases. I think of Professor Dr. Anton Carlson who did pioneer work on the physiology of the heart. There was Dr. Andrew C. Ivy who was a student of Carlson's and became internationally well known in his own right. Dr. Alexander Maximow was very brilliant and colorful and an excellent teacher. He was a refugee from Czarist Russia, at the time of the Communist revolution.

There was one professor whom I have remembered with nostalgia and vindictiveness. He had a protruding nose on which their was always perched a pair of pinching type nose-glasses. He was as arrogant and pompous as he appeared, where I was concerned. Whenever I elected to discuss a subject in his bacteriology class, I noticed a frown on his face and impatience which he did not display with the white students. With obvious cock-sureness he often expounded on the, "Inherited racial susceptibility of the Negro to tuberculosis." This, he would often say, is an inherited characteristic of all primitive races. I could not accept the great professors' thesis. It was very obvious that in his opinion, I was a member of one of those primitive races and he disliked having to tolerate my presence in his class. The subject of bacteriology was one of the easiest to comprehend in medical school. I was happy to receive the "C" which he gave and not a "D," and get out of his class.

Years later and I hope he was still living, medical science discovered the effectiveness of anti-biotics and other drugs which virtually wiped out tuberculosis and caused the closing of tuberculosis sanitaria and isolation hospitals in all industrial nations. So, the "Inherited racial tuberculosis genes of primitive races" disappeared overnight with the advancement of science.

This professor, of course, was not by himself with reference to the "Inherited racial" theory of tuberculosis and other so called "filth" diseases. It was widely taught throughout America and elsewhere. Even before the discovery of the magic drugs, I could not accept the logic and justification of this theory. Apparently it disturbed me so much that the first piece of research I performed after graduation was on the subject

231

of "Race and Tuberculosis." My studies in Chicago and in the Cook County Morgue showed a definite correlation between the incidence of tuberculosis with poverty rates, housing conditions, literary rates within the all Negro residential boundaries. Tuberculosis and socio-economic indices decreased mathematically in square mile zones from the poorest part of the inner city progressively to the outer boundaries where middle class Negroes lived. In the latter area, tuberculosis rates among Negroes were no higher than that of the white population. This study was accepted as a partial requirement for the Masters of Science degree in Pathology. During the clinical years I was very proud to have such instructors as Dr. James B. Herrick, who was credited with being the first doctor to describe coronary heart attacks. Before his classical descriptions, an acute coronary heart attack was known as "acute indigestion." He was credited also as being the first, certainly in the United States to observe sickle cell disease or sickle trait in patients. There was also the pompous Dr. Bevan, chairman of surgery, whose principal fame came from training great surgeons whose achievements exceeded those of their teacher.

I must mention, however, a few other experiences encountered by a Negro trying to make his mark in a top rated American medical school in the late 1920's. I recall with a measure of forgiveness and humor, the professor in pediatrics who would call Negro students to examine only Negro babies while calling white students to examine babies of any ethnic or racial group. Occasionally he would make a mistake and switch babies putting the students in an awkward gesture. I was embarrassed then before classmates and parents who were with their children, but I thanked God that the disease pattern was the same regardless of skin color or ethnic origin.

Obstetrical training in my day included the requirement of each student having to deliver 12 babies in the home during the last two years of training. All these patients had prenatal care in the out-patient department and a very unique sterile or aseptic delivery room package was taken into the home. Again race became a very important factor. Negro students were assigned to deliver only Negro and Mexican mothers. White students had the privilege of living in the intern's quarters of the Presbyterian Hospital and to get their cases off in about 10 days to two weeks regardless of the race of the mother. Negro students were assigned to cases which did not fall into the rapid schedule for white students launched directly from the hospital. We were called from our homes day or night and in my case assignments were scattered throughout the period of a year. Incidentally when the news broke back in the Al Capone area about the "St. Valentines Day massacre," I discovered that on the night of the tragedy, I had been busy with a delivery just two blocks away.

Patients were not separated racially for purposes of student care except as previously mentioned. I remember one case which brought forth the mixed emotions of embarrassment and humor. Three students, a white male and female and I were brought over to an examining table by an instructor for the purpose of examining the abdomen of a young white female patient. The instructor first examined the patient's exposed abdomen and said, "Here is the technic of examining a patient with a spastic colon" and as he pressed, the patient wiggled and was very obviously unhappy. He reassured her and indicated that the examination was important for her and then asked the white male student to examine the patient's abdomen and then the white girl student was called to do the same thing. And in each instance the patient almost got off the table, indicating that the examination was causing considerable discomfort. It then became my turn as the instructor called on me to carry out the examination. I didn't know what to expect. So I proceeded to examine the patient in the manner instructed. The patient relaxed completely, showed no signs of distress and finally said very loudly, "Gee your hands are nice and warm, you can stay there." We all looked at each other and finally managed a smile.

All in all I was quite proud of the training I received at Rush Medical College of the University of Chicago. While some experiences were depressing and embarrassing, it prepared me for the real world of racial attitudes and inhibitions, which I would encounter at post graduate training levels as well as the limitation I would encounter in the search for continuing growth as attending physician in hospitals, teaching and researching opportunities at all levels of my professional career.

In spite of the profound academic atmosphere at the University there were occasions for social highlights and athletic activities, particularly in football and track. I remember vividly the visit of the English Prince of Wales, later Edward VIII, to the campus. He was at that time the world's most famous and handsome bachelor. He covered the campus partly by motorcade and partly by foot, being followed by plain clothes protectors. Young co-eds came from everywhere giggling and waving as he returned a gracious bow. Middle aged women dashed out of their research laboratories wearing white coats and flat heel shoes removing their thick lens glasses to get a better look. Even the men stood in admiration of this much heralded slayer of women's hearts as he strode along wearing the neatly fitted uniform of an English Prince, decorated with all the ribbons, earned and unearned signifying his rank in the army, the navy and the royal orders of the British courts.

No fair lady seemed to make him break his stride, but of course at that time he had not met the dashing "grass" widow, Wally Simpson, for whom he, as king, gave up the English throne for "the woman I love."

As amazing as it may seem today the University of Chicago had outstanding athletic activities. In 1924 the legendary director of athletics and coach, Alonzo Stagg, produced a championship football team in the Big 10 midwestern conference of which the university was an outstanding member for many years. I managed to see the home games by scheduling my outside jobs, getting an usher's badge as pay for working the grandstand. The last year of the "Maroon" champions in 1924, I saw the famous games between Stagg's boys and the University of Illinois' Grid-Ironers led by Harold "Red" Grange. Stagg allowed to the press and the campus "pep" sessions that he would stop "Red" Grange with an unbeatable offense. His prediction came true. The Staggmen won the toss and made the first touchdown without a turnover. A halfback named McCarthy carried the ball all the way gaining five yards at a time. He repeated his act twice again earning the title "Five Yards McCarthy." "Red" only got a hold of the ball three times, but he made three touchdowns and the game ended 21–21. In Big Ten championship meets and Olympic try-outs, I saw such Black stars as Jesse Owens, Ralph Metcalfe, Eddie Tolan, DeHart Hubbard of Michigan and others, who were of special inspiration to me.

During one relay hurdle race a black hurdler got off to a slow start. On the turn he strode ahead of the leader. A white fan could not hold back his emotion and yelled out loudly, "Catch that nigger." Some white fans seemed embarrassed but quickly there came the strong voice of a short hunchbacked Negro yelling to the top of his voice, "Run, nigger, run," "run nigger run." The Black boy took the hurdles in stride, shaking a couple of them, but knocking down none. He finished with a burst of speed winning the race. I watched with all the emotion of the other fans wanting to see a good race. I watched the race from beginning to end, stride for stride. At the finish there was something inside me saying over and over, "With the Grace of God and all of the courage and strength within me; there I go in the field of medicine."

At the end of my junior medical year I went to camp Fort Snelling near St. Paul-Minneapolis. I was housed in the University of Chicago barracks. Next door on one side was the barracks of the University of Minnesota and on the other the University of Iowa and so on down the company street where practically all the medical and dental schools of the Middle West and beyond were represented. Everything was normal for the first of the 6 weeks required training period. One afternoon while my barracks mates and I were relaxing in the front camp grounds, up came the colonel, commanding officer of the fort. He stopped about twenty feet from the group and beckoned with his right hand calling my name. I left the group and reported to him maybe with a salute. Probably not because I hadn't learned too much about military courtesy and secondly my intuition told me that the old race problem was popping up. "Berry," he said, "there has been some objection to your presence in the camp. Among the 500 students we have here some came from as far south as St. Louis. They are unhappy and I am interested in your welfare. Therefore, we are arranging for a private room for you in the post hospital about a mile and a half up the road." My response was "Colonel, it's good to hear that you are interested in my welfare." "I can report to you that as far as my welfare is concerned, I am doing alright here. It therefore would seem to me that if any persons from St. Louis or elsewhere is unhappy, that ought to be their problem." The colonel bristled and responded, "I'm interested in their welfare too, and I'll have a sergeant down here before dark to help you with your baggage to your hospital room."

The practical exercise that I was suppose to receive on evacuating the wounded in combat, rendering first aid on the battle field, setting up emergency hospitals, etc., was "received" in the confines of the hospital room for five weeks rather than in the field with white students. Fortu-

235

nately there were a large number of recruits coming to the hospital from the South. Some of them had a malaria fever infection. My time was spent in the clinical laboratory studying malaria parasites, an experience which I could not have had in Chicago.

In the end, of course, I had to write the same final examinations in military medicine as anyone else. I received a first lieutenant's commission upon graduation. We had finished the courses required for captaincy which would be received automatically in five years. At the appointed time I wrote to the army authorities for my certificate of captaincy in the medical reserves. I was told that I was one year late in asking for it. It was five years since I received the M.D., but it was six years since I finished medical school requirements. The discrepancy was caused by the requirement of a one year internship before the degree was received. Because you are late the letter stated we offer you a second five years at the same grade of first lieutenant or you can drop the whole matter. I was deeply chagrined but accepted the second term as first lieutenant. The second period ended in the spring of '41, when reserve officers were being called up in anticipation of war. All doctors at that time in my age group without military training were given the rank of captaincy upon joining the army. Any doctor except Negroes trained in a medical specialty entered the army for hospital service with the rank of major or lieutenant colonel. With medical specialty and army officer training I had risk of being called to duty with the active rank I held, that of 1st lieutenant in case of war. Fortunately my commission ran out just before the Pearl Harbor attack. That solved part of my problem for the time being. There would be more problems later on.

During the last quarter of the senior year we were required to pass the "comprehensive" examination. This covered the 4 years of medicine while finishing up the work of the last quarter. Then came a near tragic experience for my buddy and classmate, now the distinguished Dr. George ("Charlie-My-Boy") Cannon of New York. He came down with tuberculosis two months before graduation. He went through the best treatment of that day, namely, bedrest at the Chicago Municipal Sanitarium, suburban fresh air and periodic injections of air into the pleural space along the inner boarder of the ribs to collapse the healing lung.

During that year I was interning at the Freedmen's Hospital, Washington, D.C. The name referred to Negro ex-slaves just after the Civil War when the hospital was established. I was in frequent contact with Cannon by correspondence. He once wrote very courageously; Temp. 100 degrees, bugs groggy, Cannon in the lead. He and I used to address each other with the salutation "What you say Charlie." After a while it was shortened to just "Charlie." Through the years and until now we call each other "Charlie." As I finished my internship "Charlie" Cannon went back to school to finish his "comprehensives" and one quarter of work. He keeled over in the process and returned to the sanitarium for a second year. At the end of the 2nd year of treatment, he again returned, finished his work under great strain and has had a long and distinguished career in the practice of medicine.

Internship and Residency:
Junior Attending Physician

THE University of Chicago in my day issued only a 4 year certificate at the end of their fourth year period of training, to be sure that their graduates had an internship. The M.D. was withheld until the completion of one year internship or supervised research. Many states did not require internships for general practice. Internships for Negro doctors were limited almost exclusively to Negro hospitals. Cook County hospital was the only so-called white hospital in Chicago which knowingly had a Black intern through the 1920's and for a considerable longer period.

Provident Hospital in Chicago established by the primary efforts of Negro doctor Dan Williams in 1892 with considerable help from white philanthropy and medical school professors, was essentially a Negro hospital. It was one of the better ones in the United States. I happened to choose Freedmen's Hospital, connected with Howard University in Washington. For one thing, I wanted to go back east and be nearer my family again. I would have been happy to have been Cook County hospital's Black quota of "one" that year but my politics failed and no other Black medical school graduate from the surrounding area was selected in 1929. I hope that some of my readers are still around who will remember that County Hospital internships required a competitive county civil service examination in those days. But all Negro and some white candidates who were successful had considerable political help in being appointed.

My internship was profitable and interesting from several points of view. I met and came to know qualified Black medical school professors

239

who were attending physicians and surgeons at Freedmen's Hospital. I met fellow Black interns from Howard and MeHarry whose training and abilities I came to respect. I made friendships which lasted through the years.

Near the end of the year at Freedmen's I decided to take the examinations of the National Board of Medical Examiners. It was given in three parts at the same time with the same questions all over the country. Candidates were identified by numbers only, except at the central headquarters where names and numbers were codified. I wanted to be able to practice medicine in all states but primarily I wanted to see what kind of grade I would get when the examiner didn't know my complexion. I received the 2nd highest grade level in the country in physiology. I felt it was a compliment to my medical school that I ranked among the very highest in this examination.

About this time I learned that my medical alma mater had formed an affiliation with Provident Hospital in Chicago. Graduate fellowships with Rockefeller money were being given to young Negro medical graduates from all over the country who had finished their internship and were otherwise qualified and interested. The plan which included "residencies or residency equivalents" were awarded with the understanding that following a three-year period of training, they would affiliate with Provident Hospital. The unannounced expectations of many of the white medical hierarchy was that these specialty trained physicians at Provident Hospital would then train "all-of-the-rest-of-them."

It should be said to the everlasting credit of the people involved at the Univ. of Chicago, led by the enthusiasm of a great physician, Dr. Franklin C. McClain that the University of Chicago-Provident affiliation brought opportunities to young Negro doctors which could not be duplicated anywhere else in the United States. McClain was an outstanding scientist who had worked at the Rockefeller Institute of Medical Research in New York City as well as at medical schools in China. He returned to the University of Chicago, where he had held an appointment years before. He was thoroughly missionary minded. At this time the university was severing its relationship with the westside Presbyterian hospital center, which held the original Rush Medical college charter. The university's plan was to set up its own hospital center on its south campus instead of sending its juniors and seniors to the westside Presbyterian center. The first and central hospital was named Billings. The plan called for a distinctly unique and different hospital; different from any in town. With vast sums of money at its disposal Billings Hospital would only have full time paid professors and teachers and hospital attending doctors, which was very unique at that time. Its interest in research and training professors for other institutions would be greater than ever. Weights and measurements would be changed to the European metric system and its thermometers from fahrenheit to centigrade of the original French scale. There would be no Black patients nor Black doctors nor Black nurses nor Black janitors.

I was called by Dean Harvey into his office for further briefing about the beginning of my junior year in the fall of 1927. The last nail had been driven in the new Billings Hospital and they would be accepting their first patients that fall. Dean Harvey, an anatomist from Canada was a very nice man, but rather naive in adjusting to the intricacies, strategies and practices of America, with its well ingrained racial mixtures.

He said to me very frankly, with no double talk or polish such as I had been accustomed to from others; he obviously meant no harm nor did he mean to embarrass me. "Mr. Berry," he said, "when the fall term opens, Billings Hospital will have its first patients, the white boys will choose either to continue to go west to Presbyterian and central free dispensary for their classes or to stay south and do their clinical work at Billings. The Black boys will have to go west to the original Rush; they will not be assigned to Billings. "Because you see, Mr. Berry, Billings is going to be a brand new type of hospital. They will have no Black patients, they won't even have many poor white patients. They are going to cater to middle class patients who can cooperate with their research." "We are sure, therefore, that these patients would not tolerate being examined by a Black doctor or medical students." I thanked him very, very quickly and beat it out of the office hopefully before he could change his mind. For me, it was like throwing a rabbit into the briar patch. For two years or more I had been hearing about the great Sippys, the Herricks, the Tices's, the Bevens, etc., the great and famous teachers of the Westside. I found no one who knew the young new professors who would open the Billings Hospital. They were well selected and trained with unusual potential as proven by their later accomplishments and fame in the profession. Months later I learned about one or two whose reputations might have challenged a few of the Westside group.

What does all this have to do with Provident Hospital three years later when I appeared on the scene to accept training in internal medicine and gastroenterology for an unsalaried position on the staff of what was then being called the "Greater Provident Hospital?"

It soon became very clear that the University of Chicago was gradually cutting loose from the westside. Their master plan which became clearly obvious as the years past, was to gradually send their Negro students across Washington Park to the "Greater Provident" following their two years of basic training on the university campus.

To the credit of missionary minded Dr. McLean the medical administration believed that it was solving a great problem, thanks to the convincing persuasion of McLean who was in the very center of the new Billings development. To be credited also are several of the Billings clinicians who felt that it was their duty to see to it that by supervising emissaries sent over to Provident Hospital the Black graduates who would wear the University seal would have had training up to the professional standards of the University. These Negro doctors saw only Negro patients and mostly Negro doctor teachers and, just like the dean said, they were not permitted access to Billings Hospital.

My graduate specialty training was received for the most part at the County Hospital with occasional guest staff rounds at Billings Hospital. This came after a few years of development of some camaraderie which developed between Provident attending staff and some of the doctors at Billings.

My training at County for three-and-a-half years consisted of daily ward rounds seeing and examining patients in internal medicine and gastroenterology, attending conferences, observing in gastrointestinal x-rays and a considerable period in the morgue assisting with autopsies and carrying out research on pathological cases for which I later received a master's degree in pathology from the University of Illinois and County Hospital.

The late Sidney A. Portis who had been a younger professor of mine during the years at Rush was my great sponsor there. He not only made openings for me at County but came to my rescue when needed in those years. My first lecture before a medical society was given before the

(Negro) Cook County Physicians Association using the slides of Dr. Portis who discussed my masterpiece after my presentation.

For ten years after my residency and while I was developing a gastrointestinal division at Provident, I looked over the shoulder of Dr. Portis while he saw his patients in the Mandel Clinic of Michael Reese Hospital. It was only then that he and his friend Heinrich Necheles had the courage to sponsor my request for membership on the staff at Michael Reese. I became a member of the "limited courtesy" staff to break the first Black ice in that institution. A few years later Dr. Portis died but through the years I have often spoken of him as my "patron saint" because of the many opportunities he sponsored for me in my very early years in medicine.

Because of the racial pattern of medical care in Chicago in the thirties, forties and fifties, Provident Hospital not only had fully accredited internships and residencies in all of the branches of medicine, but its staff with some continued help from the University of Chicago trained more Negro specialists than any other center in the country. In the 1940s the great majority of all Negro certified specialists had received all or most of their training at Provident Hospital in Chicago.

I opened my services as junior attending physician at Provident Hospital in the field of gastroenterology in 1934. At this time the Greater Provident Hospital had only 200 beds, but it had the 4th largest outpatient clinic in the city. Interns and residents in medicine did some rotation through my service and I eventually had three or four general practitioners interested in gastroenterology working with me.

In 1935 Dr. Rudolph Schindler, a gastroenterologist, who had developed the first practical gastroscope three years before, came to the University of Chicago from Munich, Germany. Hearing of the new invention and of the recent arrival of Professor Schindler at the University, I approached Dr. Sidney Portis who was kind enough to introduce me to him. Because of the University-Provident affiliation I was soon able to look over Dr. Schindler's shoulder at Billings once a week, while he gastroscoped patients and discussed in scholarly detail their stomach problems.

After about nine months of this, near the end of 1936, I induced Dr. Schindler to come over to my clinic at Provident once a week to gastroscope some of my interesting patients. He found this acceptable

243

and soon became very interested because to quote Dr. Schindler, "you have many cases and they are all very well worked up." Once a week, thereafter, I would pick up Dr. and Mrs. Schindler, who always worked with him, and transport them in my automobile to the GI clinic at Provident Hospital.

Dr. and Mrs. Schindler continued to visit my clinic for eight or nine months until I had gastroscoped a hundred patients with Dr. Schindler virtually looking over my shoulder, guiding and supervising teaching technique. There was also a wholesome clinical discussion of patients and their problems. Dr. Schindler's personal gastroscope was used during most of this period until I was able to purchase one of the earliest gastroscopes manufactured by the George Wolf Company of Berlin. It had been slightly used by a doctor in this country who purchased it while visiting in Germany but found little time to study the procedure and use the instrument in this country. Dr. Schindler taught me to number in a serial fashion a copy of the report on every patient I gastroscoped and to keep these in an organized fashion in my private files. Incidentally I have continued this practice for more than 35 years. And my serial number has reached very near 15,000. I appreciated Dr. Schindler, very much indeed as a dedicated teacher and as a friend.

Mrs. Schindler was a very charming person who handled every patient with exceptional tenderness and kindness while the doctors looked into their stomachs through rubberized semi-flexible tubes which contained lens and a tiny electric light bulb which brought into view the empty stomach blown up by the inflation of air. This instrument was called the gastroscope.

When Schindler left my clinic I went full steam ahead with this very interesting work in connection with the care of patients with digestive diseases in my free clinic as well as private patients at Provident Hospital. In a few years I had examined more patients and written as many papers as anyone in the country other than Dr. Schindler himself. I continued a very occasional visit to Dr. Schindler's clinic and once in a while when he was out of town and had a visitor at Billings, the visiting doctor would be brought across the park to my clinic at Provident.

I became interested and curious about the appearance of the lining of the stomachs of severe alcoholic addicts who lived in Chicago's skid row near the "loop" on South State and West Madison Streets. This interest developed while working part time as a police doctor at the main headquarters located at 1121 South State Street. My first approach was to get permission to examine their stomachs in the Bridewell Jail Hospital. It wasn't very long before my case load ran dry, because the nurses did not care to be bothered without ever actually saying so. The exciting observation of the first dozen patients was the remarkable lack of inflamation of the stomachs of patients who drank very heavily everyday for months or years. Very excitedly I reported this to my teacher and friend, Dr. Schindler.

A few weeks later my clinic nurse brought me a newspaper clipping describing a great professor from the University of Chicago who was trying to get permission to examine the so called vagabonds with his gastroscope. Meanwhile I had found more successful "pickings" by driving into the "loop" at 6 a.m. approaching these so-called "derelicts" coming out of their flop houses after sleeping off their drunkedness the night before. I would take them to Provident Hospital, make the examination, do further studies on their stomach secretions and blood and have their chests fluoroscoped for tuberculosis. I would then give them a supply of vitamins especially the "B" complex. While none of these men felt they were sick, I gave them advice and suggested County Hospital if and when they felt the need. I gave these patients 25 cents a head out of my family budget and a street car token to get back to the loop.

One day I picked up a man who said, "You only give two bits, the professor at the university gives 50 cents." I then knew that I was in a real research race with my chief. I reported my studies in a paper read before the American Medical Association section on gastroenterology and proctology at its annual convention in Cleveland, Ohio, 1941, two weeks before Pearl Harbor. I had made a preliminary report six months before at a meeting of the Chicago Society of Internal Medicine.

The lecture before the A.M.A. turned out to be the first presentation ever made by a Negro doctor before the American Medical Association convention. As a young man I was stunned by this confirmed news. At this point, I was ahead of my chief in the race to report studies which had never been reported before in the annals of world medicine.

It was revealed six months before that I had done many more cases than his group. He had not presented a paper before any society but after the A.M.A. meeting his friend Dr. Morris Fishbein jumped Dr.

Schindler's paper over mine which was part of the proceedings of an A.M.A. national convention and published the Schindler paper in the Journal of the A.M.A. I made a trip to see the editor, to lodge a protest. Dr. Fishbein, I said, "You may not know me, sir, but as a medical student I took your course in medical writing." I have submitted manuscripts to your journal before and had them denied because "proceedings papers took presidence." I, then, mentioned the Schindler paper which was very similar but given priority over a convention paper. "Oh yes, Dr. Berry, I know all about your fine work in gastroenterology, in fact whenever I have a patient, who has a colored maid, who has a stomache I always recommend you very highly. Fishbein published my paper the very next month with my note indicating my published preliminary report in the proceedings of the Institute of Medicine of Chicago six months before.

The Schindler-Berry friendship was sharply interrupted, but we be came friends again after one or two years. We began to quote each others research in our writings. Dr. Schindler's research was supported by the Rockefeller Foundation and the financial resources of the University of Chicago. My support at this time and for years later came out of my family budget in a bookstraps operation at Provident Hospital where research funds were not available and my private office where I established a research laboratory. The Schindler-Berry friendship continued then for about twenty more years.

Meanwhile I had become a member of the attending staff of the Cook County Hospital and a teacher of gastroscopy in the Cook County Graduate School of Medicine. Early in these appointment periods I had developed the Eder-Berry gastrobiopsy-scope which was the first direct vision suction instrument for removing diseased tissue from the stomach for miscroscopic examination. Dr. Schindler eventually returned to native Munich after some years of infeeblement, and it was there that he died. This brought to an end a long friendship with one of my great medical teachers who gave me an opportunity when there were very few available to me for which I am everlastingly grateful.

Emanuel, Portsmouth, Va.
(1921–1926)

Pop completed his Presiding Eldership years in charge of the Portsmouth District of the Virginia A.M.E. Annual Conference. This period in life of the Berrys followed Pop's pastorate at St. James where we lived on Berkley Ave., Norfolk and I attended and graduated from Booker T. Washington High School. The younger children attended Lincoln Grammar School.

As Presiding Elder, we lived in a house which Pop owned. This was a great relief to Mom from parsonages supplied to the minister's family on a temporary basis by various churches. However, at the annual conference of 1921 Pop was appointed to the pastorate of Emanuel Church in Portsmouth. I had just completed my first year at Wilberforce. It meant another move for Mom and the family.

"Berry, I have plans for you," said Bishop J. Albert Johnson. "I have watched your Presiding Eldership carefully. You can have a brilliant future in the Church. I want to give you that chance. I am taking you from presiding over small churches and sending you to historic Emanuel. Keep that under your hat."

The good bishop was reared and trained as physician and theologian in Ontario, Canada. He had served in South Africa before his appointment to the Second Episcopal District of Maryland, Virginia and North Carolina. He was highly respected as an efficient religious leader throughout the Church.

Pop became the bishop's principal "cabinet member" in Virginia and a close personal friend. The 1921 Annual Conference opened in April with communion services led by the erudite and princely Bishop J. Albert Johnson. He reconvened the Conference early the next day. Ministers wore their best bibs and tuckers. The ladies dressed in bright summer frocks, many with corsages of spring flowers and brightly colored parasols. As usual, there was a semi-festive mood as brothers and sisters showed off their socio-religious status in clothing and ecclesiastical stance. Out-of-town visiting dignitaries were introduced. Among them were Bishop A. L. Gaines of Baltimore and the Rev. Francis Gow of Johannesburg, South Africa, later to become the first African-born A.M.E. bishop.

Inside the church, the Rev. J. Mainor of Oceana had just made his pastoral report. The Reverend was highly visible with his robust stature and flowing red wig. Typhoid fever had left him without a strand of natural hair. The only reason for the red wig was its similarity to his natural red hair, which harmonized with his Scandinavian fair skin with a "touch" of African. Rev. Mainor's principal claim to fame was his talented daughter, Dorothy, studying at Hampton Institute, with J. Nathaniel Dett. Dorothy Maynor became a renowned concert singer.

Sunday night came and the church was jam packed. Congregations of the entire state wanted first-hand news of what pastor would be assigned to what church by the all-powerful, all-knowing bishop. In those days of the Methodist itinerancy, if you were a preacher you travelled. Annually, you gave an accounting of your stewardship. You took the worst with the best and you moved with your uprooted family forward and backward every one to five years.

At the appointed zero hour and after an appropriate sermon, the bishop gesticulated, the congregation rose and sang gustily with the ministerial voices ringing out above the others, "I'll go where you want me to go, Dear Lord." Somebody had to save the souls at North Snake Creek Circuit, and historic St. John's on Norfolk's Bute Street could accommodate only one head preacher at a time. Rev. I. L. Butt, Senior Presiding Elder, beckoned Rev. Berry to the pastor's study early during the evening service. "Berry, I hear its in the bag. You are moving on up to Emanuel. Your leadership role at the General Conference is paying off." The colorful Rev. Butt was a slave escapee from Great Bridge, Va. during the Civil War siege of Norfolk and served as Justice-of-the-Peace in Norfolk during Reconstruction Days.

The ever-present visiting Dean Frederick Woodson of Payne Theological Seminary at Wilberforce hobbled out on his cane, soliciting financial support for the "Educated Ministry." After a long life, his heirs exhibited some of the finest real estate and homes-for-sale along the Columbus Pike between Wilberforce and Xenia, Ohio.

"How do you do, Dean?" said one of his former students.

"Well, if it isn't the Rev. Jim Hatcher. I am just struggling along, but you look great." "Thank you, Dean."

"You remember I always said as a theological student that as long as there was something of value out there, I would get some of it." "Yes, yes," smiled the Dean.

"I remember your witty and humorous spirit. Where are you now? Are you still singing?"

"I am pastor at Roanoke," said the dapper and handsome Rev. Hatcher, "and singing and composing, too." (But for the early demise of the brilliant and personable James Hatcher, he might have been an A.M.E. Bishop like his brother Eugene.)

The Dean continued, "I often think of your fine tenor voice, and your pranks at the Seminary. We still sing your popular composition, *I Cannot Drift Beyond His Care*. "Thank you, Dean. Here's hoping the wind remains always at your back and that your foot never slips from the cross." Enjoying a mutual smile, the Dean waved so-long with his walking stick, as the dapper James Hatcher sauntered away.

When Rev. Berry's name was called, Bishop Johnson said: "One of the leading ministers in the Virginia Conference and the Second District is the Rev. L. L. Berry. He has a fine family and I am sending him where he can continue his leadership and effectiveness in the community and Church at historic Emanuel in Portsmouth, Virginia." There was great applause and expressions of satisfaction from that church membership which had known him as Presiding Elder. Rev. Berry prepared during the next several days to move his family across the Elizabeth River from Norfolk to the beautiful church and parsonage on North Street in Portsmouth. There was much joy in the hearts of the Berry family as well as in the heart of the new pastor of Emanuel. Only a small proportion of the population in the Tidewater area of Virginia had homes with electric lighting, steam heat, and hot and cold water bath. These facilities were made possible in The Emanuel Parsonage next to the church by a common heating plant and other joint arrangements.

The Emanuel Church building was picturesque. A portion of its facade near the entrance was taken from one of its earlier buildings in the days of slavery. The church began near the time of the American Revolutionary War as the "African Society." Its members had eight or nine white ministers before they had their first colored minister.

One of the earliest was Rev. George Bain. In all of this early period, the white ministers of the Monumental Methodist Church also pastored the Black congregation, mostly slaves, but some free men, in a separate and very unequal building. An important reason for the white charity was to keep a white eye on the Black slaves. Emanuel's first Black minister was Rev. James A. Handy, later a bishop, who brought African Methodism from Baltimore to Portsmouth in 1864.

A large proportion of the members in 1921 were intellectually and economically middle-class people, who enjoyed his well-prepared sermons as the imagery of community leadership. In those days a large number of Black school teachers also taught Sunday school. Other professionals, semi-professionals, business people and civil servants attended the A. M. E. Church in large numbers.

When my freshman college year ended in 1921 I went home to Portsmouth because summer resort jobs were scarce. The country was in a recession.

I found that "Mother Beulah" had been poorly for several months. I had not been informed of mother's illness. Her troubles were more or less mild and non-chronic. What was thought to be a tumor at first ended in a "problem solving delivery" in August. It was "Gerri" (Geraldine), arriving 10 years after her nearest sibling, brother Elbert. Mother, at age 42 years, was a bit embarrassed in her new pastoral setting. The church sisters came with their joyful greetings and congratulations. Mom's youngest sister, Lula, who grew up with the Berry family came from Hampton Institute in June and was briefed on coming events. "Lula," said the expectant mother, "I still find Dr. Francis' diagnosis hard to believe at my age." Lula, known for her wit and frankness, replied, "Well, Sister, you know what you've been doing, don't you?" The modest and sedate minister's wife walked slowly and silently away.

Mom and Pop celebrated their 25th wedding anniversary while at Emanuel. The occasion was beset with glamour and splendor. There was wide attendance by relatives and friends throughout the state of Virginia and elsewhere. The usual amenities for such an occasion were carried out. The Sunday school orchestra furnished background music. A very large number of silver gifts were received. Nuptial vows were repeated and I was "urged" to sing Cadman's "At Dawning, I Love You." While some of the guests were still eating silver frosted cake a few of us sneaked out the back door and over to the Churchhill's to do a little "rug cutting" to the tunes of Fats Waller's "Ain't Misbehavin'," "Moanin' Low" and other such unreligious songs.

One of the most memorable occasions at Old Emanuel was the Palm Sunday service. "Pop" was at his best in delivering the Palm Sunday message. The ritual of waving the palms while singing the anthem by the same name is well-remembered. Emanuel had an excellent choir with Professor Hiram Simmons, the notable composer and chorister directing. But, on Palm Sunday, as far back as anyone cared to remember, the talented and pompous soprano, Sister Johnsie Churchill always sang "The Holy City." No diva from the Metropolitan Opera House could have replaced her. Certainly no one else in the choir or congregation dared challenge her for the honor. In later years, as she sang "Jerusalem! Jerusalem! Hosanna in the highest," some sisters and brothers would hold their breaths in anticipation of Sister Johnsie's highest note, fearful that some day she just might not make it.

Always on the following Sunday, with the church packed with young and old wearing their Easter finery, the sacred story of the resurrection was told and retold in words and music. Classic anthems of the Old World masters were interspersed with hymns of faith and Negro spirituals. Beethoven's "Passion According to St. Matthew" or portions of Handel's "Messiah," "When I Survey the Wondrous Cross," or "Were You There When They Crucified My Lord?" were also rendered.

The text of Rev. Berry's Easter sermon was frequently taken from the Gospel of St. Matthew, Chapter 28, Verse 6: "He is not here: for He is risen as He said. Come see the place where the Lord lay." He once began by saying:

"Easter brings us to the battlefield of spiritual conflict. Here the church renews her vows and reconsecrates her faith and devotion to God our Father and Christ our Redeemer. If there are doubts in your mind as to the resurrection of Christ, you are called upon to accept the invitation of the text: "Come see the place where the Lord lay."

Meanwhile, in 1924 I had taken Pop's advice and support about going to Chicago to study medicine. This time I left the Tidewater area via the Chesapeake and Ohio railroad to travel beyond my recent haunts at Wilberforce to the far away midwestern metropolis of Chicago. Did I really know where I was going? How could I have known that it was in the destiny of the Berrys that I would "go west" as Horace Greeley advised, "go west, young man and grow up with the country."

St. John's Church
(1926–1932)

"REV. Berry, we run our church." These were the first words of greetings, received by Pop after accepting his appointment at St. John's A. M. E. Church Norfolk at the hands of Bishop J. Albert Johnson. These words came from a committee of officers at St. John's, a committee purported to have been self-appointed. Pop's reputation as a leader, organizer and A. M. E. church disciplinarian had preceded him. The response to this greeting was, "Yes, I know you do, but the Bishop has sent me here to show you how." This statement of the committee had been made previously to the Bishop, who gave them an answer similar to Pop's. The Rev. Mr. Berry, leader of the Virginia conference had been forewarned by the bishop.

St. John's church, an imposing brick structure with an equally interesting parsonage next door was located on East Bute street, not far from the business district of the city, and a block from St. Vincent De Paul Hospital at the corner of Church and Fenchurch streets. Another block away, facing the church was the "colored police station." Not that it was manned by a single person of color, but only that it was located in the Black ghetto and about 99 percent of its reluctant patronage was by black residents and it had a heavy influx of short term tenants on Sunday night. Also in close proximity to the church was the well known and popular Phillis Wheatley Ballroom, where the nearby colleges held forth during the Christmas season with their annual morning, afternoon and evening parties. Many out-of-town students spending the holidays in Norfolk would take time out to worship at St. John's and other churches. Norfolk was the social mecca for Black colleges each competing with the other during the holiday vacation.

253

In spite of many preconceived attitudes or impressions which had been advanced by the St. John's Sunday School "committee," Pop was very warmly and graciously received by the membership and congregation of St. John's as well as by ministers of the local community churches. He found that St. John's was one of the largest Sunday schools in the A. M. E. connection (many thought it was the largest). Much can be said to the credit of the Sunday school as well as the effect it had in the community. So well organized and operated was the Sunday school that it was reputed to rival the general interest in the primary church structure itself, between 1920–1925 and earlier. During this period the Sunday school had such influence and strength in the internal affairs that it dictated the policy of the church. The bishop and ministerial hierarchy were saying "at St. John's the largest A. M. E. church in the Virginia conference the Sunday school pastored the church."

In later years it was said by ministers that Berry was sent to St. John's partly to create a better balance in the church structure, where several pastors had failed. At its highest peak, St. John's Sunday school boasted a membership of several hundred with an average Sunday attendance of two to three hundred. Many of the classes were organized within themselves, having regular meetings and sponsoring fund raising events. The classes assumed names as a distinguished feature, such as "Delta Alpha," "B. F. Lee," "Anti-Can't," "Daniel A. Payne" and "Richard Allen." So circumscribed was Sunday school that many students and teachers would seldom remain for regular morning worship services; having felt their religious and spiritual needs had been fulfilled. Interestingly, for some period the Sunday school superintendent was paid a salary in the same context that the church pastor received.

Under pop's leadership there was immediate and renewed growth of the church; spiritually, financially and in membership. This posed a threat to the continuance of the Sunday school as a "hyphenated" body, presumed by many to be of greater importance. The dynamic growth and interest in the church continued yearly for three years, at which point the Sunday school "wing" apparently could stand it no longer. So, at the last quarterly conference, preceding the annual conference in 1929, the Sunday school in its report did not request the return of the pastor, which was customary, but instead recommended to presiding elder Rev. Fred Seaton that the pastor not be returned.

What followed was a series of charges and counter-charges, resulting in the resignation of the Sunday school superintendent, his assistants, several teachers, adult members and young people. Subsequently, they withdrew their membership from the church.

The effect that this scism might have on the young people was Pop's greatest concern. Naturally, this loss in membership was felt for a while; but in spite of any turbulence and descension the church survived and continued to prosper. Dormant leadership abilities, talents and skills surfaced resulting in a rebirth of a more vibrant and influential church with reasonable and customary balance in all aspects of church life.

One might ask why the development of this disproportionate growth of the Sunday school? It should be noted that a large proportion of the classes were adults "Bible classes." The likelihood is that there were strong laymen who desired to express their leadership at a greater speed and in a different direction than that of their appointed pastors. They did a good job as they saw it. Which, however, threw out of balance and caused retrogression of the authorized and organized structure of the church.

One unfortunate effect of this strong difference between the ministerial philosophy based on A. M. E. law and custom and that of some laymen, was that members of some families followed the dissenters while other family members continued their connection with St. John's A. M. E. Church.

The worship service and sermons of "the Rev. Berry" grew in popularity and stature throughout the city. Pop used to say that his sermons had to be geared to three segments in the congregation. The first part was the persons who sat in the rear of the church and would respond only to higher intellectual form of discourse. Incidentally they might even leave before the collection was lifted. The second part was persons to the center of the church whose reaction was usually mixed; and the third part was to the majority who occupied the front and amen corners." These were always the most fervently responsive and more likely to remain for the benediction.

Among the latter group was Cousin Maria who could always be dependent upon to "quote" and talk back and shout, even though she may not have known what was being said. On one Sunday morning, Cousin Maria came rushing in the church late and out of breath just as the sermon was beginning. Someone had taken her regular seat and this disturbed her religious stability. Near the end of the sermon she managed to go into her regular shouting routine and in the course of her gesticulations her hat fell off. She quickly recovered her hat, pushed it down on her head and held it down with her hands. She took her seat, remained quiet, still holding her hat down, for Cousin Maria had forgotten to comb her hair.

Pop's understanding of the foibles of humans, especially the young was quite evident when a young woman member of St. John's was charged before the Quarterly Conference with "unwedded pregnancy." Several of the older sisters and brothers proposed that the entire matter was settled simply by Pop when he reminded the accusers of the words of Christ when an adulteress was brought before Him. He further reminded them of their Christian duty to be compassionate, understanding and forgiving and to lend a helping hand to the unfortunate young lady.

The temporary setback resulted not only in a spiritual renaissance but in financial success previously not experienced. As a fourth annual conference was imminent, groups were voluntarily organized to raise conference fees. Monies poured in that far exceeded expectation.

Before leaving for the Annual Conference that year, Pop in his "farewell" remarks to the congregation said, "I thank all of you who have so loyally stood by me with increasing Christian loyalty this year. I must include in my thanks those who have fought against me in the progress of the church, even when I was temporarily confined to a sick bed. Tomorrow, I shall make my report to the conference, the best and greatest report that has ever gone out of St. John's church in its long history. I may not return here as your pastor but I will go somewhere. If I don't see those who have attempted to obstruct my program and to unfairly take advantage of me, if I do not see you anymore on this earth, I'll meet you in heaven, I'll join arms with you and walk around the Glory Land forgetting your unkind deeds here at St. John's." This produced "amens" and "hallelujahs" all over the church.

As a happy climax to all this, the members presented him a new suit of clothes (the custom in some churches but not previously at proud St. John's.) The Ministerial Alliance presented him an overcoat and hat. So Pop strutted into conference like the outstanding success that hundreds of people felt him to be. He was returned by the bishop and served two more successful years at St. John's.

During the next year many successfully and interesting events occurred at the church. One of them was the selection of St. John's for the meeting place and entertainment of the quarterly meeting of the Bishops Council of the total A. M. E. Church. Many citywide civic affairs meetings were held at St. John's. The children of Rev. Berry were always interestingly involved in church affairs except when they were away at boarding school. Pop felt that his children served the social barometer for him and that they were cognizant of the "goings on" in the community and often participated in some of them; notwithstanding the fact that they knew the "place of preachers children." The Berry children were sometimes involved in activities which attracted participation of young people from other churches and denomination.

Our sister Gladys was a member of the "BUGS Social Club." Gladys states that one day, while having a casual talk with Pop, he said to her; "Gladys, now that you are out of college and making your own money, why not on your own initiative do something that will help me here in the church work." I began to think of how good Dad had been to me and the struggle it had been to send all of his children to college, four of them at the same time. Fortunately the three boys were able to help themselves a great deal during school and the summers between. I thought this would be my big chance to show Dad some appreciation. For days I wondered just what I could do that would raise some money. I decided to call some of my friends and to see if they would help me put on a play which should be fun for all of us. I first mentioned the idea to my best girlfriend, Marilyn Hall, who later became my sister-in-law. Gladys continued, I then contacted Gaynell Clanton, Doris Dungee, Maxine Ferebee, my brother Elbert, Louis Tyler and Ellis Corbit. Everyone thought it was a good idea and wanted to take part.

It was decided that we would do a better job if we had someone specially trained in dramatics to help. I suggested Vivian Huckles, who taught English and dramatics in the junior high school. She was contacted and agreed to help. I had already selected a play called "Eyes of Love" a comedy drama in three acts, which was accepted by the group. Most of the casting was self-selected and all rehearsals were held at the St. John's parsonage. Sometimes long after the appointed hour no one had shown up and I would get on the telephone and assure them that Pop would pick them up. That he would do. We had our ups and downs, but finally general interest developed. Gladys continued, one night my boyfriend Samuel Hooper, whom I had appointed manager said; "who are we, what shall we call ourselves?" I said to the group, "let's call ourselves the Players Guild." I shall never forget the night of the dress rehearsal. Vivian was a little disgusted, bawled everybody out and we went home. Meanwhile, Pop had seen to it that there was adequate advertisement to church circles and otherwise. At the Booker T. Washington High School Auditorium the following night, we had a capacity crowd and the play went off beautifully. G. James Flemming of *The Norfolk Journal and Guide* gave us a very good write up. Pop was very proud of me and we turned in a net proceed of $50 to the church.

A little later The Players threw a big party for themselves. I presented the idea that we become a continuing organization and study dramatics. It was generally agreed, we solicited more members and we became a little theatre group. During the next year we presented two or three short plays. The "Players Guild" was on its way and has continued through the years even to the present time far beyond any of our initial expectations. Two years later my father became Secretary of Missions of the A. M. E. Church with headquarters in New York.

During the last two years at St. John's church, Elbert was active at the Booker T. Washington High School as president of the senior class, the HI-Y Club, the Philosophian Lyceum and twice delegated to the annual older boys conference at Virginia State College, and to a national YMCA conference at King's Mountain, North Carolina. For a few months after graduation he was the assistant to Mr. J. W. Anderson, secretary of the Hunton Branch YMCA. Lew was active during his high school days in Tau Beta Sigma, a high school Greek letter society and social club. He gave the general impression that he never took life too seriously considering the time that he was seen with books. He was always expected to be academically vulnerable but he always came up with decent grades. And in college and later years he was always measured up in achievements when somehow his friends seemed surprised.

This period was probably one of the toughest financially for Pop because of the educational burden of four children in college at the same time. At the college level Gladys was a senior at Virginia State while Dick and Lew were students of Wilberforce. Elbert was entering the theological seminary at Howard University and I was in medical school at the University of Chicago. As I graduated and entered my internship at Freedmen's Hospital and residency at Cook County Hospital in Chicago, Elbert was entering Howard still leaving four Berrys in college at the same time. The four boys always worked after school and during the intervening summers. Mom and Pop always maintained a strong faith and trust in the Almighty and in the belief that he would make a way. I received a scholarship during the first two years of my residency and was able to send some help to Elbert. Dick stayed out of Wilberforce for one year and worked a Larchmont, N.Y. Hotel in order to assist Lew through his senior year. He received his degree majoring in biology and was able to find work to help Dick receive his degree in business administration.

Emanuel, Portsmouth, Va.
(1932–1933)

IN April, 1932 Pop was transferred after six years from St. John's Church, Norfolk back to Emanuel in Portsmouth.

This was Pop's second pastorate of Emanuel, with St. John's of Norfolk in between. It was unusual in those days for a congregation to accept a pastor for the second time after his pastorate elsewhere. Rev. Berry's acceptance was an expression of the unusual love and respect previously developed between the pastor and the congregation which enjoyed his sermons and his community relations extremely well. A large proportion of the members consisted of intellectually and economically middle class people, who enjoyed his well-prepared sermons as the imagery of his community leadership. In those days a large number of Black school teachers also taught Sunday school. Other professionals, semi-professionals, business people and civil servants attended the A. M. E. Church in large numbers.

Among the many loyal and outstanding members was Sister Lucinda Morris, mother of the late Dr. S. S. Morris, Senior and grandmother of Bishop S. S. Morris, Jr., the eighty-ninth bishop of the A. M. E. church. She was leader of class #25 for many years. Another reason for the love and appreciation of Sister Morris by the Berrys was that she called the Reverend one of her sons, and the Berrys were always her guests for dinner on New Year's Day.

Another very fine and loyal member of Emanuel was school teacher, Mrs. Sylvia Bynum representative of the intelligence that chose Emanuel as a place for worship. Mrs. Bynum was most unusual. She enjoyed Rev. Berry's sermons so much during his presiding eldership and two pastorates that she took notes as he delivered his sermons. She presented to me a long list of his prize collections of Pop's subjects, and texts and biblical texts as they were delivered to his membership over a 5-year period. She pointed out that his sermons were well prepared and eloquently delivered, never longer than 15 to 20 minutes. Mrs. Bynum, who has remained a close family friend thru the years would not part with her notes.

Another loyal well known and picturesque gentleman called "Ye Scribe" was the church clerk, well into his eighties. He was hardly ever seen without the church record book under his arm. He held office as a young man during the Reconstruction period and went to war as a body servant to a Confederate Colonel in the Civil War.

One of the most important events in Pop's climb in community service was his election as "Most Worshipful Grand Master" of the Masonic Grand Lodge for the state of Virginia, Prince Hall jurisdiction. This occurred in 1932 following the death of the previous grand master, Dr. Caesar Bassette. Mom was a Worthy Matron of the Prince Hall Eastern Star lodge named for her. Pop received all of the degrees in masonry to the 33rd degree. He was a member of many fraternal organizations including Elks, Odd Fellows, etc. He enjoyed the fellowship of men in such organizations, all of whom were built on a background of Christianity, which was practiced in their rituals. The Masons were undoubtedly his favorite lodge. With his usual smooth persuasion, his sons became Masons; two of them acquiring higher degrees and state offices.

Pop often repeated with pride the founding of Black Masonry in America. Prince Hall came over from Barbadoes to Boston in the immediate pre-revolutionary times. When the war began, he was refused admission to join the white patriots in their fight against England. As a skilled leather worker he supplied drumheads to the Boston Artillery Regiments in 1777. During the British occupation of Boston he was initiated in the order by Masons in the British army. He then set up Black Masonry and after many fights and years, Prince Hall Masonry is now generally accepted as an official jurisdiction.

It was always interesting to Pop who was interested in Black cultural history that Prince Hall set up Black Masonry in 1787, the very same year that Richard Allen withdrew from St. George's in Philadelphia, ultimately to found the African Methodist Episcopal Church. The American Constitutional Convention was in session at the time and it was one year before the election of George Washington as President.

Pop, with others, preached that the Black church became the first and continuous repository for Black culture and history. He would hasten to explain however, that Black so-called secret organizations have played a dual role with the Black church as the bedrock of organized progress in its struggle for equality and freedom. Pop's almost total involvement in the recognition and promotion of these concepts played an important role in the destiny and successes of his family in his generation and those generations which followed.

Perhaps the most significant and dramatic event during Pop's short return pastorate at Emanuel was the 75th or Diamond anniversary of the founding of the church. There was two weeks of activities from October 31 to November 13, 1932. The pastor and members of the mother church, Monumental Methodist (white) were guests. Pop insisted that his parishioners, in spite of the Virginia state law regarding separation of the races in public assembly, would not be relegated to rear seats in their own house of worship. The compromise resulted in Emanuel members occupying the entire right side of the church and balcony while the visitors occupied the left side. This was a satisfactory arrangement without conflict. The white guest minister delivered an address and the Emanuel choir furnished the music. All sessions were attended by overflow crowds from all black denominations. Emanuel was the oldest black church in existence and second only to Monumental in existing white churches. The celebration carried out in a unique and appropriate manner was one of the great highlights in the history of the city of Portsmouth.

During one of the meetings the older members of Emanuel were called upon to give a personal testimony of their experiences in the city and church. Long remembered was the speech of one brother, Wayman Riddick, whose nickname was "Dog Take It" Riddick. He was in his late 70's. He ended his impromptu speech with the following, "I have been living in Portsmouth all my life and I am proud to say that I have one of the best police records in town." This of course brought much laughter but was correctly understood. The final day of the celebration featured an anniversary dinner. Preceding a beautiful pageant depicting the history of the church and of black people in Portsmouth and the state of Virginia. With everyone who likes sweets nibbling on a piece of diamond anniversary cake, the historic celebration came to an end.

Section Six
Secretary of Mission's Years
and Children's Careers
(1933-60)

Secretary Berry's Foreign Missionary Safari 1939

Secretary and Mrs. Berry, daughter Geraldine (r.), and South African delegation in front of Mission House, New York; Berry aboard R.M.S. *Queen Mary*, 1st leg of trip to West Africa. Berry (c.) and Rev. D. P. Talbot with faculty of A.M.E. School, Paramaribo, Dutch Guiana; A.M.E. Monrovia College, Monrovia, Liberia, West Africa; Rev. E. J. Randall, missionary and ordained A.M.E. minister, Gold Coast (Ghana), West Africa, leader of A.M.E. conferences.

Back row from l. to r.:
Richard O. Berry, Elbert J.
Berry, Homer Smith, Sidney
Barthwell (Best Man), Col-
ston LeGrande, Forest
Blount, Llewellyn Berry, Jr.,
Leonidas Berry, Alfred
Young.

Wedding of Miss Gladys Ursula Berry, daughter of Rev. and Mrs. L. L. Berry of
New York, to Atty. Charles Fisher of Detroit. Bethel A.M.E. Church, New York
City, 1940. First row from l. to r.: bridesmaids Valleta Harper, Pauline Jackson, Hazel
Fisher, Bride and Groom, Grace Brooks (Maid of Honor), Lillian Goings, Carolyn
Johnson, Naomi Cooper.

The Rev. Berry children grow up and establish their own homes.

Above: Leonidas and Emma Berry; l.: condominium home, in Chicago.

Left: Retirement home of widowed mother Berry and daughter, Gerri, Detroit; c.: Mrs. Llewellyn L. Berry, Sr.; r.: Geraldine Berry.

Right: Home of Llewellyn L. Jr. and Kathryn Berry in Washington, D.C.; l.: Llewellyn; c.: Kathryn.

(R.) LaVaughn and (c.) Gladys (Berry) Yates, and (l.) their home in Detroit.

(L.) Richard and (c.) Maryland Berry and (r.) their home in Detroit.

Elbert and Blanche Berry and their home in Hollis, N.Y.

Father and daughter.

The Leonidas Berry's at their summertime Idle-wild, Michigan retreat.

Above r.: Mother Ophelia and Judy; daughter Judith Ann on her horse "Jady;" the cottage on Paradise Lake.

50th Wedding Anniversary Celebration, Secretary and Mrs. L. L. Berry, Reception Rooms, the Mission House, New York, 1950; from l. to r.: Mrs. Emory Ross, Rev. Harris, Dr. Emory Ross, Dr. O. Clay Maxwell, Bishop John A. Gregg, Bishop S. L. Greene, Bishop R. R. Wright, Jr., Dr. and Mrs. L. L. Berry.

From Pastor
to General Officer (1933)

ON April 8, 1933, Pop received a telegram from Mr. Walter F. Walker, assistant to the Secretary of Missions. The telegram read "The Secretary of Missions died today, funeral here at Bethel Church next Tuesday." Similar messages were sent to all the bishops and general officers of the A. M. E. Church, as well as other members of the board of managers of which Pop was, at that time, the board secretary.

The death of Secretary Coit left a void in missionary office affairs because there was no authorized head to take over immediately the operation of the office. The chairman of the board of managers, Bishop H. B. Parks was confined to bed by illness in his California home. He authorized Bishop W. H. Heard, senior bishop and one of the vice presidents to call a meeting and act in his stead.

At the close of the funeral services which Pop attended on April 11, 1933, Bishop W. H. Heard, Senior Vice President of the board called an emergency board meeting. This was done at the request of Bishop H. B. Parks, President of the Board, who could not be present because of illness. Bishop Heard, finding that members present at the funeral constituted a quorum, called a meeting into session. Mr. Walker, Administrative Assistant, was questioned as to the situation of the affairs of the Missionary Department. This was considered such as to constitute an emergency which necessitated a legally empowered person to deal with the same. It was the unanimous opinion of the assembled board of managers that an interim secretary of missions should be elected. The board deemed it the best part of wisdom to elect the late Sec. Coit's successor in accordance with rules and regulations of the A. M. E. Discipline and Articles of Incorporation of the Board of Managers authorized by New York State law. All candidates who had sought the office of the secretary of missions at the previous 1932 General Conference were considered. Pop was the runner-up in that election and had lost by only a small margin. In due parliamentary form, Pop was unanimously elected secretary-treasurer of missions of the A. M. E. and proper credentials were given to him to carry out all functions of that office. He began immediately to assume his duties. He received many congratulatory messages from all over the church and officially recognized and acclaimed in all church periodicals. Likewise appropriate reports and funds were sent to him in accordance with the A. M. E. Church discipline.

Pop returned to the Emanuel Church in Portsmouth, informed the congregation of his elevation to secretaryship of missions and preached a sad sermon of farewell from this pastorate. He had said many times to his family privately that this church and its congregation in many ways was the most rewarding of his many pastorates in North Carolina and Virginia.

The arduous task of packing and moving was begun. There was both joy and sorrow connected with this leave-taking after 21 years in the Tidewater area. A cross country moving company was engaged to haul what personal effects and furniture the family owned, along with Mom's flowers which she much preferred to carry with her rather than leave them with friends. As was the custom, basic furnishing for parsonages were the purchased property of the respective churches. The Berry's had little need for house furnishings since Pop was Presiding Elder several years before. When the possessions of the Berry's were separated from those of the Emanuel parsonage the total cost of transporting the Berry's furnishings to New York was only $75.

Living in the parsonage at Emanuel with Mom and Pop at this time were Gladys who was teaching in the Norfolk public school system, Lew and Elbert who were among the unemployed of the Depression days and Gerri who was in grade school. On arriving in New York, Mom and Gerri stayed with Berthe and Sadie Sawyer, old Virginia friends, until the missionary department living quarters could be refurbished. Lew and Elbert had to "make due" as best they could with Pop at 112 W. 120th St. Dick at this time was still in college at Wilberforce and I had finished medical school at the University of Chicago and an internship at Freedmen's Hospital in Washington and was busy with a residency at

Cook County Hospital in Chicago. Brothers Dick and Lew had made frequent trips to Harlem to find summer work during their days in college which were coming toward an end by 1933.

Aunt Johanna, one of Pop's sisters was a long time resident of Harlem. She, with her husband, Uncle Clarence Mathews had a unique employment set-up which was always available for her brother Lew's sons needing temporary quarters while working their way through college. The Mathews lived in exclusive Washington Heights, where some apartment buildings had an English ground level apartment for a man-woman employment team. The man had building care-taking responsibilities and alternated with the wife in operating a telephone switchboard for the building. Uncle Clarence was a jazz pianist and leader of a jazz combo at one of Harlem's "lesser spots."

The Mathews apartment served as a "launching pad" for Dick's and Lew's work trips on the Fall River Line or resort hotels at Larchmont on Long Island Sound.

With the family moving to Harlem, Dick and Lew were "rabbits in a briar patch." They enjoyed the atmosphere of Harlem which breathed lightheartedness, joy and happiness along its avenues. They were acquainted with the "Bird Cage," "Smalls," "The Savoy," "The Renaissance," and opened faced restaurants with Negroes "munching," smoking, bouncing to the rhythm of juke boxes. Harlem's avenues and front streets were show places, even in the depths of the Depression. Squallor and poverty were hidden behind canopies and paint jobs and on off-centered streets. Rev. Berry's sons were expert at hearing the "sounds" and seeing the "sites" of this unique place without spending a cent of hard earned money for school expenses. They were acquainted with Canal St. and other places where the latest model clothes could be purchased at wholesale prices.

The new Harlem literary and cultural renaissance was settling down in 1933. Dick, Lew and Elbert participated in some activities in these categories. All of the Berry offsprings had varying degrees of literary and religious interests. Elbert having completed one year of work at the Howard University Theological Seminary continued religious activities in New York. However, he got out of the main stream of study for the ministry and into studies in the field of social work. Working with the Allen Christian Endeavor League he was later appointed New

York state superintendent by Bishop D. H. Sims. He became president of the Harlem Church Youth Council and worked with other young people in these activities, some of whom became very well-known in related fields years later. Miss Dorothy Height and Dr. Olivia Stokes were among them. These young people were encouraged and directed by the late Henry Parker of the Harlem YMCA and the late Rev. Edler G. Hawkins. Elbert's further studies and activities led to a long career with the New York State Employment Service of the Dept. of Labor and held offices as the Worshipful Master of St. John's Lodge, Prince Hall Masons in New York city and a Grand Lodge officer.

Setting up housekeeping at a new location was all taken in stride by Mom who was a "professional" at this. Missionary women of the New York Conference under the supervision of Mrs. Mary F. Edwards were wonderful in donating furnishings for the living quarters.

Winning the First Battle and Early Years (1933–37)

IN the midst of all the official and domestic readjustment at the Mission House, things were happening at the high ecclesiastical level of the A. M. E. Church. Pop learned from the grapevine that some of the bishops who were not present at his election were feeling that they did not have an opportunity to have their say. This sentiment was being expressed, although more than a quorum was present at the election.

In due time Pop received a communication from the Council of Bishops requesting him to appear at a meeting of the Council to be held at Wilberforce University, Ohio on June 7, 1933. This was four months after pop's election. He learned that all members of the Mission Board of Managers were also requested to attend the Wilberforce Meeting. It was learned that Bishops Parks, the President of the Bishops Council and also president of the Missionary Board who was still ailing at his home had not called the meeting and objected to any "review" of Rev. Berry's election which he had authorized and which was lawfully conducted according to the discipline of the Church by the Missionary Board.

To clarify what may appear to be a conflict of interest between the two governing bodies it should be explained that all bishops were ex-officio members of the Missionary Board. They attended meetings at their pleasure rarely more than two or three at a time.

It was soon learned by "leaks" from some of the bishops who disagreed with the move that the real purpose was to declare Berry's election illegal and to elect Rev. Carl Flipper, the son of the senior bishop, to the Secretaryship of Missions. As the plans were "leaked" out to church areas around the country the matter became extremely embarrassing to

271

Pop. His election had been announced thru the public press and all the church papers, to the entire Church Connection at home and in all foreign missionary areas. He had received many letters, telegrams and cablegrams of congratulation. There had been editorial comments as to his competence in missionary affairs due to his long membership on the mission board. References were made to his climb from the smallest mission churches to some of the largest metropolitan charges.

Pop discussed all the developments with Mom and the closer members of his family. All of us were extremely embarrassed and some of us were angry. Pop's immediate move was clear. He would of course go to Wilberforce; realizing the gravity of the situation. It was very discouraging for Pop who felt keenly the unfairness of the move obviously shaping up as an Episcopal junta to put into office a bishop's son by unlawfully displacing another of equal or better qualifications.

So as Pop left 112 West 120th Street, he kissed Mom goodbye and bade her take care of things there while he went forth on a trip of destiny. "I'll pray for you Hon," she said, "God will take care of us, now as He always has." "Well," said Pop, "I am still confident that my election was meant to be and it has to work out all right." Elbert helped with the bags, they got into Pop's car and were off through Central Park to the Penn Railroad Station. Elbert discharged his passenger, turned over the bags to a "Red cap" and headed out of the traffic jam of mid-Manhattan back to Harlem. Pop, having picked up his reservations, followed his porter to a Pullman bedroom on the Cincinnati Limited at 4 p.m. He was, at last, alone with himself in the quiet confines of his compartment. He sat there peering into nowhere and feeling a kind of comfort in being completely alone and away from the embarrassing presence of his family and friends. Suddenly, he realized that his uplifted feelings were not due to aloneness, but rather to the very presence of his God whom he trusted.

His favorite psalm which always came to him in times of crisis was soon running through his consciousness. "He that dwelleth in the secret place of the most high shall abide under the shadow of the Almighty." Soon he felt the motions of the big red train of the Pennsylvania Railroad smoothly moving off. It passed through the tunnel under the station and into the daylight of a sunny late afternoon. His thoughts continued to talk to him. "I will say of the Lord, He is my refuge and my fortress. My God; in him will I trust."

The train had picked up its maximum speed and at intervals he was conscious of the rhythmic clicking of the wheels. He glanced out of the window and already the Jersey industrial plants were flashing rapidly by. He had the illusion that he was passing full speed thru the town of Elizabeth. Near the station there was a playground and innocent looking carefree children busily engaged at play in the warm spring atmosphere. Rapidly telegraph posts flashed by at an ever increasing speed. The trees were in full foliage. An occasional suburban housewife was seen working in her garden, or a man sat leisurely on his porch, smoking his pipe and reading a newspaper. In a moving panarama youngsters were engaged in a baseball game, a flock of birds flying out of range of the fast moving train alighted in a nearby field. All of nature seemed at peace and the varied activities of men, women and children bespoke happiness and contentment. To "Pop," as he stared out of the window, only he seemed to have troubles and suddenly he saw nothing before his eyes and his thoughts again seemed to speak aloud and above the steady noise of grinding wheels against the rails, "Surely He shall deliver thee from the snare of the fowler and from the noisome pestilence. He shall cover thee with his feathers, and under his wings shalt thou trust; his truth shall be thy shield and buckler." Tickets Please!, from the aisle outside the room came the voice of the conductor. He was accompanied by the white coated Negro porter. They interrupted Pop's meditation to pick up his ticket. "So your destination is Xenia, Ohio?" "Yes sir, that's correct, conductor. By the way, what time do we arrive there?" Pop inquired. "If we are on time—about 7 a.m." "Thank you, sir." "You are quite welcome, Reverend. What time do you wish to be called in the morning?" This was the voice of the porter. "Suppose you make it one hour out of Xenia." "I will do that Reverend. Thank you."

Pop looked out of the window and mused to himself there is Trenton, N.J., we will soon be in North Philadelphia. Along the railroad right-of-way there were the customary Negro faces and ghetto houses of the bigger cities and the towering smoke stacks of Trenton's steel mills. Pop took off his black mohair coat, dropped his suspenders off his shoulders and relaxed in a semi-slumped position in his seat. The train stopped for a few minutes at North Philadelphia and in a short time was passing through the Western suburbs. Into Pop's view there soon came the narrow winding Schuylkill River lazily flowing eastward towards the sea. It was littered with sculls and shells, each outfitted with a full crew of oarsmen. A barking boatswain sat in each bow calling out the cadence. "Pop" could not hear the sounds, but he could see the rhythm of the oars and the effectiveness of each stroke. The University of Pennsylvania's rowing teams were practicing for the spring regatta of the Ivy league.

Pop was impressed with the power of young manhood and the effectiveness of rhythmically pulling together and he visualized their sportsmanship which would pervade their competitive games on the river. "Why can't there be more of this kind of team work and competitive sportsmanship in the church of God." He mused. "Why, especially, must there be so much of the blight of unfair play, selfishness, and not enough of genuine brotherly love in my church; the African Methodist Episcopal Church whose motto; "God our Father, Christ our Redeemer, Man our brother," inspired me as a child. This is the Church which claims to have been born out of the experience of discrimination and in protest against man's inhumanity to man, and out of moral and social intolerance." Pop continued to talk to himself. "The train on which I am riding has just passed through the *City of Brotherly Love* in which there sits at the corner of 4th and New Streets, Old St. George's Methodist Church where Richard Allen, Black founder of my Church, watched as his fellow preacher Absalom Jones was lifted from his knees in the year 1787 while praying, and escorted to his proper place in the gallery. A long thought but what I'm trying to say myself is, shouldn't the history of my Church in America and the continuing underprivileged social status of its members make it even more encumbent upon us than upon white church religionists to refrain from political chicanery and unfair play if we as ministers are to effectively point out to others the way to God and the good life?" Pop may have overstated his thesis as he mused with himself, but he had in the back of his mind not just his own personal problem but experiences at the A.M.E. General Conference one year before. He had served on the Episcopal Committee at the "bloody session" which was reminiscent of 18th century Europe and the reign of the Papacy. Bishops were "unfrocked," candidates were jockeying for power and vindictiveness rocked the church at its very foundations. Pop who had been moving

274

within the circles of the General church hierarchy for some time realized that his predicament was largely the result of cross-fire from the Cleveland sessions of one year before. Pop was jarred from his musing by two long and three short blasts of the whistle of the big oil burning locomotive. He sat up in his chair in time to see Bryn Mawr, the College town of the famous girls school and shortly afterward of the beautiful campus and stately building of Villanova Catholic College. Pop continued his view from the dining car where he had a quiet and leisurely evening meal. He returned to his room and watched the slowly sinking sun disappear over the western horizon. He perused aimlessly thru the afternoon newspaper and began thinking about retiring. He anticipated that he would not sleep well and knew that he had to "stir early," to use one of his pet expressions. He called the porter for a table, dashed off a note to Mom and Gerri which he would mail upon arrival in Xenia, and stepped into his sleeping clothes. Before he went to sleep he knew he would pass through the often treacherous looking horseshoe bend of near Altoona, Pennsylvania. It did not take him long to clear his mind of worldly thoughts and turn to his Master. This would be a long session on his knees. There came to his mind the thought expressed by the psalmist David and he repeated "The earth is the Lord's and the fullness thereof; the world and they that dwell therein. For he hath founded it upon the seas, and established it upon the floods." He thanked God for the manifold blessings of his life and prayed for the safety and well-being of his wife and children and for blessings to all mankind. He asked for divine guidance in the special problems ahead. Just as unfailingly this Psalm of Life had come to mind in other times of crisis it came to him at this time and he ended his prayer by speaking aloud the 91st Psalm where he had left off earlier in the afternoon.

Thou shalt not be afraid for the terror by night; nor for the arrow that flieth by day; nor for the pestilence that walketh in darkness; nor for the destruction that wasteth at noon day. A thousand shall fall at thy side, and ten thousand at thy right hand; but it shall not come nigh thee. Only with thine eyes shalt thou behold and see the reward of the wicked. Because thou hast made the Lord which is my refuge, even the most High, thy habitation; there shall no evil befall thee, neither shall any plague come nigh thy dwelling. For He shall give His angels charge over thee, to keep thee in all thy ways. Thou shall bear thee up in their hands lest thou dash thy foot against a stone. Thou shall tread upon the lion and adder; the young lion and dragon shalt thou trample under feet. Because He hath set his love upon me, therefore will I deliver Him; I will set Him on high, because He hath known my name. He shall call upon me and I will answer Him. I will be with him in trouble; I will deliver him, and honour Him. With long life will I satisfy Him and shew Him my salvation. AMEN

Pop crawled into bed and finally went to sleep.

The next morning Pop arrived at Wilberforce. Immediately he began to see friends and not-so-friendly members of the church hierarchy and there were whispers about the ruthless plans of the bishops assembly. Commencement and graduation exercises were in progress. Dr. R. R. Wright, Jr., a well known A. M. E. churchman and scholar in history was president of the university. He was ambitious to become a bishop. He was intimately involved between university and graduation responsibilities and the heated political affairs concerning the Secretary of Missions. He knew well that political alignments at such affairs could affect his future election possibilities. I left my medical practice in Chicago to visit my old Alma Mater and watch the goings on from a close up view. I attended the annual national Wilberforce Alumni meeting where the very busy University President Rev. Dr. R. R. Wright, Jr. failed to show up for a scheduled address.

The Bishop's Council meeting was called for 3 pm on this 7th day of June, 1933. Members of the Missionary Board, other than Bishops, were told to wait to be called into the meeting at an appropriate time. Secretary Berry was given the same instructions. The group waited in the General Reading Room of the library while the Bishops assembled in a nearby conference room.

I remembered the scene as I walked into the library. The door to the Bishops chamber was guarded by assigned ministers; a familiar sight at Secretary's Meeting (sometimes facetiously called the Palace Guard). The guardsmen were much taller and heavier than the average minister. And wore the expression of unquestioned authority on their faces.

The ministerial members of the Mission board and Rev. Berry waited three hours without being called into the Bishop's Meeting. As the Meeting came to an end, and the Bishops were seen leaving their conference an unofficial informant told the waiting Missionary Board members that the bishops had declared the election of Berry 'null and void' and elected the presiding Bishop's son, Rev. Carl Flipper, as Secretary of Missions. The informant further stated that Reverend Flipper had been instructed to go to New York at once and take over the Missionary headquarters and the office of Secretary. The Board members and Pop were saddened and chagrined. I decided to accompany Pop on his return trip to New York. There were minister friends returning to the East Coast on the same train with us. I recall how saddened and disturbed was one minister in the group who made a plea for prayer and patience. He reminded the others that as a rule, the Bishops Council is the governing authority in General Church matters between quadrennial General Conferences. "While it would seem that the Discipline clearly gives the Missionary Board the interim authority of electing a Secretary, it might be in the better interest of peace to follow the bishops ruling. "Dr. Berry" the minister said "I haven't the slightest doubt that you will be the overwhelming winner at the next General Conference three years from now."

Pop had little to say as the ministers discussed the possible alternatives. As the train came near its New York destination, Pop called the ministers into a huddle. He said, "Now, I know all of you are my friends at this time, as in the past. You have expressed the same grave disappointment which I feel very deeply. I see this matter as a challenge to my entire ministerial career.

"This is very definitely the cross-roads. My wrong decision at this time could very easily wreck my future career in the church. And there could be unrelenting embarrassment for me in the 2nd District where I have pastored, and throughout the conventional church. The matter could bring untold embarrassment to my family, affecting their decisions and the future direction of their lives. The announcement of my election has appeared in the Negro press, as well as our Church papers, which have been distributed nationally and in Africa, the Caribbean, and all the mission areas. You have all read the glowing compliments; responses to the announcement of my election.

"In all my years, I've never looked for a fight, but no one has ever

277

successfully accused me of running away from one. I am going to stand my ground through the highest courts in the land if necessary. I appreciate those of you who have expressed concurrence with this direction. Those of you who have expressed opposite views, I respect your opinion. I still feel I have your friendship."

Three days after Pop's arrival in New York, Rev. Carl Flipper appeared at the Missionary headquarters. He said he had come on the authority of the Bishops Council to take over the office.

Pop told him that he had not been officially notified of the election of his "successor" and even if he had been so notified, he would still maintain that his election was in accordance with Church regulations and would therefore refuse to relinquish the Office until the next General Conference and only then if the Conference should fail to re-elect him. Pop then referred Reverend Flipper to Attorney Harry G. Bragg of 111 John Street, New York, whom he had retained to represent his interest. Within a very short time Rev. Flipper represented by Attorney William T. Andrews of 200 West 135th Street, New York, petitioned the Courts for a 'writ of mandamus' to remove Reverend Berry from Office. After the hearing, Negro press releases reported that "The Manhattan Supreme Court late Wednesday afternoon refused to grant the petition of Rev. Carl F. Flipper of Topeka, Kansas to remove Dr. L. L. Berry, former Norfolk and Portsmouth, Virginia pastor from the Office of Secretary-Treasurer of the Missionary Board of the African Methodist Episcopal Church." Attorney Aiken A. Pope appeared in the last hearing for the defendant, Reverend Berry, when Attorney Bragg was called out of town.

The court ruled—that Pop's election was in keeping with the Church laws and was entirely legal. The Court victory brought much relief from embarrassment in the Berry household and to friends and well wishers throughout the Church Connection.

Attorney Bragg, still out of town, after guiding the case for the defense to victory, wired Pop a congratulatory message which ended with the long remembered quote in the Berry family; "The scepter shall not depart from Judah."

Pop had won this fight and became the champion and hero of the "Traveling Elders." He wore the robe of the courageous preacher in

278

the trench. He had fought his way out against the tyrannical will of the "royalty" on the Bench of Bishops.

A letter to Mom during that period shows how he felt.

July 16th, 1934

My dear Hon;

It is now 6:30 day light saving time, and I am getting ready to go to Richmond. Lew has been here all day, and we are starting off nicely. I just want to be the first to write you. I am sure you are in the Windy City and all excited. Some parcel post mail came to day and Elbert sent them on to you.

I am enclosing your mail also. I will leave tonite at 10:05 Standard time and reach Richmond in the morning at 7 o'clock. Geraldine was so happy at the train last nite. I followed you all last nite on the train and early this morning, and just about knew where you were. Please forget every thing except me and enjoy your self (Smiles) I am so happy that you have a chance to rest under a new condition, and strange scenes. I felt thankful that I was in a position to make this trip possible, because of the long strain you have been under. I think you were a real heroine with me in this long fight. I never thought you would stand with me so long in this struggle, I felt you would have given up. But your devotion and persistency in the fight meant every thing to me. I thank God and you, as well as the praying people of the A. M. E. Church to which our parents were devoted and loyal for the signal victory. Bishop Gregg wrote this morning that he is sending articles for an exhibit in Wash. They are all trying to get on the Band Wagon. Love to Leonidas and Mrs. Williams. Tell Gladys to "Strut herstuff"

Love and kisses from all of us.

Fondly yours.
L. L. Berry

For many months the funds coming to the department were very low. Partly due to the schism and partly due to the economic depression. Pop simply tightened his belt, toured the country; corralled the entrenched pockets of opposition with his pulpit eloquence. Nationwide, his popularity soared. At a conference in Jacksonville, Florida, Pop met his close friend, Rev. Charles Stewart; who followed him at historic

Emanuel in Portsmouth. Stewart said, "Berry, I've been "casing the joint" every since you arrived. You were not introduced with the other General Officers at the morning session. The snubbing was obvious. The men are huddling and whispering in the yard. When those two missionary ladies kissed you on the cheek, they hadn't noticed the Bishop not far away. Don't think for a minute, their "Royal Highnesses" are impressed! When George Singleton Jackson and the other men were slapping your back and shaking your hand, your "friendly enemies" were watching out of the corner of their eyes." "Oh pshaw! Man you're just saying that cause its true." Pop responded. Spontaneous laughter could not be held back. The jovial Rev. Stewart continued. "Listen, whenever you hear cackling from a huddle of these chicken eaters, man, you can see the ears of some o' these bishops prick up like horses listening for a rattlesnake." "Stewart, you are something. Lets go over to our stopping place and get ready for the afternoon session."

There was, in fact, a spreading atmosphere of fiendish glee. Everybody was gossiping about the hottest political issue in the entire church. A 'Little David' has apparently slain a mighty 'Goliath.' A five-foot, seven-inch, one hundred-sixty pound Virginia preacher noted for his pulpit oratory and leadership challenged a six-foot, two-inch, two hundred fifty-five pound senior bishop of the Council. However, you never count a Bishop out, in the AME Church. Certainly not the Senior of the Bench. But for the time being, the message was abroad. Berry won in the New York Court of Appeals, sustaining the legality of his election as Secretary of Mission. Berry with nine, and apparently ten points, of the law kept possession of the headquarters in New York City. This generated "fiendish glee" among ministers and laymen alike.

However, the action of the Bishops was split regarding monies for the Berry headquarters. Negroes in-and-out of the Church were very poor in 1933–34. Roosevelt's "alphabetical soup" had not trickled down to many of them. The great depression triggered by the market crash of 1929 was at its height. The hangover from Hoover's "just-around-the-corner-prosperity" was far-out-of-sight for Black people.

Pop continued his crusade for vindication. He said, "I will survive, and my program must survive until total victory is won."

Thursday night the customary occasion for the Conference mission program was eagerly awaited. The services were opened with singing

280

"Praise God From Whom All Blessing Flow." After announcements, Rev. Berry, in pulpit, was the focal point of all eyes. Would the Bishop-in-charge who claimed the Secretaryship for his son ignore Berry, as he did on opening day by not introducing him? The well-balanced choir of 50 voices sang beautifully, *Let Mt. Zion Rejoice.* The Bishop then introduced the Conference branch president of Women's Missionary Society to make the appeal for the missionary offering. It was getting near time for the Missionary Sermon. It was to be delivered by Rev. Griffin of Orlando, according to the printed program. Those who knew him noticed his absence from the pulpit. Soon an usher approached the pulpit and the Bishop announced the unavoidable delay of the Rev. Griffin. There was more singing and missionary introductions and announcements. After about 45 minutes, the usher returned with a second message to the president Bishop. A hurried conference was held in the pulpit while the congregation was led in song.

Reverend Berry was called in conference. When the music ended, the Bishop announced that the scheduled speaker regrettably would not be present for the Missionary Sermon because of an unavoidable train delay. The Bishop then announced that Rev. Berry had agreed on very short notice to speak to the Cause of Missions. "With apologies," the Bishop said, "We now present the Rev. L. L. Berry, whom you all know, to deliver a Missionary Message, as the Lord may direct him. After the choir leads us in one verse of *For A 1000 Tongues To Sing Our Great Redeemer Praise*, we ask your undivided attention while we hear from the Reverend L. L. Berry."

Pop had no time to prepare his sermon. However, he was often better in such circumstances than with a carefully constructed sermon. He once said to me, "All I need to do, son most of the time, is to get on my feet."

Pop was full of the broad aims of Christian Missions through years of study and as a member of the Missionary Board for 16 years. He was excitingly full of projections and aims for the role of the A.M.E. Church in World Missions.

In 15 to 20 minutes he put together all of these thoughts wrapped up in the kind of spiritual eloquence for which he was famous. Those present who knew his style predicted the outcome. He woke up the audience which was static from long announcements, collection of offerings and delays. They "talked back" with shouts and amen's, as he developed his discourse. When he had finished there was little doubt as to whom these people wanted as their Secretary of Missions.

The controversy over who was the legal Secretary of Missions continued throughout the long year of 1933 and the next year until the Annual Meeting of the Board of the Department of Missions on June 21, 1934. Secretary Berry was clearly in good favor for having held the Department of Mission functioning well in spite of great difficulties. Pop made his report and announced cost receipts from April 12, 1933 to March 31, 1934 amounting to $17,295.93. Rev. Flipper made his report of having received $10,364.58. After much discussion, the Board voted to confirm the previous election of Rev. Berry by a vote of 17 to 8. Upon the motion of Bishops Reverdy C. Ransom, seconded by Bishop W. A. Fountain the election was declared unanimous. Rev. Flipper was instructed to turn over the reported balance of $5,000.00 from his operation to Secretary Berry to which he complied. Releases were made to the General Church through the Associated Negro press and all the church papers. The report was taken from the weekly *Norfolk Journal and Guide* newspaper.

There was great rejoicing in the Berry family and the family clan of Berrys, Harris' and Jordans and their offsprings around the country and AME church members everywhere. All of the Bishops, many of whom attended the Board meetings, gradually acceded to the re-affirmation of the Missionary Board and directed their required funds to the Department of Missions.

The quadrennium General Conference of 1936 met at the Rockland Palace Auditorium, New York City. I was quite interested in what appeared to be the direction of the General Church. As a young physician, steeped in African Methodism, I wanted to think about what I might add professionally to help in steering the growth of the Church in the right direction. This philosophical and general policy interest was of course definitely tied to my interest in Pop's re-election. The usual activities of a general conference of the A.M.E. Church were carried out. Candidates for the office of bishop and general officers were busy in small groups and their election booths, telling the delegates why they felt they were qualified and why they desired to be elected to the office they sought. In secular quarters this would be called electioneering; in "sacred" places, a rose by any other name smells just as sweet.

Approximately two thousand delegates and visitors attended the sessions, which lasted two weeks. In addition to the election of officers the A.M.E. Discipline was revised, as was and still is the custom, every four years. I observed for the first time, being an alternate delegate, that dozens and dozens of resolutions were submitted to the revision committee, but only a relative few reached the floor of the general conference and survived three readings. Other interesting activities included the work of the Episcopal Committee. This most powerful of the Committees in the General Conference sits as a kind of ecclesiastical court to hear complaints of all kinds from the various Episcopal Districts. This Committee is the highest authority in such matters. Among its other duties is the important task of reassigning the bishops to the various Episcopal districts for another four years. The Committee consists of only ministers and laymen and offers the only opportunity during a quadrennium when churchmen of the lower echelon can crack the whip and retaliate or praise a given bishop for the manner in which he has conducted his affairs. During the long week there are social affairs, religious services, lots of visiting among old friends and a good time is had by all.

In this particular general conference a matter of general interest to a large number of delegates and of specific interest to the Berry family and their friends was the quadrennial election or re-election of the General Secretary of Home and Foreign Missions. Like all of the general officers, Pop had a booth from which he distributed reports and literature concerning the activities of his Department, programs and proposals for the ensuing quadrennial. His office report was called for in due time which he presented before the assembly of delegates. As he read his report each delegate had a printed copy in hand.

As Pop rose to report to the General Conference, his appearance was met with thunderous applause and cheers. It was obvious that his courage in defying an order issued from the Bishops Council when he felt his cause was just had been widely appreciated.

Pop's report was very well received and the committee on the examination of his presentation gave its unanimous approval. After all the reports are made, resolutions considered, new laws enacted, then comes what is of greatest interest to many delegates, the election of Bishops and general officers. When the election of the Secretary of Missions became the order of business, there were several candidates in the running including a candidate of great interest, namely the Rev. Carl Flipper, who had attempted with the support of a number of bishops to oust Rev. L. L. Berry from his interim election to the post. There was a great deal of excitement as the voting began and the old-fashioned method of calling out names from the ballot box before the employment of voting machines was used. There was more interest and excitement as the voting ended, for the so-called champion of the people, Reverend Berry had won over Reverend Flipper the hand picked candidate of the Bishop Council.

Pop, the newly elected and freely vindicated champion for Missions, all the members of his family and a number of friends assembled at the crosstown headquarters of the Department of Missions for a victory celebration.

Present were, Mrs. Lula Crawford and Nannie Sawyer, friends who were like family members who had prepared a seven course victory dinner. What would they have done with all the food if Pop had lost. That never crossed their minds. He had to win. His destiny was in the stars. Slowly they came. The large and closely knit big family. Cousins, aunts, uncles, sons, daughters and grands, missionary women and many supporting ministers until the large reception room was overflowing. There was laughter and victory talk. Finally someone lead the seven fold Amen in shout rhythm with hand-clapping. Before they sat down in various places for dinner, Pop brought the house to order with a victory speech. He praised and thanked everybody and especially certain individuals who had received and supported him during many trips in all parts of the country. He praised the courageous overt workers and those who had worked undercover when the adversaries were asleep. Pop ended his speech with what had long been his private Psalm of life, "If you get up early enough in the morning, you can catch the sun as it burns off the haze of the breaking dawn and watch a hawk soar over a beautiful horizon, before he stalks his prey.

"If you get up early enough in the morning you can be the first at the starting post and beat your adversary with fairness to the inside track. As the poet said, 'Heights of great men reached and kept were not attained by sudden flight, but they while their companions slept, were toiling upward in the night.' "

"Let us now remember that with great victory goes great responsibility. There are new challenges and new opportunities before us. We must bring the strength of the entire church back into the fold; so that the dreams of Richard Allen, Daniel Coker, William Quinn and J. Albert Johnson will come alive in increased abundance in our time to the Glory of God and Humanity."

When Pop had outwitted his political adversaries he would often smile and say, "Son, they don't get up early enough in the morning."

Foreign Missions:
Bermuda, The Caribbean,
South America,
and Africa (1937–40)

T HE "Mission House" as the headquarters was often called was always a mecca for ministers and laymen and their families either during business trips or on vacation. Many were the times when Mom and Pop were aroused during the night by unannounced visitors. But they were always welcomed as if elaborate prearranged plans had been made.

Missionaries from the foreign fields who came to the General Conference and the Quadrennial Missionary conventions were always on an extended stay and some would return home with reluctance. They, for the most part became a part of the immediate family and conducted themselves as such. This often to the extent of requesting an advance of their stipend or "allowance."

Beginning a few weeks before the assembly of the 1936 conference, missionaries from South Africa, Liberia, the Gold Coast and the Caribbean Islands were arriving at the missionary headquarters in New York. Mom and Pop were initiated into the experience which would continue for 26 consecutive years. These foreign missionaries and delegates (people from abroad finding themselves in a strange land) were greatly dependent upon direction from the secretary and needed all kinds of help from Mom. This is not to say that home missionaries did not make periodic pilgrimages to New York and include a visit to the headquarters. Mom and Pop became accustomed to these chores through the years.

It is recalled that at breakfast one morning, Rev. T. J. Hercules of Trinidad made the following pronouncement in his decided accent and much to the consternation of everyone. Said he, "Dr. Berry, I went to the doctor yesterday for an examination and I am greatly 'T.B.'" Just imagine the facial expression and responses from those around the table and with whom he had been intimately associated for several months. But Rev. Hercules quickly recognizing their physical movement away from him as if he were a leper, clarified his statement and interpreted his T.B. condition as meaning that he was totally broke. This evinced a burst of laughter and relief.

The sense of humor and camaraderie exhibited among the missionaries throughout the years never offset their Christian devotion and loyalty to the A. M. E. Church. All this was encouraged by Pop who was renowned for his conviviality.

One of the memorable events was during the prolonged stay of Mrs. Ntombi Tantsi of South Africa. The other missionaries would refer to Mrs. Tantsi as the "woman who lived in a shoe, who had so many children she did not know what to do." This started when she first produced a picture of all her children (approximately 12) and on the back she had them listed by number rather than by name. Being a humorist she enjoyed the laughter and jest. Mrs. Tantsi, while in the United States was temporarily employed by the Federal Government as an interpreter because of her ability to speak many African tribal languages. She also toured the country speaking at many schools and colleges, through arrangements made by Pop. She liked to relate an incident during a question and answer period at a predominately white New York City high school. The question—"Why do Africans have such thick lips?" The reply—"So that they will have more to kiss."

The missionaries and other friends who were at times solicitous of assisting Pop even in menial tasks frequently his reply was—"No thank you Sir, I am saving you for bigger things."

Pop became more and more energetic and dedicated to the possibilities of missionary endeavors on the part of the A. M. E. church, particularly in the foreign areas. He decided that in addition to his trips to annual conferences in many states of the union, preaching; lecturing and talking missions; he wanted to visit the foreign field before the general conference of 1940.

288

The discipline of the A. M. E. Church states that the Missionary Secretary shall supervise all of the missionary interests; and provide the church with missionary intelligence.

In obedience to that mandate, and acting upon the opinion and authority of the Board of Managers of the Missionary Department, Pop began his visits to the foreign fields.

Bermuda

In 1937, he visited Bermuda, reviewing the work there, touching all the preaching places, making a check upon the work accomplished and the future prospects for development. He found the work in a very healthy condition, with energetic pastors and loyal African Methodist members. Mom took this trip with Pop on the steamship, *Queen of Bermuda* and tells an interesting story in the following passages:

"I was quite thrilled while recovering from a broken wrist and two months illness, to learn that preparations were being made for me to accompany my husband and Bishop Heard's party to Bermuda. We left New York amid heavy snow and ice. We left Saturday a.m. on the *Queen of Bermuda*. When we reached the Gulf Stream, I had taken sea sick. I was put out on deck and wrapped in blankets where I was allowed to eat dry breast of turkey and celery, and watch the white caps at a distance mounting so high. They resembled large cities with tall buildings and steeples.

On Monday morning we arrived in beautiful Bermuda. We were met by Dr. and Mrs. B. A. Galloway and party of friends. After passing the customs, we were taken to St. Paul's parsonage in horse drawn carriages. All the way there I turned from side to side enhanced by the beauties of homes, and fruit and flowering trees (quite in contrast to ice and snow we left in New York). When we stopped in front of the parsonage, all were out but me, I sat just bewildered at a blooming tree. I was told it was a ponciani tree in full bright scarlet like blooms across the street. This was the trouble my husband had with me whenever we went out anywhere. The gorgeous flowers, hibiscus, poinsettia, oleanders and numerous others I could not pass, but stopped to admire. At times he would say, "Come with us, I want to show you something and I don't want you to stop to look at the first flower."

We were entertained in the Governor's mansion, served a repast, taken to the flower gardens, vegetable and banana groves. I found the banana blooms quite beautiful. The perfume factory where perfume was made from the real flowers, hibiscus, rose petals and so on.

The Crystal Caves were very beautiful and interesting; said to have been found by two colored boys playing ball. The ball falling in a deep hole, when the crystal was discovered and of course, taken over by the opposite race.

The white sandy seashore around the blue clean salt water edged with lilies, every tree or bush having flowers or fruit, except the cedar, which is the only timber found on the islands. We were given many useful gifts made from the famous Bermuda cedar—even caskets are made from cedar. Nothing was more thrilling than the great fields of Easter lilies in bloom.

The Annual Conference and Missionary Convention were held in St. Georges. After these meetings, we kept busy visiting other churches where my husband would hold services.

Bermuda is said to be composed of 365 small islands. The only means of getting water is from rain—so all homes and buildings are covered with lime which filters the water, as the island is surrounded by salt water.

Ten years later, 1947, we again visited Bermuda; this time by plane. It was my first plane ride, I hesitated for sometime, fearing the idea of flying. My husband finally said, in a kidding manner, alright if you don't want to fly with your husband I'll leave you here and visit beautiful Bermuda by myself. At this point, I made my mind up to fly.

We took off from LaGuardia Airport and were buckled down with belts. It was amazing that in a few minutes, automobiles, as I saw them through the windows, looked like toys, as we flew over Long Island. Out across the Hudson, towering above the clouds, the view reminded me of whipped cream on top of a dish dessert. The stewardess made us comfortable with blankets around our feet and legs. In about an hour, she returned with pillows, placed them in our laps, and served us a delicious lunch. Gliding along so peacefully, with the beautiful ocean and clouds below, the clear blue skys above, we could join with the psalmist in saying, "The heavens declare the glory of God, and the firmament showeth his handiwork."

In two hours and 45 minutes, the hostess came through announcing our approach to Bermuda. By contrast, 10 years before, it had taken two days and a night to make the trip by boat. The beautiful white and pink sand on the beaches as we flew toward the landing strip was a sight to behold. (Written in 1947.)

On November 10, 1973 Pop began his itinerary which included the West Indies, the Virgin Islands, Trinidad, Haiti, Santo Domingo and South America. Pop related that the first days on the high seas were rough and he could imagine how the disciples must have felt on the Sea of Galilee before Christ ordered the calmness. The name of the ship was the SS Nerissa, the storm struck during the first night out and continued for several days. All two-hundred and four passengers on the ship were seasick except twenty-one. The waves continued very high for the first few days. The members of the ships crew could hardly walk on deck much of the time. The rate of speed was only 7½ knots per hour. At the height of the storm the clouds blackened the sky. Pop states in his diary, "We soon learned that we were off the coast of Cape Hatteras, N.C. noted for its rough waters. As we came reeling out of the trough between high dashing waves no other ship was seen on the horizon. Finally we caught sight of a French freighter from Louisiana. We learned that it finally sank carrying to a watery grave some members of the crew. They sent out SOS messages to ships that were closer than ours.

On Saturday night, the 13th, the sea became a little calmer. The captain of the ship had not left his pilot house, remaining at the wheel for 20 consecutive hours. By sunrise on Sunday morning the sea had calmed a great deal but was still rough. The captain of the ship sent for Pop to conduct Sunday morning services in the lounge room but he was too sick to get up. That night he did conduct services in the second class division. Some people from the first class section came over.

He took a text from Genesis with a subject "Walking with God." The passengers said they enjoyed the services very much. Afterwards Pop went to his state room and was happy to have a fairly good rest for the first time in several nights. One Monday morning there came forth bright sunshine and calm seas. Most of the sick were able to take meals in the dining room. Everybody looked forward to the 16th when the ship was due to reach St. Thomas, U.S. Virgin Islands at 2:00 p.m.

Pop went ashore at St. Thomas, was met by Rev. Taylor, pastor of the local A.M.E. church and a party of church members. Pop distributed missionary, church literature and gave some of them Bibles.

After a sightseeing trip around the city and a brief look at the church, Pop was taken to see a physician for a checkup on advice of his New York physician Dr. N. H. Prichard. Back on shipboard after dinner and a rest period the ship anchored off St. Croix. Going ashore in a "tender," a small vessel for shallow waters, Pop was met and enthusiastically greeted by a group of ministers and laymen. They were happy to see the Secretary of Missions, they took him on a drive around the city and they stopped at the church at Christiansted, where he held services for the Rev. Roberson; then back to St. Croix for a service at the church pastored by a Rev. Bough. He discussed some of the broad aims of Christian missions and his plans which would involve the Caribbean areas to the extent that it would be possible as the church gave support to his programs back in the states. Pop returned to the ship at 1:30 a.m. Shortly after sunrise they arrived at St. Kitts. Pop found this a very beautiful city. The big ship remained about 2 miles out into the harbor and the small boats, "tenders" took passengers to shore. There were hundreds of people on the wharf. He saw for the first time the spectacle of dozens of people begging for handouts from the visitors. The ship remained there for only a short time. Pop had picked up some postcards at the previous stops and had written them on the ship which he mailed from St. Kitts. The next stop was Antigua at night, he did not go ashore. On Thursday morning, the 18th, he arrived at Guadeloupe around 8 a.m. This is a French city. He spent only 4 hours there as the ship continued around the other side of the island where a longer period was spent. He was impressed with the beautiful homes and businesses run entirely by French speaking Blacks. His short visit there was enjoyed with the help of French and English speaking guides. He learned of the close relationship with these people to the mother country of France. Most of the upper class of Negroes he learned received their education in France and returned to the island to work. On Friday, the 19th, the ship pulled into Martinique at 10:00 a.m. Pop's visit there was only for three hours. He saw and enjoyed the French atmosphere, similar to that in Guadeloupe.

From there he arrived at Barbados at 7:00 a.m. the next morning. He was met by Rev. W. A. Beckels minister of the A. M. E. Church. Pop had time to visit four churches on the island of Barbados. African Methodism was found to be well organized there. He gave out A. M. E. hymnals, copies of the book of Discipline and a booklet which he wrote titled "Missionary Guides."

The people were very responsive to Pop's lecture, his sermons and informal talks about church practices on the mainland and some problems experienced on this island. The people were very cordial and Pop was taken to the palatial residence of Bishop Bennett of the Church of England. He was very cordial as they chatted on the piazza overlooking the beautiful Caribbean Sea.

From there the party took Pop to the Governor's mansion where he was received by Gov. Owens. The governor was also very cordial and offered Pop a cigarette, which he refused with apologies. They talked about the British customs and life on the British controlled islands where Negroes had opportunities to participate in government and how Black and white people got along seemingly like a big family in Barbados.

It was now Saturday, May 20th and at 3:30 p.m. Pop returned to the ship, *The Nerissa* which weighed anchor and steamed off towards Trinidad. Here he saw an interesting custom for the first time. As the ship anchored out from shore, he saw dozens of little boys and girls dive into the water and swim out to the boat for coins thrown by the passengers. Both divers and passengers seemed to enjoy this custom and pastime.

The Trinidad city was Port-of-Spain; the arrival time was about 7:00 a.m. Small boats eventually took the passengers ashore. There Pop met his long time friend Rev. W. H. Mayhew who pastored the Metropolitan A. M. E. Church there. Being met by this minister of influence, the customs officer gave Pop his pass without examining his bags. There were a group of people at the parsonage waiting the arrival of the secretary of missions. A group of young girls wearing uniforms formed a double line and Pop was requested to walk through as they toasted him with welcome songs.

Pop had a fine reception in this beautiful little town. He was made to feel entirely at home by Mrs. Mayhew and other members of the pastor's family. He attended the morning 11:00 service on Sunday and afterwards the Sunday school. At 8:00 p.m. he preached to a packed house. Pulpit guests including the Bishop Allyne and Mrs. Allyne of the A. M. E. Zion Church. He was on assignment for his denomination on the island. Pop remained for four days on this interesting island inspecting the work of the A. M. E. churches.

On Monday evening a welcome reception had been arranged for the secretary of missions. The mayor of the city was presiding officer for the occasion. Men of all professions were present and gave toasts to the visitors. Bishop Allyne was again present and spoke. Pop's response was wildly received. One Presbyterian minister said he had never been so inspired.

During the next three days Rev. Mayhew took Pop on a scheduled tour to visit other churches in small towns and country areas throughout the island, where he addressed previously arranged audiences as a Christian ambassador of good will from the United States. Pop continued to pass out his literature of the church and the missionary department. Some officers and pastors of smaller churches who never got off the island were given books of discipline of the A. M. E. denomination. Pop was very much impressed with this visit, particularly the attention that apparently was being given to young people, in church schools which supplemented the educational training received in the public schools.

Pop wrote to Mom from Port-of-Spain.

Port of Spain, Trinidad, B.W.I.
Nov. 26, 1937

Dear Hon,

I have just sent my things to the ship, and will leave in about two hours from now for Georgetown, to see Dr. Tolbat, in 36 hours from now. I am a day late; my ship just arrived this morning when it should have come in yesterday morning.

Well, I am keeping well and very busy. I am really touching these islands, and doing things. It is so very hot. I am now about to melt. It is just too hot; it is like August. Mrs. Mayhew is giving me coconut water to drink, so that it will help to keep down the fever. They have told Dr. Tolbat to do likewise.

The people are very appreciative of my visit, and some just weep, and when they see there is nothing coming they quit. I am really taking in this work. I wrote Mr. Walker yesterday, and sent a report to the Church papers, and for the Negro Press. This report will tell of my travel and work up to this place. When it arrives ask Gladys to get it and let you read it.

I wrote Miss Ora Churchill today after you told me she was in the hospital. I remember how nice they were when I was in the hospital in Portsmouth. I imagine Mr. Walker will have much to talk about as he saw Bishop Davis there at the North Carolina conferences.

These people do not know when he is coming this way. He has not had the business about him to inform anyone here when the conferences will be held. Tell your Aunt Lucy, I say wait until I arrive, she has nothing to do. The Mayhews send love. I hope all are well. I am trying to think and hope that some mail will be at Georgetown for me, and if not O.K.

I will not carry all of my baggage with me to South America, will leave some here and pick it up on my return enroute to Haiti. I really like this tropical food and cooking. This food is more like America than Bermuda. Much love and many kisses toy. Love to all the children. Have not written much yet.

Your Husband
L. L. BERRY

From the exalted heights of being a very special foreign guest of the island, Pop was let down when he had to wait for his next ship which was one day late. Finally on Friday, Nov. 26, his ship sailed at 9:00 p.m. for Georgetown, British Guiana. Two days later on Sunday, Nov. 28, Pop arrived in Demarara, Georgetown, British Guiana, South America. He was met by his old friend, Rev. D. P. Talbert, with members of his family and many friends who came to meet the ship. After going through customs he went to the home of Rev. and Mrs. Talbert but only had an hour to stay before it was time to return and catch the same ship from which he had debarked. Together Pop and Rev. Talbert traveled to Paramaribo, Dutch Guiana, or Surinam. They arrived at their destination the next day at 8:00 a.m. where they were met by the Rev. Fields and friends and taken to the pastor's home.

At 7:00 p.m. on the day of arrival, Pop attended a missionary meeting and welcome reception arranged primarily by the Women's Missionary Society. Pop was somewhat surprised that many of the addresses were given in Dutch. Upon expressing this surprise to Mom when he returned home she responded, "What did you expect Hon, to hear their addresses in German." At any rate, some of them were translated for Pop's benefit. He was very pleasantly surprised to find three schools in Paramaribo organized and kept up by the A.M.E. church. One was named after Rev. Rankins, a former secretary of missions. The weather was very hot and sultry and Pop had to lie down after his visit to the schools. One of the high points on this Caribbean survey was his reception at a special 8:00 meeting held by the Paramaribo Masonic Lodge which he was received as a high ranking noble of the order. Pop was always cognizant of the close relation between the Negro church and the religious basis of Prince Hall masonry.

Pop visited the area where an African tribe a hundred years before had established itself and continued to live in it's primative culture. The Dutch authorities were never able to successfully subdue this group which broke away from enslavement established themselves in the bush and kept up a guerrilla warfare until their independence was largely established. Pop learned many things about Dutch Guiana during his short visit. He learned the interesting story that by the treaty of Breda in 1667 the Dutch gave New Netherlands which is now New York to the English in exchange for Dutch Guiana. Pop was very impressed with the interrelationship of the three schools with the A.M.E. churches. He found this to be one of the best examples of the educational welfare being conducted at the same level as that given to the spiritual interest of the community. In addition to the ranking school, there were two other important ones namely Themen with an enrollment of 727 students and a teaching staff of 13 and the Gaines School named after Bishop A. L. Gaines.

Before leaving Paramaribo, Pop wrote this letter.

Paramaribo, Dutch Guiana
Dec. 2, 1937

My dear Hon, and the rest of the family:

It is now 11:30, and I am getting ready to take a boat to Nickerie, and will get there in an over nite, where, I am to Baptize some Infants and Adults, and also give Communion. The Pastor there has not been Ordained, and the people have not had Communion in over a year, the Pastor come over One Hundred miles for me and the people want to see one of the Officials of the A.M.E. church, which will be something new to them.

This move will be off of my regular schedule, I will leave there after two hours stay of the boat, reach Georgetown Sat morning, visit three places Sunday, and leave Monday nite For Hatai by way of Tridad. Flies and musquitoes are about to run me crazy. I spoke here last nite to a great crowd, the people were so glad to see me, they, just came up and kissed my had, and some wept. Many sen d love to Sister Berry, and say that they can tell that you are a good woman and a lovely missionary from you picture. They pray for you in the churches as much as they do for me. I have been here from Monday morning, until to day Thursday, waiting for a boat, one came this morning. You stay here from five to eight days waiting for mail to come in or go out. This boat was not expected to arrive to day, so I get off sooner than was expected, Dr. Talbert is with me, and looking after me. He sees that I do not trink much water down here, and that is to be boiled, many are sic with fever. We drink beer some times for water, and to just quench thurst in this awfully hot place. I took the picture of the school people this morning, I am living in front and on the side of a big ditch, just like the one that you saw in front my father's house the first time you went to our country home, only here the water is green with malaria fever. I am feeling a little dull headach sort of feverish, but I think it is just the heat, and I have to go in the house after ten o'clock in the morning. I just want to send you this letter from this place. I have traveled ten thousand miles up to this time, including side and land trips. I have seen wonders, as though I have been in another world. I have been to people ans places where no Bishop has ever been. I had a conference with the Governore in his Mansion yesterday, also the Attorney General of the Country, and the Director of Education. I really have some data on our missions work in this field. It is providential that I came when I did to save some of our work, as well as to keep some of our people from giving up. It is no need to write in detail, becaus I could not finish. Just to say that I am well, and happy over the opportunity, to see and serve these people in this capacity. My vision is larger, and missions means more to me than ever. Will write you from Geroge town.

Love and kisses to all.

Your Lovingly.
L. L. Berry.

Pop found that the Negro citizens of British Guiana were very proud of their involvement in the management of their local government; the influence of the A.M.E. church and opportunities given in the professions and political activities. They spoke of Dr. F. G. Rose, world

authority on leprosy being knighted by the British government; Rev.
A. E. Dyett moderator in the church of Scotland; Mr. H. Wolcott, chief
pilot in the service of the government and several Black Vicars in the
Anglican church.

Pop's next stop was on the island of Haiti. The island also known
as Hispaniola or Santo Domingo. After Cuba, it is the largest of the
Caribbean islands. It is divided into two independent states, Haiti and
the Dominican Republic. Pop was very excited to be visiting this island
of rich and fascinating Negro history. It was here that an enslaved colony
of France, it's richest colonial possession, staged a slave uprising under
Toussaint L'overture and successfully defeated one of Napoleon Bona-
part's bravest army under General Leclerc. At the beginning of the
nineteenth century. The transportation of some twenty-five thousand
troops crossed the ocean from France to set down the uprising which
said to have been the largest trans-Atlantic fighting force known to
history before World War I. It was here that the great strong man
Henri Christophe proclaimed himself king and with slave labor carved
out of a mountainside a massive fortress known as the Citadel. It remains
as a tribute to Black ingenuity, often called one of the seven wonders
of the modern world. One should not forget the great hero, Dessalines
who really took over and freed the island after Toussaint was betrayed
and captured by the French.

African Methodism came to Haiti as early as 1824. Bishop Richard
Allen appointed Rev. Scipo Beane who had been a circuit riding missionary in St. Mary's and other counties of Maryland to extend his work
to Haiti. Rev. Beane became ill after a couple of years and had to return
to the states, however, he succeeded in establishing a small church. African Methodism had an up-and-down course in Haiti, partly due to the
French language. At the time of Pop's visit the very aggressive and in-
dustrious Rev. Philip Van Putten was pastoring the mother church in
Haiti, E'glise St. Paul.

Pop was told about a contingency of two-thousand American Negroes who settled in Haiti in the early 19th century. They were encouraged to settle there by President Boyer of Haiti. Many of these
people came from Philadelphia and the early spark of African Methodism
was apparently carried by some of them. Immigrants through the years
have also come from the British West Indies to Haiti. English-speaking

Haitians have been members of the A.M.E. churches there. When Pop visited Eglise St. Paul he found Rev. Philip Van Putten conducting two Sunday morning services; one in English and another in French. This bi-lingual practice was very unique. They would sing "Praise God from whom all blessings flow," in English and repeat the song in French. Rev. Van Putten would preach an entire sermon in English and immediately repeat the sermon in French. The bi-lingual service was carried out by the choir, and the recitation of the decalogue and all of the ritualistic service of the African Methodist Episcopal church.

Rev. Philip Van Putten took Pop into the mountains of Haiti where he visited some of the smaller churches. Some of these trips were made on horse back, Pop rode a mare named "Miss Michigan." The name was derived from the fact that the horse was given to the Haitian work by the Women's Missionary Society of the state of Michigan. The people were very much impressed with Pop's missionary messages and sermons. A few years after this visit the people of this community who remembered Rev. Berry and who appreciated his cooperation with their missionaries, under the leadership of Rev. Van Putten, built the L. L. Berry A.M.E. Church, honoring the Missionary Secretary.

From Haiti Pop wrote:

> Port au Prince, Haiti.
> December 18, 1937
> Saturday morning 7:30

My dear Hon, and the rest, I am up sitting up stairs in the office of the church with windows and door open trying to get the frish air, and writing this letter before it gets too hot. I know this sounds like a Fairy tale, but if you could see how I have broken out with heat, you would see that I have really suffered from the very hot weather here.

Well, I have been hard at it here, with a very full program, and every row is mine, as your Uncle Joe used to say. I have been high up in the mountains in a car, where I just could not look down, but watch the driver, and keep telling him to bear close to the mountain side so I could not see the awful abyss below. I went up to a Mission and preached to the mountain side, to many people, who had come down from their huts in those mountains on the road side to see the "Big Chief" and see him preach. (Smiles) I preached to them through an interpreter,

299

in their Picwa language, some of these people who have joined our Mission church, did know about God, they have been worshiping idols, I have some of their beeds, and trinkets, and have been shown a large tree that many of the worship. I have seen and heard many things in these parts of the world. I do not think Africa is much worse, she may have many more.

Last nite, Friday, nite, I preach at the prayer meeting here for Dr. Van Putten, a anoter minister was my interperter. I am to preach to morrow morning at 8:30 to the Frence people, called the French service, at 11, A.M. to the English people, Afternoon to the Young people of the City, and 7:30 P.M. the Christmas sermon to the mixed crowd through an interperter for all. I will be glad when this is all over, the process of preaching is too slow for me, I forget what I said last. (Smiles)

I have my picture taken on the Missionary horse, which you will see on my return. I made a visit to the American Consulate here, and talked with the American Consul a Mr Finley, we had a very pleasant brief chat, and he assured me of his pleasure in doing any thing he could for me while here. As I told you before that the Santo Domingo trip was cut out for good and sufficient reasons.

You all, may have read of the riots going on here, every body is very much upset. Most people staff off Streets at nite, and many do not go to public services. Soldiers are all around us. Our church so far, is the only church that has not had a detatchment of Soldiers stationed around for the public service, I cannot tell, it may happen to morrow. The American Consul advised me to be careful in my public expressions. I told him if I got into troubld, I would run to him and have to wrap the American flag around me. He wanted to know what size flag would I want, a coffin size or a casket size? (Smiles) and then told me a story about that. Well, I hope to leave here Monday Afternoon for Jamacia, and leave for America, or New York, on the 24th. of Dec. I have been told that it only takes Four days for the boat to reach New from Jamacia, if that is a fact I would reach N.Y. on the 28th. The Boat Officials have not told me that yet, I will see them Monday morning. I hope you all have liked my articles that I have had to scratch between times to send out. I have hardly had time to rest any time for thirty minutes unless it while on the Steamer, and it takes all of my time then to, either keep it from sinking or turning over, you should see me bearing down on my side of the boat when she leans too far the other way, of course I have to bring her back. (Smiles)

These heavy seas are too much for me, I really dread crossing that Atlantic on my way back off coast of N.C. Cape Hatteras. And everybody says it will be rough there all of this month. I guess I will not send another letter before leaving now, if I leave on the 24th. If any other communication my reach you by Cable.

I have been living in bedlum for quite some time now with all these tounges and tribes. I shall have to finish my write ups after I arrive.

Love and kisses, and love to all.

Devotedly Husband.
L. L. Berry.

Pop visited the missionary work carried on in the Republic of Santo Domingo. This part of the island which is Spanish has had a greater economic development than Haiti during the last century. It also has more A.M.E. churches than Haiti. However, the growth of African Methodism is somewhat hampered by the language barrier. Pop visited some of the churches there and was very satisfied with the progress he observed. The people received him with the same kind of enthusiasm which he had received throughout the Caribbean. He continued to distribute A.M.E. church literature and to record general impressions of all of the church communities he visited.

The next stop on the Caribbean journey was in the British West Indies. African Methodism reached the British West Indies in 1915. Early developments of the church were carried out there under Bishop John Hurst and Rev. J. W. Rankin former secretary of missions. The church in Kingston, Jamaica and several circuits in the nearby areas were visited by Pop. He was very well received and the enthusiasm of the people in the small circuits indicated their interest in African Methodism for the guidance and provisions of their spiritual needs.

Kingston, Jamaica.
Dec. 23, 1937

My dear Hon.

It is now 11:30 P. M. and I have just come from the church in the City where a recption was held for me to nite. I went over Two Hundred miles out in the country where I have spoke to three of our congregations and spoke again to nite and I am very tired. But I must write this letter to nite because the Air Mail will close early in the morning.

This letter will also say, that the schedule of my ship has been changed, so that I will not leave tomorrow Friday as formerly planned, I will leave for New York Sunday the 26th. at 3 P. M. reaching new York Thursday morning. This is a new and fast Ship just put on making the change because my other ship has been taken of the line. This is a fast ship and will make the trip in three days and a half. I am quite tired now and I feel it, but just too anxious to get data to give up. Bishop Davis is on the Sea and will hold a Conference at Georgetown Britchish Guian Dec. 31st.

I am well and keeping up.

I am rushing this so you will have an idea just when I am to arrive, I hope all will enjoy the Xmas.

Fondly yours.
L. L. Berry.

P. S. I will be on the S. S. "Talamanca" look in the papers and see as to the time of arrival.

L. L. B.

The Island of Cuba had not been touched by African Methodism until very recent times. Perhaps the principal reason for not directing missionary activities into this island has been a problem of language. However, March 31, 1939 Pop made his annual report to the board of managers of the department of missions. He spoke of the formation of the commission to Cuba. It was composed of Bishop H. C. Rankin, chairman, Bishop J. A. Gregg, E. J. Howard, D. H. Simms, H. Y. Tookes, W. A. Fountain, M. H. Davis, Noah W. Williams, Dr. John R. Hawkins, financial secretary and L. L. Berry, secretary of missions and Dr. Frank Jones, advisor.

It was stated that the commission had spent eight days in Cuba and had just touched: Havana, Pinar, Del Rio, Mantanza, Santa Clara, Camaguey and Santiago de Cuba, completely transversing the island of Cuba. The commission was greeted by large gatherings at all of these sections and with us enabling the commission to gain a good insight into the social and economical conditions of the people. This was a fitting conclusion to Pop's interesting and informative trip to the Caribbean. From this survey Pop wrote a booklet, titled *A Little Missionary Journey To A Great Missionary Area.*

Pop wrote Mom from Nova Scotia:

> Barrington Street. Y. M. C. A.
> Halifax, N. S.
> October 3, 1938

My Dear Hon;

This is Monday afternoon, and we have just come in the "Y" for dinner and little rest. We have been out all the day, with a lawyer to offset the Rev. Stewart who is trying to take our Church property. He would not let us come in the Church Sunday. He had to stay in the church to keep us out. My lawyer has the case in hand and it comes up Friday afternoon, and I cannot leave here.

I had a great thrill in my airplane trip of three hundred miles. I wrote Mr. Walker an account of my experience, ask him to let you read the letter. I will not be able to visit Bishop Williams Oct. the 5th. I have very good reasons to believe that we will win out.

Rev. Lord had a fit in that plane Sunday, and I was not much better. I will tell you what happened to him in the plane and after he landed. We were given raw cotton to put in our ears while up in the air, I failed to do so, and could hardly hear when we landed, but after about an hour I was alright.

I hope all are well, and that every thing goes well. I need my winter coat, but you need not bother with it, as it would cause too much trouble. Heat is on here now on the trains and in the buildings. We had frost here last nite.

I was staying with a white family, but things did not suit me so we are now at the "Y", white, of course. This little scrap of paper tells what Rev. Stewart put in the paper today. Most of what he states is not true.

Will close now, but if you have to contact me write me to the above address or wire, but you have to act quickly. I am just out here making history for the church and getting new experiences, many of which I thought never come to me, but you cannot tell. Please pray for me. I really want to be serviceable, and do all the good I can. Some how, I just believe the Lord is with me and is using me for what He wants me to do.

Pop's interest in missions to Africa had its origin during his child-hood. His father told him stories of how he longed to know something about the country from which his people were brought as slaves. His father would go to the seashore and look longingly and tearfully over the vast watery horizon and think of his African homeland. His father never got beyond the tearful dream at the ocean front. His son received the torch and pursued the dream as if by destiny and added a religious slant. He had heard something of the physical beauty of this tropical land. He had read something of the ancient kingdoms of Africa and its highly developed ancient culture. Mostly the history available to him in his school days pictured Africa as a land of "uncivilized" people. In religious circles they were called heathens. As a minister Reverend Berry not only wanted to see Africa for himself but he wanted to carry to these people the teachings of Christianity.

The culmination of a lifetime dream began on March 11, 1939 when he boarded the S.S. Queen Mary for a prolonged trip to Africa. Mom, Gerri, Elbert, other family members and friends were at the ship to see him off. The family boarded the vessel to inspect its palatial sur-roundings. Again they bade him bon voyage and returned home to pray for his safe return. Pop wrote in his diary that the majestic Queen Mary steamed calmly up the Atlantic coast but ran into a snow storm about midnight, off the coast of Boston. Through the port holes and glass enclosed portions of the deck the bright lights from the big metropolis of Boston could be seen through the heavily falling snow flakes. Pop read portions of the afternoon newspaper and a few verses of his Bible and retired. The big ship could be felt slowly dipping into huge troughs and then with equal slowness climbing the crest of the companion waves. Pop reduced the light in his spacious comfortable bedroom. He was often given to deep thought after retiring, especially when he was alone.

On this first night at sea he was ever mindful that at last he was indeed on his way to Africa. Quickly he thought of the eloquent surroundings of this magnificent floating hotel. He thought of the comfort of the up-holstered chairs in the dining salon; the glimmering reflected light from the crystaline prisms of swinging candelabras. He recalled that some passengers on their leisurely voyage to Paris, dressed in tuxedos and formal gowns for the evening meal.

Rapidly his thoughts returned to Africa, described by white historians as the land of the uncivilized. It is the land where unabashed nakedness and heathenism has been shrouded with pity by white Christians. "But Africa is my ancestral home," he mused, "Yes I am committed to the existence of a spiritual God of the universe. My training, my upbringing has been in the religion of Christianity. I sometimes feel that "heathenism" may in fact be just another form of religion equally acceptable in the sight of God. I believe that the culture and human progress evolved into the world today came largely with the development and spread of Christianity. Nakedness and so-called heathenism may not represent backwardness. Yet it does not represent "keeping up" with the advanced cultural and social advancement of the "privileged" in the western world. But Africa is my ancestral home."

Pop regarded underdevelopment in Africa, primarily the result of contrivance and exploitation fostered by blood-thirsty war lords of nations whom the tide of history gave superior weapons. "I cannot forget that my ancestors were brought to America and the Western World by the ruthless, gold-seeking traders in human cargo," he mused. "These traders were the ancestors of some of the wealthy, leisure seeking voyagers on the Queen Mary. The African slaves brought in chains, in the hulls of freighters (with compartments to fit the bodies of slaves). How different must have been their voyage from this elegant ride on the Queen Mary."

Finally the slow rhythmic role of "Her Majesty's ship, The Queen of the Seas" brought sleep to the frustrated heart of a Black missionary enroute to the dark continent of Africa. He said his prayers again and was off to the land of pleasant dreams.

Pop arose early on the first full day over the ocean waves. It was Sunday and the sea was calm, the sun shone brightly overhead but the March weather was cold. There were church services but Pop's diary says the "format" did not appear inviting. The half-hour scheduled service in the small chapel was of the Church-of-England "variety." I suspect that the "format" referred to was the Episcopalian regalia and the "half hour" which hardly gives a Black Methodist time to warm up.

Pop spent most of the day resting and reading. His diary says "I wrote a note to, 'Hon,' to be mailed in Cherbourg."

Mid Atlantic Ocean.
March 15, 1939

My Dear Hon;

Just a line to let you know I am feeling fine, and have not even been seasick, though it has been quite rough. We were in snow storm shortly after we entered the Atlantic Ocean Saturday After Noon, and it lasted up in Sunday. The waves lashed this great Ship, just as they do the smaller ones, throgh not as badly.

I am happy to say that I am getting along nicely, I had the Ship's Doctor to look me over to day, he detected my blood was a little, high but not too much for my years and activity. (Smiles) He says I have nothing to be bothered about. He discovered I have a mild case of Catarrh, and he has given me a treatment for that. I am eating three strong meals a day of many varieties. So you just as well to get ready to treat me like guest when I return because by this time I am accustomed to real service. (Smiles)

Just think, we had quail for dinner to day, and fish and fowl of many varieties every day. I was sorry to leave you all Saturday to the extent I felt very funny, I could have changed my mind I guess, (SMILES), but I am all right now. I felt like Geraldine did not eat her breakfast because I was going away so far, that has bothered me much. I hope I am not correct in my thoughts about it. I do not know what happened to Mr. Walker, he went off the Ship, and no one could find him, I never had a chance to tell him some of the things I wanted to say to him.

I have written him a long letter, tell him to read the notes I wrote him for the *Voice* and *Public Press*, that is one of my letters I hope to send out from time to time. I have been having peculiar dreams, since I left, well, I suppose I may hear any thing while away, and when I return. I just feel like some one is dead, or something bad, from my dreams.

I am just one day from Cherbourg, France, my landing place. I am now entering the English Channel, were Germany played such havoc during the World War. I will pass through the Bay of Biscay as I start down the Coast to Africa to see your people. If you see Bishop Davis, tell him the first Ape I see, I will tell that Bishop Davis sends love to his cousin. (Smiles)

306

I will have about a day in Paris, leave that p.m., spend the night in Antwerp, and join Mrs Smith the next day enroute to Monrovia. Send me a letter to Monrovia, Liberia, C/o American Legation, I am to arrive there Mar. 30th.

I am going to cable you, as soon as I get on land, and you will hear from me before you get this letter. Tell all the friends who ask of me that I am fine, and things are going grandly.

Tell Dr. Pritchard, that I am getting along nicely.

Well, I have never been this far away from home in my life, even before I ever met you. Some how, I feel like things are going to work out very successfully, and to the good of the work. I am just happy over the prospects of the Mission work in Africa, and that I will have a message for the people that I have never had before.

I believe that the Lord is pleased with my going, and the spirit which prompts my going. Somehow, I see a great day ahead for our Missionary in the A.M.E. Church, despite the envy and selfishness of many who are interested in missions, just shamming through.

I am praying, that Mrs Smith, and Mrs Hughes will have another slant on missions, and especially Mrs Hughes, if she can take her self out of the picture, and quit seeking an office which she will never get, and let the Lord use, her, she will get some where.

Love to all the children, and tell them I will write them from some where.

Keep evry thing going straight.

> Love and kisses.
> Lovingly your Husband.
> L. L. Berry.

During the next few days, Pop met fellow passengers and had some interesting conversations. The seas were moderately rough at times and many passengers were sea sick. Some went to the rail of the deck, braving the wintery winds to "feed the fish;" a seamen's expression for vomiting. This is said to be a cure for seasickness.

The palatial steamer sailed over the ocean waves with only moderate roughness for the next four days. On the fifth day the ship entered the English Channel and there was noticable excitement among the passengers anticipating landing in Cherbourg. Pop suffered only mild nausea, proving himself seaworthy. He felt that he had become an "old salt" by his association with seamen around Norfolk and Hampton in his younger years.

I sent you some programs that we had on the Queen Mary, Otis may be able to use some of them in working out something for his projects. I hope all things move along nicely. I will close now, my guide has come to take me down to the Office of the Liberian Consul. I am too near all this War Zone, every thing around here is talking about War. It is very fine to live in America. I may write you from Antwerp, as I will have a day and nite there. I will tell you what it looks like.

Love to every body. Good bye and good luck.

Many kisses.

> Lovingly Yours.
> L. L. Berry.

On Thursday, March 16, at 10:00 a.m. the giant Queen Mary docked at Cherbourg on the hour of 11:00 a.m. Very little time was spent there, Pop caught a 12:30 train for Paris where he arrived at 6:00 p.m. to meet his travel agent and put up at a pre-arranged hotel. His itinerary called for two days in Paris and then he would be off to Antwerp, Holland. However, he received bad news. The Dutch ship on which he was to sail to Africa was 4 days late. He cabled the scheduled change to 'Mom' and the missionary department. He received a cable in Paris from his wife, "Hon," which indicated that all was well at home. Facing a delay, he changed hotels for economy reasons. He thought it was a paradox that the name of the cheaper hotel was Astor. Pop visited many interesting sights in Paris and conferred with the Liberian council and cabled through its travel agent the rearrangement with people who would meet him at various stops in West Africa.

From Paris he wrote:

> Astor Hotel
> Rue 8, Paris, France.
> March 20, 1939

My dear Hon;

It is now Monday morning Ten Oclock and I have had breakfast, and am packing for the train to go to Antwerp, Belgium. It is just Five

O'clock in New York, and I know you are not up yet. There are Five hours difference in time here and N. Y. So I am Five hours ahead of New York, some fast to beat N. Y.

I wrote you from Cherbourg, and you should get the mail when the Queen Mary lands Wednesday. I am writing you from Paris now, as it may be some time before I can get a letter to you again, it may not be until we land in Africa some where. I have not heard from Mrs Smith, I do not know where she is.

Since my Ship is four days late in sailing, she may have gone out from London. I understand that this ship is a small Freight boat, only taking Twelve passengers, all else is freight. I know Mrs Smith will have a fit if she has to go this way, I regret it very much myself. Well, I can stand anything once.

If the Lord wants me to go I will go, and fear no danger. The people are very nice here, I have not seen a Colored person since I have been here. The people in the Hotels look at me as though I have just escaped from the Zoo. They are trying to teach me French, I just pick up some words by the contacts I have.

After three days in Paris he entrained for Antwerp, only to find that the freighter on which he would sail would now be five days late. I am sure that Pop felt at this time that he was more in "dutch" than in Holland.

He wrote from Antwerp:

> Antwerp, Belgium.
> At Hotel Century
> March 21, 1939

My dear Hon;

I have been here since last night, which will make me two days and two nites before I sail. This ship was Four days late, and to day the news came that she is another day late. I am expecting the ship in here to morrow nite.

I was at the Ticket office to day, and they have Mrs Smith listed as one of the passengers of the Freight Ship. (Smiles) I have been assured to day that the Ship will be safe, since she is so heavily loaded, that she is away down in the water, and the waves cannot toss her quite so high. (Some Consolation, Smiles)

I am anxious to see Mrs Smith, if she is on this Boat, to just see how she looks, I hope I will not have to laugh at her. Just think with all that pomp and gust, with she left New York, now she is just where she belongs, so Mrs Thomas would say. I just laugh every time I think about it, some drop down.

Well, there is not much else for me to say, as I have been saying it in part in all of my letters. My bags are all packed, and I am ready to sail. I think I will spend to morrow nite on the ship, and we sail early Thursday morning. Just as I did when I went to South America, from N. Y. C.

This is some beautiful city, I passed through Brussells, Belgium last nite. We had a typical March day for the First of Spring, it rained snowed and hailed some, and then the sun came out. I think the first time for this week I have seen the Sun. Every thing is very high in this Country, and American money is just about half of the money here in value. An American Ten Dollars will amount to about Six Dollars.

I will write as often as I can. I cannot mail much after I get on the ship. Well, So long, as Geraldine says.

The Lord bless you all.

Love and kisses.

L. L. Berry.

Finally he was aboard the Dutch ship *Reggestroon*. If this is a kingly name thought Pop, "It is a far cry from the queenly ship that brought me across to Cherbourg."

The trip to the African coast required 10 days at sea. From Antwerp the ship sailed thru the English Channel. The waters were moderately rough at times during the 24 hour trip. On Saturday the 25th the freighter cruised into the Bay of Biscay and promptly ran into heavy seas. Many passengers were seasick; Pop remained healthy but found it difficult to stand or walk, so he spent much of the time lying down reading and resting. At dinner time he chatted with passengers. Some of them were Dutch and spoke very little English.

On Sunday the 26th Pop noted in his diary that there were no religious services, so he conducted a private service in his bedroom. He read aloud the story of the "Sermon on the mount" as recorded in the book of Matthew. He threw himself into the spirit and meaning of this gospel. He was in fact on a journey and hoping to reach a mountain top in his life's career.

During the night the ship sailed out of the Bay of Biscay and into the Atlantic Ocean. After 48 hours or more they were passing the coast of Spain and the Canary Islands, one day behind schedule. Pop must have felt like the "ancient mariner" as the days wore on and he saw nothing but ocean waves and water. After three more days and nights journey, he noted that the weather was getting a little warmer. In the afternoon Pop wrote some releases for his paper "The Voice of Missions." He received a mid-ocean cablegram from Bishop Howard which said "awaiting your arrival in Monrovia." Some of the crew pointed out a group of whale boats coming in from the South Pole. It was relief to see something other than ocean waves and the foam at their crests. The captain began his instructions to passengers with reference to the use of quinine to prevent African malaria. Later that day Pop observed from the starboard deck that the ship was taking on oil from a supply tanker sailing alongside his ship at full speed.

Hopes were high that Dakar, Senegal on the west coast of Africa would be reached sometime the next day. Near 10 p.m. Saturday night March 18th many passengers were on deck rejoicing at the sight of lights shining from the distant shore. Pop retired near midnight but was up before dawn. He went to the forward deck to greet the rising tropical sun. His ship was steaming full speed ahead due east. As he stood there in the dusk of dawn, a huge blazing red sun came up with the suddenness of thunder. It appeared to rise up out of the ocean over the distant horizon. Suddenly, it was daybreak and Pop was thrilled at the glorious sight he had never seen before. He said to himself "The heavens declare the glory of God and the firmament showeth his handiwork." Pop returned to his room. The bedroom steward removed his bags to the loading deck and Pop went directly to the dining room for breakfast. It would still be a few hours before scheduled landing at Dakar.

As landing time neared Pop picked up his briefcase containing his notes, diary, passport, visas, etc. and with his winter coat on his arm he proceeded to the portside deck. Basking in the warm spring breezes with the other passengers ready for debarkation, a splendid view of the city could be seen. There were tall white buildings appearing like those of any medium sized city in the state of Florida. The members of the crew pointed out the buildings by name as they stood near some of the passengers. Pop was astounded at the beauty of this city but it soon became marred as a crewman continued his description in good and clear English. He pointed to an ancient grey stone building near the seashore. It was built like a prison with watchtowers on its top. It was centuries old and stood as a silent reminder of the atrocious slave trade. Here the unfortunate victims of slavery were stockpiled and beaten into submission before being chained into the galleys of slave ships for the North-West Passage to the Americas.

Pop spent only part of one day in Dakar. On a tour of the city he saw beautiful government and commercial buildings with red flowering plants clinging to their outer walls. He was most impressed by a marching troop of tall Black Senegalese soldiers, smartly dressed in the uniform of the French army. Pop remembered the heroic stories of these brave Senegalese fighting men against the Germans in World War I. Pop could barely get over his surprises upon seeing the beauty and flashes of history upon his first landing on the shores of West Africa. He picked up a few curios of wooden carvings made by natives and peddled along the streets. Some were carvings of the antelope, the Senegal equivalent of the eagle in America. Others were of ancient face masks and other items of the ancient culture of that country.

Pop left the city by cab in time to make the 1 p.m. deadline in boarding his ship. They soon steamed out of the harbor and were on their way southward along the Northern border of the West African "Hump." The next stop would be Freetown, Sierra Leone at about 8 a.m. Pop had a late lunch on the ship. He relaxed and read for awhile in his room. Later in the afternoon he returned to the starboard deck to enjoy the warm spring breezes. Slowly the sun was sinking in the West. Now Pop would see the most beautiful sight and most treasured of nature which he would remember and frequently describe for the rest of his life. He titled his description, "the tropical African sunset." Pop's diary records the following:

"As the blazing red sun continued its daily trip downward across the skies it was a picture of celestial beauty. Brilliant crimson reflections covered wide areas, lighting up the heavens for thousands of miles and I thought of the symbolic crimson flood that washes away the sins of the redeemed. Then came streaks of slowly moving white clouds bringing the beauty of white and red contrast. The sun continued to dip toward the ocean. To mortal eyes it gave the illusion of plunging beneath the waves into the mighty deep to close its eyes in sleep. I rested my eyes for awhile and again I watched the changing scene. There was darkness all around. I sat in awe of the omnipotent architecture of God the creator. My spirits rose even higher as I sat for a long time in the after-glow of the setting sun. Pop wrote that he thought of many experiences in life that have an after-glow. This would be the subject of many sermons and lectures to be given in the future.

He wrote:

Mid-Ocean
Friday Night March 31, 1939

My Dear Hon;

We only have one night out now before we make our first stop since we left Antwerp, March 23rd. Some time tomorrow nite we will reach Dakar, French West Africa. We will leave there some time Sunday For Freetown, when we hope to reach there some time Tuesday. I received a Cable from Bishop Howard to day Mid- Ocean, saying that he would wait for us at Monrovia.

I have sent a Second release to Mr Walker for the *Papers* and the *Voice*, which will give you an idea of my activities. I am keeping quite well so far. I have not had any sign of any illness not even sea sickness since I left New York. Mrs Smith was sea sick while in the English Channel and the Bay of Biscay. It was very rough in the Channel and the Bay. She was in bed for two days, also some others.

I am sending this letter to you from Dakar, West Africa which is a French Country with the hope that you will get it soon. As I cannot tell when you will hear from me after I get to Monrovia, and then sail for another week down the Coast to Takor, on the Gold Coast. I am sure I will have much to talk about when I return. Tell Mr Walker to let you see the article I am sending for the *Voice*, and other Papers. The Captain is requesting all to change heavy clothing for light clothing to morrow, he also started this morning giving crew and Passengers five grains of Quinine, and we will take this once a day until we get almost back to England on the home bound trip.

The Captain and I have made good friends, he is a very interested Mason, and we get together often during the day. Mrs Smith bought her Helmet and sun umbrella in London, the Chief Stweart has ordered ours at Dakar, every body has to wear one in this hot sun, at least from Eight in the morning until five in the Afternoon. I hope all are well, and that all goes well. Tell Geraldine that I will write her from some place in Africa. Tell her I am anxious to hear her play some more, and especially "Melody of Love.".

I am putting a letter in here for Gladys. Love to the rest of the family. If they are all getting married, just so you and Geraldine will be there when I return it will be alright. Well, I must not leave Gladys out, because she seems to be a home fixture. Well, she says it is her business.

Love and kisses.

Lovingly yours.
Husband
L. L. BERRY.

At 7:30 a.m. on April 4th, Pop's ship landed in Freetown, Sierra Leone. He was met aboard ship by the Reverend I. E. C. Steady an American trained minister who had visited the missionary headquarters in New York on many occasions. Pop spent one day here conducting a service and memorial at the grave of Sarah Gorham the first A.M.E. woman missionary and visiting schools established by the church. The local ministers and churchmen had a prayer service of thanksgiving for the safe arrival of the American official, Rev. Berry, from overseas. Pop carried out some of the procedures which he had followed in his trip to the Caribbean that is he gave to the people, church literature, some of them bibles, copies of the book of discipline of the A.M.E. Church, and other literature.

Pop then left Freetown arriving at his next stop Monrovia, Liberia on Wednesday, April 5th at 9:30 a.m. Monrovia had no landing docks. His steamer remained in deep water awaiting transportation to shore in tenders. The waves were very high. This required the use of the "Mammy Chair" to reach the shore. This landing method required the erection of long cables extending from the top of the big ship. A chair like contraption containing passengers would be projected along the cable to the bottom of the surf boats near the shore. Pop landed with the exclamation "Thank God!" Pop was greeted by Bishop B. J. Howard who was holding his conferences. To Pop's surprise Bishop Howard adjourned his conferences and the entire body came to meet him. There was a rousing welcome and presentation of flowers.

While in Monrovia, "Pop" was house guest of Captain and Mrs. W. D. Nabors, U.S. military adviser to Liberia. Pop visited churches in Liberia and particularly the Eliza Turner Memorial Church. He visited another interesting church in Krutown. The people there spoke practically no English. Pop was impressed with the little children singing the same church songs that we sing in America and in English rather than their native tongue.

From Liberia, Pop wrote:

Monrovia, Liberia.
April 8, 1939

My dear Hon;

On my arrival here Wednesday the 5th. I found your letter in the letter sent by Mr Walker; Mr Walton, the American Minister received it for me, and sent it to the home of Capt. Nabors at whose home I am stopping. Mrs Smith is stopping at the Home of Major Whistnant a friend of Mr Walker's.

I left Antwerp, Belgium, the day you wrote me from America. I have sent you a letter from every place I have stopped so that you might keep up with my movements. This trip has given me a wonderful experience, and a wealth of very necessary information.

This is now Saturday, P. M. and Conference has closed and I will preach in the morning at 10:30. We will remain here until the 14th of April which is next Friday, and then go to the Gold Coast, and come back to Freetown in time to leave there on the 29th. of April according to our original plans for London, and leave Southampton on the 17th. of May for New York.

I stopped in Freetown on my way here, and made a visit to all of our churches, and schools, and spoke in them and took pictures. I held a brief service at the grave of Sarah Gorham.

This is a very fine country, to be in Monrovia is just like South Boston in many respects. This country is very mountainous and plenty of water, with the Atlantic surrounding the entire place. I sleep under a blanket every nite. Very cool and pleasant in the early mornings and evenings. Cooler than Bermuda was when we were there. But mid-day mid sun just makes you sick all over. You just want to lie down any place to rest and get your strength. I am making quite a hit with the people here, will tell you about it on my return. Capt and Mrs Nabors are very nice to me. We drove out in the interior yesterday, and saw Joseps, he is doing fine and looking well. Mrs Smith went also, and she is about to have a fit over these people. I have never seen her rave over people and things as she has over these little black naked Natives. They are so black they just shine like a black snake. A little black baby just walking a little took hold of her hand in Kroo Town, and Mrs Smith wanted to almost faint over it she wanted to take it up in her arms, it of course would have been a peculiar contrast (Smiles)

It is no need for me to attempt to tell all I would like to say at this time. Just let you know that I am well and "Strutting my stuff"

I will try to send cards to the people whose names you mentioned in your letter. There are no Post cards in this Town. Very sad about Dr. Mc Gill. Love to every body.

Many kisses and kind rememberances.

Lovingly yours.
L. L. Berry.

Monrovia, Liberia.
Friday April 14, 1939

My dear Hon;

This is to say that I am quite well, and standing this mid day heat very well. We are touching much of this life here, and making history in our contacts. We are packing up to day and will leave in the morning for Takoradi, and further down the Gold Coast.

We will hold the Gold Coast Conference next week, and leave for Freetown again, and leave on the 29th. for Southampton, and take the Queen Mary on May 17th. for home. That is to say, if every thing works out well. Every body is much concerned in this part of the World, about the impending danger of war.

We are keeping informed as much as we can, since our passage from Freetown to Southampton is on a German ship, and we will be on that Ship for two weeks, and we cannot tell what may happen as to war before we land. Mrs Smith and Bishop Howard are also much concerned.

But I think every thing will work out satisfactory. I am sending a bundle of papers to you with some names. Please mail them out to the names given. It gives an account of some of the Conference activities.

Mrs Smith has gone up in the interior today to see the Firestone's Rubber Plantations, Bishop Howard and I did not go. I am just tired of getting about so much, and the mid-day sun makes you so tired. Mrs. Smith was fainty sick yesterday from the heat, but she is trying to play along, and keep up with every thing. She has proven to be a pretty good sport so far, but I know she is worn out. We will have a conference with President Barclay today at 3 p.m.

This is also a Holiday here, a Thanksgiving Day, with prayer and general Church service. We have spoken, and visited all of the Colleges here.

I suppose Mr Walker is attending Conferences, so I will not write him now. There is hardly any thing to buy in this town, save food and not much of that. We have not been able to get a post card which was very disappointing to us, as we had planned to send out many from here. We are told that some may be purchased in Takoradi, but we will not have much time there.

I hope Easter is doing well, and that the Conferences are making good reports. I just felt that some of the Bishops would take advantage of my absence from the Country. I hope I will not have any cause to loose faith in my Phila. friend. This hot sun has told on our color and especially Bishop Howard, he is applying much face powder also Mrs Smith. (Smiles)

I am sending this Air Mail, this is why I am using the thin paper to save weight. We are going out to dinners nearly every night, and many "Teas" in the day. Love to all the family, Tell Geraldine I say I know she would not like this hot sickening sun. It just makes you feel weak, though it is very cool and pleasant in early morning and nights. There is no mail going out until next Sunday, and no incoming mail until next week and we will be gone then. I hope to drop a line from the Gold Coast. I am expecting to see Bishop Brown, he sent me a Cable, and will meet me. I hope to hold the Board on the 8th. of June, so please plan to that end. I have written Bishop Young to that effect. Though this is not to be known yet. I am trying to dodge those visits from the Bishops just to get money. I am having many strange and funny dreams. I hope nothing goes wrong.

Love and kisses to all.

Yours lovingly
Husband.
L. L. Berry.

Pop and his party visited Monrovia College which was established by the A.M.E. Church through the good auspices of Bishop W. Sampson Brooks. Some years before Bishop Brooks made quite an impression on the people of Monrovia. In fact there is a section of the town called "Samson Brooks." This college was one of the more important educational institutions of the country of Liberia. After visiting more churches and conducting short services in the Bush country of Liberia, Pop and his party boarded a ship of the Holland West Africa Line for Takoradi, Gold Coast (now Ghana).

A large group of Liberian citizens and church people including the American minister, Lester A. Walton and his wife, came down to the ship to see the missionaries off to their next stop. The missionary workers were traveling on a Dutch freighter enroute to the Gold Coast. They made a couple of stops enroute. One of them was a port on the coast of Guinea. Many ships were anchored there waiting to be unloaded. Pop's ship spent a full day and night waiting to be unloaded. Arriving in the Gold Coast the party was met by Bishop Brown of the A.M.E. Zion Church who was there supervising the missionary activities of his denomination. Pop had dinner with the Bishop and by automobile they went to Accra where there was a welcome reception given for Bishop Howard and the secretary of missions. Pop stopped at the home of Mrs. Randall who was ordained Deaconness at this conference. Pop preached the annual sermon at the conference which was very well received. Several A.M.E. churches were visited including one in Seckondi.

He wrote from Accra:

Accra, West Coast of Africa.
April 21, 1939

My Dear Hon;

On my arrival here from Monrovia, I found your letter which was handed me by the Pastor Rev. Wright.

318

We left Monrovia the 15th. after spending Ten very pleasant days there among those very fine people. We were met in Takoradi, by Bishop Brown, wife and some of the Ministers of the Gold Coast Conference. After a very nice service, Bishop Brown took us 63 miles in his car, had us to a very fine dinner, and sent us in his car for 120 miles to Accra, where we reached at 8, P. M. then to church for the "Welcome Reception" all was very fine.

I have been very busy every hour I have been here, and I am staying in to nite not attending the session so I can get this letter off in the morning Air Mail, it leaves at 7:45, Bishop Howard is also in to nite, Mrs Smith said she would stay in to get off mail.

We are not sure yet as to the sailing date of our ship it is expected to sail Sunday or Monday the 23rd or 24th. for Freetown and Southampton. We are about ready to sail any time, and Bishop Howard is ready to close the Conference any time to catch the Ship. All ships are crowded to the limit, and if we do not take this German Ship it is no telling when we can get home, or start that way at least. So we have made up our minds to start, we do not expect any trouble. I am quite well, and feeling fine so far.

It is quite hot here, Bishop said he did not know he could get so black, every body is terribly sunburned, Mrs Smith is quite tanned, though she does not seem to think so.

I have not received any thing from you concerning Kate and the Hospital bill of Barrett. I wrote Bishop Sims, he will get it some time. I have written you an Air Mail letter from every place I have landed since I have been away, and I judged you were hearing from me, every time mail came in from France. I am sure you have my letters by now. I sent you two letters from Monrovia. I also sent you some papers to be mailed out. I sent you an Easter Cable, as well as the time of my Arrival in Monrovia.

When we leave here, Sunday or Monday, it may be some time before you will hear from us unless we wire as we will be on the Ship until we reach England and we will be on the Ocean for two weeks or more. Every thing is moving along nicely. I am trying to send out cards to many friends, but do not know the address of many Ministers in N.Y. Conference. While I write this letter, Bishop Howard is in the next room holding a meeting with his Finance Committee, trying to count this West African money. We are near Nigeria, and down here very near the Equator. Will close, Tell Geraldine I will see her soon, and that I am well, and I am very careful with my self, that nothing ill is to happen to me. I appreciate her interest in me very much. Mrs Smith sends love to her.

I trust this finds all well. Love and kisses.

Lovingly. Husband.

L. L. Berry.

When Pop finished his sojourn in Liberia and the Gold Coast, there were some very challenging questions which arose in his mind. How effective has been the total missionary endeavor of the A.M.E. Church by 1939?

Their Missions program began with the efforts of one very able and dedicated man, the Rev. Daniel Coker. This A.M.E. minister sailed to Africa with the first group of expatriated slaves, sponsored by the American Colonization Society in 1820. He established the first A.M.E. Church in Sierra Leone and spent the rest of his life there doing a remarkably good job until 1846.

Sarah Gorham arrived in Sierra Leone as the first A.M.E. woman missionary in 1880. The very able Bishop Henry McNeil Turner organized our first annual Conferences in these countries in 1891. These were remarkably early starts when American Negroes did not begin to have the affluence which they had in 1939.

Pop continued to recall. "In 50 years we have done a reasonably good job in helping some of the privileged peoples to develop a Christian church life. We have helped some to come to our church schools in America. Monrovia College is a very significant symbol of our help and stimulation of Liberians to help themselves. I saw in Africa a greater challenge," he thought. "We must extend our help into smaller areas of the bush and to the poorer classes in the major cities. We must increase our efforts in primary education and health. There must be more dedication by A.M.E.'s in America. The Bishopic and the hierarchy must get financial support to specific economic, social and educational programs to supplement our religious work in Africa. We cannot have maximum growth at home until we accept a fuller challenge to help our less fortunate brothers and sisters in Africa."

320

After visiting more places of interest in the Gold Coast, Pop and Bishop Howard boarded a German ship *Waddi* which was due to arrive at midnight but was delayed until 3 a.m. They boarded and retired for the long trip to Southampton, England. They arrived at Southampton fifteen days later non-stop on the high seas. During this period of the voyage three people died. They were embalmed and kept on the ship. Pop was very glad to get off of the ship on arrival in Southampton. From there they took a train ride into London. Pop found London very interesting. He visited the Houses of Parliament, St. Paul's Cathedral, Westminster Abbey, and the John Wesley Memorial Church at #49 city rhodes. He heard a short sermon there by a Reverend Cox.

From the German ship *Waddi*, Pop wrote:

Mid Ocean
April 28, 1939

Dear Hon;

I am now on my homeward stretch. I left Takoradi, Gold Coast West Africa, Mid-night Tuesday. Bishop and Mrs. Brown came down to see us off, in fact we spent Monday nite with them, they were so very nice to us. They will arrive in New York, early in June.

I am now between Monrovia, and Freetown, and will reach Freetown early in the morning. We are on this German ship, and every body is keen to hear the Broad Cast at 4 P. M. to day. I have advised a group to stay in their Cabins until it is all over. We three are the only Americans on Board, all the rest are Germans.

Every body seems to be very nice and pleasant to us on this Ship. We are to reach Southampton, May the 10th. tell Mr Walker to inform Mr Wald, so that he will have his Agent to meet us on the Waddi. All of us are just worn out. I am tired but well. I weighed to day for the first time since I left home, I tipped the scales at 171 pounds, but I think the scales are wrong, because I have fallen off in my waist.

I hope to hold the Board June 8th. We will be so glad to get to some cool weather, it is so hot. Mrs. Smith thinks that H- is no hotter than here.

I have tried to mail out many cards, but keeping so busy on programs, and plus the inconvenience of things in this part of the world, I could not send out all I wanted, then too postage is so high here. I may be able to send another letter from Dakar, or England. I hope to send this from Freetown in the morning.

Tell Mr Walker, if he thinks it is necessary as to time, he may send notices to Board members for June 8th. provided he has heard from Bishop Young and he is agreeable. If he thinks we have sufficient time, than he can wait until my arrival. Mr Wald can tell you where to write me in London, or at what Hotel.

You will know just the time we will arrive on May 22nd. if every thing goes well. I hope every body is well, and that all goes well. I suppose many things are happening in the Conferences, and especially the Va. Conference, and also Baltimore. Will close now, and write you another time. Love and kisses to all. Tell Geraldine I hope to see her soon, though nearly a month off yet.

We have put over a big job, and we have a wealth of information on Africa and the Africans.

Love and kisses.

Lovingly yours
Husband.
L. L. Berry.

Pop then did some shopping around London for gifts to carry home for his wife and other members of his family. On the 18th of May, Pop and Bishop Howard boarded the Queen Mary for the return trip to New York. The distance was negotiated in five days which was in great contrast to the two weeks aboard a freighter from West Africa to Southampton, England.

On the Bay of Biscay 2 P. M.
May 9, 1939

My Dear Hon;

I am out here have been on this ship ever since the 25th of April. We are to reach Southampton some time to morrow if all goes well. You will see that I wrote you a letter after I left Freetown, thinking that I could mail it at Las Palmas, in a Spanish City but no mail was sent out from there, and Southampton will be our first place to send off mail.

It has been quite stormy out on the Sea since we started home. We have had two deaths since we have been on this ship. One man died of something that the Dr. could not tell what it was, and the chief cook died of fever a week later. So we will go in port with two dead bodies so far.

If our schedule carries as planned, we are to leave London the 17th. of May on the Queen Mary, and arrive on the 22nd of May. I cannot tell just changes will take place until we get to Southampton or London.

I will cable if any changes, then too, Mr Wald the Agent there will know all about the change. Bishop Howard will come up home with me, and leave the same day for Texas. Mrs Smith will go on to France and other places in Europe and arrive in N.Y. on June the 1st.

We are all very anxious to get home, and to eat some American food and cooking. I hope every thing has gone forward orderly and pleasantly. We all are very anxious to know what is going on in America, and especially in the church circles. If we find it possible to leave London before the 17th. we will try to make the change and come on.

The weather is quite cold now as we are nearing Europe and we could use of the heat we left behind us in Africa. Many are sick on this ship with the fever. We are taking Quinine every morning, and have not missed since the first of April.

I will close now, and may write another word on this letter when I get to Southampton or London.

Love and kisses.

Yours lovingly.
Husband.
L. L. Berry

P.S. Southampton, Eng., May 11, 1939.

Dear Hon, I arrived here last nite stopped over, and will leave this a.m. for London. I sent a cable to Gladys last nite. I feel like I am in another world here. After having been away from real civilization so long. This is my first newspaper in weeks. Bishop Howard is with me. Mrs Smith has gone to Paris. Will see you soon. This letter will leave for America to morrow Friday. Love

L.L.B.

In addition to the church celebrities and government officials on this trip to Africa. Pop met two interesting celebrities on the Queen Mary. On the way over from New York he had lunch at the same table with

"Fats" Waller the jazz celebrity. On the way back he and Bishop Howard met the famous boxing champion John Henry Lewis and members of his family returning from Paris.

The mission fields of So. Africa were covered by Mrs. Lucy M. Hughes, president of the Women's Home and Foreign Missionary Society. One of Pop's lifetime regrets was that World War II prevented his visit to South Africa. He has met and developed many friends among missionaries and students from that missionary area. He had corresponded with others sending stipends for their work in the name of the A.M.E. Church. In the course of Pop's work he became acutely aware of the many problems of race and the difficult struggles of individuals in the Union of South Africa and the Rhodesias.

Among the best South African friends of Secretary Berry and his wife were Rev. and Mrs. Ntombi Tantsi of Pretoria. Mrs. Tantsi stopped at the New York missionary headquarters while touring A.M.E. churches in America raising funds for school and churches and informing her sisters and brothers in African Methodism about South Africa. After a few months she was stricken with illness. She was confined in the home of secretary and Mrs. Berry for a long period. Their friendship became closer. After several months of hospital and home care, Mrs. Tantsi succumbed. She was mourned by her many good friends in America and buried with appropriate dignity and respect under Pop's direction as the Secretary of Missions in the city of New York.

It was a tragic misfortune that the second woman missionary, during the administration of Secretary Berry, after a long trip from South Africa succumbed at the end of her journey. Mrs. Charles Demas really never touched American soil. She became fatally ill on the ship. Upon landing she was carried immediately by ambulance to a New York hospital where she died the next day.

Among other friends of Secretary and Mrs. Berry from South Africa was Reverend and Mrs. Francis H. Gow of Capetown who later became the first African Bishop and first lady of the A.M.E. Church. Bishop Gow's father, Rev. F. M. Gow was among the founders of African Methodism in South Africa. There was also the Reverend J. H. Makone and Mrs. Makone and their daughter Eva Makone; Reverend M. N. Tilo, Reverend Samuel LeSabe, and many others. These dedicated friends and workers from South Africa will long be remembered by the Berry family of two generations who for many years met the South African delegates to A.M.E. general conferences. South Africa can boast of Wilberforce Institute and the R. R. Wright Health facility. These conferences have more A.M.E. schools, churches and health facilities than any other foreign missionary area of the A.M.E. Church.

Secretary of Missions, Reverend L. L. Berry, Mrs. Christine Smith and Mrs. Lucy Hughes together with Bishop Howard reported their individual and collective surveys of the A.M.E. missionary activities on the continent of Africa to the general conference of the A.M.E. Church in May of 1940. For Reverend Berry, the Secretary of Missions, the trip to the continent of Africa was the culmination of a dream; a dream which began in the previous generation of his family and probably by destiny in other generations beyond. The trip was therefore stimulating, interesting and informative. For the department of missions the Secretary brought back an account of new challenges and new opportunities for the A.M.E. Church on the continent of Africa.

The Children Marry,
Have Children
and Pursue their Careers
(1937–42)

BY the time Pop had settled down to the work of his first full term as missionary secretary, 1933–34, his brood of offsprings had finished college and started on their separate ways for careers of their own.

There had been practically no talk in the family about marriage. It was understood, of course, that sooner or later in the continuing tradition of the Jenifer-Berry-Harris-Jordan clan, we would all marry and bring our families into the fold. In the schedule of Berry priorities, chasing success would have to be solidly on the way first. The old bugaboo called depression had slowed down employment which under girds marriage.

Brother Dick was the first to venture a voyage on the sea of matrimony. It happened like this: After Dick received his Bachelor of Science degree in Business Administration, he thought of a career with the North Carolina Mutual Insurance Co. in Durham, N.C. This was a logical train of thought for justifiable reasons. John Avery, the vice president of the company had been Pop's roommate at Kittrell College in 1895. Mrs. Lula Aikens Avery had been Mom's roommate at Kittrell during the same period. Dick reasoned that this gave him the right to call the vice-president of the largest Negro insurance company, "Uncle John." He would, of course, have Pop drop a word, kindle old family friendship flames which had never grown really too dim and Dick should have it made. Dick caught a train in New York, and was off to Durham, N.C.

"How do you do, Uncle John," he said to the vice-president. "I'm fine, how are you? Your Daddy has told me that you have a degree in Business Administration and you think you'd like a career in insurance." "Well, that is quite right Uncle John. In fact, knowing about you all of my life and your successes probably had something to do with my choosing a business career." "Well I am certainly glad to hear that," replied the vice-president. "You are the second son, aren't you, named after your Uncle Richard?" "Yes, that is true." "I suppose they call you Dick." "The family always called me by my middle name, Otis, but I prefer Dick." "Very well, that's what I will call you." "Dick, I have given some thought to possibilities for you since your dad spoke to me." Dick's heart was all a flutter at this point, thinking of getting a start in the home office, with the special clout of the vice president. Uncle John continued, "Dick, you lived in Norfolk a long time and your dad was a minister there, your family is well known and so are you in the Tidewater region. We need some help in developing that district. We have a sharp young man as district manager there. He is quite a go-getter. I believe with your knowledge and acquaintances the two of you as a team could soon develop one of our best debits." Dick felt somewhat disappointed but thought that he would soon work his way to the home office.

Again, there was the bugaboo of the depression and hard competition from the white Metropolitan Life and Home Beneficial Insurance Companies aiming their nickle and dime policies to the Negro community. Dick was soon snatching "defeat from the jaws of victory." He wore out a lot of shoe leather but made little money. One day in Lambert's Point, a Norfolk community, he saw the name Lydia Hall on a door bell. Remembering the name as a family acquaintance and member of St. John's Church, he rang the door bell hoping for a likely prospect. The bell was answered by Maryland Virginia Hall, a young school teacher who had been the classmate of our sister Gladys at Virginia State College. By the way, her name was derived from the birthplace of father (Maryland) and mother (Virginia). No sale was made but Dick thought he had a prospect. Two days later by mutual agreement he was back again. Soon it was obvious that he was more interested in selling himself to Maryland than selling an insurance policy, and Maryland was finding more interest in Dick, than in his sales pitch. The end of a long story

328

is that a period of courtship followed and Dick and Maryland decided on a secret marriage. This was to protect Maryland's teaching job until the end of the school year. In those days and in that town only single women could teach in public schools. Dick and Maryland delayed their marriage celebration until they had moved to New York. There members of two families who had been long standing friends joined in a rousing welcoming party for Maryland and Dick.

Now all Dick had to do was to find a job hopefully in the field of his training. He found jobs of sorts, but not always to his liking. Dick wore out some more shoe leather, dropped a lot of nickels in the subway turnstiles and wore out the Harlem "A" train. Finally Dick wrote me; "Dear "Gink" hard times are so great here that monkeys in the zoo are lining up for red pepper. Pop has set up a soup line over at the Mission House. Occasionally I've sneaked over, joined the line, to bring back a bowl or so for Maryland and the baby who make three." Dick continued with his wit; "Man I'm finding that a Negro with a Business Degree only brings a laugh. This town is owned by Jews, run by Irishmen, and "Niggers" are only spose to enjoy it. Even Roosevelt's alphabetical soup only trickles down in drops up in Harlem. I may have to move to a little industrial town and get a W.P.A. job leaning on a shovel, if I don't reach pay dirt soon."

While Dick continued "job fishing" along the Atlantic coast hoping for a good haul, he finally got one; only the "haul" was spelled differently; their baby was named Lydia Hall Berry.

Fortunately, Dick made a suitable job contact in the middle west and moved his young family to Detroit. He was employed in the business office of the Detroit Arsenal, a unit of the U.S. Department of Defense. He remained there as a Management Analyst, receiving several promotions up until the time of retirement. Dick began purchasing a house for his family as his "economics," (as he called it) became more stable. Always with a great sense of humor he paraphrased a popular song, "With Maryland and me and the baby makes three, I am happy in my blue heaven."

After a few years in Detroit, their daughter Sylvia was born. Maryland did graduate work and continued her career of teaching in the Detroit public schools. The family joined Bethel A. M. E. Church as might be expected. Dick was very active as a Steward in the church. Secretary

of Omega Psi Phi Fraternity and very active with the Prince Hall jurisdiction of Masons. He served as a local and state Masonic officer; he
obtained 32nd degree status and was active also as a Shriner.

After Dick, I was the next of Rev. Berry's sons to be bitten by the
marital bug. I spent a long time chasing success and feeling that there was
plenty of time to think about marriage. In fact, I was near the age of
confirmed bachelorhood before I finally got married. It all came to pass
in the course of my work as an occupational hazard, much like Dick's
experience. I was going along minding my own business, writing a thesis
on "Race and Tuberculosis" for a Master's Degree in Pathology. While
the research had been done at the County morgue, I occasionally had to
visit the University of Chicago Medical School. On one of my trips
there, I met an attractive young lady who was employed as a medical
secretary. On subsequent trips somehow our paths continued to cross. I
finished the research and had the thesis almost written in longhand.

One afternoon as I was leaving the university in my "jalopy," I saw
this young lady, whose name was Ophelia Flannigan Harrison, standing
on the corner waiting for a street car. It was raining and she had her umbrella raised. Recognizing her, I pulled over to the curb and asked if I
could give her a lift. I had seen her in her own little car but she stated
that it was in the shop for repairs. She accepted the ride in my car which
didn't always complete a reasonably long distance between two points
without a breakdown. Thankfully, it did not happen on this occasion. I
mentioned to her that I had been seeking a stenographer who could type
an acceptable thesis with medical terminology. She mentioned that the
university had a thesis office where she had frequently worked in spare
time and that most of the theses came from graduate students in the basic
medical sciences. "If your writing is legible, she said, maybe I can help
you." Those became famous last words. For after that I found myself
on a new project where romance was more important than thesis writing.

As the thesis project was nearly completed my new acquaintance, a
very efficient stenographer and secretary was called to a new and more
challenging job. She left the department of pathology and became executive secretary in the Graduate School of Sociology on another part of
the campus. After that our paths were no longer crossing. So I expressed
my interest in seeing her, where thesis writing would not be involved.
She replied, "Fine, I'd like to invite you to my home." "I live with my

parents, I'd like to have you meet them and I have a little boy by a previous marriage. Perhaps you'd like to meet him also." I visited her home, met Mr. and Mrs. Flannigan and her little curly-haired brown boy, Alvin. I found that my new acquaintance could play the piano and I had the occasion to loosen up my rusty vocal cords with some songs that I had not sung since Wilberforce days. On another occasion I found her knitting or crocheting a garment and she showed me some fine artistic needlework that she had created in her spare time. She was obviously a very versatile and practical person; quite different from some of the social butterflies I had been exposed to, before. The more I saw her quiet well behaved little boy the more I liked him. I began saying to myself, "Gee, with this little guy around, I could make up for lost time." Our first child would already have an older brother to play with.

Before long I met Ophelia's older sister, Zita Flannigan Headen. I was surprised to find that she was the wife of an Alpha Phi Alpha fraternity brother Dr. Leon Headen, a dental surgeon. We had lived at the Alpha fraternity house several years before. Headen was a few years ahead of me at the Northwestern Dental School while I was in Medical College at the University of Chicago. There followed a few double dates and I found myself being more and more involved.

After a while we felt there was no point in prolonging the courtship any further. We were united in a quiet ceremony by Rev. Archibald J. Carey, Jr. the pastor of Woodlawn A. M. E. Church where I was a member.

Two years later on our marriage anniversary date there was a "new recruit." Alvin had a little sister and we named her Judith Ann. The "Ann" was borrowed from my mother's name Beulah Ann, at my mother's insistence.

At the appropriate time, Rev. L. L. Berry, the Secretary of Missions journeyed to Chicago and joined the presiding Bishop, the Right Rev. John A. Gregg in christening Judy into African Methodism, at the Woodlawn A. M. E. Church. Rev. Archibald Carey and his wife, Hazel, became Judy's godparents.

From the earliest years we enjoyed summer vacations in the country side of the state of Michigan near one of Michigan's many lakes. I bought a summer home on Paradise Lake at Idlewild, Michigan. At age four, Judy joined a horseback riding class in a riding school owned by a former sergeant in the famous Negro 10th Cavalry of the United States Army. Later she acquired a riding horse of her own which she kept for a number of years. Alvin grew up fast and at the age of 17, after graduation from Parker High School he enrolled at the Tuskegee, Alabama Aviation School and became a pilot in the U.S. Air Force.

My brother Lewellyn, Jr. came to Chicago after receiving a B.S. degree at Wilberforce and entered University of Illinois Dental School. After one year he switched careers and decided to become a Medical Laboratory Technologist. He entered hospital laboratory training at Provident Hospital and the University of Chicago and after two years found employment with a Municipal Hospital in the city of New York. He stayed there for a few years and left for employment at the Freedmen's Hospital in Washington connected with Howard University. After a period, he was called into the U.S. Army during World War II.

Paradoxically he had trained to the rank of second lieutenant in infantry by way of the ROTC at Wilberforce (because it was compulsory) but never bothered to pick up his officer's commission. He entered the war as a private and was immediately given intensive training in tropical medical technology at Walter Reed Hospital, Washington, D.C. presumably for army hospital duty in the war zone. In fact he was assigned to a white hospital unit at Camp Upton in New York, just as they were ready to embark for war duty in Europe. Upon his arrival the commanding officer seem startled and almost frightened as Sergeant Lewellyn L. Berry, Jr. reported for embarkation as medical laboratory technologist. "There has been a very great mistake," he said. "I'm sure you'd be very unhappy with this unit." Contacts were made in (post haste) Washington and in a short time Lew was aboard a long camouflaged troop train enroute around the Atlantic coast from New York to Galveston, Texas. He was assigned to an all Negro Air Base Security Battalion, which was shipping immediately for duty in the Southwest Pacific. The assignment of Lew's unit was to rescue American pilots, dead, wounded, or alive when they were shot down by Japanese fighters.

Lew served in Guadalcanal and Bougainville. He had the experience of sleeping in "fox holes" during Japanese raids and listening to the propaganda broadcasts of "Tokyo Rose." "Why are you guys over here fighting?" she would ask. Did you hear about the lynching of a Negro at Sykeston, Mo. the other day?" "What do you have to fight for? You

332

will always be second class citizens in white America." "This is a race war." We are winning it, where will you be? White on the inside and Black on the outside? A great majority of the boys took this kind of propaganda in stride, Lew always said. The weather was forever hot and humid. Lew did very little of the work he was trained to do and spent many months in this infamous battleground of World War II. He finally developed a severe widespread dermatitis which was known as the "jungle itch." He became disabled completely and did not respond to war zone medical care. He was evacuated after a long period of service and returned to Washington for further hospital treatment.

At the end of the war he returned to his employment at Freedmen's Hospital. There he met Kathryn Fountaine who had graduated from Howard and trained as a laboratory technologist. She was also working at Freedmen's Hospital. Following a haunting family tradition, the third son of Rev. and Mrs. L. L. Berry became the "victim" of an occupational hazard. Lew and Kathryn were married and the Berry family fold was further increased by a very lovely lady from a very fine family. Kathryn with her quiet and smiling ways soon went over big with Mom and Pop and the rest of the family. After a year or two the Secretary of Missions and Mrs. Berry were proud to be presented with their first grandson. He was named Llewellyn L. Berry III to add to their collection of three granddaughters.

Lew and Kathryn continued their respective jobs at Freedmen's Hospital and loved the work very much. As the boy grew up, Lew decided to purchase a private medical laboratory which he ran in conjunction with his employment at Freedmen's Hospital and Howard Medical School. Lew's wide acquaintance with attending physicians at the hospital served as a "feeder" for his private laboratory. So the Lew Berrys became prosperous, bought a comfortable home and lived a quiet and interesting life in Washington.

In the Berry tradition, Lew joined the historic Metropolitan A. M. E. Church and became an active church officer. He was also active as a Mason and a member of the Omega Psi Phi Fraternity. Lew became a strong supporting arm for a number of doctors in private practice. Through him the doctors were able to keep up with newly developing medical laboratory procedures as they were used at Freedmen's, a teaching hospital. The doctors were attracted to him especially after he became supervisor of the laboratory staff at the hospital. As his private laboratory business increased Lew and a group of physicians formed a corporation representing several speciality branches of medicine. With Lew becoming director of what was named the Allied Medical Laboratories, Lew and Kathryn enjoyed their work both alternating in the private laboratory business with their employment at Freedmen's Hospital.

As the Berry family expanded there were frequent family reunions particularly at Idlewild, Michigan, the "mission house" in New York and surrounding areas. And in later years in Detroit, Michigan.

The last of Mother Beulah's quartet of boys, Elbert, surrendered his bachelorhood to a young lady by the name of Blanche Pierce who had grown up in New Haven, Connecticut and attended college there. After a short teaching stint in the South she became employed as an accountant with a social agency in Midtown Manhattan. Elbert had left Howard University Divinity School without graduating; taken more social studies at New York University and decided not to preach—not as a profession, that is. (A decision similar to that of his older brothers). Elbert ran into an occupational hazard. He was working for a government social agency, the State Employment Service of New York whose parameters overlapped the agency activities where Blanche was employed. They courted and married and have had a very happy relationship. They had no children but they have said they enjoyed very much the recreation involved in trying. They were able to do many things the rest of us couldn't do while we were rearing children.

They bought a home in Hollis, N.Y. in the borough of Queens, where there was room for a beautiful flower garden and a well kept lawn, which they enjoyed immensely. In later years they travelled a great deal around the country. They especially enjoyed visiting islands of the Caribbean and excursion boat tours. As the years passed they also joined the family reunions and as fate and Mother Beulah would have it; the reunions of related families continued to involve all of our generation of brothers, sisters, sons, daughters, cousins, aunts and uncles.

Elbert, like the rest of the Berry offspring, was very subtly inducted into religious activities, short of donning the vestments of the priesthood.

As I look back it seems amazing that there was never any strongly overt brainwashing to involve us in religion. The induction was very subtle and astute. We all seem to have been caught up in the religious atmosphere in which we were reared. None of our generation ever deserted the church throughout our lives. Elbert came "darn near" being captivated into the priesthood. Or I should say he almost became a preacher. So through the years I would occasionally get a letter stating that, last Sunday he had delivered a lay sermon for the 11 o'clock Sunday service, or he sang a sacred solo at this or that affair. Elbert found religious expression in another category which was part of the Berry family tradition, that being the Masonic Lodge. He became master of a Lodge in Harlem and was very proud of the various programs for the brotherhood. He even imported his brother Dick from Detroit to deliver a special lecture as a crowning event of his programs as master of his lodge. I remember being in New York at that time and while I wanted to hear my brother Dick's speech he and Elbert refused to allow me to attend because they said I was so rusty on the rituals of the lodge, that I would embarrass them and perhaps even be thrown out as an impostor.

Elbert possessed a degree of modesty which the rest of the family always said that his oldest brother never had. I am sure they were kidding because other people have said that I inherited quite a bit of my mother's very lovely modesty. Seriously I always felt that Elbert did a much better job than he ever talked about; giving counsel to a large number of underprivileged people of Harlem who had not only unemployment, but emotional, marital, spiritual and other problems as well.

All of the Berry brothers entered marriage with a quietness that suggested that they didn't want their bachelor buddies to realize they were leaving their ranks. This was not the case with our sister Gladys Ursula. Her romance began in a subtle manner, in that she was kindling a flame during a Detroit General Conference that had nothing to do with Pop's election campaign in which she was supposedly involved. She met a young man there by the name of Charles Fisher who was working as a law clerk and whose entree for her attentions was based on the fact that he came originally from Portsmouth, Virginia. It turned out that most members of his family attended the Emanuel church, some of them being active during Pop's pastorate there.

At the Detroit conference of 1940 the reports, speeches, sermons and the Lord's Supper soon came to an end. The agenda moved to the most exciting and emotion-filled action of General Conference; The election of Bishops and general officers.

Meanwhile, I was present and accounted for, as a lay delegate from Chicago. Brother Dick and I teamed as a kind of CIA surveillance unit to see that delegation leaders pledged to work for Sec'y Berry were keeping the faith. Dick especially took to this role like a duck to water. He continued in this role at all general conferences thereafter until father's death. I was enjoying my 4th year of climbing the ladder of success as a stomach specialist and a pioneer in gastroscopy. This was the new medical technique of looking into the stomach thru flexible illuminated tubes. Early cancers and ulcers could be seen that were missed by x-ray. The ambitions and enthusiasms of the father had really rubbed off on the oldest son. I presented a paper before the conference in Detroit one week. Three days later in advance of the General Conference assembly, I kept an appointment to speak before the South Side Branch of the Chicago Medical Society. With three days to spare I returned to Detroit for two weeks of church business. Secretary Berry was re-elected; three bishops were elevated to the bench and the young church-oriented doctor dreamed of a church related.

"Whenever the expression "Hell bent for election," came from an election among preachers can sometimes make you wonder." Dick Berry said. "It is no different in Detroit or Rome. That Black and white smoke eminating from the Vatican during the election of a Pope is the "substance of things hoped for and evidence of things unseen"." Eventually the shouting and the tumult died, the delegates rise and sing; "Lord God of hosts, be with us lest we forget."

The oldest daughter of Rev. and Mrs. Berry, Gladys Ursula was the next in line for the glamor of center stage. The former Norfolk school teacher and now secretary-to-the secretary of missions announced her resignation. While church politics in Detroit occupied others, Gladys was having a session with Cupid. A year later she announced her engagement to Atty. Charles Fisher.

Before I describe Glady's elaborate marriage event, I have something to say about our youngest sister Geraldine whom we call "Gerri." She came along 10 years after the birth of her youngest brother, when the rest of Berry chickens had flown the coop. Mom said that God sent her a child companion to take the place of the others who had sprouted their own wings. Gerri had a partial speaking and hearing handicap. She therefore received so much love and affection that it undoubtedly became an additional handicap. This she had to overcome to some extent as she neared adulthood. She grew up to be a very lovable person with a genial, affable personality which everybody in her circle of friends and acquaintances loved. She developed some talents and characteristics that were not anticipated in the earlier years. She is a good typist and plays the piano very well. She never married. At present she lives with her widowed sister Gladys in Detroit and works for the Chrysler Motor Car Company. She remains even in adulthood the pet of the entire Berry-Harris-Jordan clan.

Gladys' announcement of her engagement to Atty. Charles Fisher became firm. Wedding bells soon rang out and Pop pulled out all the stops for his beloved "daughter." The nuptials hailed as a Harlem social event was the most elaborate "hitching" in the 150-year history of the Berry-Harris-Jordan clan. The vows were read by Bishop David H. Sims before a full house at Bethel A. M. E. Church in Harlem. A detail of city police provided security and handled traffic problems. Grace Brooks, a lovely first cousin and school teacher from North Carolina, was Maid of Honor. The bridesmaids included another lovely school teacher-cousin from Camden, N.J., Lillian Goings; Valetta Harper, assistant editor of the Voice of Missions, a working associate in the Office of Missions; the sister of the groom, Hazel Fisher of Portsmouth, Va.; Carolyn Johnson of the missions department staff; Pauline Jackson, and Naomi Cooper, childhood friends of the bride. The male escorts consisted of the four Berry brothers—Leonidas, Dick, "Lew" Jr., and Elbert, brothers of the bride; also, Homer Smith, leader of the famed N.B.C. Singers, the Southernaires, Calston LeGrande, Alfred Young and Forest Blount. Sidney Barthwell, druggist of Detroit, was best man. Judy, my two-year-old daughter, was the flower girl.

The solemnity of the occasion was broken when Rev. Berry, disregarding the rehearsal, let go with his editorialized response. The presiding prelate entoned, "Who gives this bride in holy matrimony?" Pop, in a very loud voice, responded, "I do, her father, the Reverend L. L. Berry, Secretary of Home and Foreign Missions of the A. M. E. Church." He sounded like he was very anxious to give her away and he wanted it completely authenticated. The audience could not hold back the laughter.

More laughter was provoked at another point in Gladys' wedding ceremony. Judy, all decked in beautiful fluffy silk and lace with the traditional basket of flowers, hurriedly scattered them in front of the marching bride; then reversed her steps, picked up all the flowers, returned them to her basket, until she bumped into the bride breaking the rhythm of her march. The little flower girl then marched to the side of the bride, grasping the side of the bridal dress with one hand, and swinging her basket of flowers with the other. The Fishers lived in Detroit where Charles continued his work as a law clerk. Gladys' bachelor's degree in elementary education from Virginia State College and teaching experience in Norfolk brought her a teaching opportunity in a Detroit suburb. She enjoyed being a school teacher for 20 years following the tradition set by her mother in years gone by.

Meanwhile a storm had been brewing in Europe which broke with the impact of a Domino reaction in September, 1939. On this date the German army invaded Poland and World War II was set in motion. President Roosevelt was elected to a third team in 1940 and the Japanese attack on Pearl Harbor occurred on Dec. 7, 1941, a day which would live in infamy as the president expressed it. With the sudden and dramatic entrance of America into the shooting war there was overwhelming excitement everywhere. While the war was developing momentum, some normal peaceful affairs continued as previously planned.

I was all set to present a paper before the American Medical Association Convention two weeks later in Cleveland. The paper titled: *Chronic Alcoholic Gastritis Gastroscopic Evaluation of the Concept in 100 Severe Alcoholic Addicts* was duly read. It was a gastroscopic study of the stomachs of vagabonds or derelicts from Chicago's skid row. Over a period of 2 years, I had picked up these alcoholics who consumed an average of 3 pints of liquor per day. I encountered them around 6 a.m. as they came off their bouts of drinking the day before. On the canvas covered back seat of my Pontiac they were shuttled to Provident Hospital where I conducted my stomach clinic. The patients were paid 25 cents a head, plus a street car token to get back to the "loop" after examination of their stomachs with the new gastroscope. A pharmaceutical house provided vitamin B tablets. All other expenses including the gastroscope were paid from my family budget as no grants for research were available to one.

A direct view of the inflated stomach failed to reveal the severe chronic gastritis generally anticipated. Only one-third of them showed extensive gastritis. This was the first such study to appear to the world medical literature. I was equally surprised to learn that my paper was the first ever to be presented before the American Medical Association by a Negro doctor.

At a Smoker given by the local Negro doctors, I was surprised to be called on as the guest of honor. Within 24 hours, I was swamped by the news media. My report before 1,000 doctors at the American Medical Association convention was exciting. It seemed to lift the badge of incrimination against liquor. Nothing however, had been said about it's effect on the liver and nervous system. My findings were reported in "What's New in Medicine" and a news agency indicated that excerpts were released to more than 500 newspapers at home and abroad. A pathologist scheduled to discuss my report stated before the audience that he would pass us the discussion because he had no more desire to incriminate alcohol than Dr. Berry.

The following year I became the second Negro doctor to present a paper before the American Medical Association. I continued my boots straps research at Provident Hospital, supported by my personal funds. Papers were read, lectures and exhibits were presented before local and national societies for a number of years before small grants were provided by a couple of pharmaceutical houses.

World War II reached high gear for the USA quickly after the bombing of Pearl Harbor. I had prepared for this war and was anxious to join as a gastro-enterologist and gastroscopist. I had spent 16 years in infantry and medical reserved officer training corps, and active duty with 8th Inf., Ill. National Guard and the Civilian Conservation Corps.

As the result of pressure from the predominantly Negro National Medical Assoc. an army post hospital was set up for Negro officers and men at Ft. Hauchuca Arizona. There would be no further opportunities for Negro doctors in army hospitals.

Although I was the only Negro gastroenterologist in the USA by training and experience, I failed to get the appointment at Hauchuca. I was unable to qualify sufficiently as a personal friend of the Negro colonel who was given the exclusive authority to select his entire hospital staff.

Missions at Home
(1940–54)

THE general conference of 1940 was a very exciting session for the secretary of missions. After 1936 when the general church had overwhelmingly confirmed their desire to have L. L. Berry as secretary of missions. He returned to New York and began his plans for surveying the entire foreign missions field, which by 1939 he had accomplished. He thus went to the 1940 quadrennial session with a report which would establish him firmly as one of the outstanding secretaries of missions in the history of the A.M.E. church. His report on the activities of the previous quadrennium was very well received by the church hierarchy, the ministerial and lay delegates of the conference. So great was his popularity at this time that many of his friends felt that they should present him for the bishopric where he might be of greater service in missionary endeavors, to the church and as administrator and leader at the highest level.

Members of his family and his friends were soon able to see that he was so imbued with the challenges and the possibilities in the field of missions that he preferred to remain the secretary. Returning to his office in June 1940 he had a long conference with his assistant, Mr. Walter F. Walker. Pop was very fortunate to have this brilliant young man as his associate and assistant administrator.

Pop had previously announced his intentions to write a history of the first century of missions in the A.M.E. church. As he prepared to launch into this program he was further very fortunate in finding a young lady who had just earned a masters degree in English at Columbia University. She was also interested in writing. This person was Ms. Valetta Harper whose father happened to have been a minister in another denomination. The plan was developed for the organization of the book with Ms. Harper doing much of the research and assisting with the correlation. Sister Gladys with a background of training in elementary education and secretarial work assisted in the beginning of the project. While continuing with the routine duties of secretary, more than a full time chore in itself, Pop put his "shoulder to the wheel" and "burned the midnight oil." In 1941 his comprehensive book of 333 pages titled, *A Century of Missions of the African Methodist Episcopal Church (1840–1940)* was published by the Gutenberg Press, New York.

One of the highlights of father's secretaryship according to many testimonials and writings of his peers and authorities on missions was the integration of A.M.E. church missionary activity into the world missions movement. He is said to have been the first A.M.E. missionary secretary to work widely with the universal missionary endeavor. He began this work while a member of the A.M.E. missionary board of managers, ten years before his election to the secretaryship in 1933. As a result of his interest, he was appointed to committees of these groups. He held various committee appointments throughout his years of activity as secretary of missions.

He was a member of the Africa Committee of the Foreign Missions Council. He participated in their deliberations and policy-making sessions. For four years he was vice president of this committee. He was a member of the committee on reference and council for ten years, a member of the executive board of the Home Missions Conference of North America for eight years. After the formation of the National Council of Churches of Christ in the U.S.A. he was a member of its general board and its nominating committee.

Secretary Berry also felt that one of his roles should be to stimulate and help to bring together the total Black church in terms of its general policies in the area of missionary endeavor. To this end he was a founder and organizer of the missionary secretaries of the Independent Negro Church Groups operating home and foreign missionary departments. It was called officially, The Organization of Foreign Missionary Secretaries of Negro Churches. On one occasion this organization was successful in causing the U.S. Dept. of State to deal more responsibly with the Liberian government.

Pop's Canada trips to survey and attend the Missionary work there was so frequent that it seemed unlike a foreign adventure as compared with Africa. However, there were problems especially with conflicts between the A.M.E. church and the Canadian version of African Methodism, a "split off" group known as the British Methodist Church. Bishop John Andrew Gregg, a very missionary minded person was a staunch friend of Secretary L. L. Berry. They had their missionary interests and beliefs in common. In 1943 Bishop Gregg received a special appointment by President Franklin D. Roosevelt to fly to many parts of the world carrying messages of cheer and goodwill to Negro soldiers on all of the war fronts of World War II. After some high level planning and consideration, Bishop Gregg made his visits to the war fronts by special plane under the auspices and by the authority of the U.S. Dept. of War and the Fraternal Council of Negro churches of America. In Bishop Gregg's book entitled "Of Men and of Arms" describing his war services, he makes the following statement in chapter one: "I am most grateful to President Franklin D. Roosevelt for his kindly personal interest in this mission and I pledge to give to it my best endeavor. Speaking to my own church, should this mission prevent my returning in time for my annual conferences, I am asking Dr. L. L. Berry, the Secretary of Missions, to conduct the Ontario-Quebec annual conferences." Pop had conducted these conferences on previous occasions serving for and with the authority of the presiding bishop of the district.

In mid-August, 1943, Pop boarded the New York Central train in New York City enroute to Ontario, Canada by way of Chicago and Detroit. Pop had enjoyed coming to the middle-west almost annually since he first became secretary of missions. He liked the Chicago ministers and the Chicago Annual Conference. I like to think that he also enjoyed visiting me, "the young physician" as Pop often presented me in those days, and my family. On this occasion he boarded the train as usual around 4:00 p.m. at the Grand Central Station. He tucked himself away in his reserved bedroom to relax from the usual hustle and bustle preceding his leaving town. He looked forward to this relaxing time, which would carry him through the night and arrival in Chicago after an early breakfast. Pop never counted the telegraph poles as they flashed by the window of his bedroom, but his observation of other things and events through this window helped him to relax and to think. He was traveling the so-called "water level" route on the train known as the Commodore Vanderbilt. As the day faded away he observed farmers bringing their herds to the barnyards and the many farm houses and growing crops in

343

up-state New York. His train passed into Pennsylvania near sundown and it was time for him to think about the delicious dinner usually served on this train.

Around 5:30 a dining car waiter came through with the announcement, "First call for dinner." Pop checked the time on his closed-faced pocket watch and decided that he had better wash his hands and proceed to the dining car to get ahead of the crowd. He was seated in the middle of the car at a two-seat table, facing forward. "Good afternoon," said the waiter as he pulled the chair. "Fine," said Pop, "I see I'm in plenty of time." "Yessir," said the waiter, "This is the time to get the best service." As the waiter poured a glass of water, Pop began to read the menu. It did not take him long to eye the main dish of Virginia flounder stuffed with Maryland crabmeat. Certainly this old Virginian who grew up near the shores of the Chesapeake Bay never grew tired of this kind of cuisine. As Pop began to consume his preliminary cup of clam chowder, he noticed a tall blondish gentleman apparently walking away from the escorting dining car steward and heading toward his table. My affable and much travelled father proffered the first 'How do you do, sir.' "Fine sir, hope you don't mind the company of a stranger," said a smiling voice with a white southern accent. "Your smiling countenance suggests that you are a friendly type of stranger," said Pop. They smiled and continued to exchange pleasantries as the waiter pulled the chair and seated the gentleman facing Pop at the table. Before long they introduced themselves. Pop's table mate was a congressman from the second congressional district of Chicago. He had just finished his last term and had accepted a professorship in philosophy at Syracuse University. His name was Thomas Vernon Smith. A few minutes later the congressman said "The name Berry is familiar, I have a good friend in Chicago, Dr. Leonidas Berry, a physician there with offices on the southside." Well, of course, Pop smiled and said "that is my son." And so my good friend T. V. Smith explained his relationship with me which had begun nearly twenty years before. He recalled my difficulties in getting into the medical school at the University of Chicago and how he was able to help with my problem as the dean of unclassified students at that time. "Your son has developed into an outstanding specialist in digestive diseases, Rev. Berry, I am sure you must be proud of him." "Thank you, congressman, I do think that he has done quite well."

"This is certainly a pleasant coincidence, congressman, I am so pleased that you joined me for dinner. I shall certainly tell my son about meeting you." "Please give him my very best regards, Reverend, I have not seen him very much in the last few years." This ended the toast to me. Pop and Congressman Smith then shifted to the discussion of the war, the tremendous loss of life, the courageous and loyal Black and White soldiers and the inevitable conversation of race, religion and America. By this time they had leisurely finished their main course and the waiter was asking for a selection of dessert. Pop was never very much of a dessert eater but he found it quite difficult to turn down hot fresh baked apple pie with a slice of American cheese. Pop's southern table mate thought that was a good selection for himself also. They finished their dessert. The Congressman apologized for his after dinner cigarette and shortly they departed to their respective bedrooms expressing mutual pleasure at having met and having enjoyed dinner together.

Pop had been virtually taken by storm. He never hesitated to strike up a conversation in his travels in parlor cars and other places. However he didn't remember ever having a white southerner go out of his way to become his table-mate in a half-filled dining car.

The story of a racial confrontation regarding Professor Smith's first election to political office; that of Representative to the Illinois State Legislature is told in more detail later. His fairness and encouragement to Black students during his professorship at the University of Chicago, helped him to successfully combat the political "image" of a former Ku Klux Klansman.

At around 9:00 the next morning I met Pop at the Chicago 63rd Street Station of the New York Central Line, and took him to my home on Vernon Avenue. Judy was four years old and had learned to love her grandfather. She ran down the hall and leaped into his arms as he recited his special little ditty reserved for her "the sweetest girl in town when no one else is around." Pop would then repeat the first line and Judy would finish the rhyme. After a short visit Pop proceeded on to Detroit where he visited briefly with his recently married daughter, Gladys and her husband and with Dick and Maryland.

Pop arrived on time in Toronto through Windsor and into Canada by the Canadian National Railway. The conference was held at the Grant A.M.E. Church in Toronto with the Turner A.M.E. Church in

Oakville, a suburb, as the co-host church. Large congregations greeted him from the surrounding Ontario churches where he was well known. He saw many old friends who regretted that Mom could not make the trip with him as she had done on previous occasions. Among those whom he saw during the three day conference were Rev. and Mrs. C. P. Jones and their daughter, Alberta May of Oakville; Rev. J. Holland of Hamilton, Ontario; Rev. and Mrs. Perry, staunch old friends; Mrs. Rachel Hackley, devoted missionary worker; her mother-in-law, Mrs. Elizabeth Katherine Hackley, also a dedicated missionary worker and others.

While in this area Rev. Berry visited the birthplace and home of the late Bishop John Albert Johnson in Oakville. The late Bishop and Pop were staunch friends. The bishop had regarded Pop as a protégé in his early ministry and did more than any single churchman to advance his growth and development down in Virginia many years before.

Bishop Johnson had grown up in Oakville and preached his trial sermon at the Turner A.M.E. Church there. His birthplace still stands on a corner of one of the main thoroughfares in Oakville. It is a beautiful old well-kept white stucco building no longer in the Johnson family. The house and yard are encircled by large trees planted by the bishop's parents to form a fence for their home. Pop reported that these trees stand in stately dignity so characteristic of the dignified, erudite, eloquent J. Albert Johnson, one of the best loved and most respected in the long history of A.M.E. bishops. He was a member of the medical profession before he became a bishop.

This trip may have been the most significant and certainly the most authoritative visit to the Canadian area during Reverend Berry's twenty-one years as secretary of missions. Canada became a country for foreign missions early in the history of the spread of African Methodism in the pre-civil war era, mainly because many underground escapees had worshiped secretly or otherwise as A.M.E.'s in the U.S.A. and migrated as far west as Vancouver.

Organized A.M.E. Missionary endeavor was instituted by the New York A.M.E. conference in response to escapees request to have an affiliated A.M.E. church in St. Catherines, Ontario in the year 1837. Other churches were established in Nova Scotia and other surrounding towns. This broad area was essentially the terminal of the Northeast route in winter of the Underground Railroad. A.M.E. foreign missions to Canada also followed a more western route of the Underground Railroad, through Detroit, across the Detroit River, sometimes by foot over the ice, and on into Ontario.

On this conference trip, and others, to Canada Pop was unaware of his early ancestor, Doc Henry Jenifer, escaped slave from St. Mary's County, Maryland, who proceded him by Underground Railroad. This revelation had not been researched at that time. There was, however, a sort of spiritual reunion with the Negro past whenever Pop went to Canada. With a keen sense of the destiny of Black people and his own African ancestry, he was always excited when he arrived on Canadian soil. There in the Black community of Ontario especially when he visited the little A.M.E. churches started more than 100 years ago by underground escapees. He felt a closeness with the people whose previous generations came empty-handed and pennyless escaping the bloodhounds of slavery. Pop was indeed a lover of history and especially interested in the search for the truth of Black history. Especially on this trip as he stood with exalted authority he experienced a sense of rededication in his role of secretary of missions to the continued growth and development of the Negro community in Canada.

Pop had a very joyful experience in Canada conducting the Ontario-Quebec conference for his good friend Bishop John A. Gregg. He returned by the way of Chicago to visit the Chicago annual conference in its September session. While there he was asked to preach a sermon on Sunday morning of the closing day of the conference. Bishop Gregg, who had returned from his trip around the world, was in charge. In introducing Rev. Berry for the sermon, he spoke of the excellent reports which had come from Secretary Berry's conduct of the Canadian conference.

Pop announced his text to be found in Isaiah, 52:7, "How beautiful upon the mountain are the feet of Him that bringeth good tidings, that publisheth peace; that bringeth good tidings that publisheth salvation; that sayeth unto Zion thy God reigneth!" His subject was the *Christian ministry and the gospel 'of Christ.'*

The book from which this text is taken is interesting and attractive. May I say that it is interesting because of its many references to the future church. Whether the prophecies of Isaiah come by dreams, voices, or visions, it is true that God made Himself known to this man and through

347

him God spoke to his people. While chastised and warned of their sins, He also encouraged them. Jesus went forth preaching the good tidings of His kingdom, He taught the mystery of salvation in healing the sick and causing the lame to walk and casting out devils and sending forth messengers and they were men, not angels, men born of the flesh, men who had sinned, men of everyday life, men who were called of God. Some may not receive God's message. Others may be cold and indifferent but deep down in the hearts of thousands this gospel will strike a responsive cord and from every cardinal point of the globe will be heard the tramp of teaming millions coming up to Zion joining their voices with that of the Prophet Isaiah in saying "how beautiful upon the mountain are the feet of Him that bringeth good tidings."

Pop's sermon was well received in the spirit of his interest in missionary endeavors. He continued on to New York, somewhat weary of the long and busy trip but very happy to greet Mom and Gerri. After visiting his family he went down stairs to the office to check on the activities during his absence. He found work to do but took care of only essential matters. He returned to his living quarters for an afternoon nap before dinner. The next day he began his office work in earnest. About mid-morning he noticed a young man standing in front of the missionary headquarters. He paid no attention at first but fifteen or twenty minutes later the young man was still standing there staring up at the sign which said "Department of Missions, African Methodist Episcopal Church." Half an hour or more had passed and the young man had moved only a few feet, always coming back and staring at the building. Pop went outside and spoke to him. The young man said that he was an African student and was looking for a job. Pop invited him in and buzzed my mother upstairs and asked her to fix him a lunch. He ate very heartily and asked for more. This he was given very freely. He returned to the office, Pop gave him words of encouragement and wished him luck in finding a job and gave him a ten dollar bill. And said "Now if this gives out before you find a job come back and see me." The young man thanked him very graciously and left. He never returned and Pop assumed that he had found a job. This penniless hungry, discouraged African student turned out to be Kwane Nkrumah, who eventually finished his college work at Lincoln University and graduate work at University of Pennsylvania. His biographers state that he later contacted and made friends with Paul Robeson and W.E.B. DuBois in New York, met Jomo Kenyatta of Kenya, East Africa, in London, studied and held workshops with these men, planned and plotted the ambitious task of leading his countrymen in the Gold Coast to ultimate freedom from the British Empire. He returned to the Gold Coast in 1947, successfully lead the revolution which obtained that freedom and changed the name of the Gold Coast back to its ancient name of Ghana.

When he became prime minister in 1957 he told the story privately and over and over from the public platform of being befriended and encouraged by Reverend L. L. Berry in the U.S.A. when he was desperate and at the most important crossroads of his life. The story was retold to me by Dr. Peter Bright-Asare, a Ghanian physician whom I recruited for his present position of chief of the division of digestive disease at Cook County Hospital, Chicago. He said that the Nkrumah story was told by teachers in public and private schools all over the nation of Ghana. He related his personal observations that Nkrumah, would "choke up" and wipe tears from his eyes whenever he repeated the story of the beneficent Black minister in America. Nkrumah was quoted as saying that the meal in the minister's home was his first in four days, and he felt that his life was at its end. When Prime Minister Nkrumah came to New York and Harlem for a victory celebration he went to 112 West 120th, seeing the same large sign of the Department of Missions of the A.M.E. Church still there, he rushed in to greet and pay his respects to Secretary Berry and share the joy of his momentous success. Instead of Secretary Berry he met Secretary Clarke. Secretary Berry had passed away three years before in 1954. It was reported by Rev. Clarke to me that the prime minister briefly related his experience with Rev. Berry referring to it as a God send that turned his life around; he wept briefly as he stood in the vestibule before returning to his waiting limosine. Three years later in 1960 Kwane Nkrumah returned to New York as president of the Republic of Ghana. He is said to have requested his entourage to pass thru 120th Street between 7th and Lenox avenues. He stopped his limosine briefly in front of the Missionary Headquarters hurriedly walked up the steps to the entrance door, gave a symbolic and reverent bow and returned to join the parade.

Nkrumah had been a poor African student, penniless, hungry and in a foreign land; he could see no possible way out. There came to him a date with destiny that turned his life around. Reverend L. L. Berry, Christian minister, fighter for justice and parity of opportunity was an important part of that date with destiny. The story ends with the bene- factor eventually changing the course of history of the world and co- lonialism. While the good "samaritan" minister reached the end of his life without ever knowing the significant impact of his kindly deed.

During the quadrennium from 1944 to 1948 Pop as the Secretary of Missions reached the height of his career. He was perhaps better known throughout the church than any other General Officer. He had established himself as a courageous and efficient individual from the time that he first took office as the general secretary of Home and Foreign Missions. His resounding victory in the challenge to his election followed by the demonstration of his zeal for missionary endeavor by traveling the oceans to the missionary field near the brink of World War II. He developed a reputation for holding his audiences spellbound, as he de- scribed the great need in Black underdeveloped countries for elementary schooling, food to sustain life, their spiritual needs and directions and the great challenge of the Black African Methodist Episcopal Church to bring Christian aid to their brothers and sisters whose needs were far greater than our own.

Pop travelled about the United States during the years between general conferences showing movies which he had made in his African and Caribbean travels. He was a practical missionary. In the times of emergencies, he solicited and shipped by way of the missionary head- quarters, tons of clothing to hurricane victims in Jamaica, British West Indies. This was only one example of similar projects he sponsored.

At the Philadelphia conference in 1944, he introduced his compre- hensive book *A Century of Missions of the A.M.E. Church (1840 to 1940)*, and a smaller book on A.M.E. missions in the Caribbean, entitled *A Little Missionary Journey to a Great Missionary Area*.

In 1944 Pop's friends again were urging him to become a candidate for the bishopric. He appreciated their thoughts and evaluation of his leadership qualities as they expressed it. However, he very often said that the position of secretary of missions had possibilities for service to the church and to his people which far exceeded in breath and perhaps depth, the geographic confinements of an Episcopal district—the sphere of a bishop. Certainly in ecclesiastical authority, and permanency of position and temporal security, a bishop in the A.M.E. church had no peer in the field of gospel ministry. But, at this time and the years before, his vision for dedicated missions service made all other attractions become secondary.

However, as the 33rd general conference of 1948, to be held in Kansas City, drew near, Pop finally permitted his friends to enter his name as a candidate for the bishopric. It was a strange kind of candidacy. He never personally sent out a single personal letter announcing it. Discussions with Pop by ministers around the country about the bishopric, usually brought the response that he wanted to be of the greatest service in missions. "Why not be a missionary bishop with greater authority?" he was asked. As ministers and church officers gathered in various meetings around the country in 1947 such expressions as "Draft Berry for Episcopal honors," were heard. Pop finally went into the general conference of 1948 as a candidate for the bishopric. His friends including a large number of bishops had the highest enthusiasm for his election. He had no election headquarters as did the other candidates for the bishopric. His modest plaques announcing his candidacy were posted in his Secretary of Missions headquarters. Rev. L. L. Berry was not elected a bishop in the A.M.E. church. Almost with a sigh of relief he again announced his candidacy for the Secretary of Missions for the fifth consecutive election. (More than had ever occurred before.) Again he was overwhelmingly re-elected against all comers. Churchmen and churchwomen were saying that he was "unbeatable" for this position by the relatively large number of candidates in those days.

I was present in Kansas City in my fourth consecutive tour of duty as a lay delegate to the general conference of the African Methodist Episcopal Church. My wife and many of my friends especially in the medical profession marvelled at what a brainwashing I must have received growing up from childhood in A.M.E. parsonages. This often brought a smile or a facetious laugh for indeed their guess was probably right. By invitation I had written a short chapter in Pop's book "A Century of Missions of the A.M.E. Church (1840–1940)." The title of my article was "A Prospective for Further Endeavor in the Field of Missions and Public Health."

I went to the general conference of 1948 with the specific intention of getting a law passed establishing a permanent health commission which would study the feasibility of setting up some type of church-wide health activity. I had presented my proposal and acquired approval by laymen in the Chicago conference area and the Fourth Episcopal District laymen convention. The plan was to attempt to get approval of the entire lay organization at the general conference to have them sponsor a bill to enact the health program. Attorney Herbert Dudley, President of the Connectional or Church Wide Laymen's organization was very enthusiastic and this organization voted unanimous approval.

In order to symbolize our efforts, I had arranged with the Kansas state department of public health and the Kansas City health department to furnish health education literature for distribution at the conference. health department. Health education sound films were
During lunch periods of the delegates, health education sound films were provided for us by the city health department. With a tremendous amount of work, cooperation by laymen and at least the creation of a sense of awareness on the part of some bishops, the bill "creating the permanent Health Commission" was passed and printed in the book of discipline of the A.M.E. church. I learned a few months later that the modest funding request was also passed but later deleted by the compilation committee.

At all subsequent general conferences I served the health commission as chairman from 1948 to 1977. I was able to set up first-aid and health education clinics during the entire period of deliberations. An average of 400 to 500 delegates and visitors were processed through these clinics at each session. The program was largely voluntary. It has supplied an important need and has become a necessity. Liaison with local hospitals for serious emergencies and opportunities for voluntary services on the part of doctors and nurses of the church has been maintained.

At each general conference the director of the commission has been re-elected medical director and connectional officer by the commission. In 1972 the general conference elected the commission chairman, a General Officer and medical director of the A.M.E. church by acclamation. In 1976 I requested and was voted retirement as General Officer and Emeritus Consultant. A variety of health conferences and programs have been carried out in various Episcopal districts between general conferences to the extent that finances and voluntary services would permit.

352

As medical progress becomes more technical and there is a growth of awareness for health rights and return towards more personal concerns in the delivery of health care the church has an increasingly important role to play in the prevention of disease and preservation of health.

It was an interesting twist of fate that I followed Pop's trail into Canada so many years earlier as I had done in West Africa and the Caribbean, primarily involved in medical meetings or tourism. It was many years later that I extended a meeting of the "American Society for Gastrointestinal Endoscopy" in Toronto to visit A.M.E. churches in southern Ontario. I was in Toronto with my wife primarily to receive the annual Rudolf Schindler Medal of 1977, the highest award of the Society.

My wife and I first visited the Grant A.M.E. Church at 23 Soho Street in Toronto with Reverend Robert Clay the pastor. This was the co-host church with the Turner Church in suburban Oakville, where Pop held the annual conference for Bishop Gregg more than thirty years before. Rev. Clay and I discussed Black Church History in that area and my wife and I had a lunch of southern cooking, called "soul food," at the famous Underground Railroad Restaurant in Toronto. Later, Rev. Clay took us by auto to Oakville, 25 miles away. There, we met Rev. and Mrs. Myles Esterbrooks in the parsonage next to the Henry McNeal Turner A.M.E. Church which was founded in 1854 and later named after Bishop Turner.

I should have said earlier that, Reverend Joseph Brockington who lived in Detroit had served as pastor and Presiding Elder of A.M.E. churches in Canada. He and his son were very helpful in directing us in our survey of churches.

Reverend Esterbrooks and his wife are Caucasians. We were told that 40 percent of the membership of this church was white and 60 percent Black. Pop had told me about this church which had a history very dear to him. Bishop J. Albert Johnson, who really sponsored the beginning of Pop's upward climb in the church went to Sunday School as a child and entered the ministry at the Turner Church in Oakville. After discussing the interesting and integrated religious history, Rev. Esterbrooks took us into the quaint and beautiful sanctuary, through the parsonage including the pastor's study where he had many books on the Black religious and cultural experience in Canada. He had been an accountant before entering the pastorate of the Turner Church which he had held for seventeen years.

The month of May weather was very comfortable and we took a walk a few blocks away to see the house where Bishop J. Albert Johnson was born on October 29, 1857. It was kept in an excellent state of repair by the white family which presently occupied it. It was painted white with green colored window frames and shingled roof. The well-kept grassy lawn and house were surrounded by tall spruce trees symetrically arranged as a fence.

Our very interesting and enjoyable visit came to an end as Rev. Esterbrooks drove us back to the hotel where we spent our last night in Toronto.

On the next morning we flew to Detroit where my sisters Gladys and Geraldine lived. We picked them up in a rented car and drove the relatively short trip through the tunnel under the Detroit River into Windsor, Ontario. We saw the A.M.E. Church in Windsor; it was closed and we could not locate the pastor. However, we recalled that my sisters and I with Pop and Mom had attended this church from Detroit some years before while Bishop Baber was holding the Canadian Conference there and Pop was speaking on Missionary night. My wife, two sisters and I continued to drive our air-conditioned car around southern Ontario over well-kept highways to other A.M.E. churches. Our next stop was at the A.M.E. Church in Chatham where Pop had visited many times. From there we drove to Amherstburg and visited the Nazery Church named for Bishop Willis Nazery, fifth bishop of the A.M.E. church. It was founded in the year 1839 and later named for Bishop Nazery. Its early members like those of the other A.M.E. churches in Canada were for the most part escapees from American slavery usually by the Underground Railroad. My wife, two sisters and I met Mr. Melvin "Mac" Simpson and his wife who lived next door. They were very happy to meet us. Mr. Simpson recalled immediately that when he was a little boy, Rev. L. L. Berry, Secretary of Missions from the U.S.A., stopped in the home of his parents, when visiting Grant Church and other churches in the nearby community.

Mr. Simpson was organizing a museum of the "Canadian Black Identity," to be housed in the building next door to the church, with some government support. He showed us the sanctuary of the quaint little church and relics in an adjoining archives room. There was a beautiful multi-colored pipe organ which received its power from a hand-operated, hidden bellows within the organ structure. The organ, pulpit chairs and Bible stand were first used approximately one hundred years before. In discussing the history of the church, Mr. Simpson related the role played by Bishop Willis Nazery in reuniting the A.M.E. church in Canada which had split off to become British Methodist Episcopal. The reunion of the B.M.E.'s of Canada with their mother church, the A.M.E.'s, has been an "on again, off again affair," from the earliest times to the present without permanent success.

At one time when a lawsuit developed, Pop made an emergency trip to Canada as mediator, to save an A.M.E. church. He traveled by train and a twin-seated plane of an early model, with only himself and pilot as passengers. After a very pleasant visit and discussion of the past, present, and future of the Black experience in Canada, we drove back to Detroit for the night, anxiously looking forward to the continuation of our tour of A.M.E. churches and Black history on the next day. Early the next morning after breakfast and gasing up the car we were off to our return trip to Canada. We were heading for Dresden, Ontario to visit the former home and museum commemorating the life of the famous Reverend Josiah Henson. He had reached the Dresden area in Kent County, southwest Ontario, after escaping from Charles County in Southern Maryland where he was born in 1789. His escape with his family followed their sale and transfer as slaves to Kentucky. His final trip to Canada was circuitous and ingenius. Josiah Henson was a most unusual self made man. He taught himself to read, become a successful businessman, and minister, first in the African Methodist Episcopal Church, and later a well-known minister in the British Methodist Church, an offspring of the A.M.E. denomination. Rev. Henson worked as an abolitionist; established a trade school in Dresden; traveled to Europe, raised money and organized an international society to support his school.

Josiah Henson was one of several remarkable men and women who escaped from the bonds of slavery in the state of Maryland. Henson originally came from a Charles County Plantation in Maryland. He was best known as the original "Uncle Tom." It was his life story as a slave that inspired Harriet Beecher Stowe to write the classic of world literature; "Uncle Tom's Cabin." Rev. Josiah Henson is buried with members

355

of his family in a corner of a large acreage of land in Dresden, once owned by him. His Industrial Institute or Trade School was there. A house in the Dresden Memorial plot is said to be one in which he lived. There is a secret passage way to the attic where escaping slaves were hid away. Our party viewed the interior of Rev. Henson's church and a large museum of memorabilia of "Uncle Tom" and the culture in which he lived before and after his escape from slavery. This site in Dresden is preserved to his memory and for the edification of generations who have been and still are interested in Black history and culture in the western world.

Gladys, Gerri and I returned from Canada having covered an historical portion of the African Methodist Missionary area. In spirit we traveled with Pop; this was a part of our Christian heritage and destiny.

Golden Anniversary
(1950)

THE year 1950, marked the mid-point in the 20th Century. It was an interesting period in world and American history. It marked an important milestone in the destiny of the Berry family. I have often been called officious by members of the family, but never by Mom and Pop, whether or not the title was deserved. It was said that I would get an idea involving the family and "run with it." It was said that sometimes the idea was a "bubble," but all agreed that I never put the family in serious jeopardy.

In the Spring of 1950, I had one of those crazy ideas. I had been practicing medicine for 15 years. I had to attend a meeting of the Association of Former Interns and Residents of Freedmen's Hospital in Washington to preside as president. It was also the year of Mom and Pop's 50th Wedding Anniversary which would be celebrated in the Fall. I felt that I wanted to visit the scenes of my childhood down in Virginia and to collect some memorabilia which might be used at the Wedding Anniversary.

And so on the 5th of June, I rushed away from Chicago in a Roomette on the B&O Capital Ltd., for the meeting in Washington. The medical meeting was soon over and I was all excited about my decision to take the one and a half hour, 16 seater propeller plane across the Bay. I had taken a number of trips on the Norfolk-Washington Steamer since school days. They were overnight runs and I was either a white-coated "stowaway," guest of the Black chef cook, or a "Jim-Crow" passenger in a second class stateroom. All this could temporarily be forgotten as one looked over the rail of a segregated deck, or through a porthole. The moonlit silhouettes across the billowy waves were romantic and delightful sights to behold. By contrast on the plane, I felt like a ship wrecked sailor on a raft off the shores of Cape Hatteras in the dead of winter. Unfortunately, I had a round-trip ticket. The plane dipped in

357

and out of air pockets (I suppose they were), and rumbled as though it would crack up throughout the entire trip across the bay. I sat there, cramped, tense, strapped to my seat, and holding my breath with each pitch and toss toward the surface of the water. We finally landed, I, with the worst case of preemesis nausea that this gastroenterologist had ever suffered, witnessed or read about.

It did not take long to photograph old St. John's on Bute Street, St. James in South Norfolk, Emmanuel on North Street, Portsmouth, and the parsonages next door; and presiding Elder Berry's proudly possessed residence at 806 Berkley Avenue, in Norfolk. I was off by trolley car to Old Willoughby Spit and across Hampton Roads by Ferry to Old Point Comfort and Hampton. My! how memories were stirred of my childhood and school days at Abraham Lincoln Grammar, and Booker T. Washington High School along these familiar routes. As I landed at Old Point Comfort, there stood in the distance to my left the majestic and historic Chamberlain Hotel. Pop worked there as a bus boy in the summers between terms at Kittrell College in the mid-1890's. To my right and covering a wide expanse in the distance there was familiar Fortress Monroe with its grassy mounds, surrounding a labyrinthine moat and hidden casemates, the vintage of which extended quite beyond the period of John Berry's training there for the Civil War. I snapped a few pictures and leisurely hopped a trolley for the trip through Phoebus in the direction of Hampton only a few miles away.

Soon I caught sight of the broadly expanded National Veterans Cemetery at Kechotan, as the trolley approached the adjacent campus of Hampton Normal and Industrial Institute. Grandpop John Berry lay peacefully in Civil War Veterans Grave No. 38, since September of 1909. As the tall buildings of Hampton Institute came into my distant view, I caught sight of a beautiful and massive tree which I suddenly remembered from high school days. It was the famous "Emancipation Oak" under whose boughs, the first free school for Negro children was conducted by Mary Peake, a free born woman citizen of Hampton. I then remembered that a couple of hundred yards back we had passed a point where the main trolley line branched off to the right for Buckroe Beach. My memory brain cells were working rapidly. I must get a fast look at Hampton Institute Campus and its main entrance gate but I'm thinking also of Buckroe Beach where I must return to spend the night with Emmy Churchill Wilson and her husband, family friends since public school days. The trolley stopped at the Hampton Institute Gate and there it stood in all its historic nostalgic beauty.

I remember a pictorial calendar published by the school about the time of World War I. An introductory picture in the calendar of the gate carried a caption which read "H.N.I. where three races of men work out the problems of everyday life without friction." We all knew that at best that was a "white lie" in the good Old Dominion state at the time of World War I. But the white faculty-administration wrote it.

The students in World War I days, and before, were Negro and American Indians. As the streetcar lingered, I could see through the trees the beautiful brick buildings all built by students. I remembered "The Wigwam," a Dormitory primarily for Indian boys; "Winona," primarily for Indian girls; James Hall for Negro boys and Virginia Hall for Negro girls. Lula Harris Myers, Mom's youngest sister, graduated there in Home Economics in 1922. As the trolley moved on across a little land bridge that was the familiar little mountain of oyster shells beyond which there was a clear view of big steamships in Hampton Roads and the Chesapeake Bay. Soon the trolley was on King Street, the main street of Hampton. I must remember the stop that will let me off near Lincoln Street and Bethel AME Church. I had been away from these old stomping grounds for 20 years. "James Crow" is still the paragon of public law in Virginia, but I was passing through an island of moderate liberalism in a sea of white racist aristocracy. I had carefully rehearsed the signals and I was rolling with the tide.

As luck would have it I got off the trolley two blocks too soon. I passed a store as I walked, which I am sure was the Greek ice cream parlor where as youngsters, cousins John and Tom Berry and brother Dick and I bought three cent strawberry ice cream sodas en route to Buckroe Beach for a swim. I wasn't certain of the Jim Crow arrangements then nor now. So with a hard swallow I moistened my hard palate and uvular with such salivary secretions as I could muster up and kept walking. In the bright mid-afternoon sun I soon had a clear view of the impressive brick Bethel AME Church on Lincoln Street. Diagonally across the street on the corner there still stood the little house where Grandma Berry spent her last years and died.

As I walked slowly, Hampton Institute was still on my mind. The white faculty there ran a "tight ship" for discipline, but there were cultural attributes and excellent training in their trade schools. The boys wore military type uniforms and Major R. R. Moton was the commandant of the compulsory military "brigade." This was before he succeeded Booker T. Washington as President of Tuskegee. Northern white philanthropy kept Hampton on a solid base. William Howard Taft was a trustee when I was in high school. Broadway theatrical and musical professionals were brought to the Hampton Institute campus which excluded clamoring local white citizens who demanded to sit up front with the students behind. As a high school student in Norfolk I witnessed strong football teams at Hampton composed of Negro and Indian Athletes. There was a star half-back with straight black, coarse hair, and high cheek bones who walked and ran pigeon-toed. His name was "Owl." Instinctively he executed the delayed off-tackle buck for long yardage before the technique was discovered by professionals.

Big "Red" Dabney, 6'3", 225 lbs., a super giant for those days, played center except for goal line stands, when he would put the quarterback over the ball and take over fullback and make the touchdown.

I have now reached Lincoln Street and the Bethel Church. Pop went to Sunday School here in the 1880's; his father was one of the earliest members in 1870, he was an exhorter, a steward and Pop's class leader in the early days. I aimed my camera to capture the beautiful church and the adjacent church yard cemetery. There were scattered tombstones throughout the burial ground, of many sizes and shapes of grey and white granite; some were erect, others leaning at various angles. Here and there trees were distributed among the stones. There was one very large, impressive weeping willow with its high limbs drooping over the roof of the church.

I entered the churchyard following a long crooked beaten path. Pedestrians had an idea that a straight line may be the shortest distance between two points, but a crooked one is still shorter then going around the block. As I walked I met an elderly lady and I spoke. "I'll bet you're a member of this church." "Yes, for many years," she replied. I continued, "I've just noticed a stone which reads 'Mother Nancy Berry, 1847–1919' that's my grandmother's stone." "Oh!" the lady exclaimed, "I knew her when I was a little girl; so you are a Berry?" "Yes mam." "Are you one of Rev. Berry's sons?" "Yes, I am" "Are you the doctor?" "Yes, you guessed it, I am the eldest son, Leonidas from Chicago." "I am

Sister Peeden, Dr. Berry." "That's a familiar Hampton name," I said. "I'm very glad to meet you, Mrs. Peeden. I have seen no other Berry stones, but I must have several relatives buried here." "You certainly do, Doctor," said Sister Peeden as she looked around. Hesitatingly, she said, "I know where one of them is buried. You see that large weeping willow tree hanging over the edge of the church roof? Your grandmother, Sister Nancy Berry planted that tree to mark the grave of her young daughter, who died in the 1880's." A few months later, Pop, Uncle John Augustus, Aunts Catherine and Lola had confirmed Mrs. Peeden's statement. Their young sister Florence died in 1889 and their parents had no funds to purchase a tombstone.

I took several color photo shots of the church and trees long after my informant had disappeared on the next street. I'm glad I did, because ten years later on a trip to Hampton, I found that the tree had recently been cut down. I arrived there near sundown and learned the sad news from neighbors sitting on their porch across the street, after observing that the tree was missing. I stood silently there for a long time, staring and feeling a lump in my throat. I thought of a poem I knew as a boy, titled "WOODMAN SPARE THAT TREE." The poem described a young man pleading for the life of a tree under whose boughs he had spent memorable hours at play in childhood. I held back the tears of regret that I had not had the opportunity to plead for the life of that tree which had stood for three-fourths of a century as a symbol of the love of Grandma Berry for her young daughter Florence, lost in death at such a tender age. I feel sure that Grandma nutured that carefully chosen willow sprig. She must have watered and cultivated it for days and months until the sapling took root. As I knew Grandma Berry, she must have prayed at the gravesite day-in and day-out that her treasured memorial might have long and abundant life to the loving memory of her one lost sheep. Long after the planter was gone the willow tree continued its upward growth into the skies, toward the heaven that Grandma knew. Its drooping boughs appropriately called weeping willow branches, dipped majestically in symbolic reverence over the church in which Grandmother worked incessantly to establish and develop. The mother and father of little Florence, some of their sisters and brothers and playmates are gone. Some had man-made memorial stones. None will reach the enduring majesty and growing beauty of this living memorial, not made with hands, "whose hungry mouth was pressed against the earth's sweet flowing breast;" "A tree that looked at God all day and lifted her leafy arms to pray; A tree that did in summer wear a nest of robins in her hair;" but to paraphrase Joyce Kilmer, "Man may destroy but only God can make a tree."

After my spring trip in 1950 to retrace the trails of my father and his family down in Virginia, I returned to my medical practice in Chicago. During the summer, some time was spent at the family summer home in Idlewild, Michigan. As the fall approached, all our thoughts were in the direction of New York's Harlem, and Mom and Pop's 50th Wedding Anniversary.

Late in September, the Berrys everywhere were happy and expectant because a big event was in store. Preparations had followed an organized schedule in New York for about a year. It was to be a three-day event, though not a church convention. The entire house had been decorated with carefully selected harmonious appointments; the floors refinished, the small yard in back of this New York house and the so-called roof flower garden on top of the second level had been appropriately arranged. A third floor story near a window extending nearly to the floor served as an easy exit to Mom's roof flower garden. It was a rare gem in 1950 Harlem. The extensive preparations for this family affair also included engraved invitations, to the "multi-nuclear" Berry-Harris-Jordan family and many friends for the Golden Wedding Anniversary of Reverend and Mrs. Lewellyn L. Berry, on September 26, 1950. Members of the family clan and friends mostly of the ministerial world came from all directions across the country. Some came non-stop overnight by automobile. A few risked stopping overnight but they had to be careful of what hotel bell they would ring to avoid being insulted in 1950. The more daring ones would read the Ten Commandments or whistle *My Country Tis of Thee* before driving up.

D-Day was just around the corner when Dick and Maryland Berry with two fidgety pre-teen girls Lydia and Sylvia arrived non-stop by automobile from Detroit. On the next day from Washington Lew, Jr. and Kathy came with Lew III, while Ophelia, pre-teen Judy arrived, and I by automibile from Chicago. Among other members of the family attending the three-day extravaganza were Mom's sisters, Ursula and Lula and brother John. Pop's widowed sisters, Catherine and Lola, were present. His oldest brother John Augustus, Jr. and wife, Victoria, were

362

among the most visibly elated, while saying little or nothing about their own marriage of 60 years.

On the morning of the 26th, many cousins, first, second, and third from nearby towns arrived for the afternoon ceremony of renewing their marital vows. Richard Allen Brooks, his wife, and his sisters Grace and Sylvia. From Camden, N.J., Lillian Goings from Washington, Clara Rovster, her sister Nona, from Philadelphia, Marion Jordan Moore from Atlantic City, the Jordans from Newark and Orange and many others all came to the celebration.

The climactic event occurred in the Reception Room of the Mission House. The ceremony was performed by Bishop John Andrew Gregg, assisted by Bishops R. R. Wright, and S. L. Greene, former chairmen of the Missionary Board. In the reception line, in addition to the immediate family were long time friends, Dr. S. S. Morris, A.M.E. Secy. of Religious Education; Reverend Maxwell of a Harlem Baptist Church; a representative, Miss Shotwell of the National Council of Churches in the U.S.A. and the United Church Women respectively. The latter representing integrated religious groups tending to dispute the concept that religious denominations are the most segregated institutions in the U.S.A. following the exchange of vows, the Reverend Samuel S. Morris, Sr. stepped forward and said: "Let us all join with them in celebration of this glorious occasion." He then shook Pop's hand and kissed Mom on the cheek. Together Reverend Lewellyn L. and his life's marital mate Beulah Harris Berry had walked together on the golden sands of time. They walked side by side over barren fields and grassy meadows. They led their flock like shepherds and carried their young lambs in their bosoms. Let there be poetic joy for they have reached that cherished milestone on the roadway of wedded bliss; or if you prefer that distant glowing lighthouse on the rugged sea of matrimony. Following the formalities, the large audience of the extended Berry-Harris-Jordan family ate hors doeuvres, and drank golden fruit punch. Gradually the more dignified and sanctimonious people left and some of the communion "wine" being passed around became pale, pink and bubbly. At this point some of the male cousins moved over on the sofas and in the corners of the next room. Soon the conversations and laughter began to challenge and then to drown out the chatter of the teens and gossip of the older ladies in the other parts of the adjoining rooms. The men having separated from the boys reminisces of childhood and earlier years graduated to Parlor and "not-so-parlor" types of tall tales with brother Dick as usual, leading the pack, with his endless collection of observations on religious dignitaries, ordinary preachers and sanctimonious brothers and sisters of the church.

Among the milder jokes were parodies on religious songs like:
"Blest Be The Cheese That Binds"
"Amazing Grace How Sweet the Sounds"
"Ta da, ta da, etc."

The rest can only be told by preacher's sons in a corner with male cousins while celebrating their parent's Golden Wedding Anniversary.

"Now Dick, you have the floor, give us one of those good ecclesiastical ones; never mind a clue." Dick started with feigned reluctance, as usual, "Maybe this one shouldn't be told in a Mission House, has Pop gone?" "Yes," someone answered, "and remember that Uncle Lew always preached that there is a time for all things; a time to reap, to sow, to weep, to laugh, to pray, to tell jokes. Now, let's hear it Dick." "O.K. give me another swiggle of those pink bubbles." "There were two denominational preachers who enjoyed a bicycle ride each Monday morning after a hard Sunday at church. One day Preacher No. 1 walked over to the parsonage of Preacher No. 2. "Good morning Parson, why are you walking, where is your bike." "Well Rev. as you know, I always strive to live the good life, to walk the straight and narrow and it depresses me greatly when in spite of my Holy intentions I'm taken advantage of. Someone has stolen my bike." "Oh, that's terrible, you mean that new 10 speeder." "Yes sir." "I'm very sorry, but I suspect that somebody in your congregation stole that bike; the devil goes to church sometimes you know." "Why don't you preach on the 10 Commandments next Sunday and when you get to *Thou Shalt Not Steal* you just let them have it and I'll bet your bike will turn up."

The next Monday morning Parson No. 1 came riding up on his bike. "Gee, Rev., I'm glad you found the thief. Did you preach on the Ten Commandments?" I'll bet when you got to "Thou shalt not steal" you just laid 'em in the aisles." "Well—no, it wasn't quite like that—when I reached the Commandment just before that, I turned my sermon suddenly into a prayer, because I remembered just where I left my bike. Hallelujah"—"Love thy neighbor—yes Reverend. 'As thy self.'" On that note we all retired.

All the family members occupying the many bedrooms in the three-story Mission House slept late that next morning; many of the clan had returned homeward before the big family dinner late in the afternoon. This was attended only by the immediate members of the Berry family, their children and grandchildren. Now the fruits of my travel around the country months before, making photo-slides of all of the churches pastored by Rev. Berry and the parsonages occupied by the family during the pastoral years in and around Norfolk, Portsmouth, Winston-Salem, Chapel Hill and Pop's childhood church in Hampton, would be viewed.

I had robbed the family photo albums going back to the early years of Mom and Pop's marriage. These included immediate children and grandchildren at all stages of their growth and development at work or play. After dinner, these slides were shown with much laughter and endless comments. We had also collected phonograph records going back to our childhood which were played as background music for the entertainment production. Before we were tired enough to go to bed there was the final feature of the evening. Charles Fisher, Gladys' husband played the violin, Ophelia Berry played the piano. Dick sang the lead in an impromptu family quartet with Gladys singing alto, Pop singing bass and I, first tenor. We sang "Carry Me Back to Ole Virginia" with Lew Jr.—interrupting with "That's the only way they will ever get me back there." We harmonized with Negro spirituals, hymns, "Sweet Alice Ben Bolt" and finally "Auld Lang Syne," before we wearily retired, bringing an end to a glorious event in the destiny of the Berry family.

Truth Speech in 1952

THE 34th Quadrennial General Conference assembled in Chicago, Illinois in May, 1952. At an appropriate time the Secretary of the Board of Home and Foreign Missionary Department, Rev. L. L. Berry was scheduled to make his quadrennial report before the general assembly. It was customary that a committee made up of the delegates from each Episcopal district previously appointed by the bishop, would examine the report of each general officer.

On a certain day near the noon hour when the morning session had come to an end a loud voice came over the speaker, "Attention, ladies and gentlemen, attention, please!" These were the words spoken by a minister wearing the badge of the First Episcopal District. He continued, "The committee on the Secretary of Missions report has met and organized. The second meeting will be held this afternoon at 4:00 in room 25 on the second floor." The ears of the Rev. Berry "faithfuls" perked up. They did not like the sound of that announcement. None of them had known about the first meeting of the appropriate committee. A quick gathering was held at general conference headquarters of the Secretary of Missions. It was revealed that this was the first announcement of a meeting that any of those present had heard. The general opinion was there was something politically rotten in Denmark. The preachers and lay loyals converted into shock troops. With just three hours to spare in the huge Chicago Coliseum and eighteen individual delegates scattered among 5,000 people, there was no time to spare. Ecclesiastical politicians sometimes makes civilian politics look like amateurs. Exactly at the announced hour the convener opened the committee meeting by asking those assembled to rise and sing one verse of "A charge to keep I have, a God to glorify; a never dying soul to save and fitted for the sky."

As a Chicago lay delegate and official member of the committee, I was present and sat near the rear. From this vantage point I counted a clear majority of Berry supporters among those assembled. The convener recognized as the same minister who made the announcement of the meeting over the loudspeaker was presiding. He thanked all the bretheren for the fine turnout and made introductory remarks. He announced as the elected chairman and the previous meeting. At this point a late comer opened the door and I saw my brother Dick manning his post just outside. He was wearing the ordinate delegate badge of a lay delegate who couldn't get out of Johannesburg, South Africa. I gave Dick the high sign, "we had the horses" each at his designated starting gate. The previous meeting was challenged, the minutes were called for. It was revealed that only three official committee members were present at the first meeting, this was far less than a quorum. The young lady delegate selected as secretary previously, resigned at this point. After considerable discussions and attempts to find flaws in the Secretary of Missions' report, a vote was called for. The overwhelming majority approved the report. The convener of the meeting announced that there would be a minority report for the general conference.

By this time everybody knew that the convener and his supporters were backing Rev. Clark as a candidate from the First Episcopal District as the leading candidate to challenge the veteran Rev. L. L. Berry for election to the office of secretary of the Department of Missions.

At an appropriate session, Rev. Berry made his report before the general conference. It was clothed with the usual eloquence for which Pop was well known. His presentation was received by a standing ovation.

Following this, presiding Bishop Frank M. Reid called for the report of committee on the Secretary of Missions quadrennial statement. The committee reported approval including an audit of the financial statement for the previous four years. A request was then made by a committee member to read a minority report. The request was granted, the minority statement made and a "witness" from an African delegation, not acquainted with the political ways of the American clergy was called to the platform. Following his "instructions," the African delegate stated that he felt that all of the funds allotted to him by the Board of Missions had not been received from the Secretary of Missions. This caused quite an uproar. Bishop I. H. Bonner, presiding bishop of the South African district from which the complaining delegate came, was asked to make a statement. The Bishop in open session completely repudiated the statement of the African delegate and the minority report was rejected by the body, creating an embarrassing situation.

Amid loud calls from the audience presiding Bishop Reid granted the platform to Rev. L. L. Berry for a reply. The speech which became a legend in AME church circles is partly reproduced as follows:

REVEREND BERRY'S SPEECH IN DE-
FENCE OF *HIS QUADRENNIAL REPORT*
as Secretary, Department of Missions, AME Church, May, 1952 at Chicago, Ill.

Bishop Reid, and members of the General Conference, ladies and gentlemen. I come before you once again, as I have come on many occasions during my tenure of office as your Secretary of Missions, during the last 21 years. My appearance today is totally different from any that has occurred in the past. I am just as proud to be your Secretary of Missions today as at any time in the past. But like an unsuspecting partridge, shot in ambush, my pride has been wounded here today. My Christian dignity has suffered some embarrassment; my integrity has been attacked by a bold and willful misstatement of the truth. The majority report approved my stewardship with highest acclaim as stated in the releases which you hold in your hands. In the twilight of my 45 years in the Christian ministry, not in my wildest dreams could I have anticipated this nefarious attack upon my integrity. But unlike Cardinal Woosley in the days of old, I have not served a false God or an earthly King. I have served the true and living God; King of Kings and Lord of Lords, who knows the good

and evil in the hearts of men. So I am not deserted in my later years; yes my head is bloody
but it is unbowed.

Bishop Bonner's statement corroborating
the audited aspects of my report has just been
greeted by your long and overwhelming applause. I can not adequately express the sentiments in my heart more forcefully than by the
words of the poet who said, 'He who steals my
purse steals trash, but he who steals my good
name, steals that which enriches him not, but
leaves me poor indeed.' Today we witness the
fulfillment of the Holy word which says 'Ye
shall know the truth and the truth shall make
you free;' free like an eagle soaring into the light
of a rising sun; so as I bring these remarks to a
close, my Christian friends, the record of my
stewardship is before you. I have no fear of your
judgement of righteousness. 'For I believe that
Truth crushed to earth shall rise again. Truth is
forever on the scaffold, wrong forever on the
throne; Yet that scaffold sways the future, and
behind the dim unknown, standeth God within
the shadows; keeping watch above his own.'

Following Pop's speech in defense of his position a most unusual
uproad developed in the audience of some 3,500 delegates and visitors
at this conference session. The meeting took on the atmosphere of a
national political party convention. The presiding bishop could not bring
the house to order for a considerable period. Several delegates were
speaking from different microphones at the same time. Finally several
delegates were heard over the clamoring noises of the conventioneers.
The concensus was a demand to change the order of the day to stop the
report of general officers and there was a demand to procede at once
with the re-election of the secretary of missions. The presiding officer
objected but he could not get order among the delegates until they had
there way. During the uproar delegates were heard to say "They

shouldn't have let him speak." "If they wanted to defeat him they shouldn't let him speak." "We're gonna put him back in that office as long as he lives." "Re-elect him now! Re-elect him now!" The demand to change the order of the day and re-elect the Secretary of Missions prevailed by a virtual stampede.

The election machinery was set up and the voting proceeded as usual by districts from the first, involving the New York and New England conferences and proceeding to all of the mainland districts and finally the African and foreign districts.

Rev. Berry was overwhelmingly re-elected for the fifth year term.

This may not have been Pop's finest hour as Secretary of Missions, but it was a dramatic and resounding victory very similar to his first election by the general conference to the office that he loved so well. In his hour of victory no one thought that this might be his last election. As fate would have it this election turned out to be the last in the longest continuous record of service in the history of the Missionary department. It was said repeatedly by his peers that no one ever came close to defeating him for the office that he loved so well.

The Mantle Is Passed
(1954)

IT was Nov. 1954. "The year is rapidly coming to it's end," Mom told her tired and weary husband. "Do you really feel like taking this trip to Texas?" "I'll be alright Hon." he responded. Every year in Nov. for the past 26 years, Pop had taken his trip from the New York headquarters of the Department of Missions to the A.M.E. Church Fall Conferences in the South. But at this time he was under doctor's care for a weakened heart and blood pressure which was often above normal. His re-election at the last general conference in 1952 had been particularly hard on him. The ecclesiastical politics had reached a zenith not previously experienced in his entire career. Defeating his adversaries every 4 years for nearly a quarter century had produced two kinds of Christian brethren. Those who almost worshipped him for his spunk, his leadership and success, and a minority who disliked him extremely for the same reasons.

At last spring's meeting of the Mission's Board of Managers, there had been continued harassment of Pop by a bishopric representative of the defeated candidate for the secretaryship. The loyal opposition was girding their loins with vicious determination for a victory in 1956. If they had known that Pop and the family had already quietly planned his retirement in 1956, the opposition may have been different and less taxing on the ailing secretary. As it was, Elbert, who came from his home in Brooklyn for the Spring board meeting, had to complete the reading of Pop's much interrupted final report. Nitroglycerine under-the-tongue tablets had relieved Pop's attacks of cardiac anginal pain but left him temporarily exhausted.

With much reduced activity, Pop was able to rest and improve thru New York's hot and humid summer months by the gift of a new air conditioner in his bedroom window.

Pop was indeed much better when in November Mom asked "Do you really feel like taking this trip to Texas," and he replied, "I'll be alright Hon."

As usual, Elbert, always ready and willing to support his father, came from Brooklyn and drove Pop in the family car to the Grand Central Station. Mom saw that Pop was well wrapped in his winter overcoat with his white scarf protectively tucked around his neck as she kissed him goodbye and said, "Take care now! I'll be praying for you."

Elbert had long since learned that the clergy cross on the car windshield and a handshake with a police officer, crushing a dollar bill into their palm would guarantee pleasant loading time at a convenient entrance to the station. With equal treatment to the red cap and sleeping car porter, Elbert soon had Pop comfortably and assuredly tucked away in his reserved bedroom for the long express railroad trip to Texas.

The Annual Texas State Conference of the A.M.E. Church was held in Dallas. Pop shed his winter coat and felt quite comfortable in the November southern atmosphere. He was sentimentally up-lifted as usual upon greeting and renewing many old friendships among Bishops, general officers, and ministers from all around the country.

At the appointed time Pop was invited to deliver a sermon. He somehow felt better than he did when he left New York. Before a packed house, he delivered his message from the text: Isaiah 6:1. "In the year that King Uzziah died, I saw the Lord."

He announced his subject as "God, our refuge in affliction."

> In the midst of a grief sticken people over the death of their leader, God gave consolation and hope through his prophet Isaiah. The Lord of Heaven still lives, though princes die and kings and monarchs be banished from the earth. The words of the prophets ring down through the ages. 'Fear not then, O Zion, the vissicitudes of nations, for Jehovah dwells within thy palaces.' Sadness had come into the life of Isaiah because of the death of his friend, King Uzziah. The experience changed his life into one of deep

> religious faith and caused him to exclaim; 'in the
> year that King Uzziah died, I saw the Lord sit-
> ting upon a throne high and lifted up and his
> train filled the temple.'

There was rapt attention and, need I say, amens from his surroundings in the pulpit and from every corner of this African Methodist
church as he applied his subject to the daily lives of Christians. For many
years thereafter, especially at general conferences, ministers and laymen
present on this occasion have relived and reviewed with me the eloquence
of Pop's Dallas sermon in 1954.

Ten days later Pop was at his next stop, Mobile, Ala. In the interim
he had his ups-and-downs physically; relying occasionally upon nitroglycerine under-the-tongue for chest pains. From Mobile he called Mom
back in N.Y. and found everything OK. He reported that he felt well
and he really did, at that point. Pop greeted other old friends and there
was mutual back-slapping and handshaking. Pop undoubtedly felt unusually "up" for his scheduled sermon in Mobile.

Those who saw and heard him there have repeatedly said that he
appeared to be in unusually high spirits, reminiscent of his younger days
as he arose to begin his sermon. For reasons which he explained he had
decided to discuss the visit of Jesus to the bedside of Lazarus in the town
of Bethany. Jesus came at the bequest of two sisters who were gravely
concerned because of the serious illness of their brother Lazarus. And
following the scripture as recorded in the 11th chapter of St. John, the
28th verse "Mary said unto her sister as she greeted Jesus at the entrance
of the house; "The Master is come and He calleth for thee."

These words were his text as he delivered a masterful sermon on
the theological analysis of this portion of the sacred scripture. Again
many who were there to hear him have said repeatedly that it was
perhaps the greatest sermon of his eloquent career. None of the 700 to
800 said to have been present could have possibly known that they were
hearing his valedictory. It was indeed his last sermon. How prophetic
was the selection of this text for his last pulpit appearance. One can only
wonder and shudder at the unseen guidance of the hand of destiny. The
Master had come and was calling for him.

At the end of the sermon, the host pastor took Pop to the pastor's study for a requested glass of water and a short rest period on a couch. Forty-eight hours later Pop appeared to be well recuperated and was returning to New York City. He had stopped in the nearby Mobile countryside and purchased a big fresh tom turkey for his family's Thanksgiving dinner. Pop stored the bird in the chef's dining car refrigerator for the fast Mobile express ride home.

Mom knowing Pop's schedule and estimating his arrival time was looking out of the window, when Pop rolled up in a Yellow Cab. The driver carried Pop's bag and Pop carried a large cardboard box with an improvised handle. Once inside the house and having received a welcoming "peck" on the cheek, Mom came thru with; "Hon, what is that heavy box you're lugging? I'll bet you brought it all the way from Mobile." "Your guess is correct, Hon. Here is a big fresh tom turkey for Thanksgiving Day." Those we get around here could have been in cold storage for a year. Mom was used to Pop bringing "goodies" home to his family. All of their married lives, he had done this. Years before, in Virginia, there was a community legend that said, "If you see a man getting off the street car looking like Santa Claus, that's Reverend Berry."

Gerri, our younger sister, recalls the events of the next few days. She says, "Dad arrived home from Mobile on Saturday morning, Nov. 20th, 1954. He looked fine to me. He brought home a turkey which Mom cooked the same day. We had a pre-Thanksgiving turkey dinner on Sunday, the 21st. Mom invited Mrs. Lydia Hall, our brother Dick's mother-in-law who was visiting in Brooklyn and an old family friend from Norfolk, Mrs. John Riley Dungee for dinner. We enjoyed ourselves and retired to the living room where I turned on radio music. Shortly afterwards, Dad went down to the office. About 20 minutes later he buzzed two bells for Mom to come to the telephone. He had called our oldest brother 'Lee' in Chicago. We talked to him. Dad then called our brother 'Lew' in Washington. 'Dick' and sister Gladys in Detroit. Mom wondered why he called all the family at that time. I said, he just wanted to talk to them. A little while later Dad called me to the office and asked me to type a letter which he wanted to mail before his secretaries came to work on Monday. I typed the letter as he requested. Later that night we all went to bed and Pop had no complaints that we knew about. On Monday night the 22nd, Dad went to Long Island and preached the funeral of a family friend. On Tuesday, the 23rd, business was as usual in the office during the morning. In the midafternoon Dad dictated a letter to his secretary, Alberta Roberts. It was a letter to Bishop Frederick Jordan in So. Africa, who was having immigration problems in Rhodesia. After that Dad went out to mail the letter at the post office.

At 4 p.m. the secretaries left for the day and were concerned that Dad had not returned and so was I. Mom was upstairs holding a meeting of the Harlem Committee of the "World's Day of Prayer." The meeting was finished and the ladies left for home. It was now dusk and Dad had not returned, or so we thought. Shortly afterwards, Dad buzzed us from his office downstairs. He had returned without our knowledge. He said "I am sick." We hurried downstairs with Mrs. Crawford who had not left the house. We found him in great distress lying on the long conference table, used for board meetings. We were greatly surprised and frightened. Mrs. Crawford and I helped him upstairs to a couch while Mom hurriedly phoned Dr. George Cannon. His nurse said the doctor is on his way. Dad had already called him. I called my brother Elbert in Brooklyn, and he drove over at full speed. Dr. Cannon soon arrived and gave Dad a 'shot.' He was breathing hard and his face was wet with prespiration. The doctor left for his office saying he would be right back but don't let the patient move from the couch. Dad seemed to get worse. I began to cry and pray softly, "Dear God, please don't take my Dad away." Elbert went into the street. When Dr. Cannon's car was not in sight, Elbert went to the corner and called a doctor out of his busy office. He came and took one look and knew that Dad was gone. He took Elbert in the next room and told him it was too late. Elbert returned and Mom said, "What did the doctor say Elbert?" and Elbert had to tell Mom that Dad was dead. She began to sob and tremble. Our dear Dad left us on Tuesday night, November 23, 1954, two days before Thanksgiving Day. It was very, very sad for all of us."

This is the end of my youngest sister's memoir of Pop's death. Could he have had an intuition when suddenly he called all the members of his family while guests were still in the house? How can mortal man explain a planned pre-Thanksgiving Day dinner, when the head of the household is destined to die 24 hours before the national day of Thanksgiving.

When my friend Dr. George ("Charlie my Boy") Cannon called me from N.Y. and informed me of Pop's sudden death, I was stunned and speechless. "Charlie" had the good judgement of letting me have it quickly without beating around the bush. After having the medical details of an acute coronary attack, we hung up and I walked slowly away and flopped in a chair. Piercing thoughts went through my brain and soon I made the rational decision that I must gracefully bow to the will of God. He was two months from 79 years.

My life time of 52 years with Pop flashed thru my mind. How blessed I was to have had the support, the discipline, the love, advice and in later years the understanding of a strong father for more than half a century. The review of our lives together as part of a loving and closeknit family unit as I moved about in a state of trance with mixed experience of joy and sadness. As Bill Shakespeare would have said; "nothing in his life became him like the leaving it." The end was quick, on schedule, punctual, always-ahead of the crowd, seemingly always ready each day for a well thought out plan of action. He knew that procrastination was indeed the thief of time. He was "together," organized, and therefore seemed always ready to meet lifes obstacles or opportunities to the best of his ability. "Leonidas," he would say with a smile or chuckle when he had outdistanced a political adversary, in church affairs, "they don't get up early enough in the morning." The central thread of his philosophy of life as I reflected upon it was sincerity, dependability and a subtleness of love for humanity, seldom verbalized even to his dear marital mate of 54 years, but expressed *in action*, generosity and a charisma that usually attracted people as soon as they met him. He lived by the philosophy of the timeliness of things and often preached that there is a time to reap and to sow, to laugh and to weep. With his children there was a time to discipline and a time to reward. There was one disciplinary failure and that was to convince me that I ever received a whipping that did me any good. It was probably the message of the sermonette delivered before and after each stroke of the razor strap—received as a steady diet for all of his sons. Yet as we grew older he became more of an older brother. As his mantle falls on the shoulders of those he loved and inspired I am realizing for the first time how dearly I loved him. I seem to have thought that only a mother needed to be loved, that a father is taken for granted. I now have come

378

full circle to realize that Father and Mother are to be cherished and one usually necessary to the highest fulfillment of the individual potential. I can see his smile, his laughter, his sternness, his occasions of suppressed sadness, but always I was conscious of the potential song in his heart. I am sure he felt that in life, the road would never bend nor would a day ever end without a song. He never really knew what makes the rain to fall nor the grass grow tall, he only knew there is no life at all without a song.

In humble submission to an all wise Providence the large Berry family and relatives across four generations began arriving for the funeral which was scheduled to be on Friday morning, the 26th. The four Berry sons, Lee, Dick, Lew and Elbert, an adopted son, Mom's youngest brother John Harris and first cousin James Berry decided that as a final gesture of our love, we would serve as active pallbearers. Bishop I. H. Bonner, chairman of the Board of Managers of the Missions Dept. came to deliver the eulogy. Other bishops, general officers, ministers, friends and acquaintances arrived from many parts of the country.

An unfortunate episode which threatened to mar the solemnity and dignity of our father's death and burial occurred. The representative of the highest council of the church hierarchy, whose political harassment against Pop had continued, made a request for an appearance on the funeral program. The minister of the church where the services were to be held brought the request to the family and indicated the pressure upon him to effect the arrangements. When the children of the family strongly objected, the minister pleaded for reconsideration because of the hierarchical pressures upon him. When there appeared to be an impasse Mom came forth with all the majesty and charity in her heart for which she was well known. She agreed to grant the request of the high council member and asked her sons and daughters to consent. This we did in deference to her graciousness and our love for our mother. The party in question led the singing of a hymn, and differences were buried.

There was standing room only at Emanuel Church and at least 200 were family members and in-laws attending the services. The Grand Master of Prince Hall Masons of the jurisdiction of Virginia, requested the Grand Lodge of the jurisdiction of New York State to conduct appropriate Masonic funeral rites. There were in attendance Grand

Lodge officers of the jurisdiction of Virginia. Bishop Bonner delivered a very fitting eulogy reviewing more than fifty years in the ministry; the many years in the pastorate in Virginia and North Carolina and 22 years, the longest term ever held by a general secretary of Home and Foreign Missions of the A.M.E. church. He spoke of a loving and faithful wife of 54 years and the rearing of a creditable and successful family of 6 children, who occupied positions of high standing with their families in various communities of the country.

Arrangements were made for burial in a family lot at Elmwood Cemetery in Detroit, Michigan. The city where Rev. and Mrs. Berry had purchased a home for their retirement. Sister Gladys, brother Dick and their families had lived in Detroit several years. Meanwhile the family acceded to the requests of Bishops A. J. Allen and George W. Baber to have a second memorial in Detroit.

On Friday following the N.Y. memorial services most of the immediate family boarded the Wolverine N.Y. Central express train for an overnight passage to Detroit. Other family members traveled by automobile. My father's casket with all the many floral designs were placed in the baggage car and family members with the deputized Masonic official, Mr. David Muckle of Portsmouth, Va. were assigned to Pullman sleeping car facilities.

As I lay in my sleeping berth with lights burning very dimly there was an atmosphere of quietude except for the rhythmic clatter of the car wheels against the rails of the fast moving express. I reviewed with closed and sometimes tear dimmed eyes, my long life with a loving father.

Just a few hours before, I had shared the sad experience with my brothers of walking behind our father's casket at the beginning of his last journey; the long trip down the church aisle to the waiting hearse as his active pall bearers. Unabashedly, silent tears rolled down my cheeks, I had no desire to wipe them away. I recalled the ever increasing emotional strain as we reached our destination. My physical strength sagged and required assistance from an attendant as we lifted the casket into the hearse.

I recall saying to myself, everybody loves a Mother but I never realized how much I loved my father until now. Where did it all begin I mused. Then I recalled an experience at about the age of 6 years. I was lying on the parsonage floor at Chapel Hill, N.C. as Pop tickled my ribs until I went almost into hysterics with laughter. I remembered like a flash, Pop taking the family for rides with Nellie hitched to the surrey with the fringe around the top, as a boy of 10, during our 2 years at Princess Anne Court House, Va. I remembered Pop escorting some of us safely by the white school to prevent being beaten by white gangs while walking another mile to the colored school in South Norfolk, Va. when I was in 6th grade. Pop went to the sheriff's office with a dismantled pistol in his hands and served notice that he would protect his children in the pursuit of their education if the sheriff's police would not. With some special financial effort Pop then purchased a small piece of property and became a taxpayer in a nearby district. His children could then attend a better school out of easy reach of the white school.

Our funeral train rumbled along across the midwestern plains as the hours rolled by. In a state of semi-sleep, my thoughts wandered back to the day in 1920 when Pop proudly put me on a Norfolk and Western train for a 1,000 mile trip to college at Wilberforce, Ohio. I was adequately advised about the pitfalls of teenagers away from home, admonished to keep my thoughts on my goal of studying medicine with promised financial help somehow, whenever there was need.

Four years later with a Wilberforce degree I came home from work at a Long Island summer resort and cautiously revealed my desire to study medicine at the highly rated, expensive medical school of the University of Chicago. I will never forget Pop's words, as we stood in the parsonage at Emanuel in Portsmouth, "Leonidas, that is not an impossible ambition. If that is your goal, go on to Chicago and do your best, and as long as you do that I will do all I can to encourage you."

At that moment a load fell off my shoulders that has never returned and I felt like an eagle soaring thru the heights, toward a mountain top. With this incentive I attained my goal. Five months before Pop passed, I had flown to Paris to deliver a research paper at a world medical congress set up in four languages. I returned home with elected membership in the French National Society of Gastroenterology and Pop's ego nearly burst with pride.

But there were other especially fond memories of a loving father sacrificing for his family. They all came back like a flash as I rode with him on this lonesome journey to his last resting place.

While I was in medical school at the U. of Chicago two brothers, Dick and Lew were in college at Wilberforce.

In retrospect sacrificial benevolence was perhaps not Pop's most precious attribute. It was rather his sense of the fitness of things. He was a stern disciplinarian when he needed to be. He was affable, jovial and quite witty when the occasion was appropriate. But he always was ambitious for himself and family and a serious man of religion.

As the light of early dawn began seeping around the shade at the window of my sleeping room, I suddenly realized that Pop was riding with his family upon whose shoulders his mantle had fallen on his last earthly journey and that from this day forward he would live only in his service to humanity and as a precious memory in the minds and hearts of those who loved him. His influence on our lives and destiny would determine how well we would wear his mantle and pass it on acceptably to coming generations.

We arrived in Detroit early the morning after we left New York City. The oldest and most historical cemetery in Detroit had been chosen two years before Pop's passing. The Rev. Carlyle Stewart sold the idea of purchase in the integrated Elmwood as soon as lots were available for the burial of deceased Blacks. Four Berry lots were purchased next to those of the Stewart family. When the tears were dry on the family cheeks, the matter of a family stone was taken for granted. A modest three-foot tall monument for a family marker was thought to be appropriate. As arrangements were being made, the family was informed by cemetery officials that the stone could not rise higher than six inches from the ground. Elmwood Cemetery consists of rolling acres with hundreds of towering obelisks, mausoleums, beautiful and elegantly carved marble statues and statuettes interwoven between tall, spreading oak, elm and weeping willow trees. An ancient dry river bed winds its way gracefully through this burial place. Since the year 1846, the resulting hillsides were adorned with family plots extravagantly marked with artistic and reverant stones of all sizes and appropriate shapes. So the cemetery management was asked what makes the Berry plot different. The answer was, "You don't own a family plot. You have purchased only the " 'right to bury,' and that right is divided into four separate but equal parts." Of course that language sounded familiar. But the Berrys never lost an obvious racial battle that easily while Pop lived. They were not about to lose his right to a decent burial and memorial stone in death. Scores of letters, a threat to sue, and three years later, the three-foot family monument was erected, with the compromise and face-saving requirement to purchase eight rather than four lots.

Meanwhile, as more tears dried, it was decided to "case the joint" and to look into its history. Observation #1: On Memorial Days, thanks to high visibility, Blacks were seen visiting in the same cornered area of the cemetery. Management admitted that somehow sales had turned out that way. Observation #2: It was learned that a court decision permitted the cemetery trustees to re-sell unclaimed lots which were parts of large family plots. There was an obvious parallelism between the court decision and the sudden invitation to Black "integrators," preferably on a one to two separate entry basis.

Twenty-four years have passed since the burial of Rev. Berry in this picturesque and historic cemetery. Meanwhile, Mother Beulah, Brother Dick and the husband of Sister Gladys, LaVaughn Yates, have been interred in the Berry plot.

Many tours and a study of historic records have been revealing. Elijah Busch, Bernard Stroh, James Vernor and Hiram Walker, all of beverage fame and many ex-governors and mayors are buried in Elmwood. Within memory of many Blacks, including undertakers, Elmwood was generally known as a segregated, WASP (White Anglo-Saxon Protestant) cemetery until the early 1950's. However, this practice existed only for about 50 years. There was an interesting interval of integration in the 19th century. Michigan's veterans of the Civil War are grouped together with military identity only. Black veterans are unseparated, marked only with the nationally used U.S.C.T. (C.T. for Colored Troops). Elizabeth Denison Forth, a slave, was emancipated by her owner, Mayor Elijah Busch in the early 19th century. She lived until shortly after the Civil War, after accumulating much wealth with which she built St. James Episcopal Church as a landmark of an underground railroad station. D. Augustus Straker, is also a citizen of Elmwood. He was an attorney who fought the Plessy vs. Ferguson, separate-but-equal civil rights case in the 1890's, and became Michigan's beloved first Black judge. So there is always some degree of evolution in human relations as in organic life. The bitterness of today may become the joy of tomorrow, and the sorrows of yesteryear may have generated the measure of happiness in our time.

The Hand That
Rocked the Cradle
(1900–1960)

Mom'S love of family and faith in the Supreme Spirit seemed to grow stronger year-by-year. We all knew that her strength of character and personality had been the principal force in holding together a very extended Berry-Harris family for three or four generations.

Almost all of her married life, Mom had lived in A.M.E. church parsonages or the Mission House in Harlem. Every year or two except for five years when Pop was Presiding Elder there, she would uproot, pack her flowers and her other belongings and move to the next parsonage. All of her married life, especially at moving time, she expressed the longing for a home of her own so that she would not have to dig up her roses or leave them. Finally, one day, she talked to her husband. "Hon, you are now in your seventies. I don't want you working as a General Officer in the church until you are stopped by disability. I think you should retire and rest before that time comes. The children are well out of the way, except Gerri and she will be ok. I think we should buy a retirement home somewhere outside of New York, and have a few years of rest and peace."

She had talked about this "home of my own," many times in the past, and always there was that dream of a house with a garden of beautiful flowers. "I don't know about retiring," said Pop, "but of course, I might have to. Where do you think we should look for such a place?"

Shortly after their 50th wedding anniversary Mother had settled on Detroit for her son Dick and daughter Gladys and their families lived there. In contrast to the compact houses in New York City, Detroit, in those days was full of beautiful houses with tall trees shading the street, and many of them had flower gardens in the backyard. So Mom and Pop found a home at 235 Woodland in Detroit. Pop never got to live there, but Mom and Gerri moved in after Pop's death. Dick, who lived across town, visited Mom frequently and took care of the needs and maintenance of the house that could not be handled by Mom and Gerri.

Mom's love of flowers colored her entire life. I recall as a growing boy that there was always room for flowers in our house or in the yard. As I grew up I became familiar with such words as petunias, hyacinths and geraniums, although all I could really recognize were violets and roses, and the ones that grew in a shallow bowl of water with pebbles.

One day during a casual conversation at the dinner table, Mom said, "All of my life or as far back as I can remember I have always loved flowers. As a child I would hunt them wild. Often, I was teased because I would bring back all kinds of weeds with the slightest bloom or leaves with unusual shapes. My mother," she laughed, "was always afraid I would get a severe skin rash or poison ivy or even be bitten by a snake."

Her children were determined that she would indeed have that beautiful flower garden to enjoy. Our wives and Gladys' husband also thought it a good idea and all of us enjoyed many visits and family reunions at 235 Woodland, heightened by delicious meals and the beauty of Mom's many roses and other flowers.

During Mom's years in Detroit, after Pop's passing, she had the very enjoyable experience of a "This is Your Life"-type testimonial. It was sponsored by the State of Michigan Missionary Societies and the Young People's Department of the A.M.E. Church. It was organized and chaired by Mom's good friend and co-worker, Mrs. Mamie Aiken.

The program reviewing Mom's life was presented before a large audience at Bethel A.M.E. Church in Detroit. Relatives and life-long friends came from many places out-of-town where the family had lived before. Mom's many community, church and family activities were reviewed, covering her entire life. It was all a complete surprise as out-of-town visitors made their appearance to witness her long and useful career. The summary follows:

BEULAH A. BERRY

1. *Her Activities as they relate to church and her husband's work.*

She married Rev. L. L. Berry of Virginia Conference A.M.E. Church in 1900. She worked with him in small mission churches for 8 years. During the next 25 years she worked with him in the pastorates of many churches including some of the larger metropolitan churches. She was very active in most departments of the church, Sunday School and choir. Her greatest work was President of the Women's Local Missionary Society. She has served as Vice President, Assistant Secretary, member of the Executive Board of the Conference Branch for many years. She has been a delegate to the Quadrennial Conventions since 1919, at all times serving on important committees.

In the local Missionary Societies she organized committees to take care of the sick and needy of the church and community, day nursery and to pay church obligations for the students in college and the widows and stranded people passing through. She was an alternate delegate to the 1956 General Conference of the A.M.E. Church in Miami representing the 15th Episcopal District. After the death of her husband in November, 1954 she came to make her home in Detroit, in January, 1955 and soon connected with the Abatenjwa League.

2. *Her religious activities outside of her immediate parish.*

Her husband's election as a General Officer of his church, Secretary-Treasurer of Home and Foreign Missions of the A.M.E. Church with headquarters in New York City, encompassing North and South America, South and West Africa, the Bermudas and West Indies for 21½ years, opened greater avenues, fuller life and more responsibilities in her service to mankind. She served as hostess to all the missionary ministers, their families and students coming to America as delegates to General Conferences and to attend college and others who became stranded in the U.S.

She has been as a mother to hundreds of missionaries who address her as "Mother Berry." When two women missionaries passed away while in New York it became her duty to care for them during their illness and burial. Her philosophy of life, "Let me live in a house by the side of the road and be a friend to man," or "if I can help somebody as I pass along then my living will not be in vain," has been exemplified in all her life.

In New York City she was a member of Mt. Zion A.M.E. Church, the local Missionary Society and Executive Board of the Conference Branch, a member of the Home Mission Conference and Foreign Mission Council of North America, now the National Council of Churches of Christ in the U.S.A. Department of Home Missions and Foreign Missions. She served as a member of the Executive, Administrative, Personnel and Migrant Committees of the Home Missions for many years and the Executive Committee of Foreign Missions, attending conventions in various cities and Buck Hill Falls for several years. She attended the Constituting Convention of the National Council of the Churches of Christ in the U.S.A. consisting of 29 communions whose theme was "This Nation Under God" one of the greatest conventions ever held in Christiandom. While working with the Migrant Committee of the Home Missions Council she had the privilege of joining the staff and other members of the committee on a trip to a Migrant Camp at Riverhead, L.I. They traveled in the first station wagon called "The Harvester," purchased by the council, which was dedicated at this meeting. She was a member of the United Council of Church women and a voting delegate to all Biennial Assemblies until 1955, a member of Nominating and Christian World Missions Committee of the Council and active as Chairman of Harlem Group of No. 1 World Day of Prayer which led the entire 20 areas in Manhattan.

She joined the Interdenominational Ministers Wives Association in 1933, the National in 1943. In the Local she held the office of President, Vice President and Treasurer. As President in 1942 and 1943 they entertained the soldiers and sailors at Christmas and giving pocket testaments instead of having their regular Christmas dinner. Under her administration a War Bond Drive was put on at which time over $35,000 worth of stamps and bonds were sold. She received a citation from the government for outstanding work done. She is a member of The A.M.E. Minister Wives Association, The Woman's National Sabbath Alliance and has been a member of the Order of Eastern Star for 47 years.

She was a member of the 1897 class of Kittrell College and salutatorian of the class. The president of the college was the late Dr. Jno. R.

Hawkins who was then Secretary of Education of the A.M.E. Church. She was a public school teacher in Person County, North Carolina for 8 years. She substituted and taught in private and night school at many places where her husband pastored. Monrovia College and Industrial Institute, Liberia, West Africa, conferred upon her the degree of Humanities in 1955.

As a mother and minister's wife, she reared six children and her orphaned youngest sister. Of the seven all have college education except one who has a hearing handicap. All except one are married and have families. All seven are active adult church workers and have served as trustee, steward, S.S. teachers, choir members, youth workers, general conference delegates, laymen's league workers in the A.M.E. Church.

In addition to church work, her offsprings have been active participants in fraternal and civic affairs including the Alphi Phi Alpha and Omega Phi Psi fraternities, Delta Sigma Theta sorority, the Masons, Shriners and the Democratic party.

Their names and occupations are as follows: Mrs. Lula D. Myers of Raleigh, N.C., housewife seamstress and former Norfolk, Va. public school teacher; Dr. Leonidas H. Berry of Chicago, Ill., Assistant Clinical Professor of Medicine, Univ. of Ill., research authority and specialist in digestive diseases; Richard O. Berry, Detroit, Mich., Organization and Method Examiner of the Management Engineering Office, Detroit Arsenal; Mrs. Gladys Berry Yates, Detroit, Mich., housewife and public school teacher; Mr. Lewellyn L. Berry, Jr., Washington, D.C., Chief Medical Technician, Freedman's Hospital, and director of a commercial medical diagnostic laboratory; Elbert J. Berry, Hollis, L.I., Employment Counsellor, N.Y. State Employment Service, Brooklyn, N.Y.; Miss Geraldine V. Berry, keeps house for her mother.

She and husband celebrated their 50th (Golden) Anniversary, September, 1950. Mrs. Beulah Ann Berry, 54 years a minister's wife.

Two particularly beautiful tributes to Mom were given by Henrietta Sawyer, an old friend from Princess Anne, Virginia and by Valletta Harper Linnette, the young woman who had graduated from Columbia University and worked as assistant editor of the Voice of Missions which Pop edited during his years as Missions Secretary. These testimonials follow:

Beulah Berry
February 5, 1960

No one has ever endeared herself to any family as Beulah A. Berry has to the Sawyer family. When she and her family first came to Princess Anne County, Virginia, in 1912, we claimed her as Aunt Beulah; that close relationship has lasted throughout the years increasing in love and esteem as the years have rolled on. The Berry family and the Sawyers are in a way spiritually united. We have so many things in common; love for mankind, love for beautiful flowers, love and devotion for friends and family ties. Our homes have always been open to each other; our joys and frustrations have been shared.

Aunt Beulah possessed all of the virtues that were the embodiment of integrity, culture, devotion, loyalty and love that together make an unusual Christian soul. Her soft modulated voice, her forgiving attitude and beauty will be greatly missed by us. We feel that a cherished family member has left us; without Aunt Beulah we shall flounder for awhile. Our consolation will be the realization that she has gone to her deserved reward. We know her own children and family members are proud that they were blessed with such an unusual understanding, devoted mother, grandmother and sister. Her family was her pride; her work with the A.M.E. Church came next. The missionary work that she did for more than 23 years in New York making foreign missionaries and guests comfortable was a great expression of her love for all mankind. Even though this work was pleasant, Aunt Beulah could never become reconcilled to a compromise for good. In her estimation RIGHT WAS RIGHT regardless. Our family will miss her greatly. We shall always cherish the thought that we were privileged to know her and her family; our lives have been greatly enriched. We bid you adieu, au-revoir, our loved one —sleep on and take your rest.

Henrietta Sawyer & Daughters

Note: The above tribute followed death of Mrs. Beulah Berry.

Virginia State College
Petersburg, Virginia

A Tribute to a Noble Lady

To many persons on three or four continents, the Honoree on this occasion has been known for years as Mother Berry. The first time I heard that appellation used by an African delegate to the General Conference several years ago, I questioned it because the person was of the same age level or older than our honored guest. Upon inquiry, I learned that in Africa the word "mother" is used to express love, respect, high regard and deep affection. Certainly, no term could convey more appropriately the esteem in which Mrs. Beulah A. Berry is held by the thousands of persons who have been privileged to know her. From her mother role as wife of a pastor in Virginia churches, then wife of a Presiding Elder with greater responsibility and more persons under her gentle wing to the ever expanding role of mother to the many African Methodist Episcopal missionary workers and their parishoners scattered across the miles in North America, South America and Africa as the wife of the Secretary of Missions, Mrs. Berry has moved with the dignity, grace and charm so characteristic of this consecrated wife and mother. Those of us who have had the opportunity of basking in the radiance of her quietly dynamic personality have been encouraged, stimulated and inspired by the magnetic rays permeating the atmosphere created by this noble Christian woman. I am deeply grateful for the very splendid association that I have enjoyed with her as "another daughter" in the Berry family.

The women of the Michigan Conference Branch are to be commended for honoring this very deserving lady who has devoted so many useful years in the untiring Christian service of a truly missionary-minded person. Here is really a life worthy of emulation. May she continue for many years to set an example of service for the women of her beloved church. My one regret on this happy occasion is that I am unable to be present to extend my felicitations in person. The celebration is being held a few days too early. How I would like to witness the expression on the very lovely face of our honoree when she hears the words, THIS IS YOUR LIFE, BEULAH A. BERRY.

Sincerely,
Valletta H. Linnette

This demonstration of appreciation and love was treasured by Mom the rest of her life.

One Sunday afternoon during a family visit, we returned home from Bethel Church where Reverend Roberts had preached a very thoughtful sermon and the choir had sung beautifully. Upon reaching the house Mom went straight through to her backyard and the flower garden. She walked over to the rambling rose bushes covering a distance of about eight feet along the fence separating the property from that next door, which was also well kept with pretty flowers. Mom's roses were exceptional that summer and the prettiest in the block. There she stood, in full church attire, still wearing the neatly trimmed turban, carrying a large white handbag with a splash of red flowers on its front. Mom looked at her red roses, adjusting a small sagging sprig and touching a bloom or two as she enjoyed their perfume. Some of us followed her, sitting on the porch and in yard chairs watching her enjoying them, her prize roses, some in full bloom, others just beginning to bud and others losing their leaves and fading.

The short visit to her flower garden was a fitting postlude to her worship service in her church for Mom believed like Dorothy Frances Burney: "The kiss of the sun for warmth, the song of the birds for mirth. You're nearer God's heart in a garden than anywhere else on earth."

Soon Elbert, very casually, struck up a song with his first rate tenor voice,

> "Rose in the bud, the June air is warm and tender,
> Why do you shrink your petals to display?
> Are you afraid to bloom in splendor,
> lest someone comes and steals your heart away?"

Jovially, Gladys joined in the next verse of Carrie Jacob Bond's classic song,

> "Rose in the bud, the evening sun is sinking,
> Wait not too long and trifle not with fate.
> Life is so short and love is all I am thinking
> Love comes but once and then perhaps too late."

Mom soon turned and apparently thinking on these words, she went quietly into the house to relax and rest. It turned out that the last lines of the song we sang were somewhat prophetic for one of life's great dreams for Mom, her precious flower garden and a home of her own, did, in fact, come but once and only then in the last five years of her life.

So on this particular holiday weekend we found Mom's house in very fine shape. Dick had arranged a recent interior decorating and painting job throughout the house. Gladys and Dick's wife, Maryland, would not allow Mom to cook on this occasion. They had brought the food over to 235 Woodland and we all sat down in Mom's dining room and had a very delicious Sunday dinner with her. Mom had been ailing for some time and was not "too good" as she expressed it.

When dinner was over and we sat relaxed in the living room listening to stereo music, I had a private talk with Dick and Gladys. We discussed the fact that a few months later on December 12, 1959, Mom would celebrate her 80th birthday. Her physical strength, however, was gradually fading. We felt that, quietly, we should begin planning for the biggest birthday of her life.

I spoke to members of the family in various parts of the country suggesting that we share Mom's birthday through the medium of a telephone conference "hook-up." This was at once found to be very agreeable with everybody. No one could remember when Mom had had a special birthday party. She had been so much involved every year in setting up birthday parties for other members of the family, that other members had not thought about preparing a party for her. By the first of November, Mom was still dragging, but at time feeling rather well. We prayed that she would be feeling well enough to enjoy her party on December 12, 1959.

As the date approached, we children became more and more aware of the sentimental importance of that date. It would be our mother's 80th birthday. What a milestone! What a sentimental journey! And so all of her family, her living brothers and sisters, her sons and daughters and grandchildren were programmed to participate in a surprise telephone birthday party.

The largest most beautiful and sentimental mother's birthday card that we could find was purchased. It was sent through the mail as a "round robin" letter. It finally reached Mom on the eve of her birthday bearing the names and expressions of love of family members from cities, towns and villages in six states. By previous arrangement, the Detroit Berrys, Gladys and her husband, LeVaughn Yates, brought a big dinner over to Mom's house on Woodland. They sat down to a delicious meal amid flowers, gifts, cards and telegrams from dozens of friends and relatives around the country.

At the appointed hour on December 12, 1959, there were 14 telephones and extensions used in a mighty chorus singing "Happy Birthday, Dear Mother." Twenty individuals at one point or another took part in the telephone celebration during a forty minute hookup. It was a complete surprise, thanks mostly to Gerri who was able to beat Mom away from the telephone during arrangements with telephone operators. Mom was told about the telephone arrangements just twenty minutes before the zero hour. This softened the shock of a complete surprise; an audible invisible family reunion over a radius of more than a thousand miles which Mom had never realized was possible.

The hookup into Mom's Detroit home from two other Detroit residences and from Chicago, Illinois; Manhattan and Hollis, New York; Camden, New Jersey; Raleigh and Hillsboro, North Carolina and Washington, D.C. When the operator announced, "We are ready, you are on," there was an immediate shout of song and joy as the chorus of Happy Birthday's rang out. I assumed the role of moderator. Each person identified himself or herself and expressed words of love and best wishes to their sister, mother or grandmother. A few days after the celebration was over, Mom sat down and wrote the following beautiful letter and sent copies to the individual families. This was mine:

Monday, December 14, 1959

Dear Leonidas:

What a happy and thrilling surprise to hear the voices of my entire brood and their families, saying 'Happy Birthday, Mom, Grandmother and Sissie,' and then all fifteen voices joining in and singing 'Happy Birthday to you.' Such sweet remembrances to follow me thru the rest of my life. Leonidas, You are a precious sentimental jewel, (smiles).

Plus all the rest so graciously joining in these lovely sentiments. I am so proud and thankful for each of you.

Well, I am so very thankful to have been spared to reach my 80th birthday, tho I am not feeling like I'd like to, it could be worse. God has really blessed me. I think my soul looks back and wonders how I got over. I rec'd nearly 40 cards, one telegram from Grace, Sylvia, Richard and Idella in Baltimore.

Gladys stayed from school today and has gone downtown to shop for me, to try to see what she can do. How I wanted to go with her, but was not feeling strong enough to go out . . . .

Thus, the telephone birthday party was a fitting climax in the long, beautiful life of a mother who carried out her destiny of love and inspiration to so many in her natural and adopted family clan.

Six weeks later, on February 2, 1960, Beulah Harris Berry departed her earthly life leaving children, grandchildren and a host of heirs to celebrate her glorious return to the celestial spirit that sent her.

Section Seven
The Physician and
The Public Servant
(1935—)

Mrs. Llewellyn L. (Beulah) Berry, Sr., mother of the Berry family clan in her flower garden, Detroit, 1957.

Family reunion dinners have been frequent through the years in the Berry homes. Photo Detroit, 1957.

"FLYING BLACK MEDICS"

L.H. Berry Founder–President
Emplaning for Southern Illinois
"Task Force" Medical Services

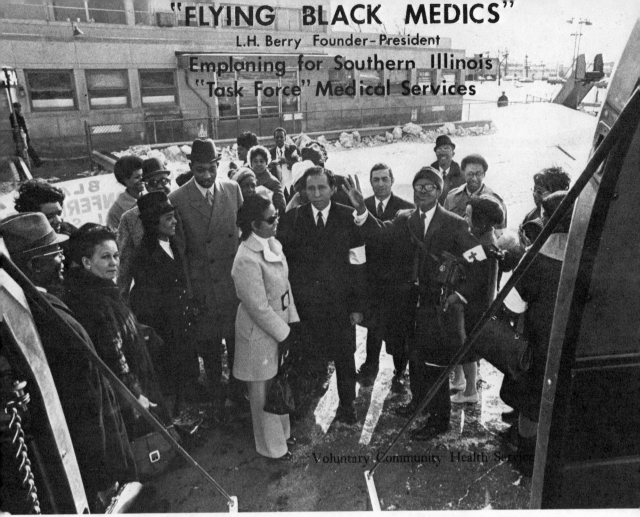

Voluntary Community Health Services

"Flying Black Medics." Dr. Berry with raised hand; Mrs. Berry, foreground left. A.M.E. General Conference. First Aid and Health Education Clinics. Founded and directed by the author for 32 years. Voluntary service rendered by doctors, nurses, teachers, and health educators.

AUSPICES
HEALTH COMMISSION
A.M.E CHURCH
DIR. L.H. BERRY, M.D.

WELCOME A·M·E CONVENTION
GET YOUR FREE CHEST X-RAY
COURTESY
Philadelphia Montgomery Tuberculosis
and Health Association

FREE CHEST FREE
X-RAY
FOR
TUBERCULOSIS ENLARGED HEART
LUNG CANCER • CHEST DISEASES
X-RAY REPORTS
ARE MAILED
TO YOUR HOME
COURTESY
Philadelphia Montgomery Tuberculosis
and Health Association
GET YOUR CHEST X-RAY EACH YEAR

FIRST AID CLINIC
39% GENERAL CONFERENCE
A.M.E.
HEALTH COMMISSION

LEONIDAS H. BERRY, M.D.
MEDICAL DIRECTOR

Rev. Charles Koen, leader of the "United Black Front" in Cairo, Ill. Dr. Berry and "Flying Black Medics" in bus from plane to one day clinic in basement, Bethel A.M.E. Church—400 poor and Black people examined and treated.

Dr. Berry teaches residents and post graduate doctors how to look into the stomach and intestines. (Cook County Hospital and graduate school, Chicago.)

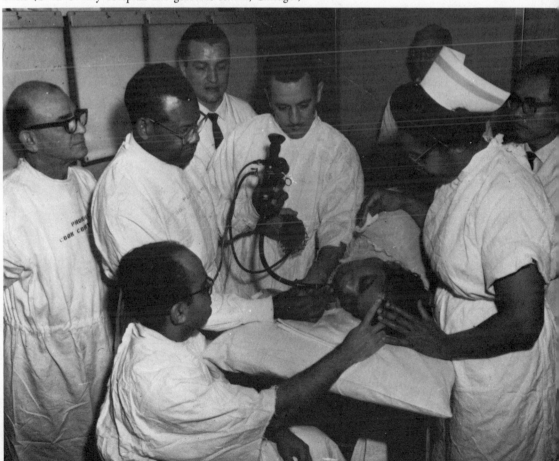

President L. B. Johnson, receiving Dr. Berry, Pres. Nat. Med. Assn. Occasion: Stag dinner at White House with president, his cabinet members and one hundred selected citizens, Nov., 1965.

President Jomo Kenyatta of Kenya, East Africa, receiving Dr. Berry (president N.M.A.), Pan-American Inaugural Flight guest and cultural exchange lecturer-demonstrator in Gastro-Intestinal Endoscopy for U.S. State Department, 1965.

Dr. Berry reports Research on Alcoholic Gastritis, with immediate translations in four languages, Paris, 1954.

Dr. Berry worked in Health-Mobile next to Martin Luther King's Church, all day meeting in Montgomery, Alabama Capital Square. He walked the last five miles of the Freedom March from Selma, 1965.

Ambassador and Mrs. Mercer Cook and secretary with Dr. Berry in front of American Embassy in Dakar, Senegal, West Africa, following luncheon while on U.S. State Department Cultural Exchange visit at University of Dakar, 1965.

Medical residents with Dr. Berry after a lecture at Kenyatta Hospital and Medical School, Nairobi, Kenya, 1965.

Occasionally there is recreation, sailfishing in Indian Ocean, off coast of Kenya, 1965.

The Career of a Multi-Dimensional Doctor

POP had come to Chicago as Secretary of Missions to attend a Conference in 1935. I had just opened an office in those days of the great depression. Pop was full of pride as he inspected my office with new unpaid furnishings. "Well, Leonidas," he said, "at last you are practicing medicine, but where is your car?" "That's okay, Pop," I replied, "I'll get one when I really need it." On the day Pop was leaving he said, "Leonidas, I have made a down payment on a car for you on a used car lot on Michigan Avenue. Here are the papers. Your monthly payments will be just $25.00, I think you ought to be able to take care of that." An attractive paint job, but the motor almost fell apart before I could finish the one year of payments. But who wouldn't love a father like that.

I recall feeling down right embarrassed. I am the first born of Mrs. Beulah Harris Berry and her minister husband and I attended school twenty-one consecutive years. While I was in medical school Dick stayed out of college and worked for one year to help Lew Jr. get his degree, than returned for his own. There were four of us in college at the same time. Pop with the help and support of Mom still had some in-put in this operation.

Pop somehow was usually able to help all of his offsprings in some special way as they moved up the ladder of success. The financial aids were never large, but always needed. Pop called them "encouragements." Pop's four boys left an after school occupational record, in those days of no scholarships: as summer dishwashers; dining car, hotel and steamboat waiters; bus boys, bell hops and janitors; construction workers and steel mill laborers.

In later years we learned that Pop borrowed on life insurance policies until they were no longer protective, made short-term bank loans, sacrificed and conserved on everything at home to help five of us through college.

How long should the benevolence of parents be sacrificially bestowed upon their children when there is need and ambition? Some say high school is enough. Others make it to college. When my Pop said, "Go on off to the best medical school you can find, do your best and I will do all I can to encourage you," he did not say until you have graduated. One day ten years into the practice of medicine, I received by mail, a timeworn discolored life insurance policy. It came from Mom and Pop. The accompanying letter worded, "I took this policy out on your life forty years ago. All the other children have similar 10¢ a week coverage. I am sending each of your policies, so you may pay them yourselves. The policy had some meager death benefits or a few maturity dollars at age 104 years. This type of insurance was the only kind available to Negroes, during the 1st century of their "freedom." Many giant insurance companies housed today in their skyscrapers in New York, Chicago and elsewhere built their fortunes largely on such exploiting policies protected by so-called "racial vital statistics."

The 1940s was a very busy decade for me in my climb to success and the realization of dreams. My study on one hundred alcoholic addicts, was the first study of its kind with the illuminated telescopic tube called the gastroscope. The presentation of my observations on the effect of alcohol on the living stomach was made in Cleveland, Ohio, June 1941 before the Convention of the American Medical Association (a Negro first). The appearance was formally discussed by outstanding authorities on stomach diseases and pathology following the presentation. The public press in addition to the medical community found the report of considerable interest. It was reviewed in the popular "Science Digest" under "what is new in medicine." The Associated Press informed me that the reviews had been released to more than 500 journals and newspapers in America and abroad. My fellow associates on the staff at Provident Hospital seemed very proud of my success. Along with congratulations, I received more referrals for consultation from the older doctors. All of this stimulated me to work harder to somehow do more research and to establish my stature as a leader in the field of digestive diseases.

I had some previous experiences reporting my earlier studies in gastroscopy. The first out of town report was made at the National Medical Association Convention at Hampton Institute, Virginia in 1938. Gastroscopy was demonstrated on a dentist patient attending the convention at the Dixie Hospital. The second presentation before the National Medical Association was made in New York City in 1939. At this convention I performed the first gastroscopic examination ever carried out at the Harlem Hospital. The first scientific exhibit of the National Medical Association was also presented at the convention. At interim periods, I had the opportunity for lectures before the Provident Hospital staff, Chicago Society of Internal Medicine and the southside branch of the Chicago Medical Society.

The attack on Pearl Harbor occurred on December 7, 1941. Everybody's plans and activities were affected by the war. The possibility of a war which would conceivably affect my life's career had been realized since my childhood witness of World War I. I began early preparations for this eventuality. I had two years of infantry ROTC training at Wilberforce. During the four years in medical school, I was involved in military medicine or medical reserve officers training corps. I should have been able to join the war effort, all other things being equal at a high professional military rank after Pearl Harbor with my professional advancement. I had long since learned that in my life, things were not otherwise equal. Every ambition, every activity would be modified by race. Like all Negro medical specialists, I was concerned that there might be no army hospital assignments when the war began.

After much petitioning by the National Medical Association, NAACP, and other pressures, the army and federal government made the great concession that Negro doctors would not be totally excluded from army hospitals as in World War I. Instead there would be one army hospital set aside for qualified Negro medical officers. This was a special army post hospital at Fort Huachuca, Arizona. This would be exclusively for Negro soldiers. The regular post hospital manned by white medical officers would co-exist with the Black hospital with superior status at the fort. This was an important period in the evolution of my thinking about race prejudice. I learned for the first time as a personal experience that not all prejudices and stumbling blocks in a Negro's career came from "white folks." A Negro doctor with general practitioner training and no military training or experience was appointed colonel and commanding officer of the 1,000 bed Negro Huachuca Hospital. Obviously he had the right political connections. He was given the authority to appoint his entire staff. The higher ranking commissions and chairmanships of divisions and departments were given to his buddies primarily for political reasons, rather than specialty training and experience. There was widespread expression of disappointment and disgust at the shutting out of qualified Negro medical specialists from higher positions since there would be no other army hospital opportunity. Protests came from Negro soldiers who felt their medical and surgical care would be less than the best.

I was offered a lower rank position to work under a general practitioner with no special training in gastroenterology. In addition I had served a period of active duty as a army medical officer in the Civilian Conservation Corps and summer active duty with the Eighth Regiment Illinois National Guard.

With ten years of experience as a practicing specialist and consultant in digestive diseases, teaching and research experience and 16 years of officers reserve military training, I was shut out of the one army hospital opportunity of continuing at my level of achievement for service to my country.

With the disappointment of failure to continue my work in the one thousand bed army hospital, I continued to work in the 195 bed Provident Hospital with a fairly large out-patient clinic. With determined effort I continued my services and "bootstraps" research and joined the voluntary Illinois reserve militia with the grade of captain, from which I was retired at the end of the war with the rank of major in the inactive reserve militia. With all of the increased work of the war years, I continued to write and read papers whenever possible. In June of 1942 I presented another paper before the American Medical Association convention in Atlantic City. I appeared as a guest lecturer at Howard University Medical School, the Mound City Medical Society, Homer Phillips Hospital in St. Louis and elsewhere. Near the end of the war, I reported 1,400 consecutive gastroscopic examinations with clinical observations before the Chicago Society of Internal Medicine. These experiences were quite rewarding. I was determined to break the racial barrier against appointments to hospital staffs in Chicago and to fight for other Black doctors.

In 1946 I achieved appointment as attending gastroscopist at the County Hospital. This served as a wedge for successful appointment as attending physician by competitive examination one year later.

It was the first appointment of a known Negro physician to the medical attending staff of Cook County Hospital. Dr. Daniel Hale Williams, performer of the world's first heart operation and Dr. A. M. Curtis, both Provident Hospital surgeons served briefly nearly one half century before as the only previous appointees to the surgical attending staff of County Hospital. During the same year and with the gracious pioneering efforts of my good friend, Dr. Sidney A. Portis, who had sponsored my fellowship training at Cook County Hospital, I received what was called a "limited courtesy staff appointment" at Michael Reese Hospital, the first for a Negro doctor. Dr. Portis acted from the vantage point of president of the staff, with special support from Dr. Heinrich Necheles, staff physiologist. Shortly afterwards Dr. Portis decided to leave Chicago and a few years later he passed. His memory is very sacred to me. I will always be grateful for his several sponsorships and courage in my behalf.

I was very proud of these achievements and determined more than ever to advance. However, at Michael Reese Hospital it required 17 years and a petition to the trustee board to advance from the courtesy appointment to the attending staff. Meanwhile no other Black internist or general surgeon, however qualified, received attending staff appointments. It became unmistakably clear that Michael Reese was not ready to extend meaningful involvement with it's attending staff to Black doctors. While this was a considerable disappointment to me it was consistant with the cultural attitudes in America. In more recent years parity of opportunity has slowly improved. I continued to work elsewhere and whenever there was a glimmer of opportunity.

My performance as attending physician and gastroscopist at the County Hospital opened an unanticipated and most grateful opportunity. In 1947, one year after the appointment to the County Hospital staff, the Cook County Graduate School of Medicine requested me to give post graduate courses in Gastroscopy to doctors registering from many states and foreign countries. Twenty five years later I had tutored nearly 500 gastroscopists and performed more than 14,000 stomach examinations with the gastroscope. At this point I produced a 640 page textbook on this subject as senior author and editor with international contributors.

Two members of the Michael Reese staff accepted invitations to write a contributing chapter in this international textbook.

The decade of the 1940's signaled a period of solid growth in the medical profession. The dreams of my parents and grandparents that there might be a doctor in the family had already come to pass. The ambitions of my youth, as if by destiny, were beginning to unfold. I remember a conversation with a pharmacist at the drug store where I worked during high school days. I said to him that I wanted to be the kind of doctor that found out and told the other doctors all about sickness and how to get people well. In later years as I remembered this conversation and my youthful thoughts, I realized that I was thinking medical research and teaching.

During the 40's and 50's progress in race relations in all fields including medicine continued to be slow. A giant leap was achieved by Blacks and liberal whites during the 1960's. I am proud to have been a part of the medical presence with the Medical Committee for Human Rights during part of the Martin Luther King march from Selma to Montgomery and elsewhere.

In the late 40's and early 50's partial success in breaking out of the racial caste system in medicine was achieved. Early comprehensive examinations, the basic certifications of the National Board of Medical Examiners, the specialty boards of Internal Medicine and gastroenterology were acquired. I became a fellow of the American College of Physicians of gastroenterology and the gastroscopic society. Credentialism and association at the highest professional level were essential to the highest level of professional growth.

I was never able to crack the racial barrier in the (important lilly-white) American Gastroenterological Association during ten years of sponsorship by my friends. At this point, I forbade any further attempts for membership. I continued to teach, to do clinical research and to maintain the highest standards of practice and service possible to my patients. Papers were published in medical journals and increasing requests came for lectures before Negro and white medical societies. Textbooks at home and abroad began to quote these publications in medical journals.

Growth and development of the digestive diseases service of Provident Hospital continued. The fight for integration into the white medical world was never designed to undercut or relinquish the work and services at the predominantly Negro and underprivileged Provident Hospital, but to broaden prospectives and growth opportunities. Then and now I regard that institution as the fundamental base for all my professional growth and achievements in the field of medicine.

Near the end of the decade of the 1940's I suppose I felt fairly solid in matters purely medical, I think I began to feel circumscribed and perhaps obsessed with the pursuit of excellence in a relatively narrow field. I felt that I wanted and needed to do more. I asked of myself what happened to the literary and philosophical interests of my high school and college years. Were not my interests in a spiritual life and my medical activities locked into separate compartments of my total life experiences? Should not they be together? Is there not a common ground? I began to think of the philosophy expressed by a great statesman who said that, "A man must be a part of the actions and passions of his times or risk being judged never to have lived." I think I must have decided that it was time to use my medical skills in social interaction in my community, particularly for the betterment of my race. There probably was a subconscious urge developing in earlier years. The Health Commission Project of 1948 for the A.M.E. Church was one of my early efforts in the interest of community health. But before that I had joined the Health Committee of the Mayor's Commission on Human Relations and was fighting to integrate Chicago hospitals.

In the early nineteen fifties, I became president of the Cook County Physicians Association, primarily of Negro physicians. I felt that this was the perch from which I could launch a major involvement in community health concerns, in which physicians themselves would be in the leadership. I led a community grass roots movement which succeeded in setting up what the news media eventually called the "Berry Plan;" officially, set up at departments of psychiatry of Provident Hospital, University of Illinois, Northwestern University, and a group therapy project inside the County jail. The project was inaugurated when the Cook County Physicians Association (C.C.P.A.) sponsored an interracial city wide group to the state legislature in Springfield and succeeded in getting special legislation to authorize the program. It was financed through the State Department of Public Health and I served an coordinator throughout the eight years of it's existence. I began to enjoy the feeling and reward of being a multi-dimensional doctor without sacrifice of the pursuit of excellence in a chosen field of specialization. From this

405

time on I would always be involved in continued medical, civic affairs. I would continue being the multi-dimensional doctor throughout my active life's career.

The program which I developed in Chicago as a medical approach to drug addiction among teenagers led to my participation in a national conference sponsored by the N.Y. Academy of Medicine. The proposal received top billing in the New York *Times* newspaper. Mom and Pop who lived in New York were very proud of this. The comprehensive two day workshop led to the publication of a book by the participants *On Drug Addiction Among Teenagers* by the Josiah Macy Foundation and the Blakiston Book Publishers.

The year 1954 was one of the most significant as well as one of the saddest years of my life. It was a time of the passing of a dear and devoted father who inspired me to do what often seemed impossible to achieve. I will always remember some happenings in the last year of my father's life. Many of the greatest dreams of my life were beginning to come true. In July of 1954, I succeeded in getting on the program of A World Congress for Digestive Diseases held in Paris, France.* This presentation was a report of gastroscopic studies and observations on the stomachs of severe alcoholics from Chicago's "Skid Row." The joyful greeting received from parents and friends upon returning from Paris will long be remembered. The accomplishment was not easy. I had to circumvent the American Gastroenterological Association which admitted its first Black member many years later. I recall being invited to a cocktail party in the home of Professor Jacques Caroli of the St. Antoine Hospital, the University of Paris. In attendance was the Secretary of the exclusive American Gastroenterological Association, a professor at the University of Michigan Medical School, who greeted me with a look of surprise and disgust with the query, "Well, how did you get here?" My reply was "By airplane sir, it was a bit rough for swimming." The program listed my fellow American for a ten minute lecture just before my ten minute presentation. As I faced the podium, I observed my compatriot walking rapidly near the exit. My lecture was very well received by the international audience listening by immediate trans-

* IV ème Congrès de L'Association des Societés Nationales Europeennes et Medilerranee es de Gastro-Enterologie 217 Juin au 7, Juillet 1954 à Paris.

lations in four languages. I was reporting the first Comprehensive Studies of the lining of the live stomachs of severe alcohol addicts according to the world literature. The following day I visited the gastroscopy clinic of the Hospital Saint Antoine as the guest of the French "dean" of gastroscopists, Professor Francois Moutier. He invited me to membership in the French National Gastroenterological Association.

Well remembered is the happiness brought to both parents and thousands of others by another important event of this period, the Supreme Court decision of 1954 banning segregation in public schools. Pop did not live to witness the slow implementation of this milestone but the decision brought happiness and hope in the last year of his life, to all of us. Following the passing of my father in November, 1954 and mother in February of 1960, many successes came to me during the next quarter of a century which I often wished they could have witnessed.

Six months before my mothers passing I began a second marriage. The young lady was the former Emma Ford Willis. We met while she had served as assistant administrator to the trustee board of Provident Hospital. Several years before she was administrative assistant to Ms. Lucy Laney, President of Haines Institute in Augusta, Georgia. As a wife she brought strong support and understanding to my bludgering activities in medical and civic affairs. Emma and members of the Berry family became very fondly attached to each other. The friendship has grown through the years as a mutual expression of family love.

The spread of family love extended even further through Emma's two sisters, Blanche, who lived in Michigan City, Indiana with her husband, David N. Crosthwait, Jr. and Evelyn, who resided in Hartsdale, New York with her husband, William E. Valentine, Jr. On many occasions these in-laws joined the family reunions of the Berrys in Detroit, Chicago and Hollis, New York. The success of my career were a high water mark in the destiny of the Berry family in its long odyssey through the generations. The strength of Afro-American culture to a great extent lies in the unique common bonds which tie together many successful Black nuclear and multinuclear families in America.

With the continuing strong support and devotion of Emma, my career continued to progress. I participated through the years in World Congresses on Digestive Diseases as lecturer in Copenhagen, Rome,

Tokyo, Chile of South American and Mexico City. On two occasions I also served as co-chairman of a session of the Congresses.

In my "spare time" I continued to work as I had done years before with the Health Committee of the Chicago Council on Human Relations. This service covered a period of 18 years including five years as chairman. Did I have any time for recreation? Yes, I went fishing once. I caught an 87 lb. sailfish in the Indian Ocean. The boat leasing company which by custom retained custody of all of the fish refused to process my "catch" and distribute it locally, as I wanted. There were several little African "ragimuffins" observing near the dock. Pityfully, two or three of them had obvious signs of kwashiorkor (protein deficiency). With disgust I departed and never returned there to recreate again. On another occasion, after morning ward rounds with Professor Ojiombo (at Jomo Kenyatta Hospital), I went "Kodak-ing" and "shot" a lioness nursing her cubs in a game park. The feat was accomplished with a telephoto camera from within the safe confines of an English landrover. Unfortunately I have loved both my vocation and my avocation of standing up for equality of opportunity and human rights in medicine. I have not felt strongly the need for other things, except as a sports observer and occasional game of golf. Like Patrick Henry I have learned that "eternal vigilance is the price of liberty." So when the wife appears neglected, I take her on the next medical trip. During a Pan-American Congress where I had an exhibit I took her to a bull fight. I enjoy other sports but neither of us enjoyed this. We then spent a few days on Copacabana beach and sightseeing in Rio de Janeiro, Brazil. Then we returned to Chicago for a symphony concert before getting back to work. We both enjoy symphonies and other concerts when I find the time.

Personal experiences and struggles in medicine led to my interest in recruitment of Black boys and girls for biomedical careers. I became a founding member of the Chicago Council for Biomedical Careers under the leadership of my good friend and community leader, Dr. Arthur Falls. This was a very rewarding endeavor involving inter-racial members working to stimulate Black youths for careers in medicine and related fields. The group began with meetings in the homes of members. The council is now a continuing funded organization in Chicago's south side ghetto. During this period I became chairman of the Council on Medical Education and Hospitals of the National Medical Association. The program of this council became tied in with the recruitment efforts in Chicago. We held annual Spring conferences for medical careers during several consecutive years. In 1965, I was elected president of the National Medical Association. It was not the result of a "draft" but friends convinced me that with their help I could make a contribution to this office. This election came after receiving the association's distinguished service award a few years before. From President Lyndon B. Johnson there came an appointment to the National Advisory Council on Regional Medical Programs, against heart disease, cancer and stroke. This was the major health project of the Johnson administration through the National Institutes of Health of HEW.

During the year of presidency of NMA, a cultural exchange, lecture-demonstration tour was made in gastroenterology and gastroscopy for the U.S. Department of State. This involved teaching hospitals and medical schools in Kenya, Uganda, Nigeria, Liberia and Senegal. In 1966 a similar program was carried out in medical schools of Japan, Korea, Hong Kong and the Phillipines. In 1970 the Saint Antoine Hospital in Paris, France, with my old friend Professor Jacque Caroli, was added to the tour. This was a most enjoyable and rewarding experience. The international teaching tour had only put my clinical research interests on a reserved schedule. I was beginning to realize that, if you dream hard and long enough and the good Lord has it in your destiny, your ultimate dreams will come true. Several months before the Paris trip I had submitted a grant proposal to the Regional Medical Programs at the National Institute of Health. The proposal was having a stormy course largely because of local medical school competition or exclusion in Chicago. But this time I had "grantsmanship power" in Washington. Thanks to the "Black presidency" of the National Medical Association and President Johnson's appointments earlier.

About this time my attentions were temporarily drawn away from the research struggle because of things happening in Cairo, Illinois. There had been racial confrontations there for years; the conflicts were getting worse because the Blacks who constituted 50% or more were almost completely excluded from participation in local government. An organization known as the "Black United Front" led by Reverend Charles Koen began continuous freedom marches and boycotts of local white businesses. This triggered resentment by Ku Klux Klan and other white organizations. Several large white businesses were forced to close but many Negroes lost jobs and there was wide Black community suffering because of the squeeze. A call for help was made to the Urban League and NAACP in Chicago. Black churches were brought into action.

I was still medical director of the Health Commission of the A.M.E. Church. I saw an opportunity for the A.M.E. Church to be of help in Cairo. I flew down to the embattled city and addressed the congregation at the Ward Chapel A.M.E. Church on a Sunday morning, under the auspices of the Health Commission of the general church. I offered to solicit drugs and food through Chicago A.M.E. churches to be distributed through the Ward Chapel Church in Cairo. In the afternoon I participated in the protest march with the members of the Black United Front under the protection of local police. During this meeting I was told that Black citizens, especially those on Federal relief were often refused medical care at the local St. Mary's Hospital, the only one in town. There were quoted instances of having to travel 25 miles to Paducah, Kentucky for emergency treatments. I was asked to try and get a clinic set up in Cairo for Black patients. On the plane enroute back to Chicago I thought of a plan; the remote possibility of a "flying health service to Cairo."

Within a week I called a meeting of a few Black doctor friends at my home. I proposed the formation of a group of "Flying Black Doctors" for servicing Cairo. I had heard of one or two instances of individual doctors traveling by plane for medical service in the bush country of Africa. My small group of Black doctor friends showed willingness to help. The proposed name of "Flying Black Medics" was approved. The financial help of Bishop H. T. Primm of the Fourth Episcopal District AME Church was received for gifts of common medicines and food staples. Arrangements were made by correspondence and telephone communication and we acquired the cooperation of Ward Chapel Church. We solicited the help of nurses, social workers, medical technicians, dieticians and doctors in all of the specialty fields in Chicago. The doctors bore the expense of two chartered 16 seater Cessna planes.

On Sunday, February 15, 1970 the "Flying Black Medics" consisting of a group of 32 doctors, nurses, and technicians flew from the Midway Airport in two sixteen seater Cessna planes to Cairo, Illinois for a

"Task Force Conference and Survey on Health." The United Front and the Social Action Committee of Ward Chapel had arranged registration of patients throughout the town and surrounding Alexander county. Many were transported by the private bus of the Black United Front. Ten thousand dollars worth of medical laboratory equipment was loaned by the Williams Brothers Clinic and carried in the belly of the planes. Areas were cordoned off in the basement and ante-rooms of the church for all of the medical specialties. Laboratory screening tests, physical examinations and history taking were performed on 300 patients in an all day and early evening session. Social workers and dieticians were also on the working teams.

The project was a great success, was very much appreciated in the Cairo Black community and the medical workers enjoyed giving the service. There was newspaper coverage throughout the state and national broadcast of the activities by NBC television, Huntley and Brinkley News. The medical power structure of the state was greatly upset. A medical advisor from Governor's Ogilvies office, an officer of the State Medical Association attempted to divert the clinic to the local hospital at the last minute. We preferred the church basement and invited the hospital doctors and nurses to join us. Two catholic nuns and token Black nurse did join. The Office of Economic Opportunity, a federal agency, agreed to provide funds for further development of the program. However, the project was bogged down by state, medical, and local politics. One evening as I sat at home in a semi-state of exhaustion I repeated the words of an appropriate prayer which I had read somewhere. "Slow me down Lord. Ease the pounding of my heart by the quieting of my mind. Steady my hurried pace, with a vision of the eternal reach of time. Give me, amid the confusion of the day, the calmness of the everlasting hills. Break the tension of my nerves and muscles with the soothing music of the singing streams that live in my memory. Inspire me to send my roots deep into the soil of life's enduring values, that I may quietly grow toward the stars of my greater destiny."

The next day I composed a letter and sent it to my patients announcing semi-retirement and drastic reduction in private practice. I had already accepted emeritus status in teaching institutions. I wanted patient's service to have priority as long as possible. I reviewed the list of patients. It became obvious that they were mostly parents, their children

411

or grandchildren. Other patients were friends of these families. Through the years, they would say "I know you are an internist and mainly a "stomach" doctor. My problem seems to be in another field; send me to the proper doctor, but I want to stay in your care."

In deciding to make this break in practice, I came to realize that my greatest reward of all of my medical activities, came from the friendship and the expressions of appreciations from patients, students and less fortunate individuals whom I have been able to serve to the best of my ability.

In prior years, I had contributed articles in five other books and monographs, which was important preparation for the larger work. During the next few years the teaching of the fundamentals of endoscopy in the Cook County Graduate School was reduced. The clinical ward service at Cook County Hospital was released in order to serve as part-time deputy for professional Community Affairs for the governing Commission of Cook County Hospitals. At this point in my career I was considerably exhausted, nearing emeritus status in teaching institutions, getting older each day.

My family had to prevail upon me to retire from the long years of a burdensome career attended by near unsurmountable difficulties. They stated "we have all known about your compelling ambitions.

You have made your contributions in civic and religious affairs. You are listed in *Who's Who in America* and the *American Men of Science* and recently you received the Rudlof Schindler Award of the American Society for Gastrointestinal endoscopy honoring the memory of your great teacher, so why don't you quit?"

What my family did not know was that I also felt the same way at times. Then out of the blue sky there would come another challenge and I would feel a surge of energy as my adrenal function was stimulated. Then I would ask myself the question; suppose I did quit and retire completely, would I be content just twiddling my thumbs? And the answer always came back, No, probably not. With this thought in mind I would soon be active at my usual pace. Then I would feel the rebound of fatigue which was increasingly difficult to throw off. At this point I would remember the admonition of my family.

Our local medical group was ready to continue the push. Fortunately, or unfortunately about this time my federal grant came through for research in cancer of the esophagus and stomach. I could not find time for further leadership, and the dissidents broke up the program.

The Federal grant of $175,000 supporting a two year clinical research study in Gastric Cancer and Esophagus with the use of Fiberoptic Endoscopes had to take precedence. It was carried out while I continued the private practice of medicine. The project was set up at the Hektoen Institute of Medical Research, associated with the Cook County Hospital. The Institute received $25,000 for rental of space and managing the funds. I served as principal investigator. The parttime personnel included five doctors trained in digestive diseases and endoscopy. There was also a full time young junior professor brought over from Tokyo Medical College in Japan. When the two year research project was a little more than half completed, we began the development of a comprehensive text book ("Under the Table"). The techniques of diagnosing diseases of the entire digestive canal with the use of fiberscope was comprehensively described at the end of three and half years as a 650 page book with color illustrations was published. I served as senior author and editor, with twenty international contributors from ten countries and four continents. This was the first book of its kind and it was very well received in the major medical centers of the world.

A unique feature was the unveiling of the book at a luncheon workshop at New York Americana Hotel during the digestive disease week in 1975. The discussants and panelists were contributors to the book from London, Germany, Japan, and the U.S.A.

The Journey

IN an assessment of my life in recent years I was unable to forget that on the back burner was my writing of the continuous odyssey of my family clan across the generations. The research and the writing would never let me go. It had been shuttled from the back burner to the front burner off and on since the death of my father twenty-five years before. I determined that this chronicle must be completed even if I were the only one interested enough to read it.

If I could only control other activities there would be more time for this project. The tragic event of the death of my father caused me to realize as never before how much admiration, love and respect I had for him. I reviewed his professional career as a minister and the very wide and sincere respect and admiration that our large family felt for him. I thought of how well known he was in the African Methodist Episcopal Church and throughout the United States and abroad. I said to myself "I must write the story of his life. I must find the time. It will not interfere with my own career and goals." I turned the idea over in my mind and discussed it with my mother. At first she gave encouragement; but observing the breadth of my plans she felt sure that I would be considerably overworked. Later Mom re-evaluated her advice saying in so many words that Pop's life spoke for itself and that he would live in the hearts and minds of those of his family who loved him and his many friends and associates.

I accepted my mother's advice respectfully but I regarded it as a challenge. I began my preliminary survey with a trip to the National Archives in Washington where Grandpa Berry had an official war service record. I had heard many stories from Pop about the escape from slavery and the Civil War experiences. I interviewed "Uncle Gus" (John Augustus Berry, Jr.). He was seven years older than my father. I talked to Aunt Kate and Aunt Lola and found Mrs. Perry who grew up with the Berry children on Butler's farm in Virginia, in the late 1880's and 1890's. She wrote a remarkably long list of Butler's farm parents and their children). I found Grandpa's story so interesting and the research so challenging that I began to wonder whose biography I should write. Mom was right, the task was overwhelming in the time it was requiring while pursuing my career as a doctor, and involvement in many other things. I went to my mother again, not to throw in the towel but to ask for Mom's help; something I learned to do in childhood. "Mom" said I, "A great idea has just occurred to me for writing Pop's biography. If you would just sit down whenever you have the time, not when you're tired, not when you have anything else to do. Just sit down, write a broad sketch, don't overwork, but sketch out a story under the title "As I Remember Him." Mom was so sure to giving in to her own brood that she said nothing about her seventy-five often weary years and her own program and responsibilities. Several weeks later when I visited Mom in Detroit, she had already written half of the story. She finished it while I was still "tooling up" for a literary masterpiece and getting lost in side issues of research.

It was many month later before I could try being a biographer again. I re-read Mom's stories. It was many many pages in long hand. Tears almost came to my eyes as I reviewed a long and loving story of her first meeting with Pop in college in 1895; graduation mixed with tragedy, child raising, school teaching on the side, hosting for a preacher husband, stretching dollars that weren't there and happy, happy times with family members and friends. I wanted to publish just that; under my name, but that would be plagarism and no one would believe I wrote it anyway. Besides my deep seated urge to compose it myself would not be satisfied.

So I would shift my hobby to a front burner again and start all over in earnest and suddenly somebody's ulcer would start bleeding; or Mrs. Peabody would have another attack of "acute indigestion" or diarrhea. It would be near time to go to General Conference and set up another first aid health clinic. "Ah! I have it," I mused. The general conference; the Bishop's Council; these would be the times to talk to many of Pop's old buddies. They loved and admired his pulpit eloquence, his ecclesiastical,

416

political shrewdness, and his sense of humor. If I could only get the help of some who bragged about his preaching or laughed about his humor or benefitted when he outwitted the hierarchy. Some help should come from the younger ministers who admitted Pop's helping hand as he moved up the ladder of success. If they would just write a tribute, I could tie it all together with what Mom had written and I would have it made.

"After all," I reasoned. "Pop was a General Officer 21 years longer than most of the bishops had been on the bench. Some of them had been general officers and traveling preachers with him. Together they had spent much time trying to outwit the bishops before they became bishops and sometimes helping the pastors after they became bishops. There was always a kind of 'side gathering' of ministers in session supposedly as the 'Connectional Council' while the bishops were in their chambers. Primarily they were trying to keep an eye on the bishops. During the first council sessions after Pop's passing our literary efforts seemed encouraging. I thought I had an 'Ace in the Hole' had not Pop hustled up 'free business' among all the preachers for me since he introduced his young doctor son in Chicago many years before?"

On the council grounds I soon ran into old friends: the Reverends S. S. Morris, Sr., Charles Stewart, The Abingtons, The John Adams, Sr., The Singletons, and the list too long to mention. I had my doctor's bag in one hand and a notebook in the other. I was expected to monitor the blood pressure of candidates and to treat everything that bothered them from hurting feet to aching hearts. "Thank you, Doc, we're going to put over your Health Commission's education program sooner than you think," they would say. "You just keep after us until we understand it real good. When we can spare the money I know it will be very fine for the church. Thank you Dr. Berry, the Lord will bless you."

Yes, I received quite a number of sincere moving tributes; they were eulogies. Not the book I had dreamfully hoped for. I became aware of the coincidental relationship between the history of the A.M.E. church and the history of our multi-nuclear family. I began with new interest. For some twenty years I continued my research, and traveled thousands of miles in the U.S.A., Africa, the Caribbean, and Canada, collecting exciting facts. I accumulated a trunk full of data and photographs all classified chronologically, geographically, genealogically, and by race. Having my mother's lifetime collection of family scrapbooks available I was finally ready to put the story in writing.

I found the story of my own professional career intertwined in this long family saga. I announced in the beginning of these writings that I would relive my own rendezvous with destiny in this written story. Many of the experiences have been recorded; many mountains have been climbed to say it rhetorically. Others have been unsurmountable largely because of race prejudice and obstructionism. I am pleased to have been personally involved in civil rights and human rights activities, and to have observed and experienced the joy of progress in race relations. I gloried in the liberal performance of Supreme Court Justice Hugo Black, a southerner, when he found himself shouldering the responsibilities of Americas' highest democratic goals for human rights and justice in spite of his alleged earlier racist record. Conversely my human dignity was crushed and I suffered along with millions of Blacks through the long years while bigoted congressmen from the South, supported by certain Northerner fellow travelers fought and filibustered for decades against antilynching bills and other measures to keep "The Negro in his place."

The good side of my journey is exemplified by the slow but progressive civil rights gains in the federal courts, especially during the 1950's and 60's. The problem of equal justice and parity in race relations in America is far from being solved. But I have many things to be thankful for as I have traveled along my life's journey. One of the darkest hours in my journey was the period and circumstances of obtaining admission to the University of Chicago Medical School in 1925. One of the happiest moments was receiving the Alumni Citation for Public Service in 1966 and the Alumni Professional Achievement Award at the University of Chicago in 1978. Very rewarding was the appointment by President Lyndon B. Johnson to membership on the twelve-man National Advisory Council Regional Medical programs against Heart Disease, Cancer and Stroke. My selection for participation in his White House conference on health and the invitation for a White House stag dinner with the President, his Cabinet and others, came while president of the National Medical Association. These honors were unique in 1965 since they represented the paradox of which America is capable; in that they came to a Black physician, from a president of the United States of Southern birth and ancestry. Like the great majority of Black Americans, I have continuing confidence in the ideals of democracy. I know no other home and I have no additional national allegencies outside of America.

One of the justifications for writing this story has been to put into perspective not only the prejudices and obstacles against minorities but to objectively and intelligently analyze and explain them and to illustrate how they can be overcome. Throughout the long period of written history there have been "those who have" and "those who have not." The prejudices and exploitations of the powerful against the weak have occurred through the ages.

I am thankful for a number of achievements which have come from very hard work and exhausting struggle. I am thankful for the strength and courage that have come from parents and my family clan across the generations. I am exceedingly grateful for the encouragements which have come from friends and well wishers across all race lines. I stand in awe and admiration for the leadership of great men and women who lived and worked in the Black Church community, and especially the first of the organized pioneers, the African Methodist, followers of Richard Allen since the year 1787. They organized, provided leadership and sustainance for a struggling race group through the last two centuries of life in America. Among them have been one hundred and one African Methodist Bishops and scores of General Church Officers elected by their peers. Hundreds of pastors trained and untrained but dedicated. There have been tradesmen, skilled and unskilled; teachers and tutors; Notary Public's and Lawyers; Justices of the Peace and Federal Judges; Medicine Men and Doctors of the healings Arts and Sciences; Magicians and Industrial scientists; Precinct captains and Congressmen, Mayors and Ambassadors and coutless numbers of worthy supporters without titles. They have been individuals who appreciated the value of a spiritual life and the essentiality of the nuclear, multinuclear and extended families that produced them in the search for the more abundant life. They have been held together and sustained to a remarkable extent by the eternal principles of Faith, Hope and Love. In the end, what is there of greater significance than Faith, Hope and Love along the pathway of life's journey?

Section Eight
The Later Years
(1954-1980)

four generations.

John Harris family and cousins.

Blanche, Kathryn Berry, Bonita.

Emma, Gladys, Sawyer sisters, Bertha, Odell, Sadie, Juanita.

Emma, sisters Blanche, Evelyn, husband Bill Valentine, Gerri.

Elbert's family, Blanche, Priscilla.

Lola Berry Innis, age 99, Mamie Berry Ross, Victoria Berry Miller.

Aunt Lola, daughters, Emma, Powell, Naomi Staton.

Kathy, Priscilla, Gerri, Blanche.

Marion Blackwell and family, Beulah, Mary.

John Harris granddaughters and Gerri.

Daughters of Marion Blackwell, Beulah, Mary.

Family Reunions Hillsboro, North Carolina

Continuing Family Reunions:
Interstate Picnics, Memorials;
Hollis, New York, Detroit,
Hillsboro, North Carolina

Marion Gordon Moore, Aunt Kate and Clara Royster.

Memorial of Rev. L. L. Berry, mother
Beulah, sons, daughters, granddaughters, in-laws.

Gladys Berry Yates, Evelyn Valentine.
Berry Brothers; Lee, Elbert, Dick, Lew.

Now Generations

Third and fourth generations that love and keep commandments

Ursula Harris Clay with children, grand and great-grands.

More Jordans, older and younger.

Young fry and future generations.

Lillian Goings Burns with favorite cousins.
4th and 5th generations.

Harris branches.

Leonidas with young cousins.

Sylvia Brooks Moore's Harris ancestry.

Under the trees at meal time.

Four first cousins, Berrys; Clay, Brooks.

Could it be a game of chess.

Leonidas with young cousins.

Grace, Sylvia, Harris lineage.   John Harris, Lula Myers, Ursula Clay,   A skit could be in order.

Now Generations

Third and fourth generations that love and keep commandments

John Berry III and young family l. to r. Shirley, Rebecca (wife-mother), Deloris, Victoria (not shown, Curtis), Philadelphia. Grandsons of Richard Berry, Sylvia's Bryan and Omar. Lydia's Mark and Daniel. Willie and Sylvia (Berry) Adams. Clarence, son of Arthur Berry.

Mrs. L. L. (Nancy) Berry III and Jenifer Berry; daughter Stephane; L. L. Berry III, husband and father.

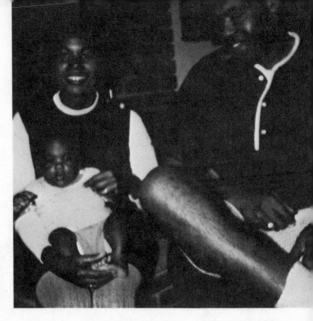

Mrs. L. H. (Emma) Berry (r.), and daughter Frances;

Alexander Jackson III, grandson Mrs. Emma Berry; Capt. Alvin Harrison II, stepson of L. H. Berry; Alvin III, and Barbara Jean, children of Willer J. Harrison and Alvin II; Judith Berry Griffin with Gilroye III and father, Gilroye II; L. H. Berry and grandson, Gil III; Gil III, medical recruit.

Continuing
Family Reunions
(1912–   )

AS far back as my unending research has taken me the concept of family reunion has always been there. When "Surrender" came after the war, kinfolks got together mo' and "ever" recalled Aint Suze, on one of her visits in the Berry home.

From the time that the children of Beulah and Rev. Berry began growing up there were always pilgrimages back to the Woodsdale farm country to visit relatives. A favorite stopping place was Aunt Carrie's and Uncle Gibbons Brooks home; mainly because there were plenty of young cousins to entertain the Berry cousins. The older ones especially Dick and I enjoyed following the men to the tobacco fields, "hand worming" or harvesting the tobacco plants on 8 foot sticks, while "minding" the cows in the nearby meadows. I still remember returning home in the late afternoon with the setting sun as our time clock. It was then that the real family reunions began. It was near evening time. The women and the girls would have supper almost ready. The delightful odors coming from the kitchen could "whip up" a "mean" appetite for active children and for us, that was the main reason for reunions in the country. As nighttime approached our bellies were delightfully empty. There was plenty of buttermilk, hot biscuits or cornbread, country butter, fresh vegetables, and various parts of the pig. Frequently, also there were apple cobbler or watermelon for dessert. Meals were not always well balanced by today's standards but oh how tasty!

Shortly after dark, sounds from overstuffed children would gradually give way to the chirps of crickets and other night country noises. The children of the Berrys and the Brooks would wash away most of the daily accumulated country soil from their bodies, say their prayers and soon be off to the land of nod.

Soundly we remained in the arms of Morpheus until awakened at sunrise by the crowing of roosters and the cackling of hens in the barn yard. Refreshed, we would soon scamper out into the weeds and grasses covered with morning dew. How refreshing this was to the boys who often trampled in their bare feet with great relief from city shoes.

As the sun rose higher in the eastern skies the families repeated their daily chores of mixing farm work with the joys of family reunions. This continued for a week or two or more; perhaps until the adults were overjoyed or exhausted or both.

Lastly, I must not forget a joy which came probably in late summer at tobacco curing time. I was allowed to go with Uncle Gibbons Brooks, Uncles Irving and John Harris, and Henry and Ernest Jordan who took turns spending the night sleeping on quilted pallets at the tobacco curing barns. There they kept the fires uniformly burning in the flues. They monitored the air temperature surrounding the mellowing leaves of the tobacco plants hanging from the ceilings and walls. Now this was reunion and sharing the joys of country fun at its boyhood best.

During 1912 the earliest summer reunion that I can remember there was great preparations for a big affair at Mt. Zion Baptist Church near McGee's Mill. The visiting youngsters were told that the event was called "August Meeting." It was held every year at the same time and lasted for a week. It was a religious revival meeting combined with the rejuvenation of family love. It was a time for family members who had moved away to return to their childhood homes and renew old friendships.

I remember having met my maternal great-grandfather on this occasion. The older people called him "Old Man" Wiley Jordan (pronounced Jurdan). Mom took me to meet him along with one of my distant cousins, Charles Stevens of Camden, New Jersey. She said, "grandpa these are your two oldest great grandsons." He was light-brown with high cheek bones, had gray hair, moustache and beard; a picturesque old man born a slave thirty years before emancipation in the very neighborhood where we met.

The closing meeting of the summer revival was always held on Sunday. I remember the country production in those days of long ago. In the churchyard, there were horse-drawn carriages, surreys and wagons. The horses were hitched to trees while the families dressed in their Sunday best gathered in church for the final worship service.

After the long services, they gathered on the outside of the church for the "love feast." Meals had been brought in baskets by each family to be shared and exchanged. I'm sure that digestion was enhanced by joyous conversation about the "good preaching," the young people who got religion and the happiness of reunion. Many had not seen each other since the year before and would not meet again for another year.

The unique way in which the food was served is well remembered. Long planks were connected to trees several feet apart and at a convenient four or five feet from the ground. These planks, about two feet wide were covered with tablecloths. The adults stood up on both sides of these improvised counters and ate their meals. The children feasted while sitting on nearby grassy areas or on pine straw from the many long leaf pine trees for which North Carolina was known far and wide.

After 1914 the war industries of northern cities, the pasttime of southern lynchings and the activities of the Ku Klux Klan forced many of our family including their in-laws, the Drumwrights, Clays, Roysters, Skinners, and earlier the Goings to cities of the northeast. Reverend L. L. Berry remained in the Norfolk-Portsmouth area in the pastorage for many years. Our family got to know the family of Uncle "Gus" (John Augustus Berry, Jr.) who lived in Hampton. There were summers prior to and during World War One, when our families spent joyful days together. The Jenifers of Hampton had died off except a few, who moved away and lost contact with our family. In the late twenties and thirties the L. L. Berry children and many of their cousins moved off to boarding schools and were busy during the summer working to support their education. Family reunions occurred in smaller groups and shorter periods.

During the Secretary of Mission years, when Pop's children married and moved into their own homes, family reunions became frequent again. They occurred on holidays and in late summer. Mom and Pop and Geraldine visited Dick and Gladys and their families in Detroit, and my family in Chicago. Many of us would gather at my summer home in the lake resort of Idlewild, Michigan.

As the years passed some of our largest reunions occurred on the sad occasions of funerals. The strength of the family bonds that held us together was always obvious on these occasions. Aunts, uncles, and cousins who had not seen each other for years would gather to support the immediate survivors. The largest of these gatherings occurred at the passing of "Pop" in 1954 and at "Mom's" memorial 5 years afterwards in Feb. 1960. Aunt Carrie Harris Brooks, who had 12 children passed in Hillsborough, N.C. in 1976. The little A.M.E. church was filled almost completely with members of the family. Many of the friends in attendance stood outside. The reunion of a large family gathering occurred at the passing of Lula Harris Myers, Mom's youngest sister a few years later, at the age of 82 years, in the same North Carolina town of Hillsborough. She had been a school teacher in Norfolk and a housewife for many years after a Hampton Institute graduation.

Our dear brother Lewellyn, Jr passed at the relatively young age of 57 years of a heart attack at University of Chicago's Billings Hospital. His memorial was held at historic Metropolitan A.M.E. Church in Washington, D.C. where he was long a member and officer. A large number of his peers at Howard University Medical School and Freedmen's Hospital and a great host of relatives paid their last tribute to a very likeable and popular person, before his interment at Arlington National Cemetery. His broken immediate family consisted of his devoted wife Kathryn who carried on his medical laboratory business and his teenaged son "little" Lew.

Our brother Dick was closest to me by age and my best childhood buddy. He was stricken with a fatal illness at age 65 years, a few months after retirement from a long held administrative post with the U.S. Department of Defense in Detroit. After the usual large family gathering, Dick was buried in the Elmwood family cemetery in Detroit beside Mom and Pop. His immediate bereaved family consisted of a devoted widow Maryland, two fine well educated daughters, Lydia and Sylvia and four grandsons.

After the passing of "Mom" and "Pop," the strong bond of the immediate Berry family appeared to get stronger. The younger families of Lewellyn, Jr. in Washington, D.C., Elbert in Hollis, N.Y., Dick and Gladys with Geraldine in Detroit and my brood in Chicago met at various times on all holidays and summer vacation periods up to the present time.

The togetherness which has involved in-laws as well, has been remarkable. The spiritual influence of the Black church has been ever present. The type of togetherness manifested in the Berry-Harris Jordan family and their in-laws has been observed through the years in many other Black families who have achieved middle class status. The so-called "disorganization" of the "statistical" Black family is purely a manifestation of economic, and social depravity under the burden of racial struggle in America.

It was Aunt Ursula, Mom's oldest sister, who took over her role in promoting many family reunions. Aunt Ursula felt that large reunions should be held annually as had been the custom many years before in the South. She began promoting these reunions in the public park of her home town of Camden, New Jersey each year on the 3rd Saturday in July. Their reunions became very popular and first, second, and third cousins, aunts, uncles, mothers and fathers began to assemble from all over the northeast where most of the older Virginia and North Carolina families had migrated.

On the third Saturday in July 1977, I attended my first of Aunt Ursula's family reunions. This was her 12th consecutive annual July picnic involving the offsprings of the Harris-Jordan-Berry clan and their in-laws. This was a far cry from the first one I attended as a little boy at the country church near Woodsdale, N.C., 65 years before.

The selected park area had been reserved months ahead each year. It was the largest in the long history of our family reunions. There were approximately 150 people present with representatives from four generations of the Harris-Jordan-Berry family clan. Aunt Ursula was 87 years old and all age groups were represented down to the age of 18 months, and all complexions and colors. They were all dressed and appropriately attired for the picnic, and brought colorful folding tables and lounging chairs which were set up for the most part in individual family groups with bright and festive table cloths or spreads for the grassy areas. Each individual family brought baskets and baskets of food which were exchanged from family to family. The temperature was near 95 degrees and practically all of the tables were arranged in the shade under the tall maple and elm trees of the area. Some brought family pictures and photograph albums which were passed around as they reminisced about parents, grandparents, great-grandparents and talked about their youngest crop of children, their ambitions, their progress in school, the business and their professional worlds. I kept very busy renewing old acquaintances, meeting people whom I had never seen, and many others about whom I had never been told.

As the families gathered and parked their cars near the picnic areas one could recognize all makes and styles of automobiles from well kept compacts to luxury family automobiles. Obviously, no one there was receiving federal welfare. After most of the groups had finished their feasts I induced several of the individual family groups to come out of the shade for color photographs in the brilliant sunlight.

The only persons remaining continuously in the very hot sunny areas were groups of teenagers sitting on colorful spreads enjoying disco and other popular music from their tape recorders and portable radios. They were relatively quiet and well behaved. After I had photographed several family groups and had them to identify their names, I called aside one of my cousins, Lillian Goings Burns, whom I had known for many years, to get the real "low down" on persons whom I did not know. I learned that people had come for this reunion from as far away as Greensboro, North Carolina, Baltimore, Washington, Atlantic City, Newark, New York, Philadelphia, and other surrounding towns, Hollis, New York and Chicago, in addition to many from Camden. I learned that the family people and their in-laws represented many professions and occupations, there were many schoolteachers, workers in government, workers with large business corporations at supervisory and lower levels. There were social workers, one college professor, a lawyer, a musician, a podiatrist, a physician, college, high school and grade school students and housewives.

My informant had lived in Camden all of her life and had just retired as a public school teacher. She named a dozen or more well known and lesser known colleges in the New York, Pennsylvania, New Jersey areas, including Glassboro Teachers College, Rutgers, Temple, University of Pennsylvania, Princeton, Yale, Harvard and several Black Colleges of Virginia and North Carolina where these family members had trained. The gathering broke at sundown, pledging to meet again, God willing, on the 3rd Saturday in July of the following year.

There were unique reunions described in prior chapters, like Mom and Pop's 25th and 50th wedding anniversaries, and Gladys' wedding in New York where friends outside of the family circle joined the celebrations and Mom's 80th birthday "Party." My brother Elbert and wife Blanche held a family gathering at their home in Hollis, New York during the summer of 1978.

428

Many members of the Berry-Harris part of the family, their in-laws and a number of close friends were present.

They came from Chicago, Michigan City, Indiana, and Detroit, Washington, D.C., New Haven, Connecticut, Virginia Beach, Virginia, Brooklyn, Hartsdale, Long Island, and New York City.

It was a splendidly enjoyable occasion. The star of this reunion was Pop's sister Aunt Lola, the last of the living children of John Berry, Sr. Aunt Lola had attained the ripe "Young" age of 98 years. She had overcome two broken hips with the help of an artificial hip joint and a bout with cancer. She pushed her two daughters, Emma Powell and Naomi Staton, aside and demonstrated her great sense of humor which seems to have been a Berry characteristic. "Take this cane," she said, "I don't need it. I'll show you how well I can walk." She walked down the driveway and some of the picnickers rushed to assist her seeing that she was walking slowly alone. She drove them away, saying, "I don't need your help. If you wish," she said with laughter, "I'll show you how to do the Susie Q." Her sense of humor lasted all of her life. This was the last time she saw a large crowd of relatives who loved and honored her. Many of them attended her last memorial one year later. She lived to within one week of her 99th birthday.

The spirit of family reunions is deeply embedded in our family clan. The passing of a senior member appears to strengthen rather than weaken the bonds.

Birthdays, mothers and fathers days, almost any prolonged holidays provide the occasions to get together. The only question seems to be who will be the next host and hostess and where. We have often been the spontaneous instigators of family gatherings in our Chicago home or elsewhere. A recent one began in the Rose Garden of Chicago's Grant Park near the famous Buckingham Fountain.

Looking back to the days of my youth—there have been numerable family assemblies thru the years. In all instances there has been the spirit of togetherness, but more than that there has been the sense of mission or goals in life for the younger members. Perseverance and achievement, love of humanity, and humility were the unspoken precepts which emanated from the family circle.

Finally, in the earlier years and today the family circle around the dinner table is never broken without a prayer of thanksgiving.

The Now Generation
and the Future

WOULD Mom and Pop be pleased if they could view the present generation of their family in America and in today's world?

Most certainly they would be happy. I can imagine the joy that would be expressed in their faces. I can almost hear their conversations. Pop, always the minister would say, "look Hon, look out on the far horizon, there is the Promise Land. There it is just as it is described in the scriptures. It looks like the distant bright star we use to see or even the North Star of our ancestors. It is much brighter now and closer." And Mom would say, "how beautiful it radiates; look at all the people moving in that direction. They are all the colors of the rainbow."

Mom and Pop would be startled by the panoramic view of America in today's world; not just by its technological changes. They would be overjoyed by the social and cultural advances, especially among the people who are called Black Americans. They would be proud of the effects of the social revolution of the 60's sparked by the leadership of an inspired minister, the Rev. Martin Luther King. They would see far less isolation of people by color among the crowds of the human race as they march in step with each other. Mom would say, "How beautiful, Hon, are the myriads of colors among these handsome people." It is God's universal beautiful flower garden.

Mom and Pop would recognize people from foreign lands, the Third World of Asia and Africa. They would recognize the robes of the people from the Gold Coast, now Ghanians. They would see the tribal attire of people from Rhodesia, now Zimbabwe. They would think of Moses and his people marching towards the Promise Land of the scriptures, seeing the new Jerusalem but not yet having quite reached it.

431

Mom and Pop would regard all they would see in the world of the new generation as a stroke of destiny, providentially ordained to help America carry out its role in a universal plan among the nations of the earth. Together they would look backwards for a moment into the dark past and survey the distance from which their united families had come. They would recount their struggles, successful survival and their contributions to the culture of their times. They would say to each other in the language of their religion, "My soul looks back and wonders how I got over." They would hear the answer figuratively ringing down across the generations; *Faith* in God; *Faith* in themselves, and *Faith* in the ultimate triumph of the ideals of American democracy.

Mom and Pop would be proud to see and recognize in the vanguard of progress and leadership of the youngest generation, the progeny of their own families. Their grandchildren, their great-grandchildren and the great-great-grandchildren to whom the future of God's plan belongs. They would be proud that nine out of 10 of their children and grandchildren were college graduates and beyond.

Pop would recognize Judy "the sweetest girl in town when nobody else is around." He would be glad to know that she earned three university degrees, two from the University of Chicago and one from Columbia University in New York City. She has worked in the field of psychology, been a suburban school principal, an administrator of the U.S. Department of Education and is the author of several children's books under her name Judith Berry Griffin. He would be ecstatic to know her brilliant preteen son, my pride and joy, Gilroye (Gill) Griffin, III.

Mom and Pop would share equal joy in auditing all of the youngest generation of their offspring.

They would remember Alvin as a very young little boy, building model airplanes. They would be proud to review his record as an air force pilot and captain in U.S.A. and Europe; commercial pilot and helicopter pilot in Canada; and chief of the aircraft maintenance base for the Federal Aviation Administration. His son, Alvin III is a Dartmouth College graduate in business and father of a fine young son. Alvin's daughter, Barbara Jean, San Jose College graduate is a photo journalist with one of the largest television networks.

There was a stepdaughter of later years whom Mom and Pop had not known. They would immediately love Frances for her charm and brilliance. She is a New York City high school teacher. She has a very fine son who calls me "Uncle Lee" and I call him my nephew. She would greatly please Mom and Pop, not just because of his two Harvard degrees but because one was a master of theology. The study of theology apparently satisfied his spiritual needs while he works as an account executive for a large brokerage firm.

Dick's smart daughters, Lydia and Sylvia are university graduates, high school teachers and each has two smart young sons. Their husbands are respectively, a school principal and a bank executive. Mom and Pop would be getting prouder and prouder.

Mom and Pop last saw "little Lew" (Lewellyn L. III) as a shy, pre-teen, a pampered only child. But after the premature loss of his father, Lewellyn Jr., "little Lew" had turned his life around. He has earned three university degrees, created and directed successful federal projects for ghetto kids and is active as a teacher of photo-journalism in Washington, D.C. schools.

Pop would be especially proud that "little Lew" (Lewellyn L. Berry III) found a wife named Nancy; since Pop's mother's name was Nancy Jenifer Berry. Besides, "little Lew" and his wife Nancy have a daughter, Stephanie and they have a young daughter born on St. Valentines Day, 1980 whom they named Jenifer Leigh Berry. Thus a prophetic Berry cycle of 113 years has been completed which began when John Berry married Nancy Jenifer, the sister of his Civil War buddy, Sam Jenifer, at Norfolk, Va. in 1867.

There is every reason to believe that life's long journey for the Berry family clan and other minorities like them is neither complete nor decadent. It will continue progressively and triumphantly on into tomorrow's world. As the sanskrit records, "yesterday is already a dream, and tomorrow is only a vision; but today well lived, makes every yesterday a dream of happiness, and every tomorrow a vision of hope."

Like my 'Aint' Suze used to sing "I wouldn't take nothin for my journey." And my Pop, the African Methodist minister used to preach, "It is only required of man to do justly, to love mercy and to walk humbly with his God."

433

Excerpts From Official Records of the Union and
Confederate Armies, Operations of the South Side of the James.
Order No. 72, May, 1864
Reports of Brig. Gen. Edward W. Hinks, U.S. Army,
Commanding Third Division of Operations, May 5–18, 1864

General: I have the honor to submit the following brief report of my
operations since landing at City Point on 5th May instant: As you are
already aware the First and Twenty-Second Regiments of U.S. Colored
Troops with Capt. Choates battery of Colored light Artillery were
landed at Wilson's Wharf. The Tenth and Thirty-seventh U.S. Colored
troops with two sections of Howell's Battery were landed at Fort Po-
watan.

Excerpts of Order No. 3, May 10, 1864.
Report of Brig. Gen. Edward A. Wild, U.S. Army,
Commanding 1st Brigade Hdqrs. First Brigade, Third Div.
18th Army Corps, Wilson's Wharf, Va., May 25, 1864

Captain: I have the honor to report that this post was attacked yesterday
at noon by a considerable force of the enemy, supposedly, to be cavalry,
having three guns, probably horse artillery. The attack was evidently
made in earnest, with a design of rushing in upon us suddenly; but they
received so decided a check from our pickets, that a large portion of the
force dismounted and made their approach more cautiously. They en-
compassed our front, and filling the woods on the James River bluff to
the north, tried to stop all communications with steamers coming to our
aid, and harassed our landing place. They also made it uncomfortable
for the gunners to serve their pieces on our gun-boat. After fighting an
hour and a half, they sent forward a flag of truce, with a note containing
a summons to surrender in the name of Major Gen. Fritzhugh Lee. This
note was forwarded to department headquarters yesterday. I declined.
We then went at it again. They massed troops on our extreme right,
concealed by wooded ravines, and made a determined charge, at the same
time keeping up a steady attack all along our front and left flank. This
charge approached our parapet, but failed under our severe crossfire.
They fled back into the ravines, out of sight, etc.

Bibliography

African Methodist Episcopal Church: *Book of Discipline*, A.M.E. Sunday School Union Press, Nashville (revisions 1936, '40, '48, '52, '76, '80.

Beitzell, Edwin: *Life on the Potomac River*, Publisher, Abell, Maryland, 1968.

Bennett, Lerone, Jr.: "Before The Mayflower," *A History of Black America*, Johnson Publishing Company, Inc., Chicago, 1969. "Great Moments in Black History," "The Private War of Harriet Tubman," *Ebony*, June, 1975.

Berry, Leonidas H., M.D.: *Human Rights and Regional Medical Programs*, Jour. NMA, Vol. 58, No. 5, pp. 387–388, September, 1966.

Berry, Leonidas H., M.D.: "Disadvantaged Populations," *Proceedings of White House Conference on Health*, Nov. 3-4, 1965–H.E.W.–U.S. Printing Office, Washington, D.C., 1965.

Berry, Leonidas H., M.D.: "Chronic Alcoholic Gastritis: Evaluation of the Concept with Gastroscopic Studies in 100 Cases," *Journal of American Medical Association*, Vol. 117, No. 26, December 27, 1941.

Berry, Leonidas H., M.D.: "Medical Counseling Clinics for Young Narcotic Addicts," *Journal of American Medical Association*, Vol. 147, pp. 1129–1132, November 17, 1951.

Berry, Leonidas H., M.D.: *Proceedings of the Annual Conference on Youth and Community Services*," Department of Public Welfare, State of Illinois, 1952, "Community Action in Narcotic Addiction."

Berry, Leonidas H., M.D.: *Conferences on Drug Addiction Among Adolescents*" (Contributing Author). Sponsored by New York Academy of Medicine and the Josiah H. Macey, Jr. Foundation, The Blakiston Co., New York, June, 1953.

Berry, Leonidas H., M.D.: "Viral Gastroenteritis" (Contributing Author), Textbook, *Current Diagnosis*, W. B. Saunders Co., Philadelphia-London, May, 1966.

Berry, Rev. Llewellyn L.: *A Century of Missions of The African Methodist Episcopal Church* (1840–1940), Gutenberg Printing, New York, 1942.

Berry, L. L.: *A Little Missionary Journey To A Great Missionary Area*," Publisher, Gutenburg Press, 1941.

437

Berry, Rev. Llewellyn L., editor: "Voice of Missions," *Quarterly Journal*, Dept. of Missions, New York, 1933–1954.

Blair, Gladys A.: *Northerners In The Reconstruction*, Hampton, Virginia, 1865–1870, a thesis, Department of History, Old Dominion University, May, 1975.

Bontemps, Arna: *The Story of the Negro*, New York: Alfred A. Knopf, c. 1948.

Boyd, William C.: *Genetics and the Races of Man*, Little, Brown & Company, Boston, 1950.

Brackett, J. R.: *The Negro in Maryland*, Johns Hopkins, Universal Press, 1889. The study of the institution of slavery.

Bradley, Chester D., M.D.: Curator, Fortress Monroe Museum, Hampton, Virginia. Personal communications to the author, 1955–1980.

Bragg, George F.: *History, Afro-American Group, Protestant Episcopal Church*, Church Advocate Press, Baltimore, Maryland, 1922.

Bragg, George F.: *Men of Maryland*, Church Advocate Press, Baltimore, Maryland, 1908.

Burton, Harrison W.: *The History of Norfolk, Virginia*, Norfolk Virginian Job Print, 1877, 264 pages.

Butt, Rev. I. L., D.D.: *African Methodism In Virginia*, Hampton Institute Press, Hampton, Virginia, 1908.

Cable, Mary: *Black Odyssey, 1839*, "The Case of the Slave Ship *Armistad*," New York, Viking Press, 1971.

Cannon, John: *History of Grant's Campaign for Capture of Richmond (1864–65)*, Longmans, Green & Co., 1869.

Catton, Bruce: *A Stillness at Appomattox*, Doubleday and Company, Inc., New York, 1953.

Catton, Bruce: *A Stillness at Appomattox*, Books Abridged, Inc., New York, 1954, pp. 133–172.

Dabney, Virginius: *Below the Potomac*, Appleton-Century Company, Inc., New York and London, 1942.

Davis, Burke: *To Appomattox*, Popular Library, New York, 1952.

Donald, Henderson H.: *The Negro Freedman*, Henry Schuman, New York, 1954.

Douglass, Frederick: *Life and Times* (written by himself), Park Publishing Company, 1882.

DuBois, W. E. Burghardt: *Black Reconstruction in America*, S-A Russell Company, New York, 1935.

DuPont, Henry A.: *Campaign of 1864 in Valley of Virginia*, New York: National Americana Society, 1925.

Dyer, Frederic H.: *A Compendium of The War of the Rebellion*, Regimental Histories, Battery "B", 2nd Regiment, Light Artillery, USCT, Vol. 111, p. 1722, Des Moines, Iowa, 1908, Dyer Publishing Company.

Ebony Success Library, Vols. 1, 11, Johnson Publ. Co., 1973.

Ellsworth, Col. E. E.: Catalogue Chicago Public Library, T. A. Oriands, p. 13.

Ellyson, H. K.: "Yellow Fever Prevalence," *Portsmouth Relief Association Report*, Richmond, 1856.

Engs, Robert: *Dissertation on Early History of Hampton, Virginia*, Dept. of History, University of Pennsylvania, Englewood Cliffs, New Jersey: Prentice-Hall, 1971.

Farrows Military Encyclopedia, 1800–1895. Vols. I, II, III, New York.

Forrest, William S.: *The Great Pestilence in Virginia*, "The Account of Yellow Fever," etc., New York: Derby & Co., 1856.

Franklin, John Hope: *From Slavery To Freedom*, Vantage Books, A Division of Random House, New York, 1969.

Green, Elmer: *The Making of Maryland*, E. & M. Green, Baltimore, Maryland, 1934.

Gregg, John A.: *Of Men and Arms*, A.M.E. Sunday School Union Press, Nashville, Tennessee, 1945.

Griffin, Judith Berry: *Nat Turner*, Coward-McCann, Inc., Publisher, New York, 1970.

Grosvenor, Gilbert: "Maryland Pilgrimage," *National Geographic Magazine*, February, 1927.

Handy, Rev. James A.: *Scraps of African Methodist Episcopal History*, A.M.E. Book Concern, Philadelphia, Pennsylvania, 1901.

Harold, Faye K.: *Our Free Nation*, McMillan Company, New York, 1956.

Heard, William H.: *From Slavery to the Bishopric*, A.M.E. Book Concern, Philadelphia, Pennsylvania, 1924.

Henson, Josiah: *Life of Josiah Henson*, Arthur Phelps, Boston, Massachusetts, 1849.

Herskovits, Melville J.: *The Myth of the Negro Past*, Harper & Bros., New York 1941.

Humphreys, A. A.: *The Virginia Campaign of 1864–65—The Armies of Potomac and James*, New York: Charles Scribners Sons, 1883.

Jackson, Luther P.: *Negro Office-Holders in Virginia (1865–95)*, Guide Quality Press, 1945.

Jenifer, Rev. John T.: *Centennial History, African Methodist Episcopal Church*, Sunday School Union Press, Nashville, Tennessee, 1916.

Johnson, Jesse J.: *A Pictorial History of Black Soldiers in the USA in Peace and War*, Hampton Press, Hampton, Virginia, 1970.

Johnson, Richard H.: *A Critical Story of Religious Work Among Negroes of St. Mary's County, Maryland Since 1865*, thesis, Howard University, Washington, D.C., 1948.

Kantor, MacKinlay: *Andersonville*, The New American Library, 1957.

Kramer, Helen: *The Amistad Revolt, 1839*, New York, 1973.

Lamb, Robert W.: *Our Twin Cities of the Nineteenth Century* (Norfolk and Portsmouth), their past, present, and future, Norfolk, Virginia: Barcroft, 1887–1888, p. 312.

Lewis, Roscoe E.: Supervisor, Virginia Writer's Project, *The Negro in Virginia*, Hastings House, New York, 1940.

Lilly, William E.: *Set My People Free*, Farrar and Rinehardt, Inc., New York, 1932.

Logan, Frenise A.: *The Negro in North Carolina (1876–1894)*, University of North Carolina, Chapel Hill, North Carolina, 1964.

Lord, Rev. S. E. Churchstone: Presiding Elder, Canadian Moritne Conf., *God in A Troubled World*, News Sentinel Press, Amherst, Nova Scotia, Canada, 1948.

Lykes, Richard Wayne: *Petersburg Battlefields*, National Park Service, Washington, D.C., 1951.

Lynch, John R.: *The Facts of Reconstruction*, Neale Publishing Company, New York, 1914.

McCake, Mrs. Gillie Cary: *The Story of An Old Town, Hampton, Virginia*, Richmond: Old Dominion Press, 1929, p. 53.

McSherry, James: *History of Maryland*, John Murphy Company, Baltimore, Maryland, 1849.

Moore, Robert W.: Maryland presents—*National Geographic Magazine*, April, 1941.

Murphy, Henry W.: *The Book of Discipline*, 40th ed. (1972–1976), A.M.E. Sunday School Union Press, Nashville, Tennessee, 1972.

Murray, Pauli: *Proud Shoes*, Harper Brothers, New York, 1956.

Nichols, Charles H. (ed.): *Black Men in Chains*, "Narratives of Escaped Slaves," New York: Lawrence Hill & Company, 1974.

Patrick, John: "Roads from Washington," *National Geographic Magazine*, July, 1938.

Payne, Bishop Daniel A.: *Recollections of 70 Years*, Publishing House, Sunday School Union Press, Nashville, Tennessee, 1888.

Payne, Bishop Daniel A.: *History of the A.M.E. Church*, Publishing House, Sunday School Union Press, Nashville, Tennessee, 1891.

Poore, Ben P.: *Life & Public Service of General Ambrose E. Burnside*, J. A. and R. A. Reed, Rhode Island, 1882.

Quarles, Benjamin: *The Negro in the Civil War*, Little, Brown & Co., Boston, 1953.

Sertima, Ivan Van: *They Came Before Columbus*, Random House, New York, 1976.

Singleton, Rev. George A.: *The Life Experience and Gospel Labors of the Right Reverend Richard Allen* (a revision of the autobiography of Rev. R. Allen written before 1831), Abington Press, New York and Nashville, 1960.

Singleton, Rev. George A.: *The Romance of African Methodism*, Exposition Press, New York, 1952.

Smith, Bishop Charles S.: *A History of the A.M.E. Church*, Vol. 2, Sunday School Union Press, Nashville, 1922.

Starkey, Marion Lena: "The First Plantation," *A History of Hampton and Elizabeth City County, Virginia, 1607–1887*, Hampton, Virginia: Houston Printing and Publishing House, 1936.

Swinton, William: *Army of the Potomac*, Charles Scribner & Sons, New York, 1882.

Townsend, Maj. Gen. E. D.: *Anecdotes of the Civil War*, D. Appleton & Co., New York, 1884.

Tyler, Lyon G.: *History of Hampton and Elizabeth City County, Virginia*, Hampton, Virginia: The Board of Supervisor's of Elizabeth City County, 1922.

Virginia Annual Conference Minutes: Vols. 1–8, 1877 to 1938. Collection of Berry, Rev. L. L., Archives (Library) Hampton Institute, Virginia. Minutes Quadrennial General Conference, 1908, '16, '20, '24, '28, '32, '36, '40, '44, '48, '52. Collections, Berry, Rev. L. L. (1908–1952), Minutes, Western N.C. Annual Conference, Random Copies.

War of the Rebellion: Official Records of the Union and Confederate Armies, Series 1, Vols. 33, 36, 40, 42, 43, 46, 47, 51; Series 2, Vol. 7; Series 3, Vols. 4 and 5. (See index of each volume for page numbers.)

Westenbaker, Thomas Jefferson: *Norfolk: Historic Southern Port*, Durham, North Carolina: Duke University Press, 1931.

White, Dr. Amos J. and Mrs. Luella G.: *Dawn in Bantuland*, The Christopher Publishing House, Boston, U.S.A., 1953.

White, Walter: *How Far The Promised Land*, Viking Press, New York, MacMillan Company, 1955.

Wilhelm's Military Dictionary & Gazetteer, Vol. 1, L. R. Hamersly & Co., 1881.

Williams, George W.: *The History of the Negro Race in America*, Putnam's Co., New Jersey, 1883.

Wilson, Charles M.: *Liberia*, Wilson Sloane Associates, New York, 1947.

Woodson, Carter G.: *Negro Makers of History in 1945* and *Negroes in Our History, 1945*.

Woodson, Carter G.: *The History of the Negro Church*, Associated Pub., Washington, South Carolina, 1921, ed. 1945, 1972.

Wright, Bishop R. R., Jr., Ph.D., LL.D.: *The Bishops of the A.M.E. Church*, A.M.E. Sunday School Union Press, 1963.

Wright, Bishop R. R., Jr., Ph.D., LL.D.: *Centennial Encyclopedia of A.M.E. Church*, Philadelphia, Pennsylvania, 1917.

Wright, Bishop R. R., Jr., Ph.D., LL.D.: *Encyclopedia of African Methodism, The Bishops of the A.M.E. Church*, A.M.E. Sunday School Union Press, Nashville, 1963. *87 Years Behind The Cotton Curtain*.

Yancey, Ernest J.: *Historical Lights of Liberia* (West Africa, etc.), Around the World Publishing House Ltd., Tel-Aviv, Israel, 1967.

Young, Whitney M., Jr.: *To Be Equal*, McGraw-Hill Book Company, New York, Toronto, and London, 1964.

Principal Persons Interviewed
1955-1980

1. Family Members Born in 19th Century:
   Rev. Llewellyn Longfellow (L. L.) Berry (letters, documents, mem-
        orabilia, etc.)
   Beulah Harris Berry
   Susie Harris Warren
   Arthur Berry
   Ursula Harris Clay
   Mamie Berry Robb
   Carrie Harris Brooks
   John S. Harris
   Lula Harris Myers
   Lola Berry Innis
   Katherine Berry Barrett
   John Augustus Berry, Jr.
   Sallie Warren
   Garner Jordan

2. Family Members Born in 20th Century:
   Katherine Berry
   Lewellyn L. Berry, Jr.
   Lewellyn L. Berry III
   Lydia Berry Mosher
   Maryland Berry
   Sylvia Berry Adams
   Elbert J. Berry
   Richard Otis Berry
   Gladys Berry Yates

Geraldine V. Berry
Victoria Berry Miller
Lillian Goings Burns
Emma Annis Powell
Blanche P. Berry
Judith Berry Griffin
Alvin E. Harrison, Jr.
Alexander L. Jackson IV
Emma F. Berry
Clara Royster
Dorothy Skinner Rice
Marian Jordan Moore
Ruth Brooks Traynham
Grace Brooks Carver
Sylvia Brooks Moore
Richard Allen Brooks
Bernice Brooks Hodge
Clarence Berry
Betty Jordan Clay
Richard Traynham

3. Members of the Clergy:

BISHOPS:	REVERENDS:
A. J. Allen	Russell Brown
I. H. Bonner	Sherman L. Green, Jr.
E. Hatcher	W. D. Johnson
R. C. Ransom	D. H. J. Thibodeaux
J. A. Gregg	J. M. Grandberry
S. L. Greene	H. D. Gregg
R. R. Wright, Jr.	Joseph L. Joyner
F. M. Reid, Sr.	W. A. Page
G. W. Baber	A. J. Carey, Jr.
J. Gomez	W. R. Howerton
W. R. Wilkes	S. S. Morris, Sr.
H. R. Primm	Charles E. Stewart
F. D. Jordan	Churchstone Lord
F. H. Gow	Charles S. Spivey, Sr.

O. L. Sherman

W. H. Ball

E. L. Hickman

S. S. Morris, Jr.

J. H. Mayo

J. Adams, Jr.

F. M. Reid, Jr.

H. N. Robinson

H. J. Bryant

H. I. Bearden

F. H. Talbot

C. A. Gibbs

F. Gow

J. H. Clayborn

Charles S. Spivey, Jr.

Andrew White

P. Van Putten

I. E. Steady

A. Lewis Williams

R. E. Peters

Robert Thomas, Sr.

A. Wayman Ward

Harvey E. Walden

C. W. Abington

D. P. Gordon

H. J. Bryant

E. J. Randell

J. W. Weeks

D. P. Talbot

J. Brockington

4. Consulted Friends and Professional Authorities:

CHESTER BRADLEY, M.D.

LOUISE GARNER PERRY

Hampton Institute, Archivist, FRITZ MALVAL

STUART WHITING

National Archives, Genealogist, JAMES D. WALKER

NANNIE SAWYER

BERTHA SAWYER

MAXINE FEREBEE

MRS. RUTH SPIVEY

MAMIE AIKEN

TOBERT MANCE, M.D.

A. S. JACKSON

LUCILLE THOMAS

SYLVIA BYNUM

G. HAMILTON FRANCIS, M.D.

DR. JOSEPH McKINNEY

U. G. DAILEY, M.D.

HOMER WILBURN, M.D.

GEORGE D. CANNON, M.D.

G. Duncan Hinkson, M.D.
Homer Q. Smith
Atty. Harry G. Bragg
Atty. Herbert Dudley
Atty. Cleveland Longmire
Lucy Hughes
Bertie Delyle
Christine Smith
Atty. Sidney A. Jones
Lula Avery
John Wheeler
Eva Morake
Mary C. Linnette
David Muckle
Esther Morphies Atwater
Malissa Jenifer
Agnes Callum

Places Visited (1955-1980)

For Family Research,
Black Medical History,
Participation in World Medical Congresses

Maryland: St. Mary's County Library, Cremona and Other Plantations, Leonardtown.

New York: Schomburg Center for Research in Black Culture.

Washington D.C.: National Archives, Arlington National Cemetery, Library of Congress, Howard University, Moorland-Spingarn Collection.

Chicago, IL: Chicago Public libraries; Main; Civil War Exhibits, George C. Hall Branch, Carter Woodson Branch, Harsh Collection of Black History, DuSable Museum of Afro-American History.

North Carolina: Woodsdale, Roxboro, Cemeteries, Farm Houses, Durham, Hillsboro, Chapel Hill, Kittrell College.

Ohio: Wilberforce University, Payne Theological Seminary.

Virginia: Norfolk, So. Norfolk, Portsmouth, Princess Anne Court House, Hampton, Fortress Monroe, Butler's Farm Site, Hampton Institute, Jamestown, Yorktown, Williamsburg, Mt. Vernon, Monticello, Arlington, Charles City, Burrowsville: Site of Wilson's Wharf, Ruins of Fort Powhatan, Site of Battle of the Crater Explosion, Petersburg, Richmond: Churches, Parsonages, Houses, Cemeteries.

Foreign Areas: Ontario, Canada; Liberia; Nigeria; Jamaica; Haiti; Trinidad; Rio de Janeiro, Brazil; Cuba; Rome, Italy; Copenhagen, Denmark; Santiago, Chile; and Mexico City, Mexico.

Sponsored by Cultural Exchange Program, U.S. Department of State

Africa, East and West (1965): Jomo Kenyatta Hospital, Nairobi, Kenya; Makerere Medical College and Hospital, Kampala, Uganda; Lagos University Medical School and Hospital, Lagos, Nigeria; Ibadan Medical School and Hospital, Ibadan, Nigeria; Firestone and Government Hospitals, Monrovia, Liberia; University of Dakar Medical School, Dakar, Senegal.

Tokyo, Japan (1966): Tokyo Medical College.

Seoul, Korea (1966): University of Seoul, National University Hospital, Yonsei University Hospital, Soo Do University Hospital, Catholic University Medical College.

Manila, Philippines (1966): Santo Tomas Medical School and College, University of Philippines Medical School, Kaiser Hospital, Honolulu, Hawaii (USA).

Paris, France (1970): Hospital St. Antoine.

Communications

United States Center of Military History, Washington, D.C.; Historical Military Institute, Carlyle Barracks, Pennsylvania; Virginia State Library, Richmond, Virginia; Person County Court House, Roxboro, North Carolina; University of North Carolina, Winston-Salem, North Carolina; Halifax County Court House, Halifax, Virginia; St. Mary's County Commissions, Leonardtown, Maryland; Seaboard Air Line; Railroad Public Relations Office; United States National Park Service, Washington, D.C.

Index

D

E

ATTENDING STAFF, RESIDE
PROVIDENT HOSPITAL

Professional Staff, Resident Staff, and Trustees; Provident Hospital and Training School, Chicago, 1938. An affiliate of the University of Chicago Medical School.

Michael Reese Hospital Medical Center, Chicago: Attending Staff Thirty Year Service Award. (l. to r.) Doctors, Max Berg, Leonidas Berry, Lloyd Matzkin, Lawrence Perlman, Jakub Schlecter, Robert Buchanan (Hospital President), Arthur Billings (Staff President), 1977.

University of Chicago Annual Alumni Awards, University President John T. Wilson and Black Awardees. L. to r.: Leonidas H. Berry, M.D., Professional Achievement Award; Benjamin E. Mays, M.S., Ph.D., Alumni Medal; Vivian Carter Mason, Public Service Citation, 1978.

Hall, James Sr.	Matthew, Henry	Smith, T. M.
Hasbrough, E. E.	McClain, Franklin	Tancil, Leon
Hightower, Jenkins	McDonald, E. K.	Tate, William
Homer, Wilburn	Mitchell, R.	Weathers, William
Howard, J. H.	Morris, Spurgeon	Webb, A. C.
Jameson, Clarence	Payne, Oscar	White, James R.
Jefferson, Ronald	Payton, Sam	Williams, O. B.
Johnson, David	Rice, Williad	Williams, W.
Johnson, Milton	Richardson, James	Wilson, Leon
Jones, William	Roberts, Carl	Wren, Charles
Kelly, Charles	Santos, Pedro	Yarber, James
Kersey, George	Scott, Roland	
Lawlah, John	Shepard, Howard	
Mason, Ira	Show, Maurice	
Mathes, Paul	Smith, Troy	

F. AND BOARD OF TRUSTEES

RL, 1938   CHICAGO

Golden (50th) Anniversary of Graduation, Rush Medical College of the University of Chicago, Class 1930. Reunion 1980 Black members. Standing (3rd from l.) Cornelius A. Alexander, Kalamazoo, Michigan; (2nd from r.) George D. Cannon, New York City. Sitting (2nd from r.) Leonidas H. Berry. Photo 1980.

Petersburg
Virginia
James R.
Chicahominy R.
York R.
Rappahan
Butlers Farm
Back R.
Hampton
Norfolk
Hampton Roads
Ocean View
Taylors Farm
Chesa
B
Eastern Shore
Atlantic Ocean